IRON IN THE SOUL

Jean-Paul Sartre – one of the best-known and most discussed modern French writers and thinkers – was born in Paris in 1905. He was educated in Paris and later taught in schools in Le Havre and Laon. In 1934 he spent a year at the French Institute in Berlin where he rapidly gained a thorough knowledge of modern German philosophy. He then taught at the Lycée Condorcet in Paris. Sartre played an active role in the Resistance during the war and afterwards left the teaching profession to spend most of his time writing and editing the magazine *Les Temps modernes*.

Sartre was a Marxist and the founder of French existentialism but he will perhaps be remembered more as a man of passion, a fighter for what he believed in rather than as an idealist. After his death in 1980 *The Times* wrote, 'His death removes from the world literary, philosophical and political scene one of the most brilliant as well as one of the most original thinkers of the twentieth century ... The most openly political of all great French writers, his sometimes intolerant and always violent passion for freedom and justice made him as hated and as loved in his own day as Rousseau, Voltaire and Zola were in theirs.' George Steiner also wrote of him, 'The importance of the man will not only prove to reside in works like *Nausea* which is a masterpiece, but in the example of trying to live rationally, day in, day out. It is the type of being he was that will influence men more than the specific declarations he made.'

Sartre's philosophical works, such as *L'Être et le néant* (1943), have had a profound effect on modern thought; and he also expounded his philosophical and political ideas through his novels and plays. His plays include *Huis clos* (1944), *Les Mouches* (1943), *Les Mains sales* (1948), *Nekrassov* (1955) and *Les Séquestrés d'Altona*, in which he put forward his own views on the need for literature to take sides which had caused so much controversy when *Qu'est-ce que la littérature?* was published in 1947. Of his novels the trilogy, *Les Chemins de la liberté* (published in Penguin as *The Age of Reason*, *The Reprieve*, and *Iron in the Soul*), is perhaps most famous. He also wrote *La Nausée* (1958) and *Words*, reminiscences of his childhood. Sartre's other works published in England include *Baudelaire* (1964), *Saint Genet, Actor and Martyr* (1964) and *Situations*, a volume of essays (1965). His *Literary and Philosophical Essays* were published in 1968. Several of Sartre's novels and plays have been published in Penguin.

Iron in the Soul

JEAN-PAUL SARTRE

TRANSLATED BY
GERARD HOPKINS

INTRODUCTION BY
DAVID CAUTE

PENGUIN BOOKS

IN ASSOCIATION WITH
HAMISH HAMILTON

PENGUIN BOOKS

Published by the Penguin Group
Penguin Books Ltd, 27 Wrights Lane, London W8 5TZ, England
Penguin Putnam Inc., 375 Hudson Street, New York, New York 10014, USA
Penguin Books Australia Ltd, Ringwood, Victoria, Australia
Penguin Books Canada Ltd, 10 Alcorn Avenue, Toronto, Ontario, Canada M4V 3B2
Penguin Books (NZ) Ltd, Private Bag 102902, NSMC, Auckland, New Zealand

Penguin Books Ltd, Registered Offices: Harmondsworth, Middlesex, England

La Mort dans l'âme first published 1949
This translation first published by Hamish Hamilton 1950
Published in Penguin Books 1963
Reprinted with an introduction 1985
9 10 8

Copyright 1949 by Jean-Paul Sartre
Introduction copyright © David Caute, 1985
All rights reserved

La Mort dans l'âme is the third volume of Jean-Paul Sartre's trilogy
Les Chemins de la liberté (Roads to Freedom)

Printed in England by Clays Ltd, St Ives plc
Set in Linotype Granjon

Introduction

I

Jean-Paul Sartre (1905–80) was a literary giant of his time. His philosophical and literary works, complex and profound, continue to attract passionate debate, while his novels and plays have lost none of their fascination for a large audience across the world. *Roads to Freedom* was his major enterprise as a novelist; a three-volume sequence followed by the unfinished fragment of a fourth that was never translated.

The Age of Reason was first published in 1945, the year of France's liberation from German occupation; *The Reprieve* later in the same year; *Iron in the Soul* and two chapters of *Drôle d'Amitié* in 1949. Sartre then abandoned the project. With the onset of the glacial era of the Cold War, his intense preoccupation with contemporary politics and the dialectics of history seems to have closed down the fictional chamber of his extraordinarily fertile imagination.

The English titles of the first two novels reflect the French originals exactly. *L'Age de raison* picks up its double meaning from the eighteenth-century Enlightenment, when the reign of God was at last supplanted by rationalism. And indeed Sartre's characters acknowledge no meaning to human existence outside of themselves and their own projects; for them, as for the author, God is dead. But Sartre also points the title at a phase of life. His 'hero', Mathieu, is reminded by his conforming elder brother that he has reached, in his mid-thirties, 'the age of reason' – to which Mathieu scornfully retorts, 'You mean the age of reconciliation', the moment of capitulation to bourgeois marriage, property, prudence and bad faith.

The Reprieve (*Le Sursis*) refers to the false reprieve from war granted to Europe by the Munich agreement of September 1938. As for the third novel, *La Mort dans l'âme* would be more accurately rendered as 'Death' – not 'Iron' – 'in the Soul'. The overall title given to Sartre's masterpiece, *Roads to Freedom*, loses some of the resonances of the original *Les Chemins de la liberté*, a more faithful translation of which might be 'The Ways of

Freedom'. For Sartre 'freedom' is only partly an end, a barricade to be stormed; it is also man's inescapable ontological condition, a permanent field of possibilities. To render 'Chemins' as 'Ways' would be to retain the sense of an odyssey while grasping also the ironic dimension – for with 'ways' goes 'waysides', the places where we sometimes fall, or drop out while declaring ourselves to have completed the journey.

The trilogy provides two obvious strands of continuity. Certain characters, most notably Mathieu Delarue – born in the same year as Sartre, 1905, and like Sartre a philosophy teacher in a *lycée* – progress from one volume to the next. There is thus a cast of principals around whom a vast chorus of subsidiaries, from humble soldiers to the great political figures of the era, state their claims on the world. History itself offers the second strand of continuity: the action of the trilogy is condensed into a period of roughly two years, from the summer of 1938 to the summer of 1940; from a Europe at peace, the Europe of private lives and insular ambitions (though the civil war in Spain was already flashing its warning to those who cared to look), to the collective catastrophe of war, defeat and Nazi occupation which caught everyone in its mesh.

For Sartre himself these events arrived as a catalyst, abruptly projecting him from philosophical speculation and literary work among a circle of kindred spirits into the company of ordinary French workers, peasants and clerks whose accepted lot was to endure, rather than to act upon events. This discovery of the 'other nation' called into question his own fastidious recoil from the compromises and demagogic slogans of politics, setting in motion within Sartre an unresolved dialogue between the 'pure' claims of the intelligence and the crude choices afforded by collective action. As novelist, playwright and journalist he wrestled with the dilemma of 'dirty hands' – the title of his play *Les Mains sales* – though the simple dualism between insular passivity and political activism is complicated by a psychological question which haunts all his writing about war and armed resistance: does one enter the Party to change the world, or to lose oneself in a comforting paternal embrace? Sartre tells us that to join the Party and *not* to join the class struggle represent two forms of escapism. The central characters of *Roads to Freedom*, the apolitical Mathieu and the Communist Brunet, are thus the protagonists in a specifically modern tragedy.

The structure of the trilogy represents a movement from the private to the public domain. The characters of *The Age of Reason* are only dimly aware of what lies beyond their personal projects, love-affairs and existential pains. Indeed the first ten chapters are the work of an artful miniaturist, not unlike the *tableaux* of an intimate stage play, as we discover what each member of a small circle needs and fears from the other. Dialogue is the crucial instrument of both action and characterization, though Sartre also used the resources of prose to describe the resistant opacity of the material universe and the hidden adventures of perception. At the heart of every personal encounter is the awareness that each self is the other for the person with whom he shares a meal or shares a bed. In Sartre's famous phrase, 'hell is other people'.

In *The Reprieve*, a panoramic and synoptic overview of Europe writhing in anticipation of war, Sartre employs a radically different literary technique. Whereas *The Age of Reason* observes the classic unities of time, place and action, Sartre now unveils the formidable resources of the modern novel (and indeed the modern cinema – he knew his Eisenstein and Pudovkin) to move from one location to the next with lightning rapidity, often in mid-sentence. What emerges is a collective stream of consciousness fashioned out of a mosaic of individual lives, each thrashing to be free of the looming fatality which is war. This helplessness applies even to the statesmen of Europe, with the single exception of Hitler, the demon orchestrator of the apocalypse.

Sartre's work as philosopher, novelist, playwright and essayist must be viewed as the motions of a multi-faceted talent across a single, though immense, field of inquiry. The artist and the philosopher remained inseparable; the first step towards cognition was invariably recognition, the pinning down of concrete experience as a prelude to abstract deduction. In one sense *Roads to Freedom* is a first-class epic; in another it is a fictional exploration of the phenomenology of freedom given philosophical form in Sartre's *Being and Nothingness*. Here three modes of consciousness are described, starting from man's initial sense of 'otherness' from everything, human or inanimate, that he encounters. This gap is what Sartre calls 'freedom', a source of anguish and alienation, yet man's distinctive faculty for fashioning a free life out of a free will. Sartre's fictional characters illustrate how we take refuge from our anguish at our failure to absorb the world, to be its sole subject, by trying to annihilate our freedom through inertia, passivity and cynicism – the syndrome described by George Orwell's 'Inside the Whale'.

Sartre calls this refuge Being-in-Itself. Alternatively we escape into a second posture of evasion, Being-for-Others, desperately assimilating the prevailing conventions and conforming to the image expected of us. Sartre was a master cartographer of the landscape of evasion, the flight from responsibility. The critic Henri Peyre compared his gift to that of Stendhal, and indeed the entry for 26 February 1940 in Sartre's *War Diaries* indicates a debt:

> Reread with deep admiration the first sixty pages of *La Chartreuse de Parme*. Stendhal's natural style, charm and liveliness of imagination can't be matched.

Men and women are 'free' whether they like it or not, insisted Sartre. He rejected all determinisms, whether Marxian, Freudian or behaviourist. Nor are freedom and authenticity medals to be won in a single battle and thereafter worn on life's tunic: each encounter is primary and demands a new choice. Mathieu, for example, tends to regard a good conscience as a faculty you fatten while waiting to make the *real* choices: too late he realizes that he has been living a lie.

Sartre's was an intelligence in constant motion, a mind propelled by an avid sense of inquiry. Had he 'frozen' his philosophy in the fashionable Left Bank cult of post-war existentialism, his writing would not have continued to generate the vitally modern radioactivity that it sustained until blindness and illness finally robbed him of his powers in the 1970s. Already in *Roads to Freedom* we are forced to confront the central question: can a man be 'free' if he suffers poverty and exploitation, or if he witnesses the misery of others but does nothing, and was Marx not right to dismiss 'freedom' as empty bourgeois rhetoric unless defined in terms of 'freedom and necessity', the central dialectic of history?

These were the great issues which in the post-war era propelled Sartre towards revolutionary socialism (though never into the Communist Party). *The Reprieve* and *Iron in the Soul* chart the early stages of an intellectual journey which was to culminate, twenty years later, in the *Critique of Dialectical Reason*. *En route* he published his celebrated essay, *What is Literature?* (1948), in which he argued that literature should be a weapon in the struggle for a society liberated from exploitation. Writing is not action but a form of 'secondary action – action by disclosure'. A committed (*engagée*) literature will not act as a sedative, a syrupy diet of consolation, but as an irritant, a provocation to change the world. Sartre's post-war politics led him into bitter conflict with erstwhile friends, notably Albert Camus and Raymond Aron, who made Sartre the prime target of his polemic, *The Opium of the Intellectuals*. 'To merit the right to influence men who are struggling,' Sartre rebuked Camus, 'one must first participate in the struggle.'

Yet an ironic paradox lurks at the heart of this secular version of liberation theology. To close the painful gap between the self and the world, to eradicate that intolerable 'lack', men resort to varying strategies. In Sartre's case – as he pointed out – that strategy was *writing*. By exercising his intelligence, by mastering the metaphysics of existence, by attempting to understand everything, Sartre sought to banish his own sense of alienation. To 'liberate' the world you have first to dominate it:

My ambition is myself alone to know the world . . . And, for me, knowledge has a magical sense of appropriation. To know is to appropriate.

It was the ultimate gambit of a short, ugly man who drank and smoked heavily, while squinting from behind his glasses with an all-seeing octopus eye.

In *The Age of Reason* the problem of Communism is a mere speck on the lens; by the end of *Iron in the Soul* it dominates almost the entire field of vision. In the 1950s Sartre's hostility towards American global ambitions and France's stubborn, rearguard colonial wars brought him close to the Communists, but the Soviet repression of the Hungarian revolution in 1956 terminated the affair. Denigrated by the 'Brunets' of the

Communist press as an agent of Wall Street and a 'hermetic philosopher', Sartre replied in *What is Literature?*: 'The politics of Stalinist Communism is incompatible with the honest practice of the literary craft.' Stalinism had replaced one form of alienation, one version of mendacity, with another. So it seems that Mathieu was right to resist Brunet's overtures, and right not to surrender himself to the consolations of a secular church.

The literary style employed in *The Reprieve* was much influenced by the 'stream of consciousness' employed by John Dos Passos, whose mammoth trilogy, *USA*, fascinated the French writer. Writing in *Atlantic Monthly* in August 1946, Sartre described the revelatory impact of Faulkner, Dos Passos and Hemingway on his own generation. The last of these reinforced his preference for a style which was lean and hard rather than bloated or baroque; he despised decorative displays just as he distrusted 'art for art's sake'.

From Dos Passos, with his 'newsreel' and 'camera eye' innovations, Sartre adopted strategies for weaving individual consciousness in and out of the onrush of events, the collision of forces larger than any individual – though he stopped short of the American writer's unpunctuated collages. Here, in Dos Passos's *Nineteen Nineteen*, the camera eye travels to Paris:

at the gare de l'Est they're singing the *International* entire   the gendarmerie nationale is making its way slowly down Magenta into stones whistles bits of iron the *International* Mort aux vaches Barricades we must build barricades . . . at a corner I run into a friend too   Look out They're shooting to kill and it's begun to rain . . .

This torrential impact is recaptured by Sartre in *The Reprieve*: a prose-onslaught both mesmerizing and sometimes over-taxing as huge, unbroken paragraphs bear down on the reader.

The cross-cutting begins in the first paragraph of the novel, which introduces us in rapid succession to Mathieu in France; to an incensed Czech nationalist, Milan, in the disputed Sudetenland; and then to the 'old gentleman', the British Prime Minister, Neville Chamberlain. Later we cut from Milan and his wife, Anna, to an illiterate French shepherd, Gros-Louis, adrift in Marseilles, searching for work and escaping from the draft and he knows not what. At another juncture the Czech nationalist takes comfort in the thought 'I'm not alone' and immediately the French homosexual, Daniel, hundreds of miles distant, reflects, 'I'm alone'. Later these same two characters, entirely unknown to each other, inhabit a single sentence: 'Tears of rage welled into Milan's eyes, and Daniel turned towards Marcelle . . .' And then immediately we are with the paralytic, crippled youth, Charles, squirming on his back: 'Where are they going to send us?'

Sartre's collage technique can be an exasperating one, not infrequently forcing us either to re-read the passage or lose our way. Yet, possessed with his marvellous freedom of manoeuvre, burdened by none of the physical constraints of the theatre, the novelist is perfectly endowed to break physical boundaries, to split and fuse the molecular structures of individual lives, and to dramatize the mysteries of 'the moment' – each clock unknown to the other, yet joined by a bondage as universal as the force of gravity. Sartre relished the endowment.

In certain respects Sartre straddles the divide between the coherent 'realism' of the eighteenth- and nineteenth-century novel on the one hand and the modernist writing of the twentieth century which has systematically fragmented human experience into a sequence of random, often futile, spasms. It was Samuel Beckett, another resident of Paris, who remarked in his novel *Molloy* that man is no more free than a slave crawling east across the deck of a ship travelling west. Sartre was always a faithful friend of experimental art and it is significant that at the beginning of *Iron in the Soul* the Spanish Republican Gomez visits the Museum of Modern Art in New York and singles out Klee, Rouault and Picasso as the artists who ask 'awkward questions'. Sartre had little love for the facile productions of Communist 'socialist realism', with their archaic literary forms washed by sentimental romanticism – Tchaikovsky in the steel works. Even so, he entertained a certain hostility towards the ivory-tower avant-garde, rejecting the surrealists' convenient doctrine that true revolt takes place within *l'esprit* or through scandalous gestures.

A recurring theme in Sartre's fiction and drama is the pseudo-revolt of the wealthy boy who loves the poetry of Rimbaud and regards himself as the privileged spirit above the common herd.

Such a character is Lucien in the story *Childhood of a Leader*; such a character, also, is Philippe, who first appears in *The Reprieve* and is seen again in *Iron in the Soul*. 'Je est un autre' ('I is another'), announced Rimbaud. Sartre regarded such declarations, when taken on board by spoiled *fils à papa*, as affectations designed to grease a sordid flight from responsibility. His own fictional characters are entirely themselves. Nevertheless, Sartrean man and woman are far from being in total command of their own capacities — hence the rapid alternations between the 'he' and the 'I', between the character as subject and as object. 'He heard them moving to and fro — almost as though they're in my room.' It's as if the character — a mere 'third person singular' to us, however deep our empathy — suddenly cries out from the page.

Such changes of camera angle were not available in the literary form that Sartre loved best, the theatre. Dramatic writing allows the portrayal of people only by what they say and do; they remain locked into the 'third person singular' even when they step front-stage and unburden themselves to the audience. The theatre was a natural medium for an existentialist philosopher who insisted that man *is*, simply, what he *does* — '*l'homme n'est rien d'autre que ce qu'il se fait*'. Indeed Sartre continued to write stage plays after he abandoned fiction in 1949. *The Flies*, *Dirty Hands*, *No Exit*, *The Devil and the Good Lord* and *Altona* remind us of his brilliant, yet always accessible, talent as a playwright.

Iron in the Soul marks a reversion to a more conventional mode of fiction than *The Reprieve*. Despite occasional cross-cutting and symbiotic fusions, we follow the story of the fall of France in June 1940 through a succession of clearly defined scenes which pay due respect to transitions of time, geography and action. The outer world is once again on its own conveyor belt. As Sartre extends the range of his narrative to encompass the ordinary *poilus*, the short-legged, demoralized, khaki citizens of the Third Republic, he increasingly resorts to the naturalistic tradition whose great French precursor was Émile Zola. It is no challenge for Sartre to reproduce the nuances of Parisian café life, but his mastery of the *argot* and *patois* of stranded workers and peasants marks a triumphal alliance of the ear and the imagination.

In the final section of *Iron in the Soul*, Sartre again adapts form to content. We are now with the Communist militant Brunet, viewing the prisoner-of-war camp exclusively as he does. To seal us hermetically into Brunet, Sartre reverts to the long, unbroken paragraphs — a tunnel of words and sensations — inside which dialogue runs on continuously, one speaker after another, like rain beating on a roof. Although we can distinguish the comrades whom Brunet ferrets out from the dispirited mass, it is Brunet's assessment of them that counts.

Novelist or playwright, the writer is sole creator (whatever his debt to the living) of his characters. The novelist, however, can in addition play 'God' to his creations in one particular manner that Sartre vigorously rejected — by providing them with a pre-set, unalterable nature, as if imprisoning them in a plaster cast, and then shamelessly confiding this image to the reader. In an essay on François Mauriac, Sartre insisted that the novelist must present his characters as free people confronting choices of their own, with a latitude for surprising both themselves and us — 'an action related from various points of view'. One can therefore read the entire length of the trilogy without finding a sentence in which Sartre sets any of his creations in a rigid mould. The preferred technique is to allow them their own internal reckoning. Thus Mathieu, waiting for captivity at the hands of the Germans, reflects:

I've spent my life reading, yawning, tinkling the bell of my own little problems, never managing to make a decision — only to find that I *have* decided, that I *chose* this war and this defeat . . . Everything's got to be done over again, and yet, there's nothing that can be done. The two thoughts interpenetrated, cancelled one another out. Only the unruffled surface of nothingness remained.

The last two sentences remind us, however, that the author lurks, huge and omniscient, behind his character's 'freedom'. One also wonders how many people, even professors of philosophy like Mathieu, ever summarize their own lives so neatly.

Similar doubts arise from a passage in *The Reprieve* where Sartre depicts the homosexual Daniel (who engineered the break-up of Mathieu and Marcelle in *The Age of Reason*) bored to death by Marcelle's company at the seaside. As his eye falls on a pretty youth digging in the sand (shades of Thomas Mann's *Death in*

Venice), he is overcome with desire. But he is also overcome with Sartrean phenomenology:

> Oh, *to be*, like a tree, like the boy's back . . . I am myself for all eternity, homosexual, mean, coward. *They* see me — no, not even that: *it* sees me. He was *the object* of looking.

Given Sartre's antipathy to definitive, god-like comment by the author, one must assume that these reflections belong to Daniel himself. But the phenomenology, strongly reminiscent of the portrait of Antoine Roquentin in *Nausea*, Sartre's first and most artistically achieved novel, must suggest that if Daniel is anyone's 'object' he is Sartre's.

Try as he may, the novelist cannot escape from his divine burden; however generously he empathizes with his creations, breathing their oxygen, in the end both we and they know only so much as he will allow us.

II

Iron in the Soul takes place in June 1940. A year and nine months have elapsed since Europe gratefully grasped the false peace described in *The Reprieve*; and nine months since Britain and France declared war against Germany and then did nothing about it. Sartre's central character, Mathieu, has been in uniform since September 1938; Sartre himself was not conscripted until a year later, his job being to send up balloons, observe them through field-glasses, and then telephone the local artillery battery with news of wind changes. This was the Phoney War, the long attrition described by Sartre in his *War Diaries*:

> The men nowadays no longer have that religious trust in their generals. To tell the truth, they have no trust of any kind. They're convinced that a total war is won for economic and political reasons . . .

It was a period of 'waiting, timidity, hesitation, withdrawal: the General Staff has deliberately accepted it all'. Sartre didn't do badly out of it. A man who by choice lived in residential hotels, read in public libraries and wrote in cafés, he established himself mornings and evenings in the 'big, cold' Hotel du Soleil at Bouxwiller and poured out a vast wordage — letters, diaries, drafts for *Being and Nothingness*, the finished text of *The Age of Reason*. Later he was taken prisoner by the Germans.

In the first chapter of *Iron in the Soul* we join Gomez, now a refugee from Franco's victory in Spain, in heat-soaked New York (the antipathetic descriptions of that city obviously draw on Sartre's own, unhappy, post-war visit). Bitterly Gomez rejoices at news of the fall of Paris; he has not forgotten that 'when Franco entered Barcelona, the French shook their heads and said it was a pity . . .' The narrative then cuts to his wife and son, Sarah and Pablo, fleeing south from Paris in a column of refugees. Their taxi runs out of petrol, the driver demands his full 200 francs, there is a harrowing scene, and one is reminded of the intensely moving episode in *The Reprieve* when Sarah drags Pablo blindly behind her through city streets after Gomez's unaffectionate return to the Spanish war and other women. Nor does Gomez in New York now give them much thought. He's more interested in shapely legs.

The homosexual Daniel exults in the defeat and degradation of France. Paris is now a ghost city as it awaits the conquerors: 'They are running and crawling. I, the Criminal, reign over the city in their stead.' Awe and joy overwhelm him as at last he sees 'them', the Germans; boldly he returns their stare, looking into 'sun-tanned faces in which eyes showed like glacier lakes'. He longs to be a woman so that he might load them with flowers.

But soon Daniel will find distraction and solace in the seduction of Philippe (the bourgeois boy pacifist of *The Reprieve*), who did in the end serve with his unit in the Nord but then ran away with everyone else. Taking the boy home, he is gratified by the admiring reaction his Mexican statuettes excite — 'And the great thing about them is that they're *genuine*,' says Daniel. He suggests to Philippe that it's not his mother he really loves but his tormentor and stepfather, the General. You want him to ride you like a mare, Daniel insinuates, your pacifism is nothing but a dialogue with the General.

Sartre offers us two contrasting seduction scenes, one 'existentialist' and dynamic, the other 'naturalist' and bogged down in helpless stasis. Every motion in Daniel's predatory pursuit of Philippe is radiated with psychological development; further east, a bombastic and ignorant soldier in Mathieu's unit, Pinette, seduces the girl in the local village post office. He has her; she clings and wails; he escapes – a succession of farmyard transactions.

Mathieu's odious lawyer brother Jacques, meanwhile, is found with his wife on the road south from Paris. As usual, Jacques reeks of Sartrean *mauvaise foi*. 'Had there been any danger,' he tells Odette, 'I would have stayed.' Insisting that he left the city for her sake, to be with her, because *she* had been frightened, he also recalls how he had been turned down for military service by an M.O.: 'Don't you remember how angry I was?' Odette, a non-smoker, is so disgusted that she steals one of his cigarettes as he snores over the wheel of the car. Enough of Jacques.

Among his comrades demoralized by military disaster, Mathieu is alone with his education and self-possession, stranded in a moronic tide drifting through supine defeat.

In the darkness they all looked alike . . . He sat down on the edge of the road because there was nowhere else for him to go. Night entered him through mouth and eyes, through nose and ears.

Out of solidarity he tries to get drunk with the lads, but can't do it: then feels ashamed of his own superiority. Mathieu is secure against physical victimization because he can swing a punch as well as any Hemingway hero if strictly necessary. And he can also, as he discovers, kill; besieged in the church tower he achieves catharsis through slaughter, a savage atonement for years of vacillation. 'Each one of his shots avenged some ancient scruple . . . He was free.' What befalls him we don't know, but it is significant that the Communist Brunet, passing through the same village, sees the church tower collapse. Brunet is taken prisoner.

The last section of 120 pages belong to Brunet and therefore to politics. Enter now the mysterious figure of Schneider, a fellow prisoner-of-war of equal composure who clearly knows a good deal about the Communist Party (banned by Daladier after the Nazi–Soviet Pact and the outbreak of war), yet is not a member. *Drôle d'Amitié*, the unfinished fourth volume of *Roads to Freedom*, will reveal that Schneider's real name is Vicarios, an intellectual who broke with the Party over the Pact. I find one specific improbability in Sartre's depiction of Brunet. 'I'm a militant,' he tells Schneider, 'and I've never wasted my time speculating about high politics. I had a job to do and I did it.' Yet we are also told that Brunet has written the leading two-page article in *L'Humanité* justifying the Ribbentrop–Molotov Pact of August 1939. Such delicate assignments, requiring the most subtle deployment of the dialectic, were never entrusted by the Party to simple militants unfamiliar with the higher politics. As novelist, Sartre here falls into the trap of convenience.

The odour of Marshal Pétain's New Order, of the Vichy regime, of collaboration, already pervades the camp. The French prisoners display an alarming gratitude for every small concession – food, a visit from relatives – offered by the conquerors. Abandoned by their own officers, they need to believe that the Germans are reasonable, fair, efficient. In Germany, says one, 'You pay your taxes but at least you know where the money goes.' Willingly they set their watches to German time. The voices of priests are heard, denouncing materialism:

And I say unto you, rejoice, my brothers, rejoice in the dark place of your suffering, for where there has been sin, there, too, is there expiation, there, too, is there redemption.

The theology which interests Sartre, however, is of that international Communism. According to Schneider, the Nazi–Soviet Pact represented Stalin's final decision to abandon the Western democracies. Brunet cannot believe it and angrily rejects the suggestion that the clandestine French Communist Party could ever condemn resistance to Nazi occupation. He insists that the solidarity between the European proletariat and 'the workers' state', Russia, is rooted in inexorable historical laws.

Brunet is destined for disillusionment, but that belongs to the fourth, untranslated volume, only two chapters of which appeared in 1949 before the project was abandoned, like Sarah and Pablo on the road south from Paris.

DAVID CAUTE

Quotations are from Jean-Paul Sartre: *War Diaries. Notebooks from a Phoney War, 1939–40.* Trans. by Quintin Hoare. Verso, 1984.

PART ONE

*

New York: Saturday, 15 June 1940. 9 a.m.

AN octopus? He pulled out his knife and opened his eyes – it
was a dream. No, it wasn't. The octopus was a reality, and
it was draining him with its suckers: it was the heat. He was
sweating. He had gone to sleep about one o'clock. At two the
heat had woken him. Streaming with sweat, he had plunged
into a cold bath, and had then got back into bed without drying
himself. Almost at once the furnace had resumed its roaring
under his skin, and he had begun to sweat again. At dawn he
had fallen asleep, only to dream that the house was on fire. The
sun must be pretty high by this time. Not for a moment did
Gomez stop sweating. He had been sweating uninterruptedly for
forty-eight hours. 'Christ!' he muttered, passing a damp hand
over his streaming chest. *This was more than mere heat* – a sickness of the atmosphere. The very air was in a fever, the very air
was sweating, and human beings were sweating within a cara-
pace of sweat. He must get out of bed: he must put on his shirt
and start sweating in that. He sat up. '*Hombre!* I haven't a dry
shirt left!' His last, the blue one, was soaked, because he had had
to change twice a day. None left. He would have to wear this sop-
ping, stinking rag until his things came back from the laundry.
Very cautiously he got to his feet, but no matter how slowly he
moved, the moisture poured from him. Great drops crept down
his legs, like lice, tickling him. His crumpled shirt lay across
the back of the armchair, a mass of creases. He felt it. Nothing
ever gets properly dry in this bloody country. His heart was
thumping: his mouth tasted like the bottom of a parrot's cage,
just as though he'd had a thick night.

He put on his trousers, went across to the window, and pulled
aside the curtains. The street glared up at him, a catastrophic
dazzle of white sunlight. Thirteen more hours of daylight to
face. In a mingled mood of suffering and fury he gazed down
at the roadway. Everywhere the *same* catastrophe. *Over there*,
blood and screams on the good, black earth, under a pall of
smoke: *here* a blinding sunlight between rows of low, red-brick

7

houses – sunlight and sweat. But the catastrophe was the same. Two Negroes were strolling along the sidewalk, laughing: a woman was just going into a drugstore. 'Oh God!' he muttered, 'Oh, God!' He looked at the screaming confusion of discordant colours. 'Even if I had the time, even if I were in the mood, how could I paint in light like this! Oh, God!' he exclaimed, 'Oh, God!'

There was a ring at the bell: Gomez went across and opened the door. It was Ritchie.

'Darned murder, that's what it is,' said Ritchie as he came in.

Gomez gave a start:

'What d'you mean?'

'This heat – darned murder. Hello!' – he went on accusingly – 'you not dressed yet? Ramon's expecting us at ten.'

Gomez shrugged:

'Didn't get to sleep till late.'

Ritchie grinned, and Gomez added hastily:

'Too hot – couldn't get off.'

'Always like that at first,' said Ritchie breezily; 'you'll get used to it.' He gave the other an appraising look: 'See here, you taking your salt-pills?'

'Of course I am, but they don't do a bit of good.'

Ritchie shook his head: there was a touch of severity in his friendliness. Salt pills *ought* to stop sweating. If they didn't stop Gomez, that must be because Gomez was different from other guys.

'Wait a minute!' he said with a frown: 'You should be acclimatized by this time: Spain's plenty hot!'

Gomez's mind went back to the dry, tragic mornings in Madrid, to the noble light of the sun above the Alcala when it was still speaking of hope. He shook his head.

'Not the same kind of heat.'

'Less humid, eh?' – there was a note almost of pride in Ritchie's voice.

'Yes, and more human.'

Ritchie was holding a newspaper. Gomez stretched a hand to take it, but his courage failed him, and he let it fall back.

'This is my big day,' said Ritchie cheerfully: 'Delaware celebrations: that's my home-town, y'see.'

8

He opened the paper at page thirteen. Gomez saw a photograph of La Guardia shaking hands with a fat man. Both of them were smiling broadly.

'Guy on the left's the Governor of Delaware,' explained Ritchie: 'La Guardia received him yesterday at City Hall: pretty big occasion.'

Gomez wanted to snatch the paper from him and look at the front page. But he thought: 'What the hell do I care!' and went into the bathroom. He started running cold water into the tub, and shaved hurriedly. Just as he was getting into his bath, Ritchie called to him:

'How you getting along?'

'Just about cleaned out: not a clean shirt to my name, and eighteen dollars left. Manuel's due back, too, on Monday, and I shall have to clear out of the apartment.'

But his mind was on the newspaper. Ritchie was reading it while he waited. Gomez could hear him turning the pages. He dried himself carefully: but it was no use: the towel was wringing wet. He put on his damp shirt with a shiver, and went back into the bedroom.

'The Giants' big game.'

Gomez looked at Ritchie. He had no idea what he was talking about.

'Baseball – yesterday – the Giants won.'

'Oh yes, of course, baseball. . . .'

He bent down to tie his shoes. He tried to read the front-page headlines upside down. Finally, he asked:

'What about Paris?'

'Didn't you hear the radio?'

'Haven't got a radio.'

'Finished, washed up' – said Ritchie without any show of excitement. 'They got into it last night.'

Gomez went over to the window, and pressed his forehead to the blazing pane. He looked at the street, at the meaningless sun, at the whole meaningless day. There would be nothing now, any more, but meaningless days. He turned away and dropped on to the bed.

'Hurry,' said Ritchie: 'Ramon doesn't like to be kept waiting.'

9

Gomez got up. Already his shirt needed wringing. He began to knot his tie in front of the glass.

'Think he'll agree?'

'In principle, yes. Sixty dollars a week – and you can do the art shows. But he wants to see you.'

'He'll see me all right,' said Gomez: 'he'll see me.'

Then he swung round.

'I've got to have an advance – is he likely to give it me?'

Ritchie shrugged. After a brief pause, he said:

'I've told him you were in Spain, and he doesn't exactly think you've got Franco written on your heart, but I didn't say anything about ... about what you'd been doing there. Better not say you were a General ... nobody really knows what he thinks about things.'

A General! Gomez looked at his shabby trousers, at the dark sweat stains already showing on his shirt. He said bitterly:

'Don't worry: I'm not likely to boast. I know only too well what it costs a man here to have fought in Spain. For six months now I haven't had a smell of a job!'

Ritchie showed signs of annoyance.

'We Americans don't like war,' he said.

Gomez stuffed his jacket under his arm:

'Let's get going.'

Ritchie slowly folded the paper and scrambled to his feet. On their way downstairs, he asked a question:

'Your wife and kid in Paris?'

'I sincerely hope not,' said Gomez briskly. 'I hope Sarah was sharp enough to leg it down to Montpellier.'

He paused for a moment, and then added: 'I haven't had any news of them since the first of June.'

'If you get this job you'll be able to bring 'em across,' said Ritchie.

'Yes,' said Gomez: 'yes – nothing for it but to wait and see.'

The street was a dazzle of windows. The sun blazed down on the flat-roofed warehouses of blackish brick. In front of every door was a flight of white stone steps. Over towards the East River there was a heat-haze. The whole city looked stunted. No shade anywhere. In no street in the world would one feel so terribly exposed. White-hot needles seemed to pierce his eyes. He raised his hand to screen them. His shirt was sticking to his body. He shivered:

'You're right about its being murder!'

'Poor old guy fell down just ahead of me yesterday,' said Ritchie: 'sunstroke – br-r! – don't like seeing stiffs!'

'You'll see enough of 'em if you go to Europe,' thought Gomez.

'It's forty blocks,' went on Ritchie: 'we better take a bus.'

They stopped in front of a yellow standard. A young woman was waiting. She fixed them with an expert, brooding eye, and turned away.

'Nice-looking dame,' said Ritchie with schoolboy eagerness.

'Pretty obvious floozie,' said Gomez, ill-temperedly.

He had felt dirty and sweaty beneath her glance. She was not sweating: nor was Ritchie, who looked pink and cool in his fine white shirt. There was scarcely so much as a trace of shine on his snub nose. Gomez the handsome! – the handsome General! The General had bent above blue eyes, green eyes, black eyes aflutter behind long lashes, but this street-walker had seen nothing but a little South-European runt earning fifty dollars a week, and sweating in a ready-made suit. 'She took me for a Dago.' All the same, he could not help staring at her long, well-shaped legs. He was conscious of a little uneasy stirring of the flesh. 'Four months since I had a woman.' In the old days desire had been like dry, hot sunlight in his belly, but now the handsome General Gomez knew only the squalid, furtive cravings of the *voyeur*.

'Cigarette?'

'No, my throat's on fire: I'd rather have a drink.'

'No time.'

Ritchie gave him a pat on the shoulder. He looked faintly embarrassed.

'Say! try and work up a smile. If Ramon sees you looking like that he'll get a fright. I don't mean be obsequious' – he added hurriedly, as he noticed Gomez's movement of irritation – 'only just to sort of stick on a grin when you go into the room, something quite impersonal you can forget about. Doesn't matter what you're thinking – only smile!'

'Oh, I'll smile!' said Gomez.

Ritchie shot him a sympathetic glance.

'Worrying over your kid?'

'No.'

Ritchie made a painful effort to apply his mind to the situation:

'Over Paris, then?'

'Paris can go to hell, for all I care!' said Gomez with sudden violence.

'It's better they should have taken it without a fight, isn't it?'

'The French could have defended it': there was a trace of emotion in his voice.

'Hell! a city like that, in the middle of a flat plain?'

'They could have defended it. Madrid held out for two and a half years.'

'Oh, Madrid!' – Ritchie repeated the word, and sketched a vague gesture: 'But what's the point in defending Paris? Why, it would have been crazy! They'd have destroyed the Louvre, the Opera, Notre-Dame. The less destruction there is, the better. As things are going now' – he wound up with an air of great satisfaction – 'the war'll be over soon.'

'Yes, to be sure,' said Gomez ironically: 'as things are going now we'll be having a Nazi peace inside three months.'

'Peace,' said Ritchie, 'is neither democratic nor Nazi; it's just plain peace. You know I don't figure to like these Nazi guys, but they're only men after all. Once they've got Europe handed to 'em on a plate, their difficulties will begin. They'll have to pipe down considerably. If they've got heads on their shoulders, they'll just let each country run itself inside a European Federation – something like our United States.'

He spoke slowly and with deliberation: 'It'll stop you folk from having a war every twenty years,' he went on, 'and that'll be all to the good.'

Gomez looked at him with a feeling of acute irritation. Unlimited kindness showed in the grey eyes. Obviously the man had a happy temperament: he overflowed with love for humanity in general, children, birds and abstract painting. It was his opinion that the only thing needed to settle all conflicts was a little common sense. He had small sympathy for immigrants from the Latin countries. He got on much better with the Germans. 'What does the capture of Paris mean to him?' Gomez turned away and studied a news-stand's multi-coloured display. He realized suddenly that there was something ruthless about Ritchie.

'You Europeans,' he was saying, 'set such a hell of a lot of store by symbols. We all of us knew, a week ago, that France was finished – and what of it? Naturally you feel a bit riled – you've had a home there, you got memories: I see all that: but what, really, does the capture of Paris matter to you, provided the place is unharmed? As soon as the war's over, we'll go back there.'

Gomez felt himself borne up on the wings of a dangerous and angry joy:

'Why should I care?' he asked in a trembling voice. 'I'm *glad*! When Franco entered Barcelona the French shook their heads and said it was a pity – but not one of them raised a finger to stop it. Well, now it's their turn, and I hope it chokes 'em! I'm *glad*!' he shouted above the din of the motor-bus which was just drawing up to the kerb: 'I'm glad!'

They got in behind the young woman, and Gomez managed to get a good look at her legs. They stood on the platform. A fat man, wearing gold-rimmed spectacles, hastily drew back, and Gomez thought: 'I must stink.' A man in the back row of seats had opened his paper. Gomez, looking over his shoulder, read: 'Toscanini acclaimed in Rio where he is conducting for the first time in fifty-four years', and, a little lower, 'New York Première: Ray Milland and Loretta Young in *The Doctor Takes a Wife*'. Here and there in the bus were the spread wings of other papers: Là Guardia Receiving the Governor of Delaware; Loretta Young; Fire in Illinois: Ray Milland: My Husband has Loved me Since I Started using Pitts' Deodorant: Ask for Chrisargyl, the Honeymoon Laxative: a man in pyjamas smiling at his young wife: La Guardia smiling at the Governor of Delaware: 'No Cake for the Miners' says Buddy Smith. All these people were busy reading. The large black and white pages spoke to them of themselves, of their worries and their pleasures. They knew who Buddy Smith was, but Gomez did not. They kept the staring headlines that said 'Paris Captured' or 'Montmartre in Flames' turned to the floor or to the driver's back. They read on, and the papers screamed their news to deaf ears. Gomez felt old

13

and tired. Paris was far away. He, alone, among a hundred and fifty million people, was concerned about it. It was no more than a small personal preoccupation, scarcely more important than the thirst burning his throat.

'Let me have a look at your paper,' he said to Ritchie.

The Germans have occupied Paris. Pressure developing towards the South. Capture of Le Havre. Assault on the Maginot Line.

The headlines screamed, but the three Negroes behind him went on laughing, not hearing a thing.

French Army Intact: Spain takes Tangier.

The man with the gold-rimmed spectacles was feeling about methodically in the recesses of his brief-case, from which, finally, he fished a Yale key. This he studied with satisfaction. Gomez felt ashamed. He wanted to put away his paper, as though it were indiscreetly trumpeting to the world his own most intimate secrets. The vast uproar of unhappy voices which set his hands trembling, the appeals for help, the death-rattles – all these things seemed crudely incongruous, like his own foreign sweat, his own unpleasant smell. *Hitler's Good Faith is Doubted. President Roosevelt Does Not Believe ... The United States will do Everything in Their Power for the Allies. ...* His Majesty's Government will do everything in its power for the Czechs: the French will do everything in their power for the Spanish Republicans. Lint, medicaments, cases of tinned milk. A drop in the ocean! *Students Demonstrate in Madrid: They Demand the Return of Gibraltar to the Spaniards.* Catching sight of that word 'Madrid' he could read no further ... 'I'm glad! ... the damn' swine ... only hope they'll set all Paris on fire, reduce the whole place to ashes ...' *Tours* (from our Special Correspondent, Archambaud): *The battle is continuing: French say enemy pressure lessening. Nazi losses heavy.*

Of course the pressure is lessening, and it'll go on lessening until the last day of the war, until the last French newspaper stops publication. Heavy losses! – mere words, hope's final little bluster that deceives nobody. Heavy Fascist losses round Tarragona: pressure lessening: Barcelona will hold out ... and then, twenty-four hours later, headlong flight.

Berlin (from Our Special Correspondent, Brook Peters):

France has lost the whole of her Industry: Montmédy has been captured. The Maginot Line has been stormed. The enemy is in flight. Paeans of triumph, sounding brass, sunlight. They are singing in Berlin, in Madrid; thousands of men in uniform: Barcelona, Madrid, uniforms: Barcelona, Madrid, Valence, Warsaw, Paris, and, tomorrow, London. At Tours gentlemen in black jackets are scurrying down hotel corridors. Grand news! grand news! – Let 'em take the whole damn' lot: let 'em land in New York – Grand!

The gentleman in the gold-rimmed spectacles was looking at him. Gomez felt ashamed, as though he had spoken his thoughts out loud. The Negroes were smiling, the young woman was smiling, the driver was smiling. *Not to grin is a sin.*

'This is where we get down,' said Ritchie, smiling.

On the posters, on the magazine covers, all America was smiling. Gomez thought of Ramon and began to smile.

'Ten o'clock,' said Ritchie: 'we shan't be more than five minutes late.'

Ten o'clock: three o'clock in Paris. Livid and hopeless, the afternoon lay hidden behind this Colonial morning.

Three o'clock in France.

'Properly stuck!' said the man.

He sat there as though turned to stone. Sarah could see the sweat trickling down the back of his neck. Her ears were filled with the din of klaxons.

'No more juice!'

He opened the door, jumped out on to the road, and stood there in front of the car, gazing at it affectionately.

'Hell!' he said between his teeth: 'Hell! Hell!' He laid the flat of his hand on the scorching radiator cap. Sarah could see him through the window standing against the glitter of the sky, in the middle of this vast hurly-burly. The cars that had been following them all morning stretched into the distance until they were swallowed up in a cloud of dust. Behind them, klaxons, whistles, hootings – a warbling of metallic birds, a hymn of hate.

'Why are they so angry?' asked Pablo.

'Because we're in their way.'

15

She would have liked to jump out of the car, but despair kept her riveted to the seat. The man looked up.

'Oh, get out!' he said irritably: 'can't you hear? Help me to push.'

They got out.

'Go round to the back,' said the man to Sarah, 'and push – push hard.'

'I'd like to push too,' said Pablo.

Sarah leaned against the car and pushed with might and main. She kept her eyes shut. It was like a nightmare. The sweat was soaking through her blouse. The sun jabbed at her eyes through their closed lids. She opened them. In front of her the man was pushing, his left hand flat against the door, his right twiddling the wheel. Pablo had flung himself against the back bumper, and was clinging to it, all the while emitting a series of wild shrieks.

'Be careful not to get dragged!' said Sarah.

The car was trundled apathetically to the side of the road.

'Stop! Stop!' shouted the man. 'God in Heaven, that's far enough!'

The klaxons had stopped. The stream of cars was once more flowing. They grazed past their broken-down companion. Faces showed, pressed to the windows. Sarah felt herself blushing beneath all those staring eyes, and took refuge behind the car. A tall, skinny driver, at the wheel of a Chevrolet, leaned out:

'Swine!'

Lorries, heavy and light, private cars, taxis with masked meters, vans. With each vehicle that passed her Sarah felt a further drop in her courage, and Gien seemed more than ever distant. Next came a procession of horse-drawn wagons, and Gien creaked away into a still more hopeless remoteness. Finally, the road became a black congestion of pedestrians. Sarah withdrew to the edge of the ditch. The crowd terrified her. The people in it walked slowly, painfully, and misery imparted to all a family likeness. Anyone who joined them would soon look just the same. I don't want to become like that. They did not look at her, but avoided the car without turning their eyes in her direction. They seemed no longer to have any eyes. A great hulking fellow, wearing a straw hat, with a suit-case in either hand, brushed the

16

car and bumped against the mudguard. He made a half-turn, and then resumed his tottering progress. His face was dead white. One of the suit-cases was covered with multi-coloured labels: Seville – Cairo – Sarajeva – Stresa.

'He's half dead,' exclaimed Sarah: 'he'll fall down at any moment.'

But he did not fall. Her eyes followed the straw boater with its red and green ribbon, bobbing along gaily above the sea of hats.

'Take your suit-case and go on without me.'

Sarah shuddered but said nothing. She looked at the crowd with terrified disgust.

'You heard what I said.'

She turned to him:

'Can't we wait until a car comes along and beg a tin of petrol? There are bound to be some more cars when this lot has gone by.'

The man gave her a nasty smile.

'I advise you to try!'

'Well, why not? why not try?'

He spat contemptuously, and for a moment or two said nothing.

'Have you looked at 'em?' he asked at last. 'They're just crawling, almost touching: is it likely any of 'em will stop?'

'Suppose I manage to find some petrol?'

'You won't. It's not very likely they'll lose their place in the line just for you.' He stared at her with a cackle of laughter. 'If you were a good-looker and twenty, there might be a chance.'

Sarah pretended not to have heard. She pressed her point:

'But suppose I did manage to get some?'

He shook his head with stubborn obstinacy:

'Nothing doing: I'm not going any further, not if you raise twenty litres, not if you raise a hundred. I've had my lesson.' He folded his arms.

'Stop and think for a moment,' he said with surly earnestness: 'braking, skidding, declutching every few yards, changing down a hundred times an hour – that's what does a car in.'

There were brown stains on the wind-screen. He took out a handkerchief and began rubbing at them with anxious care.

'I oughtn't to have let you persuade me to come.'

17

'You only need very little more petrol,' said Sarah.

He shook his head without answering. She would have liked to scratch his face, but controlled her temper. Keeping her voice calm, she said:

'What are you going to do, then?'

'Wait here.'

'Wait for what?'

He did not answer. She seized his wrist and gripped it as hard as she could:

'I suppose you know what'll happen if you stay here? The Germans will deport all men of military age.'

'Will they really? – and I suppose they'll cut off the kid's hands, and rape you into the bargain – if they're brave enough. Just a lot of blarney – that's what all that is. I bet they're not half as bad as they're made out to be.'

Sarah's throat was dry, and her lips were trembling. In a perfectly colourless voice she said:

'All right: where are we?'

'Twenty-four kilometres from Gien.'

Twenty-four kilometres! I won't let this brute see me crying! She went back to the car, pulled out her suit-case, and took Pablo by the hand.

'Come along, Pablo.'

'Where to?'

'Gien.'

'Is it a long way?'

'Quite long enough: but I'll carry you when you get tired.' Then, defiantly, 'We'll find some kind people who'll help us.'

The man stepped in front of them, barring the way. He was frowning and scratching his head uneasily.

'What do you want?' Sarah asked him grimly.

He did not know what he wanted. He looked first at Sarah, then at Pablo. He seemed to be hunting for an answer to her question.

'Going off like that, are you?' he said in quavering tones: 'without so much as a thank you.'

'Thank you,' said Sarah, hurriedly; 'thank you.'

The man had found what he was looking for – anger. He was working himself up into a fury: his face had gone scarlet.

18

'And how about my two hundred francs? – where are they, I'd like to know?'

'I don't owe you a penny,' said Sarah.

'Didn't you promise me two hundred francs this very morning at Melun, in my garage?'

'Yes, on condition you took us to Gien: but you're abandoning me and the child half-way.'

'I'm not abandoning you: it's the old bus.' He shook his head. The veins were standing out on his temples. His eyes were glittering, and he looked thoroughly pleased with himself. Sarah was not in the least frightened of him.

'I want my two hundred francs.'

She fumbled in her bag.

'Here are a hundred: I don't owe you them, and you're certainly a great deal richer than I am. I'm giving them to you just for the sake of peace and quiet.'

He took the note and put it in his pocket. Then, he held out his hand again. His face was very red, his mouth was hanging open, and there was a brooding look in his eyes.

'You still owe me a hundred francs.'

'Not a penny more will you get from me! Let us pass!' He made no move, but stood there, caught in the trap of his own ill-temper. He did not really want the hundred francs. He didn't know what he wanted. Perhaps it was just that the boy should give him a kiss at parting. These various confused feelings he translated into his own language. He took a step towards her, and she guessed that he was going to take her suit-case.

'Don't you touch me!'

'I want my hundred francs. If you don't pay me, I shall take the case.'

They stood staring at one another. It was quite obvious that he did not want to take the case. Sarah was so tired that she would gladly have given it to him. But since the scene had reached this stage, it had got to be played out. They hesitated, as though they had forgotten their parts. Then Sarah said:

'Just you try to take it! just you try!'

He seized the case by the handle, and began to pull. He could have twisted it free with a single jerk, but did no more than pull, keeping his face averted. Sarah pulled as well. Pablo started to cry. The crowd of foot passengers had already receded into the distance, and the procession of cars had begun again. Sarah knew that she was making a fool of herself. She tugged violently at the handle. He tugged more violently still, and succeeded in wrenching the suit-case free. He stared in astonishment, first at Sarah, then at what he held. Perhaps he had not really wanted to take the thing at all: but it was done now. He was within arm's reach of her.

'Give me back my case,' said Sarah.

He made no reply. He was looking foolish and obstinate. Anger flared up in Sarah and set her running towards the cars.

'Thief!' she shouted.

A long black Buick was passing at the moment.

'You stow it!' said the man.

He took her by the shoulder, but she wrenched herself away. Ease of speech and movement had come back to her. She jumped on the running-board of the Buick, and clung to the handle of the door.

'Thief! thief!'

A hand shot out of the car and pushed her off.

'Get away! you'll get yourself killed.'

She felt she was going mad. It was rather a pleasant sensation.

'Stop!' she shouted: 'Thief! Help!'

'Get away! How can I possibly stop? I'd be bumped into from behind!'

Sarah's anger ebbed suddenly. She jumped to the ground and stumbled. The garage-man caught her and set her on her feet. Pablo was crying and yelling. The game was up. Sarah wanted to die. She fumbled in her bag, and brought out a hundred francs.

'Here you are! you'll be ashamed of yourself later on!'

The man took the note without raising his eyes, and let go of the suit-case.

'And now let us pass!'

He stood aside: Pablo was still crying.

'Don't cry, Pablo,' she said; but there was no tenderness in her voice. 'It's all over now, we're going.'

They walked away, leaving the man grumbling behind them.

'Who'd have paid for the juice, I'd like to know?'

The long-bodied, dark-coloured ants filled the whole width of the road. Sarah tried at first to walk between them, but the bellowing of klaxons drove her stumbling into the ditch.

'Keep behind me.'

She twisted her foot and stopped:

'Sit down.'

They sat in the grass. The insects crawled past, enormous, slow, mysterious. The man turned his back on them: he was still clutching his useless hundred francs. The cars creaked like so many lobsters, scraped like so many crickets. Human beings had become reptiles. She felt frightened.

'He's a bad man!' said Pablo: 'bad! bad!'

'No one is bad!' said Sarah with passionate conviction.

'What for did he take our case then?'

'You mustn't say "what for": *why* did he take the case.'

'Why did he take the case?'

'He was frightened,' she said.

'Why are we waiting?' asked Pablo.

'We're waiting until the cars have gone by, so's we can walk in the road.'

Twenty-four kilometres! Eight would be about the limit of the boy's strength. Acting on a sudden impulse, she climbed to the top of the bank and stood there, waving her hand. The cars swept past her, and she had a feeling that she was being looked at by concealed eyes, by the strange eyes of flies and ants.

'What are you doing, mummy?'

'Nothing!' said Sarah, bitterly: 'just being silly.'

She returned to the ditch and took Pablo by the hand. Together they gazed at the road in silence, at the road, and at the shelled tortoises moving over its surface. Gien, twenty-four kilometres. After Gien, Nevers, Limoges, Bordeaux, Hendaye. At Hendaye, consulates, formalities, humiliating periods of waiting in official ante-rooms. It would be a stroke of luck if they found a train for Lisbon, and at Lisbon nothing short of a miracle if they found a boat for New York. And what good would it do them if they did get to New York? Gomez hadn't a brass farthing. For all she knew, he might be living with some woman: if that were so, her cup of misery and shame would be filled to the brim. He would open her telegram. 'Christ!' he would say, and turn to the fleshy blonde sitting with a cigarette between her coarse lips: 'my wife's turned up again,' he'd say: 'that's about torn it!' He'd be on the dock. All round, people would be waving handkerchiefs – but not he. He'd be scowling at the gangplank. 'If there was only myself to consider,' she thought, 'you'd never hear another word from me, but I've got to go on living in order to bring up the child you wished on me.'

The cars had vanished: the road was empty. Opposite, on the other side, were burned-up fields and hills. A man passed on a bicycle. He was pale and sweating, and was pedalling for dear life. He gave Sarah a wild look, and called to her without stopping:

'Paris is burning! – incendiary bombs!'

'What?'

But he had already caught up with the crowd of cars, and she saw him hitch himself to the back of a Renault. Paris burning? Why go on living? why protect the young life at her side? What future was there for him except to wander from country to country, bitterness and terror in his heart, chewing for fifty years the curse that lay upon his race, or machine-gunned at twenty on some stretch of road, lying with his guts in his hands. From your father you inherit pride, sensuality, and a bad character; from me, your Jewish blood. She snatched at his hand.

'Come along! It's time we were moving.'

A vast crowd was sweeping over road and fields, close-packed, mulish, implacable; a human flood. Not a sound but the susurration of boot-soles on hard earth. Sarah had a moment of panic. She wanted to run somewhere – anywhere – into the open countryside. But she pulled herself together, took a firm grip on Pablo, and dragged him along, letting herself be swept forward. Stench: the hot, stale stench of human beings, the sweet, acrid stench of destitution, the unnatural stench of thinking animals. Between two red necks topped by bowler hats, she could see the last of the cars vanishing into the distance: her final hope. Pablo began to laugh and Sarah gave a start: 'Ssh!' she said shamefacedly, 'this is no time for laughter.'

But he kept on, noiselessly.

'What are you laughing at?'

22

'It's just like a funeral!' he explained.

She felt the presence of faces, of eyes, to right and left of her, but dared not look at them. They plodded on, clinging to their plodding as she to life. Walls of dust rose in the air and broke upon them. They kept on plodding, Sarah, very upright, her head high, kept her eyes focused far ahead, staring between the two necks in front. She kept on saying to herself: 'I won't become like them!' But, in a very short time, the collective plodding seemed to have become part of her very being. It mounted from her thighs to her belly, beating within her like a huge labouring heart, the heart of those about her.

'The Nazis would kill us, wouldn't they, if they could catch us?' Pablo asked suddenly.

'Hush!' said Sarah: 'I don't know.'

'They'd kill everybody, wouldn't they?'

'Oh, do stop talking! I've just told you I don't know!'

'It'd be better to run.'

She tightened her grip on his hand:

'Don't run; stay where you are: they won't kill us.'

There was a sound of rasped breathing on her left. She had been hearing it for the last five minutes without giving it any serious thought. It seemed to have worked its way into her own body, to have settled in *her* lungs, to be *her* breathing. She turned her head and saw an old woman with grey, sweat-matted locks, an ancient crone of the cities, with bloodless cheeks and heavy pouches under her eyes. It was she who was breathing so heavily. She had probably lived for sixty years in some Montrouge slum or some back-shop of the Clichy quarter: and now, here she was, turned loose upon the road. She was clutching to her side an elongated bundle. At every step she staggered, lurching forward first with one foot, then with the other. Her head moved in sympathy with her legs. Who on earth suggested she should come away, at her age? Haven't people got enough unhappiness as it is, without deliberately going out of their way to find more? Kindliness surged in her breasts like milk: I'll help her: I'll take her bundle, her weariness, her misery. Very gently, she asked:

'Are you all alone, madame?'

The old woman did not so much as turn her head.

'Are you alone, madame?' asked Sarah more loudly.

The old woman looked at her with expressionless eyes.

'Let me carry your bundle,' said Sarah.

She waited a moment, eyeing the bundle with lustful greed.

'Do give it me: I'll carry it for as long as my little boy's able to walk.'

'I ain't a-giving of me bundle not to nobody!' said the old woman.

'But you're completely exhausted: you'll never get to where you're going.'

The ancient creature shot a glance of hatred at her, and sidled away.

'I ain't a-giving of me bundle to nobody!'

Sarah sighed and said no more. Her unused kindliness distended within her like gas. They don't want to be loved. Several heads turned towards her. She flushed. They don't want to be loved, they're not used to it.

'Is there still a long way to go, mummy?'

'Almost as long as it was just now,' replied Sarah, her nerves on edge.'

'Oh, mummy, *do* carry me!'

Sarah shrugged her shoulders. 'He's pretending he's jealous because I offered to carry the old woman's bundle.'

'Try to keep on walking for a bit.'

'I can't, mummy: *please* carry me!'

Angrily she snatched her hand away. 'He'll exhaust all my strength and I shan't be able to help anybody.' She would end by carrying the child as the old woman was carrying her bundle; she would become one of them.

'Carry me!' he said, stamping his foot: 'carry me!'

'You aren't tired yet, Pablo,' she muttered with a show of severity: 'you've only just got out of the car.'

The boy resumed his jog-trot progress. Sarah walked on, staring straight before her, forcing herself not to think of him. At the end of a few moments she glanced down out of the corner of her eye, and saw that he was crying. He was crying very quietly, making no sound, as though keeping his tears to himself. Now and again he raised his small fists and rubbed his

24

cheeks. She felt ashamed; she thought: 'I'm being too hard: kind to everybody else, out of pride, hard to him because he belongs to me.' She had an impulse to give herself to everybody. She had forgotten her own troubles, forgotten that she was a Jewess, one of the persecuted. She had found a way of escape into a huge movement of impersonal charity, and for that reason she hated Pablo because he was flesh of her flesh, and the mirror of her race. She laid her large hand on the boy's head. 'It's not your fault,' she thought, 'if you've got your father's face and your mother's blood.' The old woman's whistling inhalations were in her own lungs. 'I have no right to be generous.' She changed her suit-case into her left hand and bent down.

'Put your arms round my neck,' she said, good-humouredly, 'and make yourself as light as you can. Upsadaisy!'

He was heavy. He laughed aloud. The sun dried his tears. She had become just like one of the others, a beast of burden in the general herd. With each breath she took, it was as though there was fire in her lungs. A sharp, a half-imaginary pain gnawed at her shoulder. A weariness that was neither generous nor willingly incurred set her heart thumping – the weariness of a mother, the weariness of a Jewess – *her* weariness, *her* destiny. Hope died in her. She would never get to Gien: not she nor any of them. None of those around her had any hope left, not the old woman, not the two necks crowned with bowlers, not the couple pushing a tandem bicycle with flat tyres. We are just caught up in the crowd: the crowd is walking and we walk with it. We are no more than the feet of an interminable insect. Why walk when hope is dead? Why live? When the screaming started she was scarcely even surprised, but stood quite still while the others scattered over the road, scrambled up the bank, flung themselves flat in the ditches. She dropped her suit-case and stood in the middle of the road, alone, proud and upright. She heard the roaring in the sky. She saw her shadow already lengthening from her feet, she clutched Pablo to her breast. There was a deafening din in her ears: for a moment she was as though dead. Then the noise lessened: she had a glimpse of tadpoles in the watery spaces of the sky. The others were climbing from the ditches. She must start once more to live; start once more to walk.

'He was pretty swell, you know,' said Ritchie: 'he bought us lunch, and he's given you a hundred dollars advance.'

'True,' said Gomez.

They were on the ground floor of the Museum of Modern Art, in the Gallery devoted to Loan Exhibitions. Gomez turned his back on Ritchie and the pictures. He leaned his forehead against the window and looked out at the tarmac and at the meagre grass of the tiny garden.

'Perhaps now I shall be able to think of something else than my own bit of tragi-comedy,' he said, without turning round.

'You ought to be pretty pleased with life,' said Ritchie expansively.

The words contained a discreet hint: you've found a job: everything's for the best in the best of all possible new worlds, and it's up to you to show proper enthusiasm. Gomez glanced gloomily at Ritchie over his shoulder: pleased? It's you who feel pleased because I'm not going to be an old man of the sea on your back any longer.

He felt thoroughly ungrateful.

'Pleased?' he said; 'that remains to be seen.'

A touch of hardness showed on Ritchie's face.

'Well, aren't you pleased?'

'That remains to be seen,' said Gomez again, with a mirthless chuckle.

He resumed his former position, pressing his face to the window and looking out at the grass in a mingled mood of longing and disgust. Until this morning, thank God, colours had left him cold. He had buried the memory of the days when he had wandered the streets of Paris spellbound, mad with pride at the thought of the destiny awaiting him, saying to himself a hundred times a day – 'I'm a painter!' But Ramon had given him money. He had drunk Chili white wine. For the first time for three years he had talked about Picasso. Ramon had said: 'I don't see there's much a painter *can* do after Picasso,' and Gomez had smiled. Gomez had said: 'But I do!' – and a dry little flame had started once again to flicker in his heart.

When they came out of the restaurant, it was as though someone had operated on him for cataract. Every colour had suddenly, and at the same moment, blazed into life to do him honour: '29 was back with its dance-halls – the Redoute, the Carnaval, the Fantasia. People and things had shown a rush of blood to the surface: a violet dress had glowed to purple, the red entrance to a drug-store had deepened to crimson, colours had drummed in every object with a mad pulsation. The world had thrilled and vibrated till it seemed that it must burst. It was as though everything were on the point of exploding, of falling down in an apoplectic fit. The air had sounded a shrill cacophony of brilliance, had whirled and dazzled like a merry-go-round.

Gomez had indulged in a shrug. Here was destiny pouring colour on his head just when he had ceased to believe in his destiny. *I know perfectly well what ought to be done about it, but somebody else will have to do it.* He had clung to Ritchie's arm, walking quickly, with a fixed stare in his eyes. Colours had thrust at him from every side, bursting like tiny flasks of blood and gall. Ritchie had pushed him into the Museum: and here he now was, with there, on the other side of the glass pane, the spread of *Nature's* green, crude, unrendered, an organic secretion like honey or curdled milk. There it was, to be *taken*, to be *handled*. *I'll take it, and work it to a pitch of incandescence. ... But what business is it of mine?* I'm no longer a painter. He heaved a sigh. An art critic is not paid to spend his time worrying about the imperfect colour-sense of wild grass. His business is to think about what other men have thought. At his back were other men's colours displayed on squares of canvas; concentrations, essences and thoughts. *They* had had the good fortune to be *achieved*. Somebody had taken them, inflated them, breathed life into them, pushed them to the very limits of their nature, and now, their destiny accomplished, there was nothing more for them to hope, save to be preserved in museums. Other men's colours: that was now his lot.

'Oh, well,' he said: 'I'd better start earning my hundred dollars.'

He turned round. Fifty pictures by Mondrian were set against white, clinical walls: sterilized painting in an air-conditioned gallery. No danger here, where everything was proof against microbes and the human passions. He went up to a picture and

27

stared hard at it. Ritchie was watching his face and smiling in anticipation.

'Doesn't say a thing to me!' muttered Gomez.

Ritchie stopped smiling, but the expression of his face was one of conscientious understanding.

'Sure,' he said tactfully: 'you can't expect it to come back all at once: you got to give your mind to it.'

'Give my mind to *that*?' Gomez echoed the words ill-temperedly: 'not me!'

Ritchie turned and looked at the picture. On a grey ground was a black vertical line crossed by two horizontals. At the left-hand extremity of the upper horizontal was a blue disk.

'I sort of had a hunch you *liked* Mondrian.'

'So did I,' said Gomez.

They stopped in front of another picture. Gomez stared at it and tried to *remember*.

'Have you *got* to write about these?' inquired Ritchie nervously.

'I haven't got to: but Ramon would like my first article to be about Mondrian ... thinks it would strike the required highbrow note.'

'Oh, I do hope you'll watch yourself,' said Ritchie: 'it wouldn't do to start off by being too destructive.'

'Why not?' asked Gomez, beginning to bristle. Ritchie's smile spread a gentle irony:

'Easy to see you don't know the American public. The one thing it can't take is being startled. Weigh in by making a name for yourself: say simple, sensible things, and say them with charm, and, if you *must* attack someone, then for Pete's sake don't let it be Mondrian: he's our god.'

'Naturally,' said Gomez: 'he doesn't ask any questions.'

Ritchie shook his head and made a clucking sound with his tongue. This he did more than once, to express disapprobation.

'He asks the whale of a lot.'

'Yes, but not embarrassing questions.'

'Oh, I see what you're getting at: you mean questions about sex and the meaning of life, and poverty – things like that? I certainly was forgetting you done your studying in Germany.

Gründlichkeit – eh?' he said, slapping the other on the back: 'don't you think all that's a bit dated?'

Gomez made no reply.

'As I see it,' said Ritchie, 'it's no part of the painter's business to ask embarrassing questions. If some guy came along and asked me whether I wanted to go to bed with my mother, I'd fling him out on his ear – except he was carrying out a piece of scientific research. I don't see why painters should have the right to ask me questions in public about my complexes. Like everybody else,' he added in a more conciliatory tone, 'I got my troubles. But when I think they're getting me down I don't slip off to a museum – no, sir, I put through a call to a psycho-analyst. Folk ought to stick to their jobs. A psycho-analyst gives me confidence, because he's started off by being psycho-analysed himself. So long as painters don't do that, why, they're talking at cross-purposes, and I sure don't ask them to give me a look at myself.'

'What do you ask them for?' asked Gomez, more for the sake of saying something than because he wanted to know. He was looking at one of the pictures with surly hostility. He was thinking – 'transparent as water, nothing in it.'

'I ask them for innocence,' said Ritchie: 'take this one, now . . .'

'Well, what about it?'

'It's just seraphic!' said Ritchie ecstatically: 'we Americans like painting to be something that appeals to happy folk, or to folk who are trying to be happy.'

'I'm not happy,' said Gomez, 'and I should be a rotter if I tried to be, with all my friends either in prison or shot.'

Ritchie repeated the clucking sound.

'See here,' he said: 'I know all about your personal troubles – fascism, the defeat of the Allies, Spain, your wife and kid – sure I know! But it's a good thing to get *above* all that occasionally.'

'Not for a moment!' said Gomez: 'not for one single, solitary moment!'

A slow flush spread over Ritchie's face.

'What would *you* paint, then?' he asked in an offended voice: 'strikes, massacres, capitalists in high hats, soldiers firing on the people?'

Gomez smiled.

'I've never much believed in revolutionary art,' he said: 'and just now I don't believe in it at all.'

'Well then,' said·Ritchie: 'we're in agreement, aren't we?'

'Perhaps we are. The trouble is, I'm not at all sure that I haven't lost my belief in art of any kind.'

'And in revolution?' asked Ritchie.

Gomez said nothing, and Ritchie resumed his smiling.

'You know, you European intellectuals, you get me laughing. Where action's concerned, you all suffer from an inferiority complex.'

Gomez swung round suddenly and gripped Ritchie's arm.

'Come along! I've seen all I want to see here. I know Mondrian by heart, I can turn out an article on him any time I like. Let's go upstairs.'

'Where to?'

'The first floor. I want to see the others.'

'What others?'

They walked through three galleries devoted to the Loan Exhibition. Gomez pushed Ritchie ahead of him, and did not stop to look at anything.

'What others?' asked Ritchie again: he was in a bad temper.

'All the others: Klee, Rouault, Picasso – the ones who ask awkward questions.'

At the foot of the stairs Gomez stopped. He looked at Ritchie with a puzzled expression.

'This is the first time I've looked at pictures since '36,' he said almost timidly.

'Since '36?' Ritchie was taken aback.

'That was the year I went to Spain. At that time I was trying my hand at copperplate engravings. I hadn't time to finish the one I was working on. I left it on my table.'

'Since '36! But what about Madrid, what about the Prado?'

'The pictures had all been packed up, hidden away, dispersed.'

Ritchie shook his head.

'You sure have had a plenty rough time! Why, it must have been terrible not to see any pictures!'

Gomez burst into a guffaw of laughter.

'Not a bit of it!'

There was a hint of disapproval in Ritchie's astonishment.

'Take me now,' he said: 'I never touched a brush in my life, but I just *have* to go to all the exhibitions: it's a necessity of my nature. How can a painter go four years without looking at any pictures?'

'Wait a moment,' said Gomez; 'in a few seconds I shall know whether I am still a painter.'

They climbed the stairs and entered one of the galleries. On the left-hand wall there was a Rouault, all red and blue. Gomez came to a halt in front of it.

'That's one of the Magi,' said Ritchie.

Gomez said nothing.

'I don't care all that for Rouault,' said Ritchie: 'but I can see you like him.'

'Oh, shut up!'

He looked at the picture a moment longer, then dropped his eyes.

'Come along.'

'If you're fond of Rouault,' said Ritchie, 'there's something of his at the end of the room which I consider to be more beautiful.'

'Not worth bothering,' said Gomez: 'I've gone blind.'

Ritchie looked at him, opened his mouth, but said nothing. Gomez gave a shrug.

'No man who's shot a rifle at his fellow men can look at these properly.'

They went downstairs again, Ritchie holding himself stiffly and looking very formal. 'He thinks there's something odd about me,' reflected Gomez. Ritchie, no doubt about it, was an angel. The obstinacy of an angel showed in his limpid eye. His great-grandparents – who had been angels too – had burned witches on the public squares of Boston. 'I'm dripping with sweat, I'm poor, my thoughts are dubious because they are European thoughts. The nice-looking angels of America will end by burning me too.' Over there, across the Atlantic, were the concentration camps; here, the stake. He had a wide range of choice.

They had reached the counter, close by the entrance, where postcards were sold. Gomez was absent-mindedly glancing through an album of reproductions. Art is optimistic.

31

'We have brought photography to a high level,' said Ritchie: 'look at these colours: might almost be the original.'

A dead soldier, a shrieking woman. The recorded images of a heart at peace. Art is optimistic. Suffering is justified as soon as it becomes the raw material of beauty. I am *not* at peace: I *don't want* to find justification for the sufferings I see. Paris. . . . He turned sharply to Ritchie.

'If painting isn't *everything*, it's no more than a bad joke.'

'What's that?'

Gomez slammed the album shut:

'One can't paint evil.'

Ritchie's expression had frozen into distrust. The look he turned on Gomez was that of a country cousin. Suddenly he gave a full-throated laugh and dug his companion in the ribs.

'Don't think I don't understand, boy. Four years of war. What you need is to be re-educated!'

'It wouldn't be worth the trouble,' said Gomez: 'I'm just about ripe to be a critic.'

They relapsed into silence. Then Ritchie, speaking very quickly, said:

'Did you know there's a cinema in the basement?'

'I've never set foot in the place before.'

'They show film classics and documentaries.'

'D'you want to pay it a visit?'

'I've sure got to hang round here,' said Ritchie: 'I've a date at five, seven blocks away.'

They went across to where a panel of varnished wood was hanging, and read the programme:

'*The Covered Wagon*, seen it three times,' said Ritchie. 'But *Diamond-Mining in the Transvaal* might be interesting. You coming?' he added without any great show of eagerness.

'I don't care for diamonds,' said Gomez. Ritchie appeared to be relieved. He grinned broadly, confidingly, and gave his friend a slap on the back:

'See you again,' he said in English, as though he were recovering his native language along with his freedom.

'This is where I ought to say thank you,' thought Gomez. But he could think of no form of words, and contented himself with a silent handshake.

32

Outside, the octopus was in full operation. A thousand suckers closed upon him. He was dripping with moisture: his shirt was soaked through in a moment. A white-hot blade danced before his eyes. But he did not care, so happy was he to have got out of the Museum. The heat might be cataclysmic, but at least it was genuine. The fierce Indian sky, too, was genuine, thrust upward by the tall peaks of skyscrapers until it looked higher than all the skies of Europe. The brick houses between which he was walking were genuine, and so ugly that no one would have thought of painting them. A soaring block in the distance looked like one of Claude Lorrain's ships – a faint brush-stroke on canvas. But it was genuine: Claude Lorrain's ships were not. Pictures are just dreams. He thought of the village in the Sierra Madre where they had once fought a battle from dawn to dusk. There had been genuine red on the road. I shall never paint again, he thought with a stab of bitter pleasure. Here, on this side of the glazed frames, just *here, here*, crushed by the descending heat, on this blazing pavement, Truth had reared high walls. Truth stood blocking every vista.

There was nothing in the whole world but *this* heat, *these* stones, nothing at all – save dreams. He turned into Seventh Avenue. The human tide flowed over him, its waves crested with a fine spray of bright, dead eyes. The sidewalk vibrated. Incandescent colours spattered him as he passed; steam rose from the crowd as from a damp sheet laid out in the sun. Eyes and grins everywhere: *not to grin is a sin*: eyes vague or definite, flickering or slow moving, but all of them dead. He did his best to go on pretending that these were real men: no, impossible! Everything was falling apart in his hands; his feeling of happiness ebbed. These eyes were like the eyes of portraits. Do they know that Paris has fallen? Do they give a thought to it? They were all walking with the same hurried concentration, splashing him with the white spume of their looks. They're not real at all, he thought: they're make-believe. Where *are* the real people? – certainly not here. No one here is real; *I'm* not real. A make-believe Gomez had ridden in the bus, read the paper, smiled at Ramon, talked of Picasso, looked at the Mondrians. I am striding through Paris. The Rue Royale is deserted; the Place de la Concorde is deserted; a German flag is flying over the Chamber

33

of Deputies, an S.S. Regiment is marching under the Arc de Triomphe, the sky is dotted with aeroplanes. The brick walls crumbled, the crowd returned to the bowels of the earth, and Gomez walked lonely through the streets of Paris: through Paris, through the Truth, the only Truth, through blood and hate and defeat and death. 'French swine!' he muttered, and clenched his fists: 'couldn't take it, just ran like rabbits: I knew they would; I knew they were lost.'

He turned right into Fifty-Fifth Street, and stopped in front of a French café-restaurant, *À La Petite Coquette*. He looked at the red and green façade, hesitated a moment, then pushed through the door. He wanted to see what Frenchmen were looking like today. Inside it was dark and almost cool. The blinds were lowered, the lamps lit.

It was a pleasure to find himself in artificial light. At the far end, plunged in silence and shadow, lay the restaurant. A great hulking fellow, with his hair cropped *en brosse*, was seated at the bar, staring fixedly through a pair of pince-nez. Every now and again his head dropped forward, but he recovered himself at once with a great show of dignity. Gomez sat down on one of the bar-stools. He knew the barman slightly.

'Double Scotch,' he said in French: 'got today's paper?'

The barman pulled a *New York Times* out of a drawer and handed it to him. He was a fair young man, melancholy and precise. But for his Burgundy accent he might have passed for a native of Lille. Gomez made a pretence of glancing through the *Times*, then, suddenly, raised his eyes. The barman was looking at him with a tired expression.

'News not too good, is it?' said Gomez.

The barman shook his head.

'Paris has fallen,' said Gomez.

The barman gave a melancholy grunt, poured whisky into a small glass which he emptied into a larger one. He went through the operation a second time, and pushed the large glass in front of Gomez. The American with the pince-nez momentarily fixed them with a glassy stare, then his head dropped gently forward, as though he were bowing.

'Soda?'

'Yes.'

34

Gomez continued unabashed:

'Afraid France is a goner.'

The barman sighed but said nothing, and Gomez thought with a stab of cruel joy, that he was probably too unhappy to speak. Nevertheless, he stuck to his point, almost tenderly:

'Don't you think so?'

The barman poured mineral water into Gomez's glass. Gomez's eyes never left the lachrymose moonface. How delicious to choose his moment, to say in quite a different voice, 'What did you and your lot do for Spain? It's your turn now to dance on hot bricks!'

The barman looked up with finger raised. Suddenly he began to talk. His voice was thick, slow and peaceable, slightly nasal, and marked by a strong Burgundian accent.

'One pays for everything sooner or later,' he said.

Gomez chuckled.

'Yes,' he said, 'one pays for everything.'

The barman stabbed with his finger at the air above Gomez's head – a comet announcing the end of the world. He did not look at all unhappy.

'France,' he said, 'is going to learn now what it costs to abandon her natural allies.'

'And what precisely does that mean?' thought Gomez in sudden astonishment. He had meant to stare the other out of countenance with a look of insolent, rancorous triumph, but it was in the barman's eyes that triumph showed.

He picked his words carefully, feeling his way. 'When Czechoslovakia ...'

The barman broke in with a shrug:

'Oh, Czechoslovakia!' he said, and there was contempt in his voice.

'Well, what about Czechoslovakia?' said Gomez: 'It was your fault that it fell.'

The barman smiled.

'In the reign of Louis-the-Well-Beloved, sir, France had already committed every fault there was to commit.'

'Ah,' said Gomez: 'you're a Canadian.'

'I'm from Montreal,' said the barman.

'Are you now?'

Gomez laid the paper down on the counter. After a brief pause he said:

'Don't you ever get any French in here?'

The barman pointed with his finger at a spot behind Gomez's back. Gomez turned. Seated at a table covered with a white cloth, an old man was dreaming over a newspaper, a *real* Frenchman, with a worn, lined, stocky face, hard, bright eyes, and a grey moustache. Compared with the florid cheeks of the American with the pince-nez, his own looked as though they had been carved out of some inferior material. A *genuine* Frenchman, with genuine despair in his heart.

'Ah,' said he: 'I hadn't noticed him.'

'The gentleman's from Roanne,' said the barman; 'comes in here regular.'

Gomez gulped down his whisky and got off his stool.

'What did you do for Spain?'

The old man saw him approaching without manifesting the least show of surprise. Gomez planted himself in front of the table, and stared greedily at the face before him.

'Are you French?'

'Yes,' said the old man.

'You must have a drink with me,' said Gomez.

'Thank you, no: the occasion scarcely calls for drinks.'

Gomez's heart began to thump in an access of cruelty.

'Because of that?' he asked, pointing to the newspaper headline.

'Because of that.'

'It's because of that I'm offering you a drink,' said Gomez. 'I lived in France for ten years: my wife and son are still there. Whisky?'

'All right, but without soda.'

'One Scotch without soda, one with' – Gomez gave his order.

They relapsed into silence. The American with the pince-nez had swung round on his stool and was silently looking at them.

Suddenly the old man asked a question:

'You're not an Italian, are you?'

Gomez smiled.

'No,' he said; 'no, I'm not an Italian.'

'Because the Italians are a lot of swine,' said the old man.

'What about the French?' asked Gomez in his suavest tones: 'you got anybody there?'

'Not in Paris. My nephews live at Moulins.'

He looked attentively at Gomez.

'I can see that you've not been here long.'

'What about you?' asked Gomez.

'I settled over here in '97: that's a goodish while.' He added: 'I don't like them.'

'Why do you stay, then?'

The old man shrugged:

'I'm making money.'

'You in business?'

'Hairdressing – got a shop two blocks away. I used to spend two months in France every three years. I was due to go again shortly, and now all *this* has happened, so that's that.'

'Yes, that's that,' said Gomez.

'There've been forty customers in my place this morning. Some days it's *like* that, and they all of them wanted a haircut, shampoo, and electric massage. You'd think, wouldn't you, that they might have said something about my country? – well, you can think again! – just sat reading their papers, the lot of 'em, without a word, and I looked at the headlines while I shaved 'em. Some of them have been coming to me for twenty years, and even they didn't say anything. Ought to thank their stars I didn't cut them – my hand was trembling so! Finally, I put up the shutters and came round here.'

'They don't give a damn,' said Gomez.

'It's not so much that they don't give a damn as that they don't know what to say. The name Paris means something to them – so they don't talk, just because it does mean something to them. They're like that.'

Gomez remembered the crowd on Seventh Avenue.

'D'you suppose all those people in the street are thinking about Paris?'

'In a way – yes. But they don't think in the same way as you and me. Americans don't like thinking, so, when they do think, it takes the form of doing their darnedest not to think.'

The barman brought the glasses across. The old man took and raised it for a toast.

'Your health,' he said.

'Yours,' said Gomez.

A melancholy smile showed on the old man's face.

'Difficult to know what sort of health to drink, isn't it?' – then, with sudden determination:

'I drink to France,' he said: 'to France, no matter what's happened!'

Gomez did not want to drink to France.

'To the day when the United States comes into the war!'

The old man uttered a sharp bark of laughter:

'What a hope!'

Gomez drained his glass and turned to the barman.

'Same again.'

He needed a drink. A while back he had thought that he was alone in his concern for France. The fall of Paris had been *his* affair, a private worry – at once a misfortune for Spain and a just punishment for the French people. But he knew now that France was in this bar like a real presence, that it was eddying, in no matter how vague and abstract a form, in six million minds. It was almost more than he could bear. He had broken his *personal* link with Paris, and now here he was, an immigrant of only a few weeks' standing, preyed upon, like the rest of them, by a sort of collective obsession.

'I don't know,' said the old man, 'whether you'll get my meaning when I say that although I have lived in this country for more than forty years, this is the first time I have had the sensation of *really* being abroad. I know these people, I have no illusions about them, but I confess I thought that *somebody* would stretch a friendly hand or say a sympathetic word to me.'

His lips began to tremble:

'Customers who've been coming to me for twenty years,' he said again.

'He's a proper Frenchman all right,' said Gomez to himself; 'one of those Frenchmen who used to call us the *Frente crapular*.' But he could take no pleasure in the thought. 'He's too old,' he decided at last.

The old man was staring before him with unseeing eyes. In a voice that lacked conviction, he said:

'It may, of course, be their form of tact.'

'Hmm!' said Gomez.

'It's quite possible,' said the old man: 'entirely possible. With them everything is possible.'

In precisely the same tone he went on: 'I owned a house, at Roanne. It was my intention to go back and live there when I retired. But now I feel I'm fated to die here, and that changes one's point of view.'

'*Of course*,' thought Gomez, '*of course* you'll die here.'

He turned away his head. He wanted to escape somewhere. But he pulled himself together with an effort, went rather red, looked the old man straight in the eyes, and hissed at him:

'Were you in favour of intervention in Spain?'

'What intervention do you mean?' asked the old man in obvious bewilderment. He looked at Gomez with sudden interest:

'Are you a Spaniard?'

'Yes.'

'You too have had a lot to put up with.'

'The French didn't do much to help us,' said Gomez in a colourless voice.

'That's true: and the Americans aren't doing much to help *us*. It's with nations as it is with individuals: every man for himself.'

He didn't lift a finger to help Barcelona, and now Barcelona's fallen, Paris has fallen, and we're both of us in exile. There's not a pin to choose between us.

The barman put the two glasses on the table. They reached for them without, for a moment, ceasing to look at one another.

'Here's to Spain,' said the old man.

Gomez hesitated before saying between clenched teeth: 'Here's to the liberation of France.'

Silence fell between them. It was a pitiable situation: two old broken dolls in a New York bar, drinking to France and Spain. What a farce!

The old man carefully folded his paper and got up:

'I'm due back at the shop: that last drink was on me.'

'No,' said Gomez: 'no: barman, chalk up all the drinks to me!'

'Many thanks ...'

39

The old man reached the door. Gomez noticed that he walked with a limp. Poor old devil, he thought.

'Same again,' he said to the barman.

The American got off his stool and staggered towards him.

'I'm plastered,' he said.

'Ah?' said Gomez.

'Hadn't you noticed it?'

'As a matter of fact, I hadn't.'

'And d'you know why I'm plastered?'

'I couldn't care less,' said Gomez.

The American belched noisily and collapsed on to the chair which the old man has just vacated:

' 'Cos the Huns have taken Paris.'

A gloomy look came into his face:

' 's worst news since 1927,' he said.

'What happened in 1927?'

The man laid a finger on his lips:

'Ssh!' he said: 'tha's personal matter.'

He laid his head on the table. He seemed to have fallen asleep. The barman came across from the counter.

'Keep an eye on him for a coupla minutes,' he said: 'this is his reglar time – I'd better go find his taxi.'

'Who is he?' asked Gomez.

'Works on Wall Street.'

'Did he really get drunk because Paris has been taken?'

'If that's what he says, I guess it's true. But he was the same way last week, and then he said it was because of what was happening in the Argentine, and the week before that because of the Salt Lake City disaster. Gets drunk every Saturday, but never without some reason.'

'Too sensitive, that's his trouble,' said Gomez.

The barman hurried out. Gomez rested his head in his hands and stared at the wall. He had a clear vision of the engraving he had left unfinished on his table: it had needed a dark mass on the left to give it balance. Something like a bush: yes, a bush, that was it. He saw in memory the table, the big window – and he began to cry.

'THERE! Just over the trees!'

Mathieu was asleep and the war was lost. Even in the ultimate
privacies of sleep it was lost. The voice woke him with a start.
He lay on his back, eyes fast shut, arms pressed close to his body,
and he had lost the war. His mind was rather hazy about where
precisely he was, but he knew that he had lost the war.

'To the right!' shouted Charlot excitedly: 'over the trees!
haven't you got eyes in yer head?'

Mathieu could hear Nippert's slow drawl:

'What's the hurry?'

Where are we? – lying in the grass – eight townees in the
country, eight civilians in uniform rolled in army blankets, lying
in pairs on a spread of canvas, in the middle of a kitchen-garden.
We've lost the war. They gave it us to do something with, and
we've lost it. It had slipped through their fingers and got itself
lost somewhere up north to an accompaniment of a great deal of
noise.

'What's the hurry?'

Mathieu opened his eyes and stared at the sky. It looked a sort
of pearl grey, cloudless, bottomless, a mere negative presence.
Another morning was slowly gathering like a drop of light
which, sooner or later, would fall on the earth and drench it
with gold. The Germans are in Paris and we have lost the war.
Another morning, another beginning. The world's first morning: precisely like every other morning: everything waiting to
be done: all the future in the sky. He freed one hand from the
blankets and scratched his ear. The future didn't concern him:
other people would have to bother about that. In Paris the Germans were looking at the sky, reading in it the signs of victory
and the promise of many morrows. I've got no future. The silky
texture of the morning stroked his face: but against his right
hip he could feel the warmth of Nippert's body, against his left
thigh the warmth of Charlot's. Years and years still to be lived:
endless expanses of time to be killed. He had got to kill every
detail, all the successive minutes, of this triumphant day now

starting, light breezes in the poplars, midday sun on the corn-fields, the smell of warm earth at evening. When night comes the Germans will take us prisoner. The sound of booming grew louder: he saw the aeroplane in the eye of the rising sun.

'It's a wop,' said Charlot.

Sleepy voices tossed insults into the sky. They had grown used to the lazy patrolling of German aeroplanes, to a war that had become cynical and inoffensive. It was what they expected of *their* war. The Italians didn't play the game. The Italians dropped bombs.

'A wop, eh?' said Lubéron: 'you're telling me! Can't you hear how reglar that engine's running? it's a Messerschmidt, take *my* word – Model 37.'

Tension relaxed beneath the blankets. The faces, turned sky-wards, smiled at the German aeroplane. Mathieu heard a few muffled explosions, and four small round clouds blossomed in the sky.

'The buggers!' said Charlot: 'shooting up Jerry *now*!'

'Enough to bring a basketful of eggs on *us*!' said Longin, irritably.

Schwartz added a contemptuous comment:

'Won't them chaps never learn?'

There came the sound of two more explosions, and a couple of dark fluffy clouds appeared over the poplars.

'The buggers!' said Charlot again: 'the buggers!'

Pinette had raised himself on one elbow. His bright little cockney face looked pink and clean. He fixed his companions with a disdainful expression.

'Just doing their job,' he said dryly.

Schwartz gave a shrug:

'What's the point – now?'

The ack-ack had gone silent. The two little clouds were shredding out. Nothing could be heard but the regular and triumphant throb of an engine high up.

'Can't see 'im no longer,' said Nippert.

'I can – there he is – just where I'm pointing.'

A white vegetable thrust from the ground in the direction of the aeroplane. Charlot crouched naked under his blankets.

42

'Keep still!' said Sergeant Pierné nervously: 'You'll give us away if you aren't careful!'

'Oh yeah? – in this light they'll take us for a field of cabbages!'

All the same, he withdrew his arm as the machine passed overhead. His pals grinned as they followed the bright little speck of sunshine across the sky. It was a morning's distraction, the first event of the day.

'Getting up an appetite, that's what he's doing,' said Lubéron.

There were eight of them there who had lost the war, three orderly-room clerks, two observers, and a meteorologist, all lying side by side among the leeks and carrots. They had lost the war much as a man loses an hour – without noticing it. Eight of them: Schwartz, the plumber; Nippert, the bank-clerk; Longin, the tax-collector; Lubéron, the bank messenger; Charlot Wroclaw, the sunshade and umbrella merchant; Pinette, the ticket-puncher; and two teachers, Mathieu and Pierné. They had spent nine boring months, first in the pinewoods, later among the vineyards; and then, one fine day, a voice from Bordeaux had announced the news of their defeat, and they had realized that they had backed the wrong horse.

Mathieu felt the touch of a clumsy hand on his cheek. He turned to Charlot:

'What is it, angel-face?'

Charlot was lying on his side: Mathieu could see his healthy pink cheeks and open mouth.

'What I want to know,' said Charlot in a low voice, 'is shall we be moving today?'

A worried look was chasing round and round over his cheerful countenance, as though it did not know where to perch.

'Today? I don't know.'

They had left Morsbronn on the 12th. Then had come a period of disorderly retreat and, finally, this halt.

'What are they buggering about here for?'

'Waiting for the P.B.I., so they say.'

'If the P.B.I. can't make it, is that any reason why we should let ourselves get nabbed with 'em?'

He added, apologetically:

'You see, I'm a Jew, and I've got a Polish name.'

'I know,' said Mathieu gloomily.

'Shut up,' said Schwartz, 'and listen.'

A continuous muffled rumbling reached their ears. The day before, and the day before that, it had gone on from dawn to dusk. No one knew who was firing, or on what target.

'Can't be far off six o'clock,' said Pinette: 'Yesterday they started at 5.45.'

Mathieu raised his wrist above his eyes and turned it round in order to see his watch.

'Five past six.'

'Five past six,' said Schwartz. 'It'd surprise *me* if we moved today.' He yawned: 'Oh, well, another day on the veldt.'

Sergeant Pierné echoed his yawn.

'Better show a leg,' he said.

'Yes,' said Schwartz: 'suppose so – better show a leg.'

No one moved. A cat streaked past them, stopped and crouched as though ready to pounce, then suddenly, all purpose forgotten, stretched itself lazily at full length. Mathieu, propped on his elbow, was watching it. All at once he became aware of two legs in khaki puttees set astraddle, and raised his eyes. Lieutenant Ulmann, with arms folded, was contemplating them. His eyebrows were raised: Mathieu noticed that he had not shaved.

'What the devil d'you think you're all doing? Have you gone mad? – answer me, what d'you think you're doing?'

Mathieu waited a few moments, then, seeing that no one had attempted to reply, said, without moving:

'We thought it'd be nicer to sleep in the open, sir.'

'Indeed! – with the sky full of enemy planes. That happy thought of yours might have cost us dear and set them gunning Divisional H.Q.'

'The Germans know perfectly well we're here. All our moves were made in full daylight,' said Mathieu patiently.

The lieutenant seemed not to have heard him. 'I issued strict orders that you were not to leave the barn,' he said: 'and what the hell d'you mean by lying down in the presence of a superior officer?'

There was a lazy stirring at ground level, and the eight men sat up on their blankets, blinking sleepily. Charlot, who was stripped to the skin, covered his nakedness with a handkerchief.

The air was fresh. Mathieu shivered and felt round for his tunic to throw over his shoulders.

'So, you're there too, are you, Pierné! You ought to be ashamed of yourself. N.C.O.s are supposed to set a good example!'

Pierné compressed his lips and said nothing.

'Never seen such a thing in m'life!' said the lieutenant: 'perhaps you'll be good enough to explain why you left the barn?'

He spoke without self-assurance. His words were violent but their tone was weary. There were dark shadows under his eyes, and his fresh complexion looked blotchy.

'We were too hot in there, sir – couldn't sleep.'

'Too hot, were you? – an air-conditioned bedroom's more in your line, I suppose! – You'll spend tonight in the schools, with the others. Don't you realize there's a war on?'

Longin gestured with his hand:

'War's over, sir,' he said with an odd little smile.

'Over, my foot! You ought to be ashamed to talk about its being over when less than twenty miles away there are chaps trying to cover our retreat and getting killed for their trouble.'

'Poor buggers,' said Longin: 'just set down there to be pooped off while the armistice is being signed!'

The lieutenant flushed angrily:

'You're still soldiers, and, until you've been demobilized and sent home, you'll go on being soldiers, and you'll obey your officers.'

'Even in a prison-camp?' asked Schwartz.

The lieutenant said nothing, but looked at them with mingled timidity and contempt. They returned his gaze without embarrassment or impatience. It seemed doubtful whether they even felt the novel thrill of unexpectedly seeing themselves as objects of fear. After a brief pause, the lieutenant gave a shrug and turned on his heel.

'I should consider it a great favour if you would consent to get up – at once' – he threw back at them over his shoulder.

He moved away, holding himself very upright, and walking trippingly, like a dancer. 'His last dance,' thought Mathieu: 'in a few hours there'll be German shepherds herding us eastwards, higgledy-piggledy, officers and men alike.' Schwartz yawned till his eyes watered. Longin lit a cigarette. Charlot was tearing up handfuls of grass. They were all of them afraid to get up.

'You noticed what he said about us sleeping in the schools tonight?' said Lubéron: 'that means no move.'

'That was just for something to say,' remarked Charlot: 'he doesn't know no more than us.'

Suddenly Sergeant Pierné burst out with: 'Who *does* know – who knows anything?'

There was no reply to this question. A moment later Pinette jumped to his feet:

'Anyone coming along for a wash?' he inquired.

'O.K.,' said Charlot with a yawn.

He got up. Mathieu and Sergeant Pierné followed his example.

'The Cadum Kid!' exclaimed Longin.

In his pink and hairless nakedness, with his fresh complexion and his prominent little belly gleaming in the golden light of dawn, Charlot did look exactly like France's No. 1 Baby.* Schwartz, as usual, padded along behind him.

'You've gone all goosefleshy,' he said, tickling him. 'You've gone all goosefleshy, baby-face!'

Charlot put on his regular act of squealing and wriggling, but this morning there was something half-hearted about the performance. Pinette turned to Longin, who was smoking with a mulish look on his face.

'You not coming?'

'What for?'

'To get a wash.'

'Why the hell should I want to wash!' said Longin. 'Just to please the Jerries? They can take me as they find me!'

'Who said anything about being took?'

'You make me sick!' said Longin.

'We may make a getaway,' said Pinette.

'And Santa Claus *may* come popping down the chimney!'

'Even if they do take us, that's no reason for staying dirty.'

'You don't catch me washing for them!'

'That's all balls,' said Pinette.

* Those familiar with Paris before 1939 will remember the huge baby who used to proclaim, from half-way up the Eiffel Tower, the merits of Cadum Soap. (Translator.)

Longin chuckled but said nothing. He lay there, snuggled in his blankets, with a look of superiority on his face. Lubéron, too, had stayed where he was, and was making believe to be asleep. Mathieu took his haversack and walked over to the trough. There were two metal pipes from which water flowed into a stone basin. It was cold and stark like a naked body. All night long Mathieu had heard its hopeful, childish, and interrogative murmuring. He plunged his head into the trough. The babyish song became a silent, glittering freshness in his ears and nostrils, a bouquet of wet roses and water-plants in his heart: bathing in the Loire – rushes – a small green island – childhood. When he stood up again Pinette was savagely soaping his neck. Mathieu smiled at him: he was very fond of Pinette.

'What balls Longin does talk,' said Pinette. 'If the Fritzes do turn up we got to be clean.'

He stuck a finger in his ear and twiddled it vigorously.

'If you've got such a thing about being clean,' shouted Longin from where he was lying, 'better wash yer feet as well!'

Pinette looked at him pityingly. 'No one sees one's feet.'

Mathieu started to shave. The blade was an old one and made his skin smart. 'When I'm a prisoner I shall let my beard grow.' The sun was getting higher. Its long beams struck obliquely through the grass. Under the trees the green was young and tender, a hollow of sleep in the morning's flank. Heaven and earth were full of signs – signs of hope. Among the poplar leaves the birds, obedient to some invisible signal, struck up a full-throated chorus, a metallic storm of quite extraordinary violence. Then, mysteriously, they fell silent. A feeling of insecurity seemed to be wandering about the grassy expanse, about the patches of vegetables that were as chubby as Charlot's cheeks – uncertain where to alight. Very carefully Mathieu dried his razor and put it back into his haversack. His heart was in league with the dawn, the dew, the long shadows. Deep within him was a feeling as of a feast-day. He had got up early and had shaved as though for some special, some gay occasion – a party in a garden, a first Communion, a wedding-feast with lovely dresses flickering in pleached alleys, a table spread on the lawn, warm droning of sugar-drunk wasps. Lubéron got up and went over to the hedge to relieve himself. Longin went into the barn, carrying his blankets under his arm. A moment later he came out again, wandered idly across to the trough and wetted the tips of his fingers with a mocking, idle expression on his face. Mathieu had only to look at him to realize that there was no feast-day in the offing, not now or ever again.

The old farmer had come out of his house. He stood smoking his pipe and looking at them.

'Mornin', daddy!' cried Charlot.

'Marnin' t'ye,' said the farmer, with a shake of his head: 'marnin' t'ye.'

He came forward a few steps till he was close to them, and halted.

'Not gone, then?'

'Obviously not,' said Pinette drily.

The old fellow chuckled. He looked in no very good humour.

'' Tis just as I did say: no chance of you a-going.'

'We might.'

He spat between his feet and wiped his moustache.

'What about them Boches – we likely get a squint of 'em today?'

They broke into a laugh.

'Maybe yes, maybe no,' said Lubéron. 'We're all in the same boat – just waiting – and dolling of ourselves up to say how-d'ye-do.'

The old man gave them a funny look.

''Tain't the same fur you: you'll be a-coming back.'

He sucked at his pipe and added:

'Reckon you didn't know as I'm from Alsace.'

'We ought to: you've told us often enough,' said Schwartz: 'what about putting on another record?'

The old man shook his head.

'Funny sort of war,' said he: ''tis the civilians now as gets killed, and the soldiers as goes scot free!'

'Come off it! You know as well as we do that they won't kill you.'

'I be from Alsace, I tell 'ee.'

'So'm I,' said Schwartz.

'Maybe,' said the old man: 'but that be different. When I left Alsace it belonged to 'em.'

'They won't do you any harm,' said Schwartz: 'they're human like the rest of us.'

'Like the rest of you, eh?' said the old man with a sudden spurt of indignation: 'would you go 'bout a-chopping of kiddies' hands off?'

Schwartz burst out laughing.

'Filled up with all the nonsense of the last war, that's what he is,' he said with a wink at Mathieu.

He took his towel, dried his great muscular arms, and turned to the farmer.

'They're not a lot of loonies, you know. They'll give you cigarettes and chocolate – propaganda, that's what they call it. And you needn't be afraid of taking it all either – it won't commit you to anything.'

Still laughing, he went on:

'Good deal better, as things are, to be a native of Strasbourg than of Paris.'

'I don't want to become no German, not at my age I don't,' said the farmer: 'rather they stuck me up and shot me.'

Schwartz slapped his thigh.

'Hell, boys, d'you hear that? Rather be a live German than a dead Frenchman, say I,' he finished, imitating the old man's voice.

Mathieu jerked up his head and looked at him. Pinette and Charlot were looking at him, too. Schwartz stopped laughing, went very red, and wriggled his shoulders. Mathieu turned away. He had no wish to sit in judgement. Besides, he liked this great strapping, good-tempered, hard-working lout. Not for anything in the world would he have added to his embarrassment. No one spoke. The old man shook his head and glanced round the circle with a resentful expression.

'Didn't ought to 'ave gone and lost this 'ere war: didn't ought for to 'ave gone and lost it.'

They were all silent now. Pinette coughed, went over to the trough and began playing with the tap, looking foolish. The old man knocked out his pipe on the gravel path, trod on the ash, then turned round and went slowly back into the house. There was a long silence. Schwartz stood very stiffly, his hands on his hips. After a few moments he seemed to wake up. He forced a smile:

49

'I was only kidding!'

No answer. The others were looking at him. Then, quite suddenly, though nothing had visibly occurred to change the situation, some obstruction seemed to give way. It was as though a stretched spring had been eased, as though there had been a sort of motionless dispersal of energy. The sullen little group broke up. Longin began to pick his teeth with his knife. Lubéron cleared his throat, and Charlot, with a look of angelic innocence, started to hum. They could none of them long harbour a grievance except in matters of leave or rations. Mathieu caught a brief whiff of aniseed and mint. Following the example of the birds, grass and flowers were coming awake and flinging wide their smells, as the birds their cries. 'I'd forgotten the smells,' thought Mathieu: fresh gay smells, sharp and acid. They would grow sweeter, more lush, more feminine, as the blue of the sky deepened and the German caterpillar trucks drew nearer. Schwartz sniffed noisily and looked at the bench which they had pulled up against the wall of the house on the previous evening.

'Oh, well!' he said.

He walked over to it and sat down, his shoulders hunched, his hands hanging between his knees. But he kept his head up and stared in front of him with a hard look in his eyes. Mathieu hesitated for a moment, then went and sat down beside him. A few moments later, Charlot detached himself from the group, and planted himself on the path in front of them. Schwartz looked up at him, unsmiling.

'Better start washing my things,' he said.

There was a silence. Schwartz was still looking at Charlot.

'*I* didn't lose the war. . . .'

Charlot had an embarrassed air. He began to laugh. But Schwartz was hard on the heels of his thought.

'If everyone had behaved like me we might have won it. I've nothing to reproach myself with.'

He scratched his cheek. A surprised look had come into his eyes.

'It's a fair bugger!' he said.

That's just about it, thought Mathieu: a fair bugger. He gazed into nothingness, and thought: I'm a Frenchman ... and that's a bugger, he reflected for the first time in his life; a *fair bugger*: we've never really *seen* France: we've only been in it. France has been the air we breathed, the lure of the earth, having plenty of elbow room, seeing the kind of things we do, feeling so certain that the world was made for man. It has always been so *natural* to be French, the simplest, the most economical, way in the world, to feel that one is universal. One didn't have to explain things: it was for the others, the Germans, the English, the Belgians, to explain by what piece of ill-luck, by what fault, it had come about that they were none of them quite human. And now France is lying on her back, and we can take a good look at her, can see her like a piece of large, broken-down machinery. And we think – so *that*, all the time, is what it was! – an accident of locality, an accident of history. We are still French, but it no longer seems natural. It needed no more than an accident to make us realize that we were merely accidental. Schwartz thinks that he is accidental – and no longer under-stands himself, finds himself embarrassing. He thinks – 'How comes it that one is French?': he thinks, 'With a bit of luck I might have been born a German.' And then his face takes on a hard look, and he sits listening to the approach of his adoptive country. He sits waiting for the coming of the glittering armies that shall gleefully celebrate his change of heart: he sits waiting for the moment when he will be able to trade our defeat for their victory, when it will seem *natural* to him to be victorious and German.

Schwartz got up with a yawn:

'I'm going across to do some washing,' he said.

Charlot swung round and joined Longin, who was talking to Pinette. Mathieu was left alone on the bench.

It was Lubéron's turn to yawn noisily:

'Christ! it's a boring life!'

Charlot and Longin yawned. Lubéron watched them yawning and yawned again himself.

'What we need,' he said, 'is a bit of skirt.'

'Mean to tell me you feel like that at six o'clock in the morn-ing?' asked Charlot indignantly.

'Always feel like it.'

'More'n I do. I'd as soon get a kick in the arse as start muck-ing about with a woman at this time of day.'

51

Lubéron gave a cackle of laughter:

'If you was a married man, you little cissy, you'd have learned to do the job any old time, whether you felt like it or not. Great thing about having a woman is you needn't think about nothing.'

They stopped talking. The poplars rustled; an antique sun trembled among the leaves: from far away came the companionable rumble of artillery – such a daily familiar, so reassuring, that it had come to seem like one of the sounds of nature. Something detached itself from a point above their heads: a wasp struck at their group in a long, quivering dive.

'Listen!' said Lubéron.

'What to? . . .'

There was a sort of emptiness about them, a strange tranquillity. The birds sang, a cock crowed in the farmyard: far away, someone was hammering rhythmically on metal. But these sounds did not break the overwhelming sense of silence. The guns had stopped.

'Oh boy!' said Charlot.

'Mmm.'

They strained their ears. They stared at one another.

'That's how it'll begin,' said Pierné without any particular show of interest: 'at a given moment, over the whole front, there'll be silence.'

'What front? There isn't a front.'

'Everywhere.'

Schwartz came towards them, rather shyly:

'*I* rather think there's got to be some sort of bugle call first,' he said.

'Balls!' said Nippert: 'communications have all broken down. It might be twenty-four hours before we heard they'd signed.'

'P'raps the war ended at midnight,' said Charlot with a hopeful grin. 'They always give the cease-fire at midnight.'

'Or at midday.'

'Nonsense, you chump! midnight – zero hour – get it?'

'Stop talking,' said Pierné.

They stopped. Pierné sat listening intently, his face nervously twitching. Charlot's mouth was hanging open. Across the rustling silence they listened to peace: a peace without glory, without drums, without trumpets. A peace that was like death.

'Hell!' said Lubéron.

The rumble had begun again. It sounded less muffled, less distant, more threatening. Longin clasped his long fingers and made the joints crack. He gave vent to a little spurt of bitterness:

'God in Heaven, what are they waiting for? Don't they think we've been beaten *enough*, that we haven't lost enough men? Has France got to be completely buggered up before they decide to stop the slaughter?'

They felt nerveless and flabby, spinelessly indignant. Their faces had the leaden look which comes from indigestion. A sound of drumming on the far horizon was enough to make them feel that the great tidal wave of war had swept down on them again. Pinette swung round and faced Longin. There was a darkness of storm clouds in his eyes: his hand was gripping the lip of the trough.

'*What* slaughter? – tell me that : *what* slaughter? Where are the dead and wounded? If *you've* seen any you've been in luck's way. All *I've* seen is a lot of windy buggers like you careering along the roads in a blue funk!'

'What's biting *you*?' inquired Longin (there was a note of spitefulness in his assumed air of concern). 'Not feeling too good?'

He shot a conspiratorial glance at the others:

'Our friend Pinette's always been a nice guy. We used to like him because he was as good a hand at swinging the lead as the rest of us. He was never one to put himself forward when there was dirty work to be done. Pity he's started being a fire-eater just when the war's over!'

There was an ominous glitter in Pinette's eyes: 'Who says I'm being a fire-eater?'

'I do – coming the old soldier, that's what you're doing.'

'Well, it's better than s—ing one's bags, like you!'

'So I'm s—ing me bags, am I, just because I say the French army's taken a beating?'

'You seem to know a lot about the French army.' Pinette was so angry that his words tumbled over one another: 'I suppose Weygand's been talkin' things over with you!'

Longin's smile was lazy and insolent:

'I can see what's happened to the French army without any help from Weygand – half of its effectives in flight, and the other half surrounded. What more d'you want?'

Pinette swept the words away with a gesture: 'We shall regroup on the Loire and make contact with the Northern Armies at Saumur.'

'You really think that, do you, you fathead?'

'It's what the Captain said: ask Fontainat.'

'Well, the Northern Armies had better get a move on, that's all I can say, with the Boches already nibbling at their backsides. As to our turning up at the rendezvous – well, I'm not taking any bets!'

Pinette looked as black as thunder. He was breathing heavily and shuffling his feet. He looked at Longin, shaking himself as though to free his back from some load, and when he spoke it was with the blind fury of a cornered man:

'Even if we have to retreat as far as Marseilles, even if we have to march right across France, there's always North Africa!'

Longin folded his arms with a contemptuous smile:

'What's wrong with Saint-Pierre-et-Miquelon, you bloody fool?'

'Think yerself damn' clever, don't you? – *damn'* clever,' said Pinette advancing towards him.

Charlot jumped between them.

'Come off it, chaps,' he said: 'what you want to scrap for? Everyone knows fighting doesn't settle anything, and that there's not going to be any more of it – no more war, never again' – he declared with burning conviction. He was staring hard at both of them and trembling with passion – with a passionate desire to make peace – peace between Pinette and Longin, peace between the Germans and the French.

'It *ought* to be possible,' he went on – and there was a note almost of supplication in his voice – 'to come to an understanding with them. After all, it's not to their interest to trample on us.'

Pinette diverted his fury on to this new target:

'If the war's been lost, it's chaps like you as is responsible!'

Longin gave an ugly laugh:

54

'Just another as can't see straight!'

There was an interval of silence, then, slowly, the faces of all those present turned in the direction of Mathieu. He had been expecting this to happen. Whenever there was an argument they looked to him to settle it, because he was a man of education.

'What's your opinion?' asked Pinette.

Mathieu lowered his eyes and said nothing.

'You deaf? I was asking what your opinion was.'

'I haven't got an opinion,' said Mathieu.

Longin crossed the path and came to a halt in front of him:

'You don't say? I thought school-teachers always had an opinion. Their brains are working away the whole time, aren't they?'

'Not the whole time.'

'You're not quite a fool: *you* know perfectly well that further resistance is impossible.'

'How should I know that?'

Pinette came across in his turn. The two of them were standing one on either side of Mathieu, like his good and evil genius.

'There's nothing of the heel about you,' said Pinette: '*you* can't want the French to lay down their arms without fighting the thing out to a finish: you don't, do you?'

Mathieu gave a shrug.

'If *I* was the one who had to do the fighting,' he said, 'I might have an opinion, but it's the other chaps who are getting knocked over. If there's going to be a scrap it'll be on the Loire. I can't decide for them.'

'So you see,' said Longin, with a sneering look at Pinette, 'it's not for us to decide whether the other blokes are to get it in the neck.'

Mathieu looked at them uneasily:

'That's not what I said.'

'What d'yer mean that's not what you said? you've just bin and gone and said it.'

'If there were the slightest chance,' said Mathieu: 'one chance in a thousand . . .'

'Well?'

Mathieu shook his head:

'How can one possibly know?'

'What'you mean?' asked Pinette.

55

'He means,' said Charlot, 'that there's nothing for it but to wait and see and not get all worked up.'

'No!' exclaimed Mathieu; 'no!'

He jumped up, clenching his fists:

'I've done nothing else but wait ever since I was a child!'

They stared at him. They had not the slightest idea what he was talking about. With an effort he calmed himself:

'How can it possibly matter what we decide or what we don't decide?' he said: 'Is anyone asking for our opinion? D'you realize the situation we're in?'

They recoiled from him. They felt frightened.

'Oh, we realize it all right,' said Pinette.

'You said it,' remarked Longin: 'the P.B.I. don't have no opinions.'

His cold, slobbering smile gave Mathieu the creeps:

'And prisoners even less,' he said dryly.

Everything's asking us our opinion; *everything*. We're encircled by questions. The whole thing's a farce. Questions are asked as though we were men, as though somebody wanted to make us believe that we still *are* men. It *is* a farce – this shadow of a question put by the shadow of a war to a handful of make-believe men.

'What's the use of having an opinion? *You're* not going to be called on to make a decision.'

He stopped talking. He thought suddenly: 'life's got to go on. Day after day we have got to gather in the rotten fruit of defeat, work out, in a world that's gone to pieces, that total choice I've just refused to make. But, good God! – *I* didn't choose this war, *I* didn't choose this defeat: by what trick of fortune have I got to take responsibility for them? He was conscious within himself of the panic fury of the trapped beast, and, looking up, saw the same fury in their eyes. Let them shout together to the far heavens: 'We've nothing to do with all this!'

His passion ebbed. Oh yes, to be sure, innocence was in the morning sunlight, innocence was on the blades of grass – an almost tangible presence. But it was a lying presence. What *was* true was the fault that they had *all* committed, an indefinable fault, *their* fault. A phantom war, a phantom defeat, a phantom guilt. He looked in turn at Pinette and Longin, and his clenched

hands relaxed. He did not know whether what he wanted was
to help them or to beg them to help him. And they, too, looked
at him, then, averting their eyes, slunk away. Pinette was staring
at his feet. Longin was smiling at some private pleasantry, but
the smile was stiff and embarrassed. Schwartz and Nippert were
standing a little apart, talking together in the Alsace dialect.
Already they had the look of conspirators. Pierné was spasmodically opening and closing his right hand. Mathieu thought: 'So
this is what we've become!'

Marseilles: 2 p.m.

IT was true, of course, that he *thoroughly disapproved* of being
melancholy, but when the mood was on one it was the very
devil to get quit of it! 'I must have an unhappy temperament,'
he thought. There were many reasons why he should rejoice. He
ought, above all, to congratulate himself on his narrow escape
from peritonitis, and on the fact that he was now quite well
again. Instead of which he was thinking: 'I've come through,'
and the knowledge was bitter to him. When one is melancholy
all reasons for rejoicing become melancholy too, so that one rejoices in a melancholy way. Besides, he thought, I am, in fact,
dead. For all practical purposes he had died at Sedan in May
1940. The years of life remaining to him were a long vista of
boredom. He sighed again, following with his eyes the progress
of a large green fly moving across the ceiling, and enunciated his
conclusion: I'm a second-rater. The thought was profoundly
disagreeable to him. Until now, Boris had made it a fixed rule
never to indulge in introspective questionings, and it had always
worked very well. Besides, so long as his main problem had been
merely that of getting decently and neatly killed, the fact that
he was a second-rater had not very much mattered. Actually, it
had been an advantage, since it had meant that he would have
less to regret. But now, all that was changed. Destiny had decided that he was to live, and he was being forced to realize that
he had no vocation, no talents, and no money – none of the qual-
ities, in short, which are necessary for living, with the single

exception of good health. How bored I'm going to be, he thought. He was conscious of a sense of frustration. The fly made off, buzzing loudly. Boris put his hand under his shirt and stroked the scar which seamed his stomach in the neighbourhood of his groin. It gave him pleasure to feel the little gully in his flesh. He stared at the ceiling, stroked his scar, and remained in a state of gloom. Francillon came into the ward, strolled with unhurried steps between the empty beds in Boris's direction, and came to a sudden halt, simulating surprise.

'I've been looking for you in the yard,' he said.

Boris said nothing, and Francillon folded his arms with an indignant air.

'Two o'clock in the afternoon, and still in bed!'

'I'm fed up,' said Boris.

'Got a fit of the blues?'

'I've not got a fit of the blues: just fed up.'

'Well, snap out of it: you'll soon feel different.'

He sat down by the bed and started to roll a cigarette. He had large, prominent eyes and a beaked nose. He was an odd-looking creature, and Boris was very fond of him. There were moments when the mere sight of him produced an uncontrollable fit of laughter.

'Won't be long now,' said Francillon.

'How long?'

'Exactly four days.'

Boris did the sum on his fingers.

'That means the 18th.'

Francillon utter a confirmatory grunt, licked the gummed paper, lit the cigarette, and leaned forward confidentially.

'No one here?'

All the beds were empty. The boys were out in the yard or off into the town.

'Look for yourself – unless, of course, there are spies under the beds.'

Francillon leaned still closer to him.

'On the night of the 18th,' he explained, 'Blin will be on duty. The old crate'll be on the runway ready to take off. All aboard by midnight, airborne by two, London by seven. What d'you say?'

Boris made no reply. He fingered his scar and thought – they're in luck's way. The reflection made him feel gloomier than ever. He's going to ask me what I've decided.

'Well, what about it?'

'I think you're lucky devils,' said Boris.

'What d'you mean lucky? You can come along if you want to. Don't say you've not been invited.'

'No,' admitted Boris, 'I won't say that.'

'All right, then: what's your decision?'

'Nothing doing,' said Boris morosely.

'But you aren't going to stay on in France?'

'I don't know.'

'This war's not over yet,' said Francillon, and there was an obstinate look in his face. 'Those who say it is are cowards and liars. You've got to be where the fighting is: you've no right to hang on in France.'

'No need to tell me that,' said Boris bitterly.

'Well, then?'

'Nix. I'm waiting for my girl to turn up, as I told you. When I've seen her, I'll decide.'

'You can't let a girl stand in your way. This is a man's job.'

'Well, that's how it is,' said Boris briefly.

Francillon had a scared look and said nothing. Wonder whether he thinks I've got cold feet? Boris tried to read in Francillon's eyes what was going on in Francillon's mind. A trusting smile reassured him.

'Seven, you say, is when you'll get there?'

'Seven.'

'The English coast'll look grand in the dawn. There are big white cliffs at Dover.'

'Ah!' ejaculated Francillon.

'I've never been up in a plane,' said Boris.

He brought out his hand from under his shirt.

'Scratching your scar?'

'No.'

'I keep on scratching mine: it tickles.'

'This one's rather awkwardly placed for scratching in company.'

There was a silent pause: then Francillon said:

'When's your girl arrive?'

'Don't know: she's got to get here from Paris.'

'She'd better get a move on,' said Francillon: 'we can't wait.'

Boris sighed and turned over on his stomach. In a somewhat impersonal voice, Francillon continued:

'Haven't breathed a word to mine, though I see her every day. I'll drop her a line the evening we take off. By the time she gets it we shall be in London.'

Boris nodded his head but remained silent.

'You amaze me!' said Francillon: 'honestly, Serguine, you amaze me!'

'You wouldn't understand,' said Boris.

Francillon stopped talking, stretched out his hand and picked up a book. They'll be flying over the cliffs of Dover in the dawn – doesn't bear thinking about! Boris had no belief in miracles. He knew that Lola would say no.

'*War and Peace*' – said Francillon: 'what's that?'

'Novel about war.'

'The 1914 one?,

'No, another – but they're all alike.'

'Yes,' said Francillon with a laugh, 'they're all alike.'

He had opened the book at random and was frowning over the pages. The expression on his face was one of pained interest.

Boris let himself relax upon the bed. He thought: I *can't* do that to her – can't go off for the second time without even asking what she feels about it. If I stay on here because of her, he thought, it'll be a proof of love. But, good gracious me, he thought, what a very odd proof of love! On the other hand, had anybody the *right* to stay behind for the sake of a woman? Francillon and Gabel, of course, would say no, but they were too young really to know what love was like. What *I* want someone to tell me, thought Boris, is not what love's like – I know that already – but what it's *worth*. Has one any right to stay behind just to make a woman happy? Put like that, I should be inclined to say no, too. But has one any right to go away if by going one hurts somebody? He remembered something Mathieu had once said: 'I'm not such a coward that I should be frightened of hurting somebody should it be really necessary to do so.' All very well: the trouble with Mathieu was that his actions were always at variance with his words: he had *never* had enough courage to make anyone miserable.

Boris caught his breath and came up short against a sudden doubt. What if all this is just a mad impulse? Suppose my anxiety to get away is just pure egotism? – because I funk getting bogged down in civil life? Maybe I'm out for nothing more than adventure. Maybe it's easier to get oneself killed than to go on living? On the other hand, suppose I'm staying on because I want to be comfortable, because I'm frightened, because it's nice to have a woman handy when one wants one? He turned over. Francillon was bent over the book. There was something mistrustful in his concentration, as though he had made up his mind to unmask the author's lies. If only I could say 'I'll come'. I wonder if I can. He cleared his throat, opened his mouth, and waited. But the words hung back. I can't hurt her like that. It came to him that he didn't *want* to go unless he could first consult Lola. She's bound to say no, and that'll be that. But suppose she didn't arrive in time? – he thought: that was a possibility that had not so far occurred to him. Suppose she doesn't get here by the 18th? Shall I have to make up my mind independently? What if I stay and she turns up on the 20th, and says – I'd have let you go. A pretty sort of fool I shall look then! Still another variant – I go, she arrives on the 19th, and kills herself. Oh hell! His mind was a whirl of conflicting thoughts. He closed his eyes and dozed off.

'Serguine!' shouted Bergin from the door: 'there's a girl outside asking for you.'

Boris started up: Francillon raised his eyes.

'Probably her.'

Boris got out of bed and rumpled his hair:

'Too good to be true,' he yawned: 'no, it's my sister's day for visiting.'

'Oh,' said Francillon with a dazed sort of look: 'your sister's day – was that her the last time I was here?'

'Yes.'

'Good-looker,' said Francillon without any show of enthusiasm.

Boris rolled his puttees and put on his tunic. He waved a couple of fingers at Francillon, crossed the ward, and went downstairs, whistling.

61

Half-way, he stopped and began to laugh. What a bore, he thought, that I'm feeling so gloomy. He wouldn't get much fun out of seeing Ivich. She's no damn' use to a fellow when he's got a fit of the blues: only makes 'em worse.

She was waiting for him in the courtyard of the hospital. Some soldiers walking round eyed her casually, but she took no notice of them. While he was still some way off, she smiled.

'Good afternoon, little brother!'

At the sight of Boris the soldiers broke into speech and laughter. He was very popular. He waved his hand at them, but felt vaguely disappointed that none of them said, 'It's your lucky day!' or 'Wouldn't mind finding *that* in my bed!' The truth was, Ivich had aged a good deal and lost most of her looks since her miscarriage. Boris, of course, was still proud of her, but in a different way.

'Good afternoon, you little horror,' he said, with a flicker of his fingers on her neck.

There was always about her these days an aura of fever and eau de Cologne. He studied her dispassionately.

'Don't look too good,' he said.

'I know: I feel lousy.'

'Given up using lipstick?'

'Yes,' she said, and there was a hard note in her voice.

No other words passed between them. She was wearing a blouse of ox-blood red with a high collar – a very Russian affair, which accentuated her pallor. It was a pity that she wouldn't show more of her shoulders and throat. She had beautifully rounded shoulders, but she had taken recently to high-necked dresses and excessively long skirts. It was as though she were ashamed of her body.

'We going to stay here?' she asked.

'We can go out if you like, I'm allowed to.'

'The car's waiting,' said Ivich.

'*He's* not with you, is he?' Boris sounded scared.

'Who?'

'Your father-in-law?'

'Is it likely?'

They went across the courtyard and out through the main gate. At the sight of Monsieur Sturel's immense green Buick, Boris felt a little spasm of annoyance.

'Next time, tell him to wait at the corner,' he said.

They got into the car. It was absurdly large; so large that they felt lost.

'Big enough to play hide and seek in,' muttered Boris.

The chauffeur looked over his shoulder and smiled at Boris. He was a thickset fellow with obsequious manners and a grey moustache.

'Where to, madame?' he asked.

'Where'd you like to go?' said Boris.

Ivich thought for a moment:

'Somewhere where there's a lot of people.'

'How about the Canebière?'

'Oh, *not* the Canebière – but I don't really mind, let's go if you like.'

'Take us down to the harbour – corner of the Canebière,' said Boris.

'Very good, Monsieur Serguine.'

Slimy beast! thought Boris. The car started, and he sat looking out of the window. He did not want to talk because the chauffeur could hear everything.

'What about Lola?' asked Ivich.

He turned towards her. She looked completely unruffled. He put a finger to his lips, but she repeated the question in a loud, clear voice as though the chauffeur were of no more importance than a turnip.

'Have you heard anything from Lola?'

He shrugged his shoulders, but said nothing.

'Have you?'

'No.'

All the time that Boris was under treatment at Tours, Lola had established herself within easy reach of the hospital. At the beginning of June he had been evacuated to Marseilles, and she had made a brief visit to Paris with the object of drawing all her money from the bank just in case the worst happened. She had meant to rejoin him later. Since then 'things had happened', and he had heard no more of her whereabouts. A jolt threw him against Ivich. They took up so little room on the back seat of the Buick that he was reminded of the time when they had first landed in Paris. They had played at being two orphans lost in the capital, and had often sat close together, as they were doing now, on a settee at the Dôme or the Coupole. He raised his head, meaning to tell Ivich what he was thinking, but at sight of her dejected expression, confined himself to saying:

'Seen the papers? Paris has fallen.'

'Yes, I know,' said Ivich with indifference.

'What about your husband?'

'I've heard nothing, either.'

She leaned across and said in a low, hurried whisper: 'I jolly well hope he's dead!'

Boris took a quick glance at the chauffeur and saw that he was watching them in the driving-mirror. He nudged Ivich with his elbow and she said no more. But there was an ugly smile on her lips which she did nothing to conceal. The car stopped at the rear end of the Canebière. Ivich jumped out on to the pavement, and said to the chauffeur with an air of regal disdain:

'Come back for me to the Café Riche, at five.'

'Good afternoon, Monsieur Serguine,' said the chauffeur in a syrupy voice.

'Good afternoon!' replied Boris curtly.

He thought: I'll go back by tram. He took Ivich's arm and they set off up the Canebière. Several officers passed them. Boris did not salute, and they appeared to take no notice of the omission. He felt annoyed by the way in which the women turned to stare at him.

'Given up saluting officers?' inquired Ivich.

'What's the point?'

'The women are taking a lot of notice of you,' she went on. Boris said nothing. A dark-haired girl smiled at him. Ivich turned sharply.

'He is good-looking, isn't he?' she called after the retreating back.

'Ivich!' Boris begged her: 'for Heaven's sake don't draw attention to us!'

This was his latest ordeal. One morning, somebody had remarked that he was good-looking, and, ever since then, the thing had become a sort of game. Francillon and Gabel had nicknamed him the Pocket Cupid. Naturally, he did not take any notice, but it was annoying, all the same, because good looks are not a very manly attribute. He would far rather all these bitches had concentrated their attention on showing their legs, and that the men had done a bit of ogling – though not too much – at Ivich – just enough to make her feel that she was attractive.

Almost every table outside the Café Riche was occupied. They sat down in a crowd of bold, dark-haired trollops, elegant officers, soldiers, and middle-aged men with podgy hands – an inoffensive, conventional world of folk who'd much better be killed, though as painlessly as possible, of course.

Ivich was tugging at her short hair.

'Things not too good?' asked Boris.

She answered him with a shrug. He stretched his legs and thought how bored he was.

'What are you going to have?' he asked.

'Is their coffee drinkable?'

'So-so.'

'I'm dying for a cup of good coffee. The stuff they make up at the house is perfectly foul.'

'Two coffees,' said Boris to the waiter.

He turned to Ivich. 'How are you getting along with the in-laws?'

All feeling seemed to die out of Ivich's face.

'Not too badly. I'm becoming just like them,' she said.

'Only the other day,' she went on with a little laugh, 'my mother-in-law told me I had a look of her!'

'What d'you do with yourself all day?'

'Yesterday I got up at ten, dawdled as much as possible over dressing – which took me to half past eleven, read the papers . . .'

'You don't know how to read the papers – not properly,' said Boris with severity.

'I know I don't. At lunch they started talking about the war, and Mamma Sturel shed a few tears at the thought of her darling son. When she cries her lips curl upwards: I always think she's going to laugh. Then we settled down to our knitting and she bared her woman's heart to me. Georges was a delicate child, you'll be interested to hear, and had an attack of enteritis when he was eight. She would find it terrible to have to choose between husband and son, but she'd rather it was her husband who died because there is more in her of the mother than the wife. Then

65

she discussed her ailments – womb, bladder, and bowels. It seems they're not behaving at all as they should.'

A delightful witticism occurred to Boris. It had slipped into his mind so suddenly that he felt sure it wasn't anything he had read. On the whole, he thought, *not 'Les femmes entre elles parlent de leur intérieur ou de leurs intérieurs'*. In that form it sounded rather pedantic, rather too much like one of de Rochefoucauld's *Maxims. 'Une femme, faut que ça parle de son intérieur ou de ses intérieurs'*, or, *'Quand une bonne femme ne parle pas de son intérieur, c'est qu'elle est en train de parler de ses intérieurs.'* That, on the whole, was the version he liked best. He wondered whether he should tell Ivich. On the whole, no: she had little taste for jokes, these days. Instead he merely remarked:

'I see? – and then?'

'I went up to my room and stayed there till dinner.'

'And what did you do?'

'Nothing. After dinner we all listened to the radio, and then discussed what we had heard. It seems that nothing is lost, that we've got to keep cool, that France has been through worse crises. Then I went back to my room and brewed myself some tea on the electric heater. I keep it hidden away, because it usually fuses the light. I sat in my armchair until they were all asleep.'

'And then?'

'I breathed more freely.'

'You ought to take out a library subscription,' said Boris.

'When I read, the letters dance about in front of my eyes,' she said. 'I'm for ever thinking of Georges. I can't keep myself from hoping we'll hear that he's been killed.'

Boris had no liking for his brother-in-law, and had never understood why on earth, in September 1938, Ivich had run away from home and flung herself into the arms of that lanky nonentity. But he had to admit that the fellow had shown up well. As soon as he realized that she was in the family way, he had really behaved admirably. It was he who had insisted on marrying her, but by that time it was too late. Ivich hated him for getting her with child. She said that the sight of herself gave her the horrors, and hid herself away in the country. She refused even to see her brother. She would almost certainly have committed suicide if she had not been so afraid of dying.

'Muck!'

Boris gave a start:

'What's muck?'

'This!' she said, pointing to the coffee.

Boris took a sip and said quietly: 'It certainly is not very good.' He sat there for a moment or two, thinking: then he remarked: 'I expect it'll get worse and worse from now on.'

'Land of the conquered!' said Ivich.

Boris glanced nervously round, but nobody was paying any attention to them. The people at the various tables were all talking about the war, calmly and rather sadly – as though they had just come back from a funeral. The waiter passed them, carrying an empty tray. Ivich glowered at him.

'It's lousy!' she spat at him.

The man gazed at her in surprise. He had a grey moustache and might have been her father.

'This coffee, I mean: it's lousy: take it away!'

There was manifest curiosity in the waiter's stare. She was a great deal too young to intimidate him. When he realized what the trouble was about, he grinned rudely.

'Like a Mocha, I suppose? Haven't by any chance heard there's a war on?'

'*I* mayn't know anything about it,' she said with deliberate emphasis, 'but my brother, who's just been wounded, probably knows a great deal more than you do.'

Boris, scarlet with embarrassment, looked away. She had become a pretty tough customer, and never failed to give as good as she got. He could not help regretting the time when she had been in the habit, when angry, of shaking her hair over her face and saying nothing. It had caused a good deal less trouble.

'*I* shouldn't choose the day the Boches entered Paris to complain about a cup of coffee,' grumbled the waiter, by this time thoroughly out of humour.

He walked off. Ivich stamped her foot.

'They never stop talking about the war – or getting beaten, either. I'm beginning to think they're proud of it. I only hope they'll lose their war once and for all, and stop nattering about it!'

Boris stifled a yawn. Ivich's sallies no longer amused him. When she had been a young girl, it had been a pleasure to see her tugging at her hair, stamping her foot, and squinnying up her eyes. The sight had made him feel happy for the rest of the day. But now, there was a dead look in them: it was as though she were remembering something. When she was like that she resembled their mother. 'She's a married woman,' he thought with shocked awareness: 'a married woman with parents-in-law, a husband at the front, and a family car.' He gave her a puzzled stare, and looked away because he felt that she was becoming horrible to him. 'I'm going to clear out!' He sat up with a jerk: he had made his decision. 'I'm going to clear out – with them: *I can't stay in France* any longer.'

Ivich was saying something.

'What's that?' he asked.

'The parents.'

'What about them?'

'I said they ought to have stayed in Russia: you're not listening.'

'If they'd stayed, they'd have been put in jug.'

'Well, at any rate, they oughtn't to have had us naturalized, then we should have been able to go home.'

'Home's France,' said Boris.

'No, it's not: it's Russia!'

'It's France, since we *have* been naturalized.'

'Exactly – that's why I said we oughtn't to have been.'

'All right – but we were.'

'That makes no difference to me. Since they oughtn't to have done it, it's the same as though they never had.'

'If you were in Russia, you'd get the shock of your young life!'

'I shouldn't care, because Russia's a great country and I should feel proud. Here I spend all my time feeling ashamed.'

She stopped for a moment and seemed to hesitate. Boris looked at her rather primly. He felt no wish to contradict her. 'She'll have to stop soon,' he thought hopefully: 'I don't see there's much more she can say.' But Ivich had a fund of inventiveness. She raised one hand high in the air, and then made an odd little plunging motion, as though she were flinging herself into water: 'I detest the French,' she said.

A gentleman next to them, who was reading his paper, looked up with a dreamy stare. Boris returned his gaze. But almost at once the gentleman got up. A young woman was coming towards him. He bowed and she sat down. They shook hands with mutual smiles. Boris, reassured, turned to Ivich. There was no holding her now.

'I detest them,' she muttered between her teeth: 'I detest them!'

'You detest them because they make bad coffee!'

'I detest them for everything!'

Boris had hoped that the storm would abate of itself, but he saw now that he had been wrong, and that he would have to screw up his courage and face her on her own ground.

'I'm extremely fond of them,' he said. 'Now that they've lost this war, everyone's ready to jump on them. But I've seen them fighting, and I know that they did everything possible.'

'There,' said Ivich: 'you see!'

'What d'you mean, I see?'

'Why do you say *they* did everything possible? If you felt like a Frenchman you'd have said *we*!'

It was from a sense of modesty only that Boris had not said 'we'. He shook his head and frowned.

'I don't feel either French or Russian,' he said. 'But when I was up there with the boys, I felt glad to be with them.'

'They're a lot of rabbits,' she said.

He deliberately pretended to have misunderstood her:

'They certainly are tough.'

'I don't mean that. They *run* like rabbits – in this way' – and she set her right hand scuttling across the table.

'You're like all women,' said Boris: 'the only thing you think about is military valour!'

'It's not that at all. But they chose to have this war, and, that being so, they ought to have fought it to a finish.'

Boris raised his hand in a weary gesture: 'since they chose to have this war they ought to have fought it to a finish.' He knew all about that. It was what he had said only yesterday evening, when he and Gabel and Francillon had been discussing the situation. But ... he let his hand drop. When other people don't think as you do, it is difficult to prove them wrong, difficult and tiring. But when they share your point of view, and you've got to explain that they're mistaken, it's hopeless.

'Leave me alone!' he said.

'Rabbits!' said Ivich, with a little grin of anger.

'The chaps I was with weren't rabbits,' said Boris: 'they were rather unusually tough.'

'You've told me already that they were afraid of dying.'

'Well, aren't you afraid of dying?'

'I'm a woman.'

'Certainly they were afraid of dying, and they were men,' said Boris: 'that's what real courage is. They knew the risks they were running.'

Ivich looked at him suspiciously.

'You're not going to tell me *you* were afraid?'

'I wasn't afraid of dying, because I happened to believe that that was what I was there for.'

He looked at his nails, and added, in a completely impersonal tone:

'But that didn't prevent me from being windy – which was a bit of a bore.'

Ivich gave a start.

'Windy – but why?'

'I don't really know – probably because of the noise.'

As a matter of fact his windiness had lasted for not much more than ten minutes – perhaps twenty, and that had been at the very beginning of the attack. But he did not in the least mind Ivich thinking him a coward. It would give her a salutary jolt. There was bewilderment in the way she was looking at him. She was flabbergasted at hearing that anyone who was a Russian could be frightened, and not only a Russian, but a Serguine, and her own brother. He felt ashamed, and hastened to add:

'Anyhow, I wasn't frightened all the time.'

Her relief expressed itself in a smile. Gloomily, he thought: 'We no longer see eye to eye about anything.' There was a short period of silence. Boris swallowed a mouthful of coffee, and very nearly spat it out again. It was as though he had poured gloom down his throat. He reflected that he was about to go away, and felt comforted.

'What are you going to do?' asked Ivich.

'I suppose they'll demobilize me,' said Boris. 'As a matter of fact, we're most of us quite fit now. They're keeping us here because they don't know what to do with us.'

'And later on?'

'I . . . shall try to get a job as a teacher.'

'But you haven't got a degree.'

'I know . . . but I might teach in a high school.'

'Would you enjoy teaching small boys?'

'I should jolly well think not!' he said emphatically.

He flushed, and added humbly, 'I'm not cut out for that.'

'What *are* you cut out for, brother of mine?'

'I sometimes wonder.'

A gleam came into Ivich's eyes.

'Would you like me to tell you what we were cut out for – you and me? – to be rich!'

'What utter nonsense!' he said irritably.

He looked at her for a moment, and said again: 'What utter nonsense!' – holding his cup between his fingers.

'What for, then?'

'I was trained to the last ounce,' he said; 'and then I was done out of being killed. I'm completely at sea! I've got no gifts and no preferences.'

He heaved a sigh and relapsed into silence, ashamed at having been tricked into talking about himself. What I can't face is eking out a mean, obscure existence. I suppose that's, fundamentally, what she meant just now.

Ivich seemed to guess what he was thinking.

'Hasn't Lola got any money?' she asked.

He gave a start, and banged the table with his fist. She had the power to read his mind, and to translate his thoughts in the most intolerable manner.

'I don't want Lola's money!'

'Why? She used to give you money before the war.'

'Well, she's not going to give me any now.'

'Then we'd better both of us commit suicide,' she said passionately.

He sighed. Now she's off again, he thought wearily. If only she'd be her age.

Ivich was smiling at him.

'Let's take a room down by the old harbour and turn on the gas.'

Boris did not bother to answer. He negatived the proposal with a movement of his finger. Ivich did not press her point, but looked down and began tugging at her hair. Boris saw that there was something she wanted to ask him. At the end of a few moments, she said, avoiding his eye:

'I've been thinking . . .'

'The devil you have!'

'I've been thinking that you might let me join up with you. The three of us could live together on Lola's money.'

Boris all but choked.

'So that's what you've been thinking!'

'Boris,' said Ivich with sudden passion: 'I just *can't go on* living with those people!'

'Do they ill-treat you?'

'On the contrary, they keep me wrapped up in cottonwool – their son's wife, and all that. But I loathe them, I loathe Georges, I loathe the servants!'

'And you loathe Lola,' remarked Boris.

'Lola's different.'

'She's only different because she happens to be far away and because you haven't set eyes on her for two years.'

'Lola's a singer, she drinks, and she's lovely to look at . . . Oh, Boris!' she cried: 'they're so *ugly*. If you leave me with them, I shall kill myself! No, I shan't kill myself – it'll be much worse than that! If you only realized how old and bad I feel sometimes!'

There we go, with all the stops out! – thought Boris. His mouth felt dry, and he took a sip of coffee to help him to swallow. One can't make *two* people miserable, he thought. Ivich was no longer tugging at her hair. There was a little colour in her large, pallid face, and she was scrutinizing him with an expression in which determination fought with anxiety. There was something in her face now which reminded him of the old Ivich. Perhaps she might get back her youthful appearance, who could say? Perhaps she might once more be pretty? He said:

'All right, provided you do the cooking, you little she-devil!'

She seized his hand and pressed it as hard as she could.

'Do you really want us all to live together, Boris, really and truly?'

I shall be teaching at Guéret – no, not Guéret, that's a secondary school – at Castelnaudary. I shall marry Lola. A schoolteacher can't live with a woman who isn't his wife. I'll make a start tomorrow on working up my subjects. ... He passed his fingers through his hair, clutched a handful of it, and pulled, as though to make sure that his thatch was strongly anchored. I shall go bald, he decided; not a doubt of it. My hair will fall out before I die.

'Of course I want it.'

He watched an aeroplane catch the morning light as it turned, and to himself he said: 'The cliffs, the lovely white cliffs, the cliffs of Dover.'

Padoux: 3 p.m.

MATHIEU was sitting on the grass. He watched black smoke eddying above the wall. Now and again a flame would leap up, turn the thick cloud blood-red, and then disperse. Each time that happened, sparks leapt upwards, like fleas.

'They're making the hell of a blaze,' said Charlot.

Small butterflies of soot were fluttering all about them. Pinette caught one and crushed it pensively between finger and thumb.

'All that's left of one of the half-inch-to-the-mile sheets,' he said, displaying his blackened thumb.

Longin pushed open the trellised gate, and came into the garden: his eyes were streaming.

'Longin's crying!' said Charlot.

'Them swine was nearly the death of me!'

He flung himself down on the grass. He was holding a book with a torn cover in his hand.

'Made me work the bellows while they chucked all their bumph on the fire. The smoke blew in my face.'

'Job finished?'

'Not on your sweet life it isn't! Just cleared us out because they was starting on the secret stuff. Secret! my foot! Why, I typed them orders meself.'

'What a filthy stink,' exclaimed Charlot.

'Just a smell of burning.'

'No, it's not – it's a filthy stink – and d'you know 'cos why? – 'cos they're a-burning of Divisional records.'

' 'xactly – filthy stink – smell of burning – just like I said.'

They laughed: Mathieu pointed to the book.

'Where'd you find that?' he asked.

'Oh, over there,' said Longin vaguely.

'When you say over there, d'you mean the schools?'

'Yes.'

He clutched the book to him mistrustfully.

'Any more where that came from?' asked Mathieu.

'There were some more, but the blokes from the Q.M. stores 's been helping theirselves.'

'What is it?'

'History book.'

'What history book?'

'Haven't looked to see.'

He gave a quick glance at the cover and remarked with a bad grace:

'*History of the Two Restorations.*'

'Who by?' asked Charlot.

'Vau-la-belle,' read out Longin.

'Who the devil's Vaulabelle?'

'How should I know?'

'Will you lend it me?' asked Mathieu.

'When I've read it.'

Charlot crawled through the grass and took the book from him.

'Hey, chaps – it's Volume III!'

Longin snatched it back.

'What's that matter? – only want something to occupy me mind.'

He opened the volume at random and pretended to read, the better to stake his claim. That formality accomplished, he looked up.

'Skipper's been burning his wife's letters,' he said.

He raised his eyes and goggled at them like a village idiot, giving with eyes and lips an advance performance of the astonishment he knew his words would produce. Pinette emerged from a fit of the sulks and looked at him with a sudden show of interest.

'Not pulling our legs are yer?'

' 'Course not – and all her photos as well – saw 'em in the flames. Comes from near Bordeaux, she does.'

'Coo! not really!'

' 'Course it's really if I say so.'

'What'd he say?'

'Didn't say nothing – just watched 'em burn.'

'And the others?'

'Didn't say nothing neither. That Ulmann, 'e pulled a lot of letters out of his wallet and chucked 'em on the fire.'

'That's a funny thing to do,' muttered Mathieu.

Pinette swung round on him.

'Wouldn't you burn your girl's photos?'

'I haven't got a girl.'

'That's not the point.'

'What about you?' asked Mathieu: 'have you burned your wife's?'

'I'm waiting till Jerry turns up.'

There was silence. Longin was reading in good earnest. Mathieu gazed across at him enviously, and got up.

Charlot touched Pinette on the shoulder.

'What you say to having your revenge?'

'All right.'

'What's the game?' asked Mathieu.

'Beggar-me-neighbour.'

'Can three play at that?'

'No.'

Pinette and Charlot sat down astride on the bench. Sergeant Pierné, who was writing on his knees, moved along to make room for them.

'Writing yer memoirs?'

'No,' said Pierné, 'I'm studying physics.'

They began to play. Nippert was sleeping on his back with his arms flung out. The sound of his breathing was like water going down a drain-pipe. His mouth was wide open. Schwartz sat apart, day-dreaming.

No one spoke a word. France was dead. Mathieu yawned. He watched the secret documents going up in smoke; he looked at the rich black earth between the growing vegetables; his mind felt completely empty. *He* was dead: the afternoon was bleached and dead. It was a tomb.

Lubéron came into the garden. He was eating and blinking his big albino eyes. His ears moved in concert with his jaws.

'What you eating?' asked Charlot.

'Bit of bread.'

'Where'd you find it?'

Lubéron said nothing but pointed vaguely beyond the wall and went on with his munching. Charlot suddenly stopped talking and looked at him as though scared. Sergeant Pierné, his pencil raised, his head thrown back, was also looking at him. Lubéron went on eating stubbornly, without any sort of hurry. Mathieu noticed his air of importance, and realized that he had news to tell. He caught the infection of the general nervousness and took a step forward. Lubéron quietly finished his meal and wiped his hands on his trousers. 'It wasn't bread,' thought Mathieu.

Schwartz sauntered up. They were all of them silently waiting.

'So that's that,' said Lubéron.

'Say what you mean,' said Pierné roughly: 'what's what?'

'That...'

'The ...'

'Yes.'

A dazzle off steel, then silence. The blue, flabby flesh of the afternoon had taken eternity like the sweep of a scythe. Not a sound, not a breath of air. Time had become frozen; the war had withdrawn. ... No more than a moment ago they had all been in it, though temporarily sheltered; had all been in the mood to believe in miracles, in France the immortal, in American aid, in defence in depth, in the possibility of Russia coming into the war. And now the war was behind them, finished, accomplished, lost. Mathieu's last dregs of hope had turned to the mere memory of hope.

Longin was the first to pull himself together. He stretched out his long hands as though to touch the news with extreme caution. Very timidly, he asked:

'Has it really been signed?'

'This morning.'

For nine months Pierné had been longing for peace, for peace at any price. Now he stood there pale and sweating. The shock made him lose his temper.

'How d'you know?' he burst out.

'Guiccioli's just told me.'

'How does *he* know?'

'Radio: news came through just now.'

He had assumed the patient, impersonal voice of an announcer. It amused him to play the part of inexorable fate.

'Why's there been all that gunning, then?'

'Cease fire's not till midnight.'

Charlot's face was red, but his eyes were shining. 'Not having us on, are yer?'

Pierné got up.

'Any details?' he asked.

'No,' said Lubéron.

Charlot cleared his throat.

'How about us?'

'What yer mean, how about us?'

'When are we going home?'

'I've just said there weren't no details.'

There was a silence. Pinette kicked a stone into the carrots.

'The armistice!' he exclaimed angrily: 'the armistice!'

Pierné nodded his head. His left eyelid had started to flutter in his ashen face, like a window shutter on a gusty day:

'The conditions will be hard,' he said with a chuckle.

They all began to laugh.

'You said it!' remarked Longin: 'you said it!'

Schwartz joined in the laughter. Charlot turned and looked at him in surprise. Schwartz stopped laughing, and went very red. Charlot kept on staring at him. It was as though he were seeing him for the first time.

'So now you're a Jerry,' he said quietly.

77

Schwartz made a vague, violent gesture, turned on his heel and left the garden.

Mathieu felt suddenly overcome with weariness. He dropped on to the bench.

'How hot it is!' he said.

We're being looked at. A crowd that grew more and more numerous with every passing moment was looking at them, was watching them swallow this pill of history. It grew older, it backed away from them, a low muttering came from it – 'the conquered of '40, the army of defeat – it's their fault that we are in fetters'. There they stood, unchanged beneath the changing scrutiny, judged, summed up, explained, accused, excused, condemned, imprisoned with this ineffaceable day, buried beneath the drone of insects and the rumble of guns, in the hot smell of growing things, with the air quivering above beds of carrots, guilty for ever in the eyes of their sons and grandsons and great-grandsons – the conquered of '40 to all eternity. He yawned. Millions of eyes were watching him yawn. 'He's yawning: ever see anything like that? – one of the conquered of '40 who's got the effrontery to yawn!' Mathieu bit back the yawn that would never end. He thought: we're not the only ones!

He looked at his comrades, and his mortal eyes met the timeless, petrified eyes of history. For the first time the robe of greatness had fallen upon their shoulders: *they* were the fabulous soldiers of a lost war, human no longer, but statues! I've spent my life reading, yawning, tinkling the bell of my own little problems, never managing to make a decision – only to find that I *have* decided, that I *chose* this war and this defeat, that today has been waiting for me since the beginning of time. Everything's got to be done over again, and yet, there's nothing that can be done. The two thoughts interpenetrated, cancelled one another out. Only the unruffled surface of Nothingness remained.

Charlot make a quick little movement of head and shoulders. He began to laugh, and the flow of time was resumed. Charlot was laughing, laughing in the teeth of history, making of his laughter a defence against petrifaction. There was a glint of malice in his glance.

'Pretty good fools *we* look!'

They turned towards him, stunned. Then Lubéron joined in his laughter. He wrinkled his nose as though in sudden pain, and snorted down his nostrils.

'You said it, chum! Proper fools they've made of us!'

'Biffed, buggered, and bewildered!' exclaimed Charlot with a sort of drunken gaiety.

Longin took up the laughter:

'The soldiers of '40 or the champs of the running-track!' he said.

'Giants of the open road!'

'Speed-kings of the Olympic Games!'

'I should worry!' said Lubéron: 'nice sort of welcome *we're* going to get when we turn up at home! – oh, lots and lots of congratulations!'

Longin indulged in a squeal of delight:

'A deputation to meet us at the station, complete with the local glee-club and representatives of the athletic societies!'

'And I'm a Jew!' said Charlot, laughing till the tears poured down his face: 'What a time the anti-Semites down our way are going to have!'

Mathieu caught the infection of this hateful merriment. He had had one appalling moment, had been flung, shaking with fever, between icy sheets. Then his statuesque eternity had cracked, and flown apart in a thousand fragments of laughter. They were making the great refusal, spurning, in the name of all the guttersnipes of the world, the obligations of greatness. Why worry so long as one had good health, and enough to eat and drink? I despise one half of the world, and sh—t on the other! Their austere lucidity had driven them to put aside the consolations of greatness. They were denying even their right to suffer, were refusing to strut as tragic or even historic figures. They could not so much as bring themselves to say we're just a lot of cheap heels, a bundle of predestined failures: could not even comfort themselves with the thought that life was a gamble. All they could do was laugh, blundering against the walls of Absurdity and bouncing back from them. Their laughter was an instrument of self-punishment, of self-purification, of vengeance. They were, at one and the same moment, less than human, and more. They had stopped short of despair and transcended it. They were men. For a fleeting moment their open mouths displayed to high Heaven the black horror of their sores. Nippert was still snoring, goggling at the void, an outrage in the very fashion of his gaping. The laughter drooped under its own weight, drew out to a stretched length, shook to a standstill. The ceremony was over; the armistice consecrated. Officially now it was the moment *after*. Time flowed smoothly on, a sun-warmed infusion of weak tea. Life had got to be lived.

'So that's that!' said Charlot.

'Yes, that's that,' said Mathieu.

Furtively, Lubéron withdrew his hand from his pocket, raised it to his mouth, and began to masticate. Beneath his rabbity eyes, his jaw moved spasmodically.

'That's that,' he said: 'that's that.'

Pierné's attitude was fussy and triumphant.

'What did I tell you?'

'Well, what *did* you tell us?'

'Don't pretend to be bigger fools than you are! What did I say after Finland, Delarue? and after Narvik? – you chose to regard me as a bird of ill-omen, and, because you're cleverer than I am, you tied me into knots.'

His cheeks were flushed. Behind his spectacles his eyes glittered with spitefulness and triumph.

'We ought never to have started on this war. I always said so. If it hadn't been for this war we shouldn't be where we are now.'

'We might be even worse off,' said Pinette.

'We couldn't be: nothing's worse than war.'

He rubbed his hands with unction, and his face shone with the light of innocence. He rubbed his hands, cleansing them of war. He had taken no part in it: it had formed no part of his life. For ten months he had sulked, refusing to see, refusing to speak, refusing to feel. The very alacrity with which he had executed orders had been a protest. He had lived in a constant state of absent-mindedness, strung to a pitch of tension, his thoughts elsewhere. And now he had his reward. *His* hands were clean: what he had foretold had come about. It was the others who had been defeated – Pinette, Lubéron, Delarue, and the rest: not he.

Pinette's lips began to tremble:

'I suppose,' he said, 'you think everything's all right?' His words sounded choked: 'I suppose you're satisfied?'

'Satisfied?'

'You've got your defeat.'

'*My* defeat? It's yours just as much as mine.'

'You wanted it, it's yours. We never wanted it: you can have it.'

Pierné smiled at his lack of comprehension:

'Who says I wanted it?' he asked in the tones of one who has long suffered from being misunderstood.

'You did, only a moment or two back.'

'I said I'd foreseen it. To foresee a thing isn't the same as wanting it.'

Pinette looked at him but said nothing. His face was a mask of obstinacy, of animal mulishness. He rolled bewildered eyes. Pierné pursued his advantage:

'Why should I want it? – tell me that. You'll be saying next that I'm a fifth-columnist.'

'You're a pacifist,' said Pinette with an effort.

'Well, what of it?'

'It comes to the same thing.'

Pierné raised his shoulders and spread his hands in a gesture of hopelessness. Charlot ran to Pinette and put his arm round his neck:

'Stop arguing,' he said good-naturedly: 'what's the point? We've lost – and it's nobody's fault. No one's got anything to be ashamed of. It was bad luck, and that's all there is to it.'

Longin smiled knowingly:

'Bad luck?'

'Yes,' said Charlot, eager to conciliate: 'let's be fair? It *was* bad luck, damn' back luck, but what of it? Everyone has his turn. Last time it was we who won, this time it's them. Next time it'll be us again.'

'There won't be a next time,' said Longin. He raised his finger, and added with a paradoxical air:

'We're the last of the bunch: no getting away from that. Conquerors or conquered, it all comes to the same in the end. The boys of '40 have succeeded where their fathers failed. After

81

this there won't be any more nations or any more war. We've been beaten to our knees. Tomorrow it'll be the turn of the English. The Boches are the masters now. They'll restore order everywhere, and then full speed ahead for the United States of Europe.'

'United States, my foot!' said Pinette: 'we shall be Hitler's slaves!'

'Hitler? – what's Hitler?' asked Longin rhetorically: 'There had to be someone like him, of course. How d'you expect the nations to get together if they're free to do what they like? They're the same as individuals – see? each out for himself. Who's going to talk about Hitler in a hundred years' time? He'll be as dead as a doornail, and Nazism, too.'

'You're just a chump,' said Pinette: 'What's a hundred years got to do with it?'

Longin seemed scandalized:

'That's no way to talk,' he said: 'We got to learn to see farther than our noses. We got to think about the Europe of the future.'

'Is the Europe of the future going to put food in my belly?'

Longin raised his hand in a gesture of pacification. It hung poised in the sunlight over their heads:

'Bah!' he said: 'Bah! – there's always a way out for those as has got their wits about 'em.'

The episcopal hand, descending, played with Charlot's hair. 'Don't you agree?'

'There's only one thing I agree about,' said Charlot: 'If this armistice has got to be signed, then the sooner the better. In that way there'll be fewer dead, and the Jerries won't have any call to get really wild.'

Mathieu looked at him in amazement. So they were all slinking away, were they, every man jack of them? Schwartz was changing his skin, Nippert taking refuge in sleep, Pinette in anger, Pierné in innocence. Lubéron, grounded in the here and now, was giving all his attention to food, was stuffing every hole and cranny of his carcass. Longin was embarked on the seas of futurity. Each one of them had hurriedly assumed the attitude that would make it possible for him to go on living.

He sat up with a jerk and said in a loud voice:

'You make me sick!'

They showed no surprise, but looked at him with shoddy little smiles. He was far more surprised than they were. The phrase still echoed in his ears, and he wondered how on earth he had come to speak it. For a moment he hesitated between confusion and anger, then opted for anger. Turning his back on them, he pushed open the wicket and crossed the road. It was blinding and empty. He plunged into the brambles. They caught and clung to his puttees. He ran down the copse-crowned slope until he reached the stream. 'Hell!' he said aloud. He stared at the water and said again, 'Hell! Hell!' without knowing why. A bare hundred yards from him a soldier, stripped to the waist and dappled with sunlight, was busy washing his shirts. There he stands, whistling and kneading his lump of soggy dough. He has lost the war and he doesn't know it. Mathieu sat down. He felt ashamed. What right have I to take this high line? They've just heard that the bottom's been knocked right out of everything, and they're shifting for themselves in the best way they can. They're not used to such situations: I am, and much good does it do me! If it comes to that, I'm just as much an escapist as any of them. What's anger but a way of escape?

He heard a faint crackle in the undergrowth, and Pinette hove in sight. He sat down on the bank and smiled at Mathieu. Mathieu smiled back, but for several moments neither of them spoke.

'Look at that bloke down there,' said Pinette at last: 'he doesn't know a thing.'

The soldier, bending above the water, was washing his shirts with a thoroughness that had suddenly become unnecessary. An anachronistic aeroplane thrummed above their heads. The soldier looked up through the covering of leaves at the sky with an expression of apprehension which made them both laugh. The whole scene had the picturesque quality of a piece of historical reconstruction.

'Shall we tell him?'

'He'll hear soon enough,' said Mathieu.

They stopped talking. Mathieu put his hand in the water and waggled his fingers. His hand looked pale and silvery against the encroaching blue of the reflected sky. Bubbles rose to the

83

surface. A twig, carried downstream by the current, clung to his wrist, rotating. It drifted away, came back, and clung to him. Mathieu withdrew his hand.

'It's hot,' he said.

'Yes,' said Pinette: 'Makes one feel sleepy.'

'You feel like that?'

'No, but I'm going to try to go to sleep all the same.'

He stretched himself on his back, his hands clasped behind his head, and shut his eyes. Mathieu thrust a dead branch into the stream and moved it to and fro. After a few moments Pinette opened his eyes again.

'Oh, bugger it all!'

He sat up and ruffled his hair with both hands.

'I can't sleep.'

'Why not?'

'Too angry.'

'There's no harm in that,' said Mathieu: 'shows a healthy state of mind.'

'When I'm feeling really angry,' said Pinette, 'I've got to hit something or else I choke!'

He looked at Mathieu with curiosity.

'Don't you feel angry?'

'Yes.'

Pinette leaned forward and began to unlace his boots. 'Didn't even get a chance of letting me rifle off,' he remarked bitterly.

He took off his socks. He had the small, soft feet of a child. They were streaked with dirt.

'I'm going to wash me feet.'

He wetted his right foot in the water, took it in his hand, and started to rub. The dirt came away in little rolls. Suddenly he glanced up at Mathieu.

'They'll round us up, won't they?'

Mathieu's only answer was a movement of the head.

'And take us away to their country?'

'Probably.'

Pinette put a fury of energy into the rubbing of his foot.

'If it hadn't been for this 'ere armistice they wouldn't have got me so easy.'

'What would you have done?'

'Made 'em pay for it!'

'Quite the little lionheart!'

They exchanged smiles, but suddenly Pinette's face grew dark, and a defiant look came into his eyes.

'You said we made you sick.'

'I didn't mean you.'

'You meant the whole lot of us.'

Mathieu was still smiling.

'Is it me you'd like to hit?'

Pinette hung his head and said nothing.

'Hit away,' said Mathieu, 'and I'll hit back. Perhaps that'll calm us down.'

'Shouldn't like to hurt you,' said Pinette gloomily.

'That's a pity.'

Pinette's left foot was a-glitter with water-drops and sunlight. Both of them were looking at it. Pinette wriggled his toes.

'What comic feet you've got,' said Mathieu.

'Small, aren't they? I can take a matchbox and open it.'

'With your toes?'

'Yes.'

He grinned. But suddenly a gust of fury shook him, and he gripped his ankle violently.

'I'd feel better if I'd knocked a Jerry over. I suppose they'll just come along and mop me up.'

'That's about the size of it.'

'It's not fair . . .'

'It's neither fair nor unfair . . . it's just how things are.'

'It *isn't* fair. We're paying for what others have done – for the chaps in Corap's army, for Gamelin.'

'If we'd been in Corap's army, we'd have done exactly as they did.'

'Speak for yourself.'

He flung his arms wide, drew a deep breath, clenched his fists, threw out his chest, and looked at Mathieu with arrogance.

'D'you think I'm the sort of bloke who'd turn tail?'

Mathieu smiled at him: 'No.'

Pinette flexed the long biceps of his fair-skinned arms. He seemed to be silently glorying in his youth, his strength, his courage. He smiled, but there was a smouldering light in his eyes, and his brows were drawn together in a frown.

'I'd have been shot down where I stood.'

'That's easy to say.'

Pinette smiled and died. A bullet pierced his heart. Dead but triumphant, he turned to Mathieu. His statue, the statue of a man who had died for his country, said:

'I *would* have been shot down!'

Then the hot stream of life and anger flowed back into his momentarily petrified body.

'No one can blame me. I did everything I was told to do. It's not my fault if they didn't know how to use me.'

Mathieu looked at him with a sort of tenderness. Pinette, lying there in the sunlight, was transparent. One could almost see the life rising and sinking and eddying up and down the blue branchings of his veins. How spare, how healthy, how light he must be feeling! It was difficult to believe in the painless illness which had already begun to gnaw at him, which, sooner or later, would bow his young body above the potato fields of Silesia, or, on the Pomeranian motor-roads, would fill him to overflowing with fatigue and heaviness and melancholy. Defeat is a lesson that has to be learned.

'I didn't ask anything of no one – just did me job without complaining. I wasn't against the Jerries – hadn't so much as seen the backside of one of 'em. I hardly knew what Nazism and Fascism was about. As to Danzig – why, I was already called up before I even saw the place on a map. It was Daladier who declared war and Gamelin as lost it. What had I got to do with it? You don't suppose they asked *my* opinion?'

Mathieu shrugged.

'We've seen it coming for fifteen years. We ought to have taken steps either to avoid it or to win it.'

'I'm not a member of Parliament.'

'But you had a vote.'

'Of course,' said Pinette, though without enthusiasm.

'For whom did you vote?'

Pinette said nothing.

'You see,' said Mathieu.

'I had my military service to do,' said Pinette morosely: 'and

86

after that I was ill. There was only one occasion on which I *could* vote.'

'And when that occasion came, did you?'

Pinette made no reply, and Mathieu smiled.

'I'm in the same boat,' he said quietly. 'I didn't vote either.'

The soldier rinsed out his shirts in the flowing current, wrapped them in a red towel, and climbed up to the road, whistling.

'Recognize that tune?'

'No,' said Mathieu.

' "We'll hang out our washing on the Siegfried Line".'

They laughed. Pinette seemed to have lost something of his tenseness.

'I've worked hard,' he said, 'and I didn't always have as much to eat as I should have liked. Then I got this job on the railway, and I married my wife. Had to make a home for her, hadn't I? She comes of a good family, I'd have you know. Things weren't too easy at first, but they settled down later,' he added quickly: 'a chap can't do everything at once, can he?'

'Of course not,' said Mathieu.

'What else could *I* have done?'

'Nothing.'

'I hadn't no time to bother about politics. Used to get home dead beat, and then there was the family arguments, and, besides, when a chap's married, his wife expects him to make love to her every night – don't you agree?'

'I suppose so.'

'Well, then?'

'There was nothing more you could do. That's the way wars get lost.'

Pinette was shaken by another spasm of anger.

'*You* make *me* sick! Suppose I *had* took up politics, suppose I'd give all me time to 'em, what difference would that have made?'

'At least you would have done all you could.'

'Did you do all *you* could?'

'No.'

'And if you had would you still say it was you what lost the war?'

'No.'

'Well, then?'

Mathieu said nothing. He heard the quivering buzz of a
mosquito, and flapped his hand in front of his face. The buzzing stopped. When this war started, I, too, thought of it as
a disease. What idiocy! It's me, it's Pinette, it's Longin – it's
each one of us, made in our image. Men have the war they
deserve.

Pinette gave a prolonged snuffle, but his eyes were fixed un-
blinkingly on Mathieu. Mathieu decided that he looked stupid,
and a great surge of anger broke over him, filling mouth and
eyes. 'I'm through! yes, I'm through! I'm fed up with always
being the one who understands, who sees straight!' The mosquito shrilled about his forehead – a derisive crown of glory! 'If I
had fought, if I had pressed my finger on the trigger, somewhere,
someone would have fallen.' He raised his hand sharply and
gave his temple a resounding smack, then lowered it and saw
on his finger a tiny bloody filament, someone bleeding his life
away on a stony field, a smack on the temple, a pressure on the
trigger, the coloured glasses of the kaleidoscope stop dead, blood
spreads across the grass – I'm fed up! – fed up with plunging
into blind action as into a forest: Action – something that com-
mits one and that one never wholly understands.

'If there were only *something one could do*! . . .'

Pinette's stare showed sudden interest:

'What sort of thing?'

Mathieu gave a shrug:

'There isn't anything,' he said: 'not for the moment.'

Pinette put on his socks. His pale eyebrows drew together in
a high-pitched frown:

'Have I showed you my wife?'

'No,' said Mathieu.

Pinette sat up, fumbled in the pocket of his tunic, and took
a photo from his wallet. Mathieu saw a prettyish woman with a
hard mouth and the hint of a moustache at its corners. Across
the picture she had scrawled – 'Denise to her Babyface, 12 Jan-
uary 1939'. Pinette went scarlet:

'That's what she calls me: can't get her to drop the habit.'

'She's got to call you something.'

'It's because she's five years older than me,' said Pinette with dignity.

Mathieu gave him back the piece of pasteboard.

'She's nice.'

'She's terrific in bed,' remarked Pinette: 'you've no idea!'

His blush had deepened. With a hint of perplexity he added: 'Comes of a good family.'

'So you said before.'

'Did I?' – Pinette's voice expressed astonishment. 'Did I tell you that her father was a drawing-master?'

'Yes.'

Pinette carefully restored the photograph to his wallet.

'It's getting me down.'

'What's getting you down?'

'Pretty lousy – to go back home, like this, I mean.'

'Bah!' exclaimed Mathieu.

'Her father was one of the heroes of '14,' said Pinette: 'three mentions and the Croix de Guerre. Talks about it all the time, he does.'

'Well, what of it?'

'Just that it's lousy to go home like this.'

'Poor little devil,' said Mathieu: 'the best thing you can do will be not to go back at once.'

'She's fond of me,' said Pinette, 'but she's not easy to get on with. Thinks a deal of herself, she does, and her mother eggs her on. Don't you think one's old woman ought to respect one? If she doesn't, there's never no peace in the house.'

He got up suddenly.

'Had enough of it here: you coming?'

'Where to?' asked Mathieu.

'Don't know: let's join the others.'

'All right,' said Mathieu without enthusiasm.

He followed Pinette's example. Together they climbed to the road.

'Hullo!' said Pinette; 'there's Guiccioli.'

Guiccioli, his legs straddled, and making a peak of his hand, was looking at them and laughing.

'It's a proper have,' said he.

'What is?'

'A proper have – well out in your reckoning you was!'
'What *are* you talking about?'
'That there armistice,' said Guiccioli, still laughing.
Pinette's expression brightened.
'Nothing doing?'
'You said it! Lequier's just been along asking for news. We gave him all the news he wanted.'
'Armistice napoo, eh?' with high satisfaction.
'Sweet F.A.'
Mathieu glanced at Pinette out of the corner of his eye.
'What difference does it make?'
'You'll see what difference it makes!' said Pinette: 'It makes all the difference in the world!'

4 o'clock

NOBODY on the Boulevard Saint-Germain: in the Rue Danton, nobody. The iron shutters had not even been lowered. The windows glittered. The proprietors had just removed the handles from the doors – and gone. It was Sunday. For the last three days it had been Sunday. The whole week now, in Paris, consisted of one day, a ready-made, colourless sort of day, rather stiffer than usual, rather more synthetic, over-marked by silence, and already filled by a secretly working rot. Daniel approached a large shop (knitted goods and textiles); the multicoloured balls of wool, arranged in pyramids, were in process of turning yellow. They smelt of old age. In the establishment next door a display of baby-linen and ladies' blouses was rapidly fading. White dust was accumulating, like flour, upon the shelves. The plate-glass was stained with long white streaks. Daniel thought – 'The windows are weeping.' Behind them all was festival. Flies were buzzing in their millions. Sunday. When the Parisians returned they would find their dead city motionless beneath the weight of a stagnant Sunday. *If they return!* Daniel gave free rein to that irresistible desire to laugh which had been with him all morning as he stalked the streets. *If they return.*
The tiny Square of Saint-André-des-Arts lay abandoned in the

sunlight, lifeless. Black night reigned in the heart of noon. The sun was a fake; a magnesium flare concealing darkness. In a split second it would go out. He pressed his face to one of the big windows of the Brasserie Alsacienne. I lunched here with Mathieu. That had been in February, when Mathieu was on leave. It had been swarming with heroes and angels. After a while he managed to distinguish in the darkness of the interior a number of ambiguous blotches, mushrooms growing in a cellar. They were paper napkins. Where are the heroes? where are the angels? There were still two iron chairs on the terrace: Daniel took one of them by its back, carried it to the edge of the pavement, and sat down, a gentleman of leisure beneath the military sky, in a white glare that was alive with childhood memories. At his back he could feel the magnetic pressure of silence. He looked at the empty bridge, at the padlocked book-boxes on the quay, at the clock-face that had no hands. 'They should have knocked all this about a bit,' he thought: 'dropped a few bombs, just to make us realize what was what.' A shadow slipped past the Prefecture of Police on the further bank of the Seine, as though on a moving roadway. Paris was not, strictly speaking, empty. It was peopled by little broken scraps of time that sprang here and there to life, to be almost immediately absorbed again into this radiance of eternity. 'The city is hollow' – thought Daniel. He was conscious, beneath his feet, of the caverns of the Underground; in front, behind, above, of tall cliffs pierced with openings. Between heaven and earth thousands of Louis-Philippe boudoirs, Empire dining-rooms, and cosy corners, echoing to the secret sounds of emptiness. It was enough to make one die of laughing! He turned sharply. Someone had tapped at the window. He stared at it for a long time but could see only his own reflection. He got up. There was a curious lump in his throat, but he did not feel particularly unhappy. It was amusing to be afflicted with night-fears in broad daylight. He walked across to the Saint-Michel fountain, and looked at the green bronze dragon. He thought: there is nothing now that I can't do. He could take down his trousers beneath the glassy stare of all these darkened windows, pull up a paving-stone and heave it through the plate-glass of the brasserie, could shout 'Long Live Germany!' and nothing would happen. At the most, high on

91

some sixth floor, a frightened face might be pressed to a window-pane, but that would be all. They had lost the power even to be indignant. The respectable gentleman in that remote eyrie would turn to his wife and, in a tone of complete detachment, would say, 'Fellow down there has just taken off his trousers,' and she would reply from the far end of the room, 'Don't go showing yourself at the window: one never knows what might happen.' Daniel yawned: should he smash the window? Bah! there'd be *better things that that* to see when the looting began. 'I only hope,' he thought, 'that they put the whole place to fire and sword.' He yawned again. He felt himself filled with a sense of vast and pointless freedom. Now and again his joy turned sour within him. As he moved away, a procession emerged from the Rue de la Huchette. 'Travelling in convoy now.' It was the tenth he had met that morning. He counted nine individuals – two old women carrying rush baskets, two young girls, three dried-up, gnarled old men with moustaches, and, bringing up the rear, a couple of young women, one of them pale and beautiful, the other superbly pregnant, and with the hint of a smile about her lips.

They were, all of them, walking slowly, and not a word was spoken. Daniel coughed and they turned, as one person, to look at him. There was neither sympathy nor condemnation in their eyes, only an expression of incredulous astonishment. One of the two girls leaned towards her companion without shifting her gaze from Daniel, and whispered something, whereupon they both laughed, seeming greatly surprised. Daniel felt himself in that place to be as strange as a chamois bending its slow and virgin stare upon a party of alpine climbers. They passed him by, figures of a fantastic and an outworn age, drowned deep in soli-tude. He crossed the road and, at the near end of the Pont Saint-Michel, leaned his elbows on the stone parapet. The Seine was a glitter of sunlight. Far away to the north-west, smoke was rising above the houses. All at once he found the whole scene intoler-able, turned away, retraced his steps, and started to walk up the boulevard.

The procession had vanished. Everywhere, as far as eye could reach, was silence and emptiness, an abyss stretching horizontally away from him. He felt tired. The streets led nowhere. Without human life, they all looked alike. The Boulevard Saint-Michel, but yesterday a long southward spread of gold, seemed now like a stranded whale, belly upwards. He made his feet ring out upon the great, sodden, hollow carcass. He forced a shudder of delight. Out loud he said – 'I always hated Paris,' but in vain. No sign of life save the greenery, the long, leafy arms of the chestnuts. He had the stale, sickly impression of walking through a forest. The disgusting wing of boredom was already brushing him, when, by a lucky chance, he noticed a poster printed in white and red, stuck on a hoarding. He went up to it and read the words WE SHALL WIN BECAUSE WE ARE THE STRONGER. He flung out his arms, grinning with a sense of delight and release: They're running, running: they've never stopped running. He raised his head, laughing to high Heaven, and drew deep breaths. For twenty years he had been on trial. There had been spies even beneath his bed. Every casual passer-by had been a witness for the prosecution, a judge, or both at once: every word he spoke could have been used in evidence against him. And now, in a flash – stampede! They were running, the lot of them, witnesses, judges, all the respectable folk, running beneath the blazing sun, the blue sky, and a threat of aircraft over their heads. The walls of Paris were still clamorously extolling their merits and their pride: we are the stronger, the more virtuous, the sacred champions of democracy, the defenders of Poland, of human dignity, or heterosexual love: the wall of steel will be un-breached, we shall hang out our washing on the Siegfried Line. The posters on the Paris hoardings were still trumpeting a hymn of triumph that had gone cold. But *they* were running, mad with terror, flinging themselves flat in the ditches, begging for mercy – honourable mercy, needless to say – all is lost save honour: take everything – in the way of honour: I'll kiss yours if only you will let me have my life. They are running and crawling. I, the Criminal, reign over their city in their stead.

He walked with his eyes on the ground. He thrilled with pleasure. He could hear the cars swishing past him on the road-way. He thought: Marcelle's pupping at Dax; Mathieu's prob-ably a prisoner: Brunet's almost certainly got himself bumped off. All the witnesses against me are dead or thinking of other things. It's I who am making a come-back. ... Suddenly he said to himself: 'What cars?' He looked up; his heart began to thump so violently that he could feel it in his head, and then he saw *them*. They were standing upright, images grave and chaste, fifteen, twenty of them together in long camouflaged lorries, moving slowly towards the Seine, effortlessly gliding, standing stiffly, letting the inexpressive glances of their eyes rest momentarily on him. And after them came others, other angels, exactly alike, looking at him in precisely the same way. He could hear a military band in the distance. He had a feeling that the sky was suddenly filled with banners, and leaned for support against a chestnut tree.

In the whole length of the avenue he was the *only* Frenchman, the *only* civilian, and the whole of the enemy army was looking at him. He had no sense of fear. He surrendered with confidence to these myriad eyes. He thought: 'Our conquerors!' – and was caught up on a wave of happiness. Boldly he returned their stare, taking his fill of their fairness, of the sun-tanned faces in which eyes showed like glacier lakes, of the narrow waists and the unbelievable length of the muscular legs. He murmured: 'How beautiful they are!' He felt no longer earth-bound. They had lifted him in their arms and were clasping him to their chests, to their flat bellies. Something came hurtling down from the sky – the Ancient Law! Fallen the Society that had judged him, erased the sentence that it had pronounced. Those horrible little khaki soldiers, those champions of Man and the Citizen, were running for their lives. 'What blessed freedom!' he thought, and his eyes grew moist. He was the sole survivor of disaster, the sole *man* left, and he stood there confronted by the angels of hate, fury, and extermination whose gaze was heavy with the gifts of childhood. 'Here are new judges,' he thought; 'there is the New Law!' How ludicrous now seemed above their heads the gentle beauty of the heavens, the innocence of all its fluffy clouds. This was the victory of contempt, of violence and bad faith: this was the victory of Earth.

A tank moved past him, slow, majestical, covered with branches and scarcely so much as purring. At the back of it, his tunic thrown loosely about his shoulders, his shirt-sleeves rolled above his elbows, was a very young man with folded arms. Daniel smiled at him. For a moment or two the young man looked at him with impassive face and sparkling eyes, then, suddenly, as the tank drew away, smiled back. Hurriedly he felt in the pocket of his breeches and threw a small object in Daniel's direction. The latter caught it – a packet of English cigarettes. So tightly did he clasp it that he could feel the cigarettes snap beneath his fingers. He was still smiling. An intolerable, a delicious thrill mounted in him from thighs to head : there was a mist before his eyes : his breath was coming in pants. To himself he said : 'Just like butter ! – they are going through Paris just like a knife through butter !' Other faces passed before his dimmed vision, more and more of them, each as beautiful as the last. They have come here with intent to do evil : today the Reign of Evil begins. What joy ! He longed to be a woman so that he might load them with flowers. . . . A roaring in the sky – Christ ! – get down – quick ! In a flash the street was empty. A clatter of old tin cans filled it from end to end. A dazzle of steel tore through the sky – they passed between the houses. Charlot, pressing close to Mathieu, shouted, 'They're hedge-hopping !' The indolent and greedy gulls made a half-turn above the village, seeking their feeding-ground, then flew off, trailing behind them a metallic din that echoed from roof after receding roof.

Cautiously a few heads were lifted. Men came out from barns and houses, others jumped from the windows. The place was swarming like a fair-ground. Silence. Silence brooded over them – a hundred all told – sappers, wireless-operators, sound-rangers, telephonists, orderly-room clerks, observers – specialists of every kind, except the drivers who had been at the wheels of their cars since the evening before. They settled down as though in expectation of some show – but *what* show ? They sat cross-legged in the middle of a road that was dead now and without traffic, on the edge of the pavement, on window-sills. Others stood leaning against the house-fronts.

Mathieu had found a place on a small bench in front of the grocer's shop. Charlot and Pierné joined him. No one spoke. They had come together for company, and exchanged silent looks. They saw themselves as they were, a crowd on a fair-ground, unnaturally quiet, a hundred grey faces. The street was a burned-up, incandescent ribbon, twisting away under the gutted sky, burning hot to heels and buttocks. But they were careless of the heat. The General was billeted in the doctor's house: the third window on the first floor was his eye – but to hell with the General!

They looked at one another, and what they saw filled them with fear. They were chafing under the imposed delay: they were longing to be off. No one put the thought into words, but its presence was like a throbbing in their chests; they could feel it in arms and legs, like the ache of strained muscles; it droned dully in their hearts. Someone gave a little whimper, like a dog in a dream, and murmured, half-awake, 'There are tins of bully in the Q.M.'s stores.' Mathieu thought – 'No doubt there are, but they've posted M.P.s at the door,' and Guiccioli replied: 'Don't be daft! they've mounted a guard!' Someone else took up the refrain in a drowsy, impersonal voice: 'And there's bread at the baker's – saw the loaves meself – but he's barricaded the shop!' Mathieu was sunk in the same dream, but said nothing. He had a vision of a piece of steak, and his mouth watered. Grimaud propped himself on his elbow and pointed to the rows of shuttered windows: 'What's going on in this dump?' he said: 'Yesterday they was nattering away to us, and now they're hiding.' Only twelve hours before, the houses had been agape, like opened oyster-shells, now they were all tight shut. In those secret rooms men and women were lying low, sweating in the shadows, and filled with hatred of them. Nippert said: 'It's because we've been beat that they're treating us like a lot of plague-spots.' Charlot's stomach rumbled. Mathieu said: 'Your stomach's singing,' and Charlot replied, 'shouting's more like it!'

A rubber ball fell in the middle of their little group, and Latex caught it. A small girl of five or six approached and stood staring at him with frightened eyes. 'This your ball?' asked Latex: 'come and get it.' They all looked at her. Mathieu would have liked to take her on his knees. Latex tried to make his rough voice sound soft: 'Come along! come and sit on my knee!' – a quiet ripple of voices went round the circle – 'Come along, come along, come along.' The child stood her ground: 'Come along, chicka-biddy, come along, my pretty.' 'Christ!' Latex burst out: 'Even the kids are scared of us now!' The others laughed: 'It's your ugly mug she's scared of,' they said. Mathieu laughed.

Latex went on with his sing-song plea – 'Come along, my pet.'
Suddenly he lost his temper: 'If you don't come I shall keep it!'
He held the ball above his head, so that she could see it, then
made pretence of putting it in his pocket. The child started to
scream. They all scrambled to their feet, and all began to shout:
'Give it her, you great chump! – making a kid cry – no, don't do
that, put it in your pocket! – chuck it over the roof!' Mathieu was
on his feet, gesticulating, Guiccioli, with blazing eyes, pushed
him aside, and strode across to Latex. 'Give it back, for Christ's
sake – we're not a lot of savages!' Mathieu stamped his foot in a
white heat of anger. Latex was the first to recover his temper. He
lowered his eyes and said, 'Pipe down – I'm giving it back all
right.' Clumsily he threw the ball from him. It struck the wall
and rebounded. The child pounced on it and took to her heels.
Peace returned. They all sat down again. Mathieu sat down, too.
His anger had died, but he felt melancholy: 'We're not plague-
spots,' he thought. His mind was nothing but a sounding-board
for what they all were thinking. At one moment he was just an
emptiness filled with vague forebodings, at another, he became
just everybody else. His forebodings faded; the general mood
welled sluggishly up in his mind and oozed from his mouth;
we're not plague-spots.

Latex held out his hands and eyed them mournfully: 'Got six
of me own,' he said: 'eldest's seven, and I've never lifted me
'and to any of 'em.'

They had sat down again, a little huddle of plague-spots, a
collection of foodless, shabby creatures beneath a peopled sky,
propped against the walls of houses sweating hate. They said
nothing, for what could they say, so many abject vermin, dirty-
ing the fair surface of the June day? Patience! – the exterminator
would come, spraying all the streets with Flytox. Longin pointed
to the shuttered windows, and said: 'Waiting for the Jerries to
come along and take us off their hands!' Nippert said: 'Bet your
sweet life they'll be a damn' sight more friendly to Jerry!' – and
Guiccioli: 'Hell – if one's got to be occupied, better be occupied
by the winning side: it's more cheerful, besides, it's better for
trade. We do nothing but bring bad luck.' 'Six kids,' said Latex:
'eldest's seven, and I've never given 'em no cause to be scared of
me.' Grimaud said, 'They hate us.'

A sound of footsteps brought their heads up; but they hurriedly looked down again as Major Prat crossed the street between averted eyes. No one saluted him. He stopped in front of the doctor's house. The heads jerked upwards once again, and the assembled eyes came to a focus on his padded shoulders, as he lifted the iron knocker and rapped three times. The door was opened a crack, and he slipped through the narrow space into the house. Between five-forty-five and five-forty-six all the officers of the headquarters staff walked one by one, stiff and embarrassed, through the group of silent soldiers. Every head was lowered as they passed, every head was raised as soon as they had gone by. Payen said: 'General's throwing a party.' Charlot turned to Mathieu and said: 'What d'you think they're hatching?' to which Mathieu replied: 'Oh, shut up!' Charlot looked at him and said no more. Ever since the officers had put in an appearance the men had looked greyer, drabber, more shrivelled. Pierné glanced at Mathieu with an expression in which surprise was mixed with anxiety: he sees his own pallor in my cheeks.

There was a sound of singing. Mathieu gave a start. The singing drew nearer:

> *'Traine tes couilles par terre*
> *Ça puera dans la chambre.'*

Thirty or so fellows, without rifles, tunics, or caps, and all drunk as lords, came round the corner. They rolled down the street, singing, and in a mood half-way between blissful happiness and bellicosity. Their faces were red with wine and sun. At sight of the greyish grub creeping along the ground and looking at them with its many faces, they stopped dead and broke off their singing. A great chap with a beard stepped forward. He was stripped to the waist and covered with black hair. He had bulging muscles, and he wore a gold chain round his neck.

'You barstards dead?' he inquired.

No one answered. He turned his head and spat. He seemed to have great difficulty in keeping his balance. Charlot peered at him short-sightedly, screwing up his eyes.

'You belong to our outfit?' he asked.

'Ask me old man wot *'e* thinks 'bout it!' said the bearded one, patting his privates. 'Bloody well think we're *not* one o' your stinkin' outfit! – very idea makes me want t' cat!'

'Where you from?'

He replied with a vague gesture:

'Over that way.'

'Been a bit of trouble?'

'Damn' all – 'cept our skipper did a bunk when things began to look nasty, and so did we, only not in same d'rection, f'fear we might run into him!'

The bearded man's pals began laughing in the background, and two great hulking fellows started singing, defiantly:

> *'Traine tes couilles par terre*
> *Prend ta pine à la main, mon copain*
> *Nous partons en guerre*
> *À la chasse à putains.'*

Every face was turned towards the General's eye. Charlot made a frightened gesture with his hand:

'Stow it!'

The singers stopped, and stood, swaying on their feet, their mouths open. They looked suddenly exhausted.

'Officers in there,' explained Charlot, pointing to the house.

'T'hell with your officers!' said the man with the beard in a loud voice. His gold chain twinkled in the sun. He looked down at the men seated in the road, and added:

' 'f you chaps feel bored, better come along o' us – won't be bored then.'

' 'long o' us!' chanted those behind him: ' 'long o' us! – 'long o' us!'

There was a moment's silence. The bearded one's gaze was fixed on Mathieu. Mathieu looked away.

'Who's coming? Goin' – goin' – gone!'

No one moved. The man with the beard threw them a few last contemptuous words:

'They're no' men! – they're lorof barstards! C'mon the lads! – 'm not going to stay here and rot, f— me if I am!'

They started off again, the others drawing back to let them pass. Mathieu put his feet under the bench.

> *'Traine tes couilles par terre –'*

99

Every head was turned towards the General's eye. A few faces were pressed to the window, but the officers did not show themselves.

'Nous partons en guerre –'

The newcomers disappeared. No one spoke a word. The sound of singing died away. Only then did Mathieu breathe freely.

'Well, any'ow there's no *proof* we're not going to move,' said Nippert, without looking at the others.

'Yes, there is,' said Longin.

'Proof of what?'

'That we're not going to move.'

'How d'yer make that out?'

'No juice.'

'Plenty for the officers, all right,' said Guiccioli: 'tanks are full.'

'But the lorries ain't got any.'

Guiccioli laughed drily:

' 'Course not !'

'We've been betrayed !' shouted Longin at the full pitch of his weak voice: 'betrayed, handed over to the Germans, betrayed !'

'Left high and dry !' said Ménard wearily.

'High and dry !' repeated Mathieu: 'high and dry !'

'What's the use of talkin' 'bout a move?' said one of the telephonists: 'Just left, that's what we're goin' to be, just left, you see if we're not.'

Mathieu had a vision of them wandering along the road, singing, perhaps picking flowers. He was conscious of a feeling of shame, but it was a shame in which all of them were involved. The prospect was not altogether unpleasant.

'Barstards ! – that's what that narsty bit o' work called us,' said Latex: 'and me the father of a family ! See that cissy chain the bugger'd got round 'is neck?'

'Hark !' said Charlot: 'hark !'

They could hear the throb of an aeroplane. A tired voice murmured:

'Get down chaps ! – here they are again !'

'That's the tenth time this morning,' said Nippert.

'You keeping count? I gave that up long ago.'

They rose to their feet in a leisurely way, flattened themselves in doorways, slipped into houses, and stood in passages. An aeroplane swept over them at roof-level: the noise diminished; they came out from cover, glanced at the sky, and sat down.

'Fighter,' said Mathieu.

From far away they caught the dry rat-tat of a machine-gun.

'Ack-ack?'

'Ack-ack my foot! – that's the plane pooping off!'

They looked at one another.

'Not healthy on the road in daylight,' said Grimaud.

They said nothing, but their eyes were sparkling, and the hint of a smile was showing at the corners of their mouths. A moment later, Longin said in conversational tones:

'Can't have got very far.'

Guiccioli got up, stuffed his hands in his pockets, and did one or two knee-bends to loosen his joints. He glanced up at the sky. His face was empty of expression, but there was a wicked little crease round his lips.

'Where you off to?'

'Just going to have a nose round.'

'Where?'

'Over there: want to see what happened.'

'Keep an eye open for wops.'

'I'll be all right.'

He moved off at a lazy shuffle. They would all have liked to go with him, but Mathieu dared not get up. There was a prolonged silence. Colour had returned to their faces, and there was animation in the looks that they exchanged.

'Bit of all right it'd be if one could just take a little stroll like in peacetime.'

'What did they expect? – to get a hitch-hike back to Paris? – some guys never learn.'

'If there'd been a chance of that, we wouldn't have needed them to show us the way!'

There was another silence. They felt nervy and tense. They waited. The hands of a thin, gawky fellow leaning against the grocer's iron shutters were shaking. A few moments later Guiccioli came back, still moving in the same unconcerned way.

'Well?' exclaimed Mathieu.

Guiccioli shrugged. The boys sat up and looked at him with shining eyes.

'Done in.'

'All of 'em?'

'How should I know? I didn't count.'

He was pale and retching silently.

'Where were they – on the road?'

'Hell, why don't you go and have a dekko for yerselves if you're so curious!'

He sat down. Round his neck a gold chain caught the light. He raised his hand and fiddled with it – then suddenly let it alone. Almost regretfully he said:

'I passed the word to the stretcher-bearers.'

Poor devils! The chain sparkled. It held their eyes fascinated. Which of them would speak the words: 'poor devils'? They were on every lip, but who would be hypocrite enough to speak them? Poor devils, but would it be hypocrisy? The gold chain sparkled on the brown neck. Cruelty, horror, pity, rancour made the round of the group, an atrocious feeling, yet a comforting one. We are a vermin's dream: our thoughts are becoming muddied, are becoming less and less human: thoughts, hairy and clawed, were scurrying around, jumping from head to head; the vermin was on the point of waking up.

' 'Strewth, Delarue, you deaf!'

Delarue: that's me. He turned his head sharply. Pinette was smiling at him. *He's looking at Delarue.*

'What's up?'

'Come along.'

He shivered. He felt suddenly naked and alone, a man, *I*. He waved Pinette away, but already the group had closed its ranks against him. The vermin eyes had ostracized him, were looking at him with an air of astonished solemnity, as though they were seeing him for the first time, as though they were looking up at him through layers of slime. I'm not better than they are: I've no right to judge them.

'Come along.'

Delarue got up. Delarue the unspeakable, Delarue the scrupulous, Delarue the school-teacher, moved slowly across to where Pinette was waiting. Behind him, the swamp, the beast with the hundred feet. Behind him two hundred eyes. He had a feeling of fear in his back, and, once again, of anguish. As always, it began very gently, almost like a caress, and then settled down, a modest, familiar presence, in the pit of his stomach. It was nothing positive at all – merely a sense of emptiness, scarcely even that: emptiness within and emptiness without. He seemed to be moving in a world where there was nothing to breathe but an atmosphere of rarefied gas. The gallant warrior Delarue took off his regimental cap: the gallant warrior Delarue passed his hand through his hair: the gallant warrior Delarue turned to Pinette with a weary smile.

'What's up?' said Delarue.

'You getting any kick out of this?'

'No.'

'Then why stay?'

'We're all much of a muchness.'

'Who is?'

'They and us.'

'Well, what of it?'

'Just as well to stick together.'

Pinette's eyes showed fire.

'Not much of a muchness between me and them!' he said with an upward jerk of the head.

Mathieu was silent: Pinette said:

'Come along of me.'

'Where to?'

'Post office.'

'Didn't know there was one.'

'You bet there is – branch office, at the end of the village.'

'And what are you going to do at the post office?'

'Just you wait and see.'

'Almost certain to be shut.'

'It'll open up for me all right,' said Pinette.

He linked arms with Mathieu and led him away.

'I've found a girl,' he said.

His eyes were shining with excitement. His smile expressed self-satisfaction.

'Want me to introduce you?'

'Whatever for?'

Pinette gave him a stern look.

'You're my pal, aren't you?'

'Certainly I am,' said Mathieu. 'This girl of yours the post-mistress?' he asked.

'She works at the post office.'

'I thought you didn't want to have anything to do with women.'

Pinette forced a laugh.

'Got to pass the time somehow now there's no fighting.'

Mathieu turned and looked at him. He had an air of complacency.

'Don't recognize you, old man: you fallen for this girl?'

'Might 'a picked on worse,' said Pinette. 'You wait until you see what she's got up front: nice a pair of apples as ever I clapped eyes on! Educated kid, too: geography and sums, got it all!'

'How about your wife?' asked Mathieu.

Pinette's expression changed.

'Aw, she can go f— herself!' he said roughly.

By this time they had reached a small, single-storey house. The shutters were closed, and the handle had been removed from the door. Pinette knocked three times.

'It's me!' he yelled, then, turning to Mathieu with a grin, 'Scared of being raped,' he said.

Mathieu heard the sound of a key being turned.

'Come in, quick,' said a woman's voice.

They dived into a thick, composite smell of ink, gum, and paper. A long counter with a wire grille divided the room into two parts. At the back, Mathieu could just make out an open door. Through this the woman retreated, and they could hear her shoot the bolt. For a few moments they were left in the narrow passage-way reserved for the use of the public. Then the woman reappeared, this time at the little window in the protective grille. Pinette leaned forward, pressing his forehead against the wire.

'Keeping us at a distance, eh? Why you being so unkind?'

'A girl can't be too careful these days,' she said. She had a nice voice, deep-toned and warm. Mathieu noticed that her black eyes were shining.

'You scared of us?' asked Pinette.

She laughed:

'Not scared, but not too trusting, either,' she said.

' 'Cos I've got a pal with me? You ought to get on well together, you ought – he's a public servant, same as you. That ought to stop you worrying.'

He had assumed a mincing manner of speech and a well-bred smile.

'Come on,' he said; 'put a finger through the bars, just one finger.'

She passed one long, thin finger through the grille. Pinette kissed the tip of it.

'You behave,' she said, 'or I'll take it back.'

'That wouldn't be polite,' he said: 'I want my pal to shake hands with you.'

He turned to Mathieu.

'Allow me to introduce Miss Won't-tell-her-name, a plucky little French girl who could have been evacuated, only she wouldn't abandon her post in case she might be needed.'

He wriggled his shoulders and smiled. He never stopped smiling. He spoke in a soft sing-song with a faint English accent.

'How d'you do, mademoiselle,' said Mathieu.

She agitated the finger which she had pushed through the grille. He clasped it in his hand.

'Are you a civil servant?' she asked.

'I am a teacher.'

'And I'm a postmistress.'

He was feeling hot and bored. His thoughts were with the dull, grey faces which he had left behind.

'Mademoiselle is responsible for all the love-letters of the village,' said Pinette.

'We don't have many love-letters here,' she said with a bashful expression.

'If I lived in this dump,' said Pinette, 'I'd write love-letters to all the girls round, just so's they might pass through your hands. You should be the postmistress of love.'

He laughed rather wildly.

'The postmistress of love! the postmistress of love!'

'I should have to work overtime!' she said. There was a long pause. A nonchalant smile still showed on Pinette's lips, but there was a tenseness about him, and his eyes were darting inquisitive looks round the room. A penholder was attached to the grille by a piece of string. Pinette took it, dipped it in the ink and scribbled a few words on a money-order form.

'There!' said he, pushing the form under the grille.

'What's that?' she said, but did not touch it.

'Take it!' he said: 'You're in charge here: do your job.'

She obeyed him and read out what he had written: 'Pay one thousand kisses to Mademoiselle Won't-tell-her-name ...'

'Ah,' she said, torn between annoyance and a desire to laugh, 'now you've spoiled one of my forms.'

By this time Mathieu was thoroughly fed-up.

'I'll leave you here,' he said.

Pinette seemed disconcerted by his remark.

'Not going, are you?'

'I'd better be getting back.'

'Then I'll go with you,' said Pinette hurriedly: 'yes, I will.'

He turned to the girl behind the grille: 'Back in five minutes: you'll open the door again, won't you?'

'How tiresome you are!' she grumbled: 'First you want to come in, then you want to go out. Why can't you make up your mind?'

'All right, then, I'll stay. But don't forget, now – it's you as asked me to!'

'I didn't ask you anything!'

'Oh yes, you did!'

'I didn't.'

'Oh, hell!' muttered Mathieu between his teeth. He turned to her:

'Good afternoon, mademoiselle.'

'Good afternoon,' she replied coldly.

Mathieu went out and walked along thinking of nothing. It was getting dark. The soldiers were sitting just where he had left them. He joined the group. A number of voices spoke from the ground.

'Any news?'

'Nothing at all.'

He went back to his bench and sat down between Charlot and Pierné.

'Officers still with the General?' he asked.

'Yes.'

Mathieu yawned. He looked gloomily at the others. They were only half-visible in the darkness. *We*, he muttered, but the word had no meaning for him. He was alone. He threw back his head and gazed at the first stars. The sky was as soft and gentle as a woman. All the love in the world seemed to have taken refuge in the sky. He blinked.

'A shooting-star, chaps: wish!'

Lubéron broke wind.

'That's my wish,' he said.

Mathieu yawned again.

'As good as any other. Well, I'm going to turn in: you coming, Charlot?'

'Don't know: might be moving tonight; just as well to be ready.'

Mathieu uttered a harsh laugh:

'Don't be a bloody fool!' he said.

'All right, all right,' said Charlot hastily: 'I'll come.'

Mathieu went into the barn and flung himself fully dressed on the hay. He was dropping with sleep. He always felt sleepy when he was oppressed by gloom. A red ball started to spin before his eyes; women's faces were leaning from a balcony. They, too, started to spin. Mathieu dreamed that he was the sky. He leaned over the balcony and looked down at the earth. The earth was green. It had a white belly and was jumping about like a flea. He thought: mustn't let it touch me. But it stretched out five enormous fingers and gripped his shoulder.

'Get up, quick!'

'Wha's time?' he asked. He could feel warm breath on his face.

'Ten-twenty' – the voice was Guiccioli's: 'Get up quickly, go to the door and take a look. But don't show yourself.'

Mathieu sat up and yawned.

'What's the matter?'

'Officers' cars are waiting in the road a hundred yards off.'

'What of it?'

'Do as I say: you'll soon see.'

Guiccioli disappeared. Mathieu rubbed his eyes: in a low voice he called out:

'Charlot! Charlot! – Longin! Longin!'

No answer. He got up and tiptoed sleepily as far as the door. It was wide open. There was a man hiding in the shadows.

'Who's there?'

'It's me,' said Pinette.

'Thought you were busy love-making.'

'She's being a bit difficult. Shan't make it till tomorrow. Christ! my lips feel stiff with all that grinning!'

'Where's Pierné?'

Pinette pointed to a dark entry across the street.

'Over there, with Charlot and Longin.'

'What are they doing?'

'Don't know.'

They waited in silence. The night was cold and clear. The moon was shining. Opposite, in the dark entry, a confusion of shadows moved vaguely. Mathieu turned and looked towards the doctor's house. The General's eye was shut, but a faint light showed under the door. *I am here.* Time, with its great fanning future, collapsed. All that was left was a tiny flickering patch of local moments. There was no such thing as peace or war: no such entity as France or Germany, only a faint light under a door that might or might not open. Would it open? Nothing else mattered. Mathieu was deprived of everything now but this tiny scrap of the future. Would it open? A sense of delicious adventure flooded his dead heart with light. Would it open? The question seemed terribly *important.* If the door opened, all the questions that had haunted him all his life would at last be answered. He felt that the little shudder of delight was about to start in the pit of his stomach. He felt ashamed. He said to himself with deliberate care – we have lost the war. Instantly, the reign of Time was restored: the tiny pearl of the future swelled until it became an immense and sinister vista. The Past, the Future as far as eye could reach, from the Pharaohs to the United States of Europe. His joy was extinguished. The light under the door was extinguished. The door creaked, swung slowly back and stood open to the night. The shadow in the dark entry quivered; the street crackled like forest undergrowth, and then was silent. Too late; adventure was dead.

After a moment or two shapes appeared on the entrance steps.

One after another, the officers descended. The first to reach the bottom stopped in the middle of the road, waiting for the others, and the street became immediately metamorphosed: 1912, a street in a garrison town under snow, very late at night: the General's party had just broken up: handsome as pictures lieutenants Sautin and Cadine stood arm in arm. Major Prat had laid his hand on Captain Mauron's shoulder. They threw out their chests; they smiled, obligingly posing under the moon's magnesium – one last exposure, gentlemen – this time the whole group – thank you. Major Prat turned sharply on his heels, looked at the sky, raised two fingers in the air as though blessing the village. The General came out: a Colonel closed the door gently behind him. Divisional Headquarters Staff was present in full strength, twenty officers all told – a snowy night – a clear sky – they had danced till midnight – one of the best of the garrison evenings, long to be remembered. The little group started to move, very quietly. On the first floor a window was noiselessly opened: a figure dressed in white was leaning out, was watching their departure.

'Whoever would have believed it!' muttered Pinette.

They were walking without any show of excitement. There was a smooth solemnity about their movements. Upon those statuesque and moon-drenched faces showed so much loneliness and so much silence that it seemed a sacrilege to look at them. Mathieu felt at once guilty and cleansed.

'Yes, indeed, who would have believed it!'

Captain Mauron hesitated. Had he heard? His tall, graceful figure with its stooping shoulders, slightly faltered, and made a half-turn in the direction of the barn. Mathieu could see his eyes glitter. Pinette uttered a sound like a snarl, and made as though to run into the street. But Mathieu snatched at his wrist and held it in an iron grip. For another moment the Captain raked the shadows with his gaze, then turned away and yawned with an air of indifference, tapping his mouth with the tips of his gloved fingers. The General passed them. Mathieu had never before seen him so close. He was a stout, imposing-looking man, with a deeply lined face. He was leaning heavily on the Colonel's arm. Next came the officers' servants with their valises. A whispering and laughing party of subalterns brought up the rear.

'Officers!' said Pinette in a voice that was barely kept low.

'So it seems.'

Pinette's lips began to tremble. Mathieu was afraid that he might burst into sobs.

'Come, don't be a little fool,' said Mathieu: 'get a hold on yourself.'

'If I hadn't seen it with me own eyes, I'd never've believed it! There's the bottom dropped out of everything,' said Pinette.

He gripped Mathieu's hand as hard as though it were his last hope.

'Perhaps the drivers 'll refuse to start?'

Mathieu answered with a shrug. They could already hear the sound of engines, like the pleasing note of grasshoppers very far away. A moment later the cars started, and the sound of the engines died. Pinette folded his arms.

'Officers! now I really do believe that France is done for!'

Mathieu turned. Masses of shadow were moving away from the walls. Soldiers were silently creeping from alley-ways, wagon-entrances, and barns, real soldiers of a second-line formation, ill-kempt, ill-fed, slipping past the shadowed whiteness of the house-fronts. All of a sudden, the street was full of them. So sad were their faces that Mathieu felt a lump in his throat.

'Come along,' he said to Pinette.

'Where to?'

'Outside, with the others.'

'Oh, hell!' said Pinette: 'I'm going to doss down: I'm in no mood for talking.'

Mathieu hesitated. He was sleepy and his head was aching. He longed for sleep and the obliteration of all thought. But they looked so downcast, their backs made such a whitened huddle in the moonlight, that he felt one of them.

'I am,' he said: 'good night.'

He crossed the street and mingled with the crowd. The chalky moonlight shone on faces that seemed to have been turned to stone. Suddenly the sound of car engines came distinctly to their ears.

'They're coming back!' said Charlot: 'they're coming back!'

'Don't you believe it! That was them turning into the main road.'

They listened, however, with a vague sense of hope. The purring died away: vanished. Latex sighed:

'Well, that's the end.'

'Now we're on our own!' said Grimaud.

No one laughed. Somebody, in a low and anxious voice, put a question.

'What happens now?'

There was no answer. They did not much care what was going to happen. Something far different was worrying them, an obscure unease for which they could find no words. Lubéron yawned. After a long interval of silence, he said:

'No good hanging about here – let's turn in.'

Charlot made a vague, despairing gesture.

'All right,' he said: 'I'm for the hay: but it's bloody awful.'

Every face expressed anxiety. They did not want to separate, but there seemed no point in sticking together. Suddenly a voice was heard, a voice edged with bitterness:

'They never liked us!'

Its owner was expressing a general thought. Everyone started talking.

'That's right – you said it – they never liked us, never! For them, the enemy wasn't Jerry, but us. We fought this war together, and they've gone and left us standing!'

Mathieu's voice made one of the general babble:

'They never liked us, never!'

'When I saw 'em go past,' said Charlot, 'it was such a shock you could've knocked me down with a feather.'

A buzz of talk drowned him. That wasn't what they wanted to hear. The abscess had got to be drained. Tongues were loosened: talk had become a necessity. No one likes us, no one: the civilians blame us for not defending them, our wives have got no pride in us, our officers have left us in the lurch, the villagers hate us, the Jerries are advancing through the darkness. What was in their minds had got to find words. We are the scapegoats, we are the conquered, the cowards, the vermin, the offscourings of the earth: we have lost the war: we are ugly and we are guilty, and no one, no one in the whole world, likes us. Mathieu dared not find expression for all this, but Latex, behind him, spoke it calmly and unemotionally:

'We're pariahs.'

There was a sputter of voices. Everywhere the word was repeated, harshly, pitilessly:

'Pariahs!'

Silence fell. Mathieu looked at Longin, for no particular reason, but simply because he was his nearest neighbour. Charlot and Latex exchanged glances. All present stared at one another: all present seemed to be waiting, as though something still remained to be said. Then, suddenly, Latex smiled at Mathieu, and Mathieu returned his smile. Charlot smiled. Latex smiled. On every face the moon brought pallid flowers to birth.

Monday, 17 June

'COME along,' said Pinette.

'No.'

'Oh, do.'

'For God's sake, leave me alone!'

They were both of them under the trees in the middle of the square, with the church opposite and the Mairie to their left. Charlot was seated on the bottom step of the Mairie, deep in a day-dream. There was a book on his knee. Soldiers were slowly sauntering up and down, alone or in small groups. They did not know what to do with their freedom. Mathieu's head felt heavy and painful as though he had been drinking.

'You look fed up.'

'I *am* fed up,' said Mathieu.

At first there had been the exhausting intoxication of brotherly love – a glow of affection beneath the moon. Life had seemed worth living. Then the light had begun to burn low. They had gone to bed, because there was nothing else to do, and because they were unused to the claims of mutual affection. And now it was the morning after, and they all felt like suicide.

'What's the time?' asked Pinette.

'Ten past five.'

'Hell, I'm late!'

'Get a move on, then.'

'I don't want to go alone.'

'Afraid she'll give you a flea in your ear?'

'It's not that,' said Pinette: 'it's not that.'

Nippert walked past, not seeing them. He was deep in some secret thought.

'Take Nippert along,' said Mathieu.

'Nippert? – you crazy?'

They followed Nippert with their eyes, made curious by the unseeing look upon his face, by his tripping step.

'What's the betting he goes into the church?' asked Pinette.

He waited a moment and then slapped his thigh:

'He *is* going in! I've won!'

Nippert had disappeared. Pinette turned to Mathieu and looked at him with a puzzled expression.

'I've heard as there's fifty or so inside: been there since this morning. Now and then one or two come out to ease theirselves, and then they go back again. What's cooking? – you know?'

Mathieu did not reply, and Pinette scratched his head.

'I'd like to have a dekko.'

'You're already late for your appointment.'

'That can go to hell,' said Pinette.

He sloped away. Mathieu went across to one of the chestnuts. Just an untidy bundle left lying by the roadside – that was all there was left of the Divisional Headquarters Staff. And there were others like them in all the villages of France. The Jerries would mop them up without bothering to stop. 'What in God's name are they waiting for? Why don't they hurry?' Defeat had become a part of every day: it was the sun, the trees, the very air they breathed, and, deep down, this longing for death. Nevertheless, he was conscious of a sort of hangover from the previous night, a taste of brotherly love that had gone cold in his mouth. The post-orderly was coming towards him, walking with the two cooks, one on each side of him. Mathieu looked at them. In the darkness, beneath the moon, they had smiled friendship at him. But all that was a thing of the past. The hard secrecy of their faces seemed to say, 'Beware the madness of the moon, the ecstasies of midnight: each man for himself and the devil take the hindmost: we're not in this world for fun.' They, too, were suffering from the morning after. Mathieu took his knife from his pocket and began cutting at the bark of the tree. He felt a sudden need to write his name somewhere in the world.

'Carvin' yer name?'

'As a matter of fact, I am.'

'Ha! Ha!'

They laughed and walked on. Some other soldiers were close behind them, fellows Mathieu had never seen before. They were unshaven; there was a glitter in their eyes and a strange look on their faces. One of them was limping. They went across the square and sat down on the pavement in front of the baker's closed shop. Gradually, others turned up, a great many others, none of whom Mathieu knew by sight, without rifles or puttees, their faces grey, and with dried mud on their boots. He ought, he felt, to have been able to look at them with affection. Pinette strolled up. As they passed him he scowled.

'Well?' asked Mathieu.

'Church's full' – then, with an air of disappointment: 'they're singing!'

Mathieu shut his knife.

'Writin' yer name?' asked Pinette.

'I was going to,' said Mathieu, slipping his knife into his pocket: 'but it takes too long.'

A great lout of a fellow stopped close by them. He looked tired, washed-out. His face seemed a blur above his unfastened collar.

'Hello!' he said, but no smile accompanied the greeting.

Pinette stared at him.

'Hello!' said Mathieu.

'Any officers round about here?'

Pinette began to laugh:

'Hear that?' he said to Mathieu. He turned to the newcomer: 'No, m'lad, you won't find any officers here, we're a republic, we are.'

'Oh,' said the other.

'What division you from?'

'Forty-second.'

'Forty-second?' grumbled Pinette: 'never heard of it. Where's it hang out?'

'Épinal.'

'What you doing here then?'

The soldier gave a shrug. Pinette, suddenly uneasy, put a question:

'Not coming here, is it, with officers and the whole bag o' tricks?'

It was the other's turn to laugh. He pointed to four men seated on the pavement.

'Them's the division,' he said.

Pinette's eyes sparkled.

'Things pretty hot Épinal way?'

'They were, must have calmed down by now, though.'

He turned on his heel, and went off to join his companions. Pinette stared after him:

'Forty-second, tell that to – ! Ever heard of that lot? – can't say I had, till now.'

'That's no reason for snubbing him.'

Pinette shrugged.

'Blokes keep on turning up from God knows where!' he said contemptuously. 'Don't know where y'are any longer!'

Mathieu said nothing. He kept his eyes fixed on the scratches in the bark of the chestnut.

'Oh, come along!' said Pinette. 'We'll have a day in the country, just the three of us. Won't see another soul: that'll be nice.'

'Why d'you want me? I shall only be in the way. When you're out for what you're out for you don't need anybody else.'

'We shan't get down to it at once,' said Pinette rather gloomily: 'have to have a bit of a talky-talk first.'

He broke off sharply:

'Look, over there – another bleeding foreigner!'

A soldier was coming towards them, a short, stocky man, walking very stiffly. A blood-stained handkerchief hid his right eye.

'P'raps there's a big battle going on!' said Pinette in a voice shaken by hope: 'Maybe things are going to get tough!'

Mathieu said nothing. Pinette gave the man with the bandage a shout:

'Hey, you!'

The man stopped and stared at them with his one eye.

'Stuff flying about over there?'

There was no reply. Pinette turned to Mathieu:

'Can't get a thing out o' the buggers!'

The stranger went on his way. After walking a few steps he stopped, leaned his back against a chestnut tree, and slid to the ground. He sat there with his knees drawn up to his chin.

'Doesn't look too good,' said Pinette.

'Come on!' said Mathieu.

They went across:

'Not feelin' too good, chum?' said Pinette.

The man said nothing.

'Hey, you, anything wrong?'

'We've come to give you a hand,' said Mathieu to the soldier.

Pinette leaned down, made as though to put his arm round him, but stood up again.

'Not worth the trouble.'

The man was still squatting under the tree, his one eye staring, his mouth hanging open. He seemed to be quietly smiling to himself.

'What do you mean not worth the trouble?'

'Take a good look at him.'

Mathieu stooped down and put his head to the man's chest.

'You're right,' he said.

'Better close his eyes,' said Pinette.

This he proceeded to do. There was an intent look on his face, his shoulders were hunched, his lower lip was thrust forward. Mathieu looked at him, not at the dead man. The dead man no longer mattered.

'One might think you'd been doing that all your life,' he said.

'Seen plenty of stiffs in my time,' said Pinette: 'but this is the first I've come across since the war started.'

The dead man sat there with closed eyes, smiling at his secret thoughts. How easy it seemed to die, easy and almost gay. 'Why go on living, then?' The whole scene took on a wavering and insubstantial look: the living, the dead, the church, the trees. Mathieu gave a start. A hand had touched him on the shoulder. It was the tall man with the blurred face. He stared at the dead soldier with his washed-out eyes.

'What's up?'

116

'He's a goner.'

'It's Gérin,' he explained.

Then, turning towards the east:

'Come over here, you boys: jump to it!'

The four soldiers got up and started to run.

'Gérin's got his!' he called to them.

'Hell!'

They stood about the dead man, staring down at him suspiciously.

'Funny he didn't fall.'

'Happens like that sometimes.'

'Sure he's dead?'

'These blokes here says as he is.'

All of them, simultaneously, leaned over the dead man. One
felt for his pulse, another listened to his heart, a third took a
mirror from his pocket and held it in front of the dead lips – as
is always done in detective novels. Then, they straightened
themselves, satisfied that it was indeed a case of death.

'Poor old bugger!' said the tall man with a shake of the head.

All four shook their heads, and repeated in chorus: 'Poor old
bugger!'

One of them, who was short and stout, turned to Mathieu:

'Twenty kilometres he done on his flat feet: if he'd lain
doggo he'd a'been living now.'

'He didn't want Jerry to get him,' said Mathieu by way of
excuse.

'Oh yeah? – well, the Jerries've got ambulances, haven't they?
I walked with him for a bit and tried to get him to act sensible.
Bleeding like a pig, he was, but yer could talk till yer was blue
in the face, an' he wouldn't listen. Quite all there he was, too,
said as he wanted to get home.'

'Where was that?' asked Pinette.

'Cahors: he was a baker in them parts.'

Pinette shrugged:

'Well, anyhow, this isn't the road to Cahors.'

'No, 'tisn't, is it?'

They stopped talking and looked down at the dead man with
an air of embarrassment.

'What do we do now, bury 'im?'

117

'Nothing else we can do.'

They lifted him by the shoulders and the knees. He was still smiling up at them, but with every minute that passed he looked more dead.

'We'll give you a hand.'

'Don't bother.'

'Yes, we will,' said Pinette eagerly: 'we've nothing to do and it'll help pass the time.'

The tall soldier eyed him sternly.

'No,' he said: 'that's our job. He was one of us, and it's up to us to bury him.'

'Where you going to put 'im?'

The small, stout chap nodded in the direction of the north: 'Over there.'

They got under way, carrying the corpse between them. They looked almost as much dead as he was.

'Might've been a religious bloke, mightn't he?' asked Pinette.

They looked at him in amazement. Pinette nodded towards the church.

'Any number of padres in there.'

'No – no – we'll see to it.'

He turned and followed the others. They crossed the square and vanished.

'What's up with that bloke?' shouted Charlot.

'He's dead – that's what's up.'

'That's a f—ing bad show, that's what that is,' said Charlot. 'Didn't think to take a dekko at 'im. Didn't see 'im, 'cept when they was carrying 'im away. Well, he wasn't one of our lot, was 'e?'

'No.'

'That's all right, then,' he said.

They moved away. The songs and shouts coming through the Mairie windows were like nothing human.

'What's going on in there?' asked Mathieu.

Charlot grinned.

'That's the knocking shop, that is,' he said, as though it were the most natural thing in the world.

'Can you read?'

'Not very well,' said Charlot apologetically.

'What's that book you've got?'

'It's the Vaulabelle.'

'I thought Longin was reading that.'

'Longin!' said Charlot ironically: 'Not half he isn't! Longin's in no state to read nothing!'

He jerked his thumb over his shoulder in the direction of the building.

'He's in there; tight as an owl!'

'Longin? he never drinks anything stronger than water.'

'Have a look for yourself! You'll soon see whether he's tight or not.'

'What's the time?' asked Pinette.

'Five-thirty-five.'

Pinette turned to Mathieu:

'You're not coming? – quite sure?'

'Quite sure: I'm not coming.'

'Go and booze, then.'

He looked at Charlot with his short-sighted eyes:

'I'm going to be properly browned off.'

'Why are you going to be browned off?'

'He's got a pick-up,' said Mathieu.

'If you don't want her, pass her on to me.'

'Nothing doing!' said Pinette: 'she adores me.'

'Well, then, get out of your own mess.'

Pinette, with a furious gesture, turned his back and took himself off.

Charlot grinned at his retreating back.

'He's a favourite with the girls.'

'I know that,' said Mathieu.

'Well, he can have her,' said Charlot. 'Don't fancy girls just now.'

He looked at Mathieu curiously.

'They do say as when a chap's windy he can't do nothing in that line.'

'Well, what of it?'

'But that's not what's the matter with me: I just don't want it.'

'You windy?'

'Not on your life I'm not! simply a sort of weight on me stomach.'

'I see.'

Charlot suddenly gripped Mathieu's sleeve. In a low voice he said:

'Sit down, I've got something to tell you.'

Mathieu sat down.

'There's a lot of f—ing talk going round,' said Charlot in secretive tones.

'What sort of talk?' asked Mathieu.

Charlot showed embarrassment. 'Just a lot of proper f—ing nonsense.'

'Go on.'

'Well, Corporal Cabel's going about saying as how the Jerries cut off your you-know-whats.'

He laughed, but his eyes were still fixed on Mathieu's face.

'That certainly is a lot of nonsense,' said Mathieu.

Charlot was still laughing.

'I never did believe it. Too much like bloody hard work for the Jerries.'

They stopped talking. Mathieu had taken the Vaulabelle, and was turning over the pages. He was hoping that Charlot would let him keep it. With assumed carelessness, Charlot said:

'They do that to the Jews, don't they? – in their own country, I mean.'

'Of course they don't!'

'I've heard it said as how they do,' said Charlot in the same tone of voice.

Suddenly, he seized Mathieu by the shoulders. Mathieu could not bear the sight of the naked terror in his face, and looked away.

'What'll they do to me?' asked Charlot.

'No more than they'll do to everybody else.'

There was a pause, and Mathieu added:

'Tear up your Army book and chuck your identity disk away.'

'I've done that already.'

'Well, then, why worry?'

'Look at me,' said Charlot.

Mathieu could not bring himself to obey:

'Come on! – look at me!'

'I am looking at you,' said Mathieu: 'what's the matter?'

'Do I look like a Jew?'

'No,' said Mathieu: 'you do *not* look like a Jew.'

Charlot sighed. A soldier stumbled out of the Mairie, descended three steps, missed the fourth, staggered between Charlot and Mathieu, and collapsed in the road.

'Hullo, what's up with him?' said Mathieu.

The man raised himself on his elbow and vomited. Then his head fell back and he lay there, motionless.

'They been pinching wine from the Q.M.'s stores,' explained Charlot. 'Saw 'em, I did, with a lot of jugs they'd cadged from somewhere, and a great tin full of ration booze. A pretty disgusting sight, I can tell you!'

Longin appeared at a ground-floor window and belched loudly. His eyes were bloodshot and one side of his face was black and blue.

'Nice state *you're* in!' Charlot shouted at him disapprovingly.

Longin blinked at them. When he realized who was there he raised both arms in a gesture of tragedy:

'Delarue!'

'Hello.'

'I'm bloory disgrace!'

'Well, then, you'd better go home.'

'Can't go home by m'self.'

'I'll go with you,' said Mathieu.

He got up, clutching the Vaulabelle.

'You're a decent bloke,' said Charlot.

'Well, it's something to do, anyway.'

He had reached the second step when he heard Charlot shouting after him:

'Hi! give me back my Vaulabelle!'

'All right, but don't make such a row!' said Mathieu angrily.

He threw the book to him, pushed open the door, found himself in a corridor with white walls, and stopped dead, in sudden horrified surprise. Someone was singing 'L'Artilleur de Metz' in a sleepy and discordant voice. He was reminded of the time in 1924 when he had gone to see his mad old aunt in an asylum at Rouen. Some of the lunatics had been singing at the windows. On the left-hand wall there was a notice under a wire screen. He went up to it and saw the words – GENERAL MOBILIZA-

TION. I was still a civilian – that was a long time ago. He looked at the two crossed flags at the top of the notice, and suddenly had a vision of himself in an alpaca coat and a stiff collar. He had never worn either, but that was how he envisaged civilians. 'I should hate to be a civilian again,' he thought: 'anyhow, they belong to a dying race.' He heard Longin's voice shouting 'Delarue!', saw an open door on his left, and went through it. The sun was already low, and its long, dusty beams cut the room in two but did not lighten it. A strong smell of wine caught him by the throat. He blinked his eyes, seeing nothing at first but a wall-map, which showed as a dark square on the white plaster. Then he noticed Ménard seated on top of a small cupboard, with his legs hanging over the edge. He was swinging his army boots in the red glow of the evening sun. It was he who was singing. There was a wild gleam of gaiety in his eyes, which were rolling from side to side above his open mouth. He seemed to have no control over his voice. It was like some huge parasite feeding upon him, sucking up his blood and guts and transforming them into song. He sat there, an inert figure with dangling arms, watching with horrified amazement the vermin that was issuing from his mouth. The room was completely devoid of furniture. Somebody must have made a clean sweep of tables and chairs. A roar of greeting welcomed him.

'Delarue! How'ya, Delarue!'

There were others to his right, not quite so far gone. Guiccioli was sitting on the floor, a canteen full of wine between his spread legs. Latex and Grimaud were squatting tailor-wise. Grimaud was holding his quart-pot by the handle and banging it on the floor in time to Ménard's singing. Latex had got his hand half-hidden in his gaping flies. Guiccioli said something, but it was impossible to hear him through the noise.

'What's that?' asked Mathieu, curving his hand round his ear.

Guiccioli turned furious eyes on Ménard:

'For Go's sake, pipe down, ca' hear oneself speak!'

Ménard stopped singing:

'Can't leave off!' he said tearfully.

Dragged at the heels of his voice, he started on 'Les Filles de Camaret'.

' 's off again!' said Guiccioli.

He seemed not to mind much and looked at Mathieu with pride.

'Feeling gay – tha's wha's the matter with 'im. We're all feeling gay! lo' o' tramps, hot-heads, dish-smashers – that's wha' *we* are!'

Grimaud nodded approval and laughed. Very carefully as though speaking a foreign language he said:

'No-thing me-lanch-oly 'bout us.'

'So I see,' said Mathieu.

'You wan' drink?' asked Guiccioli.

In the middle of the floor there was a large tin filled with rough ration wine. Various objects were floating about in it.

'That's a jam tin,' said Mathieu: 'Where'd you find it?'

'No bus'ness o' yours,' said Guiccioli: 'Have drink or getta hell outa here!'

He expressed himself with difficulty, and was having considerable trouble in the matter of keeping his eyes open. But his mood was aggressive.

'No,' said Mathieu: 'I've just come to fetch Longin.'

'Fetch'm? whereto?'

'To get a breath of air.'

Guiccioli gripped his canteen in both hands and drank.

'*I'm* not going t' stop yer: does nothin' but talk 'bout 's brother: 'nough t'make feller cat – we're the rip-roarin' lads, we are – don' wan' anyone can't 'joy 's liquor!'

Mathieu took Longin by the arm.

'Come along!'

Longin shook himself free.

'Wha's the hurry? Can't yer gimme time t'dress meself?'

'Take all the time you want.'

He turned on his heel, and went across to have a look at the cupboard. It had glazed doors, and he could see a quantity of cloth-bound books inside. Something to read. At that moment he would gladly have read anything – even the Civil Code. The doors were locked. He tried to open them, but without success.

'Smash glass!' said Guiccioli.

'I certainly shan't!' said Mathieu angrily.

'Why no'? Jerries won' be sho conshiderate.'

He turned to the others:

'Jerries'll burn whole dump, and here's Delarue won' smash bi' of glash!'

The rest of the room roared with laughter.

'Borjwah!' said Grimaud contemptuously.

Latex caught hold of Mathieu by the tunic.

'Hey, Delarue, come'n have a look!'

Mathieu turned round:

'Have a look at what?'

Latex exposed himself:

'Take'n eyeful o' *that*, an' raise y'hat! Made six, I have, with tha' ole man.'

'Six what?'

'Six kids – an' good 'uns too – twenty pounds they weighed: don' know who's finding 'em in grub now! But you'll make summore' – he went on, looking down affectionately, 'dozens of 'em, y'ole devil, you!'

Mathieu looked away.

'Ta' off y'hat – y'r nowt but a beginner! – ta' it off!' said Latex in a sudden fury.

'I haven't got a hat on,' said Mathieu.

Latex stared round the room.

'Six in eight years. Anyone here do berrer tha' that?'

Mathieu turned back to Longin.

'You coming?'

Longin gave him a nasty look.

'Don' like bein' pushed around!'

'*I'm* not pushing you around! It was you who called me in here!'

Longin thrust a fist under his nose:

'Don' mush like you, Delarue – don' mush like you!'

'The feeling is reciprocal,' said Mathieu.

'Good!' said Longin with satisfaction: 'now we can ge' along fine! Why shou'n't I drink?' he asked with a suspicious look at Mathieu. 'Wha's point in m'not drinking?'

'Don' 'joy y'liquor,' said Guiccioli.

'Sh'd feel worse if I d'int drink.'

Ménard was singing:

> *'Si je meurs, je veux qu'on m'enterre*
> *Dans une cave où y a du bon vin.'*

Mathieu looked at Longin.

'You can drink as much as you like,' he said.

'Wha's that?' said Longin: he seemed to be nonplussed.

'I said,' shouted Mathieu, 'that you can drink as much as you like for all I care!'

He thought: 'I'd better get out of here,' but could not make up his mind to go. When he bent down he could smell the sticky sweetness of their drunkenness, of their wretchedness. He thought: 'But where can I go?' He felt dizzy. They did not disgust him, these beaten men who were draining defeat to the dregs. If he felt disgust at anyone it was at himself. Longin bent down to take hold of his mug, and fell forward on his knees.

'S—!'

He crawled as far as the tin, plunged his arm into the wine up to the elbow, drew out his mug, full to the brim, dripping, and bent forward his head to drink. The liquor trickled back into the tin from the two corners of his trembling mouth.

'Don' feel too good!' he said.

'Cat't up!' said Guiccioli.

'How?' asked Longin: his face was white, and he was breathing stertorously.

Guiccioli stuck two fingers down his own throat, leaned sideways, retched, and brought up a small amount of viscous fluid.

'Li' that!' he said, wiping his mouth with the back of his hand.

Longin, still on his knees, passed his mug across to his left hand, and thrust the fingers of his right down his throat.

'Hey!' cried Latex, 'you'll bring up in th' booze!'

'Delarue!' cried Guiccioli, 'giv'm a shove! – quick! – giv'm a shove!'

Mathieu pushed Longin, who slumped down on his backside, but without removing his fingers from his mouth. The rest of the party gave him encouraging looks. He pulled out his fingers and retched.

'Keep on li' that!' said Guiccioli: 'here't comes!'

Longin started to cough, and his face went scarlet.

'Nothing's coming!' he protested, still coughing.

'Y're a barstard!' cried Guiccioli in a sudden fury: 'if y' can't cat, y' shou'n't drink.'

Longin felt in his pocket, scrambled to his knees again, and squatted close to the tin.

'Warra you up to?' said Grimaud.

'Go'ng to make compress,' said Longin. He withdrew his wine-soaked handkerchief from the tin, laid it on his forehead, and said in the voice of a small child:

'Please, Delarue, will you tie it behind my neck?'

Mathieu took the two corners and fastened them in a knot.

'Tha's berrer,' said Longin.

The handkerchief lay like a bandage over his right eye. Red wine was trickling down his cheeks and along his neck.

'You loo' li' Jesus Christ!' said Guiccioli, with a splutter of laughter.

'You're ri' – shame kind of feller!'

He held out his mug to Mathieu to be refilled.

'You've had quite enough,' said Mathieu.

'Do's I tell yer!' cried Longin: 'do's I tell yer. Oh God!' he went on plaintively, 'I feel awful!'

'For Chri' sake giv'm something t'drink!' said Guiccioli, 'or'll be starting in 'gain 'bout's brother!'

Longin gave him a haughty stare:

'Why shou'n't I talk 'bout m'brother if I want to? Who's goin' t'shtop me?'

'Oh, getta hell outta here!' said Guiccioli.

Longin turned to Mathieu.

'Bro's at Hoseggor,' he explained.

'Isn't he in the army?'

'Not 'alf he isn't! – got his discharge. He an's lil wife go walking unner the trees, an' they say poor Paul's no luck – have their bi' of fun an' think 'bout me *all* the time, they do. *I'll* give'm poor Paul!'

He thought deeply for a moment, then:

'Don' like m'brother,' he said.

Grimaud laughed till the tears rolled down his cheeks.

'Wha' you got ter laugh at?' asked Longin aggressively.

'You wan' stop'm laughing?' demanded Guiccioli with a show of indignation. 'Carry on, chum,' he said to Grimaud with paternal solicitude: ''joy yerself, have goo' laugh, tha's what we're here for!'

126

'Laughing 'bout my wife,' said Grimaud.

'T' hell with y' wife,' said Longin.

' 'f you can talk 'bout y'brother, I c'n talk 'bout my wife.'

Grimaud put a finger to his lips.

'Ssh!' he said. He leaned across to Guiccioli and announced confidentially:

'My ol' woman's ugly as a duck's arse.'

Guiccioli tried to say something, but: 'Noraword!' said Grimaud imperiously: 'as a duck's arse – no two 'pinions 'bout it. Wairermoment,' he added, raising himself slightly and stretching his left hand underneath his bottom in order to reach his pistol pocket: ' 'll show yer – make you proper cat, it will.'

After making a number of vain efforts to achieve his purpose, he let himself fall back into his former position.

'Wha'th' hell – ugly as duck's arse – ta' my word fo't. Why shou' I lie 'bout it – nothin' to gain by lyin'!'

Longin seemed to be interested:

'She *really* ugly?' he asked.

' 've told you: as a duck's arse!'

'Wha's so ugly 'bout her?'

'Whole bag o' tricks: bubs hang down to 'er knees, borrom's on 'er heels – an' you sh'd jus' see her legs – bloory awful!'

'Berrer hand 'er over t'me,' said Longin with a laugh: 'jus' woman for me. Never 'ad nowt but whores – m'brother's always go' the good 'uns.'

Grimaud produced a sly wink:

'Norronyourlife, chum: 'cos if I passer over t'you, can't be sure o' getting 'nother, seeing I'm no beauty m'self. Tha's life tha' is,' he concluded with a sigh. 'Gorrer put up with wha' one's got!'

'*Et voilà*,' sang Ménard, '*la vie, la vie Que les bons moines ont.*'

'Yes, tha's life,' said Longin. 'We're jus' lorrer stiffs remembering their lives – an' pretty bloory lives too.'

Guiccioli flung his canteen in his face. It grazed Longin's cheek and fell into the tin.

'Pipe down,' said Guiccioli in a sudden fury: ' 've had me troubles same as everyone else, burri don' spill 'm out wherever I go! We're ou' for birrof fun, see?'

Longin turned despairing eyes on Mathieu:

'Gemme out of here,' he said in a low voice: 'gemme out of here.'

Mathieu bent down to put his hands under his armpits, but Longin wriggled free like a snake.

Mathieu lost all patience with him:

'I'm fed up!' he said: 'you coming or aren't you?'

Longin had turned over on his back, and was lying on the floor eyeing him maliciously.

'You'd *like* me t'go with yer, wc u'n't you?'

'I don't give a damn whether you come or not. I only want you to make up your mind one way or the other!'

'Have drink!' said Longin: 'plenny o' time t'have drink while 'm thinking 't over.'

Mathieu made no reply. Grimaud held out his mug to him.

'Lay hold!'

'No, thanks,' said Mathieu, waving it away.

'Why'r yer no' drinking?' asked Guiccioli, flabbergasted by this refusal: ' 'nuff for all, no need t'be shy!'

'I'm not thirsty.'

Guiccioli started to laugh:

'Says' no' thirsty! don' you know we're the boysasdrinkwen-they'renotthirsty?'

'I don't want to drink.'

Guiccioli raised his eyebrows:

'Why don' yer wanner drink li' rest of us? – why' – he looked at Mathieu severely–'thought y' was goo' guy– dis'pointed in yer.'

Longin propped himself up on one elbow.

'Don' y'see he despises us?'

There was a silence. Guiccioli looked at Mathieu inquiringly. Then, suddenly, he slumped, and his eyelids drooped. He smiled miserably, and said, still with his eyes closed:

'Anyone despises us berrer ge' out. Don' wanner keep anybory 'gainst his will. All pals here.'

'I don't despise anybody,' said Mathieu.

He stopped. 'They're drunk and I've not had a drop.' The fact that that was so endowed him with a superiority which made him feel ashamed. He was ashamed of the long-suffering voice which he had been compelled to adopt in speaking to them. 'They've got drunk because they're at the end of their tether.' But no one could share their wretchedness unless he shared their drunkenness too. 'I oughtn't to have come,' he thought.

'Despises us,' said Longin again with a sort of angry apathy. ' 't's like going to the pictures for 'im – amuses'm t' see lot of drunks a-s—ing of theirselves.'

'Speak for y'self,' said Latex: 'I'm no' s—ing.'

'Oh, shurrup!' said Guiccioli wearily.

Grimaud looked thoughtfully at Mathieu.

'If he despises us, 'e can go t'hell!'

Guiccioli broke into a guffaw of laughter.

'Y'can go t' hell!' he said. 'Y'can go t' hell!'

Ménard had stopped singing and now slid off the top of the cupboard. He stared about him with a hunted look, then, seeming suddenly reassured, heaved a sigh of relief and passed out on the floor. Nobody paid any attention to him. All those present were gazing straight in front of them. Every now and then they turned and gave Mathieu a nasty look. Mathieu had not the least idea what to do next. He had come here with the innocent intention of helping Longin. But he should have known that shame and embarrassment would inevitably bear him company. Merely because of him, all these chaps had suddenly become self-conscious. He had ceased to speak their language, but, nevertheless, without wishing to, had become their judge, and a witness for the prosecution against them. The sight of the tin, filled with wine and floating filth, gave him a feeling of acute disgust, though, at the same time, he blamed himself for feeling as he did. 'Who am I to refuse to drink when my friends are in this state?'

Latex was musingly fingering his groin. Suddenly he turned on Mathieu, his eyes blazing defiance. Then he put his canteen between his legs, and proceeded to dangle himself in the wine.

'Giving th' ole man a drink – it's strengthening.'

Guiccioli gave a guffaw. Mathieu turned away and met Grimaud's ironical gaze.

'Jus' won'ering what sort o' hell-of-a-place you've tumbled into, aren't you?' he asked. 'You don't know what we're like, m'lad, anything mi' happen with us around!'

He leaned forward and cried with a knowing wink:

'Warrer 'bout 'nother lil drink, Latex?'

Latex returned the wink:

'Don' mind 'f I do.'

He raised his canteen and drank noisily, keeping his eyes on Mathieu. Longin giggled. Everyone was grinning. 'They're starting again because of me.' Latex put down his canteen and made a smacking noise with his tongue.

'Tha' was good, tha' was!'

'Warrer 'bout it?' said Guiccioli: 'lorrer dam' good fellers, aren't we? Who says we don' 'joy ourselves?'

'You seen nothin' yet!' said Grimaud: 'you ain't seen nothin'!' – and he began fumbling at his flies with trembling hands. Mathieu leaned across to Guiccioli:

'Give me your canteen,' he said quietly: 'I'm going to join in the fun!'

' 's fallen into the tin,' said Guiccioli morosely: 'fish't out fer yerself.'

Mathieu plunged his hand into the tin, felt about with his fingers, touched the bottom, and brought up the canteen full to the brim. Grimaud's hands ceased to move. He looked at them, then put them in his pockets and stared at Mathieu.

'Ah,' said Latex in friendlier tones: 'knew as you wou'n't be able to stand out!'

Mathieu drank. There were lumps of some soft, colourless substance floating about in the wine. He spat them out and refilled the canteen. Grimaud laughed good-humouredly.

'No one can't look 't us and not drink! gives 'im a thirst jus' t' see us!'

'Berrer be copied than pitied,' said Guiccioli, his good temper now fully restored.

Mathieu busied himself with saving a fly that was struggling in the wine: then he drank. Latex looked at him with an appraising eye.

'Norrer a drunk, that'n – 's a suicide.'

The canteen was empty.

'I'm finding it rather hard to get drunk,' said Mathieu. He filled the canteen for the third time. The wine was heavy and had a curious, sweet taste.

'Not done anything in it, have you?' he asked, struck by a sudden suspicion.

'You nuts?' asked Guiccioli indignantly. 'Don' think we'd spoil goo' booze, do yer?'

'Oh well,' said Mathieu, 'what the hell . . . !' He emptied the canteen at a gulp and drew a deep breath. Guiccioli looked at him with interest. 'Feel berrer?'

Mathieu shook his head.

'Haven't got there yet.'

He took the canteen and was leaning with clenched teeth over the tin when he heard Longin's mocking voice behind him:

'Wants ter show 'e can carry's liquor berrer nor us.'

Mathieu swung round.

'That's not true. I'm getting drunk because I want to have a good time!'

Longin had sat down again, holding himself very stiffly. The bandage had slipped down his nose. Above it, Mathieu could see his eyes, round and staring, like those of an ancient hen.

'Don' mush like you, Delarue!' said Longin.

'You've said that once already!'

'Boys don' mush like you either,' said Longin: 'you scare 'em 'cos y're an eddicated bloke, bu' don't run away with idea tha' they *like* you.'

'Why shouldn't they like me?' asked Mathieu between clenched teeth.

'Y'do things different fr'm everyone else – even when y'ge' drunk, 't's no' th' way *we* ge' drunk!'

Mathieu gave him a puzzled look, then, turning round, he flung the canteen through the glass front of the cupboard.

'I *can't get* drunk!' he said in a loud voice. 'I can't. Don't you see I can't?'

No one uttered a word. Guiccioli removed a large fragment of glass which had fallen on his knees, and laid it on the floor. Mathieu went across to Longin, took his arm, and pulled him to his feet.

'Wha's the marrer? what've I done? – mind y' own business – y' bloory toff!'

'I came here to take you away, and take you away I will,' said Mathieu.

Longin struggled violently.

'Lemme alone! for Chri' sake lemme alone, or I'll let y' have it!'

Mathieu started to drag him from the room. Longin shot up his hand and tried to poke his fingers in the other's eyes.

'You bloody barstard!' said Mathieu.

He let go of Longin and gave him two not very hard hooks to the jaw. Longin went limp and spun round. Mathieu caught him before he fell and hoisted him on to his shoulders like a sack.

'I can do a bit of rough-housing too, when I give my mind to it,' he said.

He hated the lot of them. He went out and down the stone steps with his burden. Charlot burst out laughing as he passed.

'What's bitin' you, brother?'

Mathieu crossed the road and unloaded Longin against the trunk of a chestnut tree. Longin opened one eye, tried to say something, and was promptly sick.

'Feel better?' asked Mathieu.

Longin was sick again.

'Feel fine!' he said between hiccups.

'I'm off,' said Mathieu: 'and when you've finished catting you'd better try to get some sleep.'

By the time he arrived at the post office he was out of breath. He knocked. Pinette opened the door and greeted him with a look of rapture.

'So you decided to come after all!' he said.

'Yes,' said Mathieu.

The postmistress showed up in the darkness of the interior, behind Pinette.

'This young lady's not shy of me any longer: we're going for a stroll in the fields.'

The girl glowered at him. Mathieu returned her stare with a smile. He thought: 'She's not very friendly,' but he felt reckless.

'You stink of booze,' said Pinette.

Mathieu laughed, but said nothing. The postmistress put on a pair of black gloves, double-locked the door, and the three of them set out. She took Pinette's arm, and Pinette took Mathieu's. They passed a number of soldiers who greeted them.

'Off for a Sunday walk!' shouted Pinette.

'Now there's no officers,' they shouted back, 'every day's Sunday.'

Silence of moonlight in the sun's glare. Crude plaster effigies set in a circle about a deserted space *will tell to generations yet unborn what men once were*. Sooty tears streaked the faces of tall white ruins. To the north-west stood a Triumphal Arch; to the north, a Roman temple; southwards, a bridge led to another temple. Water lay stagnant in a fountain's basin. A stone knife stood on end pointing to the sky. Stone: imitation stone made from the sugar-loaves of history: Rome, Egypt, the age of stone. That was all that remained of a celebrated open space. He said: 'All that remains,' but the edge had gone from his pleasure. Nothing is more monotonous than catastrophe. He had begun to get used to it. He leaned against the iron railings, happy still but tired, with the taste of summer's dry heat in his mouth. He had been walking all day. His legs could scarcely carry him, but he felt the need to go on walking all the same. One can do nothing in a dead city but walk. 'I deserve a bit of luck,' he said to himself: what sort of luck did not matter, so long as some flower showed suddenly at the corner of a street for his own private delectation. But nothing happened. All around him stretched a desert: little flickers of sunlight from the windows of great buildings, small objects, black and white pigeons, and immemorial birds long turned to stone as a result of feeding on statues. The only gay note in all this mineral landscape was struck by a Nazi flag flying over the Hôtel Crillon.

Oh! le pavillon en viande saignante sur la soie des mers et des fleurs arctiques.

In the middle of the blood-red rag, a circle – white as that of the magic-lantern shining on the sheets of childhood: in the middle of the circle a knot of black serpents: the Monogram of Evil, *my* monogram. A red drop kept forming in the folds of the standard, detaching itself, and falling on the macadam of the roadway. Virtue was bleeding. He murmured – 'Virtue is bleeding.' But the idea seemed to him now less amusing than it

133

had done on the previous evening. For three days he had spoken to nobody, and his pleasure had grown hard. Fatigue had momentarily clouded his vision, and he wondered, now, whether he had not better go home. No, he couldn't do that: my presence is needed *everywhere*. He must go on walking. The strident rending of the sky brought him relief. The aeroplane gleaming in the sunlight was an easing of his burden. The dead city had found another observer, could parade for other eyes its myriads of dead faces. He smiled. It was him that the machine was seeking among the tombs. It is for me, for me alone, that it is there! He wanted to rush into the middle of the Place and wave his handkerchief. Let them drop their bombs! That would bring resurrection; the city would reverberate with blacksmith bangings, as in the days when it had laboured, and lovely weeds would sprout upon its walls. The aeroplane turned away. All about him was once more swallowed in a planetary silence. He must walk, walk unceasingly, over the surface of a cooling planet.

He moved off again, dragging his feet. The dust whitened his shoes. He gave a start. A General was standing, his face pressed to a window, idly victorious, his hands behind his back. Maybe he was watching this native wandering aimlessly through the museum of Parisian antiques. The windows all about him had turned to German eyes. He threw back his head, and imparted to his walk a springy movement, swaying his hips in a faintly comic manner. I am the guardian of the cemetery. The Tuileries; the river embankment by the Tuileries. Before crossing the road he looked right and left from force of habit, but saw nothing except the long tunnel of greenery. He was just about to walk over the Solférino bridge when suddenly he stopped, his heart thumping. Here, at last, was his stroke of luck! A little tremor ran all the way up his body, from his hams to the back of his neck. His hands and feet went cold. He stood perfectly still, holding his breath. All his life seemed concentrated in his eyes, and, with his eyes, he devoured the slim young man who, in all innocence, had his back towards him and was leaning over the river.

'A *miraculous* meeting!' Daniel would have been no more deeply moved if the evening breeze had spoken his name in

134

human accents, if the clouds had written its syllables on the mauve heavens, so manifest was it that this youth had been placed there *for him*, that the long, broad hands, blossoming from silken sleeves, were the words of his secret language. He has been given to me! The boy was tall and smoothly fleshed, with fair, tousled hair and sloping, almost womanish shoulders, narrow hips, a small, firm rump, and ears that were small and exquisitely formed. 'A miraculous meeting,' he thought, and felt something that was akin to fear. In every fibre of his body he *aped* death, like certain reptiles at the approach of danger. For me, the worst danger of all is beauty. His hands grew colder and colder. Metal fingers fastened on the back of his neck. Beauty that most treacherous of all snares, lay in wait for him with a smile of connivance, a proffered ease; beckoned to him, seemed to have been waiting for his coming. How lying were appearances!

The back of that soft, that sweet, that inviting head was waiting for no thing, for no person. The pleasure it found in rubbing against the coat collar was a private pleasure, and private, too, was the pleasure of those warm, fair thighs at whose presence he could guess under the grey flannel of the trousers.

The river fills his vision: he is looking at the river, he is lost in solitary and unaccountable thought, like a lonely palm-tree. He is mine: yet does not know me. Daniel felt sick with anxiety, and, for a moment or two, grew dizzy. The boy, a tiny, distant figure, seemed to be calling to him from the bottom of a pit: beauty was calling to him, beauty, my destiny. He thought: 'Everything is going to begin again, everything – hope and wretchedness, shame and madness.' Then, suddenly, he remembered that France was finished: 'All things are permissible!' Warmth radiated out from his stomach into his finger-tips, weariness left him, the blood beat in his temples. 'We are the sole visible representatives of the human species, the unique survivors of a vanished nation. It is inevitable that we shall speak to one another: what more natural?'

He took a step towards the stranger whom he had named, already, The Miracle. He felt young and sound and heavy with his gift of exultation. And almost at once he stopped. He had just noticed that The Miracle was trembling in all his limbs, now leaning backwards with a convulsive movement, now pressing his belly to the balustrade, leaning his head forward above the river. 'The little fool!' thought Daniel in a sudden fit of irritation. The boy was not worthy of this extraordinary moment, was not really, in a full sense, present at the rendezvous. This being, who should have been drained and empty, ready to receive the good news, was allowing himself to be distracted by puerile anxieties. The little fool! ... All of a sudden, The Miracle raised his right foot in an odd, encumbered movement, and made as though to climb across the parapet. Daniel was preparing to leap forward when the boy turned, a prey to uncertainty, his leg still raised. He saw Daniel, and what Daniel saw was a pair of smouldering eyes in a face of chalk. For a moment, the boy hesitated: then, his foot dropped to the ground, scraping the stone as it did so, and he started walking with assumed nonchalance, his hand on the edge of the parapet. So you want to kill yourself, do you?

Daniel's sense of wonder froze on the moment. So that was all it was, a grubby, terror-stricken lad unable to endure the results of his own idiocy! A hot wave of desire moved in him: he set off behind the young man with the cold lust of a prowling lecher. His very exultation had gone cold. He felt delivered, cleansed, and full of a sly malice. Deep down he preferred the thing to be so, though it amused him still to bear a grudge against the stranger he was following. You want to kill yourself, you little idiot! – as though it were as easy as all that! You'd be surprised to know how many, far more experienced than you, have failed to do it! The boy seemed to be aware that there was somebody behind him. He was striding along like a high-stepping horse, with a stiff, self-conscious exaggeration in his movements. In the middle of the bridge he suddenly noticed his right hand trailing along the parapet. It rose, seemingly of its own volition, stiff, prophetic, at the end of its attendant arm. He forced it down, stuffed it in his pocket, and walked on, hunching his shoulders. 'There's an equivocal look about him,' thought Daniel: 'that's how I like them!' The young man began to walk faster. Daniel followed suit. He wanted to laugh. 'He's suffering, he's longing to get it over, but he can't, because I am *behind him*. Go on, go on, I shan't leave you!'

At the far end of the bridge, the boy hesitated before turning down the Quai d'Orsay. He reached a point where there was a flight of steps giving access to the bank, stopped, turned impatiently towards Daniel, and stood waiting. Daniel had a momentary vision of an exquisite pale face, a short nose, a small, sagging mouth, and eyes that were eloquent of pride. He lowered his own with hypocritical modesty, slowly drew near, passed the boy without looking at him, and then, a few steps farther on, glanced back over his shoulder. The boy had disappeared. In a leisurely fashion, Daniel leaned over the parapet and saw him down on the river bank, contemplating with hanging head and absorbed attention a mooring ring which he was pensively kicking. The first thing to do was to get down there as quickly and unobtrusively as possible. Fortunately, twenty yards ahead, there was another staircase, a narrow iron ladder, concealed by a buttress. Slowly, noiselessly, Daniel made the descent. He was enjoying himself madly. Having reached the bottom of the ladder, he flattened himself against the wall.

The boy was standing on the very edge of the bank, looking down at the water. The Seine, a greenish surface, with livid lights, was carrying on its flood a number of dark, flabby objects. To plunge into that evil-looking stream was not a tempting prospect. The young man bent down, picked up a stone and let it fall into the water. Then he relapsed into his former mood of morbid brooding. Nothing doing today: in five minutes' time he'll be like a pricked bubble. Ought I to let things take their course, stay hidden, wait until he has tasted the very lees of his humiliation, and then, when he has turned away, burst out laughing? Pretty risky! – he might develop a permanent loathing of me. On the other hand, if I fling myself on him as though saving him from a watery grave, he'll be grateful to me for thinking him capable of such an act, even though he may protest, for form's sake, and especially for sparing him the necessity of making up his mind! Daniel passed his tongue over his lips, drew a deep breath, and jumped out of his hiding-place. The young man, startled, swung round. He would have fallen had not Daniel seized him by the arm.

He said: 'I . . .'

At the same moment he took note of Daniel, and seemed to pull himself together. The look of fright in his eyes gave place to one of rage. It's *somebody else* he's terrified of.

'What do you want?' he asked with haughty aloofness.

Daniel could not answer him at once. Desire caught him by the throat and checked his speech.

'Young Narcissus!' he said, bringing out the words with difficulty: 'Young Narcissus!'

After a moment's pause, he added: 'Narcissus leaned over a bit too far, my lad, and fell into the water!'

'But I'm not Narcissus,' said the youth: 'I've got a perfectly adequate sense of balance, and I don't need your help.'

He's a student – thought Daniel. He put his question with brutal directness:

'Were you contemplating suicide?'

'Are you crazy?'

Daniel started to laugh, and the boy flushed.

'Leave me alone!' he said gloomily.

'In my own good time,' said Daniel, and tightened his grip. The young man lowered his handsome eyes, and Daniel jumped back just in time to avoid his kick. So that's his little game! he thought, regaining his balance. Kicking out wildly, without so much as looking at me! He was delighted: both of them were breathing heavily. Not a word passed between them. The boy kept his head down, and Daniel noted with admiration the astonishing silkiness of his hair.

'So that's it – kicking, eh? – a woman's trick!'

The boy moved his head from side to side as though in a vain effort to raise it. After another moment's silence he said, with studied roughness:

'Get to hell out of here!'

There was more of mulishness than assurance in his voice, but he had managed to raise his eyes and now stared Daniel straight in the face with a frightened insolence. Then his gaze slid sideways, and Daniel could contemplate at his ease the handsome, vulnerable face. 'Pride and weakness,' he thought: 'and bad faith into the bargain! A little bourgeois face overwhelmed by an abstract melancholy; charming features but with no touch of

138

generosity.' At the same moment, a kick on the calf made him grimace with sudden pain.

'Bloody young fool! I've half a mind to put you across my knee and give you a thundering good spanking!'

'Just you try!'

Daniel started to shake him:

'And suppose I do? Suppose I feel like taking your trousers down here and now, who's going to stop me?'

The boy blushed scarlet and began to laugh:

'I'm not frightened of *you*!'

'We'll soon see about that!' said Daniel.

He gripped the back of the young man's neck, and tried to force his head forward.

'No! no!' cried the boy in tones of despair: 'no!'

'Are you going to try to kick me again?'

'No – let me go!'

Daniel relaxed his hold and straightened his back. The boy said nothing. All the fight had gone out of him. 'A young horse that's already felt the bit: someone's done the breaking-in for me, I see – a father? an uncle? A lover? – no, not a lover, that's still to come – and he'll revel in it. Just for the moment he's virgin.'

'So you wanted to kill yourself?' he said, still maintaining his grip: 'why?'

The boy remained mulishly silent.

'Sulk as much as you please,' said Daniel: 'it doesn't matter to me. You've bungled it this time, at any rate!'

The boy was smiling to himself. There was something at once knowing yet indeterminate in his expression. 'This is just treading water,' thought Daniel, by this time thoroughly put out – and he gave his victim a violent shake.

'What are you grinning at?'

The other looked him straight in the eyes:

'You'll have to let me go sooner or later.'

'True enough,' said Daniel: 'so I'll do it now.'

He let go of him and put his hands in his pockets. 'Well?'

The boy made no attempt to move. He was still smiling.

'He's laughing at me.'

'I may as well tell you that I am an excellent swimmer.

I've got two rescues to my credit – one of them in a high sea.'

The boy gave a girlish giggle, mocking and sly.

'It seems to be a mania with you!'

'Maybe it is,' said Daniel. 'Jump,' he added, spreading his arms: 'go on, jump if that is how you're feeling. I'll let you swallow a nice mouthful, then I'll take my clothes off at my leisure, dive into the river, give you a clout over the head, and fish you out more dead than alive.'

He started to laugh.

'When people have failed to bring off a suicide, they don't often indulge in a second attempt. Once I've brought you round, you won't feel like having another shot.'

The boy took a step forward as though meaning to strike him.

'What right have you to speak to me like that?'

Daniel continued to laugh:

'Ha! ha! – what right? – you may well ask?' Suddenly he gripped his wrist:

'So long as I am here you are quite incapable of killing yourself, no matter how much you may want to. I have the power of life and death over you!'

'But you won't always be there,' said the boy with an odd look.

'That's where you are wrong! I *shall* always be there.'

He had a little thrill of pleasure. He had caught a sudden flash of curiosity in the lovely hazel eyes.

'Suppose I *do* want to kill myself, what's that got to do with you? You don't even know who I am!'

'Just a little mania of mine – as you said yourself,' replied Daniel jovially. 'I happen to have a passion for preventing people from doing what they want to do.'

A look of kindliness came into his eyes: 'Are things really as bad as all that?'

The boy made no reply. He was doing all he knew to keep from crying. Daniel felt so profoundly moved that tears came into his own eyes. Fortunately, the other was too much concerned with his feelings to notice. For a few seconds more Daniel managed to control his longing to stroke his hair; then, his right hand came out of his pocket as though independently of his will, and rested for a moment, with the fumbling uncertainty of a blind man, on the golden head. He snatched it back as though he had touched fire. 'Too soon! – that was a false step!' ... The boy shook his head vehemently, and walked a few paces along the bank. Daniel waited, holding his breath. 'Too soon, you fool, much too soon!' In a sudden spurt of self-punishing anger, he completed his thought: 'If he makes off now, I'll let him go.' But at the first sound of the other's sobs, he ran to him and took him in his arms. The boy yielded without a struggle.

'You poor dear!' said Daniel, overcome by emotion: 'you poor dear!'

He would have given his right hand to be able to console him or to share his fit of weeping. In a second or so, the boy raised his head. He was no longer crying, but two tears were trickling down his adorable cheeks. Daniel would have liked to lick them off, to drink them down, to feel in his mouth the salty taste of the other's grief. The young man looked at him distrustfully:

'How was it you happened to be there?'

'I was just passing.'

'Aren't you in the army?'

Daniel heard the question with no sense of pleasure.

'I am not the least bit interested in their war.' He hurried on: 'Look here, I'll make you a proposal. Are you still determined to commit suicide?'

The boy said nothing, but a dark obstinate look came into his face.

'All right,' said Daniel: 'just you listen to me. I found it amusing to frighten you, though, in point of fact, I've nothing whatever against suicide so long as it is the fruit of ripe reflection. I take a sort of sporting interest in your death, since you are a perfect stranger to me. I see no reason why I should stop you from killing yourself, if you have a valid reason for wishing to do so.'

He saw with pleasure that the colour had ebbed from the young man's cheeks.

'You were feeling safe,' he thought.

'Take a look at this,' he went on, displaying the thick bezel of his ring. 'Inside there I carry a poison that brings sudden death. I wear this ring always, even at night, and, if it so happened that I found myself in a position that was intolerable to my pride . . .'

He stopped talking, and unscrewed the bezel of the ring. The boy stared at the two brown capsules with an expression in which repulsion fought with distrust.

'Tell me your motives. If I decide that they are valid, I'll make you a present of one of these. Would you like me to give it to you now?' he asked, as though he had suddenly changed his mind.

The boy passed his tongue over his lips without speaking.

'Do you want it? It is yours for the asking. You can swallow it in my presence, and I promise not to leave you.' He took the young man by the hand: 'I'll hold on to you, and close your eyes.'

The boy shook his head.

'What proof have I got that it really is poison?' he asked with an effort.

Daniel's laugh was young and gay.

'You're afraid it may be just an aperient? Swallow it and see!'

The boy made no reply. His cheeks were still pale, the pupils of his eyes dilated, but he gave Daniel a sidelong smile that was at once sly and coquettish.

'You don't want it, then?'

'Not at once.'

Daniel screwed up the bezel of his ring.

'Just as you like,' he said coldly: 'what's your name?'

'Must I tell you my name?'

'Yes, your christian name.'

'Well, if I must . . . Philippe.'

'Well, Philippe,' said Daniel putting his arm through the young man's, 'since you want to talk about yourself, you'd better come home with me.'

He pushed him towards the staircase and hurried him up the steps. At the top, they turned along the Embankment, arm in arm. Philippe obstinately kept his eyes lowered. He had started to tremble again, but made no effort to keep an interval between himself and Daniel, whose leg he brushed with his own at every step. Smart suède shoes, almost new but obviously bought at least a year ago, well-cut flannel suit, white tie, blue silk shirt –

the whole turn-out, Montparnasse, vintage 1938: hair carefully disarranged – his whole appearance reeking of narcissism. Why isn't he in the army? Probably too young: still, he may quite well be older than he looks: childhood is prolonged in the case of young men with dominant parents. Obviously it wasn't poverty that drove him to the idea of suicide. As they passed the end of Henri IV bridge, Daniel suddenly shot a question at him:

'Was it because of the Germans that you wanted to kill yourself?'

Philippe looked surprised and shook his head. He was as pretty as a painted angel. I'll help you, thought Daniel with a little surge of passion: I'll help you! He longed to save Philippe, to make a man of him. I'll give you everything I have, you shall know all that I know.

The Markets were dark and empty. Gone was their old familiar smell. But the city looked wholly different. An hour ago the scene had been set for the end of the world, and Daniel had felt himself to be a character in history. Now, slowly, the streets were becoming themselves again, and he was at the heart of a pre-war Sunday, at that turning-point of the afternoon when the promise of a brand-new Monday begins to emerge from the death-agonies of the week and the sinking sun. Something was about to begin: a new week, a new love-adventure. He threw back his head and smiled. A window blazed with the scarlet of the last light – an omen. The exquisite smell of crushed strawberries suddenly filled his nostrils – another omen. In the distance, a shadow crossed the Rue Montmartre at a run – yet a third omen. Each time that Fortune brought him face to face with a boy of angelic beauty, Heaven and Earth invariably indulged in knowing winks. He felt weak with desire and caught his breath with every step; but so used had he become to walking silently in the company of the unsuspecting young that he had grown to love for its own sake the long-drawn-out patience of the paederast. I am watching you, you are naked in the hollow of my gaze; I possess you, though we are not touching, merely through the medium of sight and smell, giving nothing of myself in return.

He leaned his head sideways, the better to breathe the fragrance of the bent neck, and was suddenly brought up short by a strong smell of naphthaline. At once he straightened his back, feeling his passion cool, conscious of a little flutter of amusement. He adored such alternating moods of thrill and aridity, adored the sense of *exacerbation*. Detection's my strong suit, he thought with a flicker of gaiety. A young poet plans to throw himself into the river on the day the Germans enter Paris; why? I have but one clue to the problem, but it is central: his suit smells of naphthaline – obvious deduction, he hasn't been wearing it. Why should he change his clothes in order to commit suicide? Because he *could no longer wear* what he had on yesterday. *Ergo* it was a uniform, which would have given him away and led inevitably to his being made prisoner. He's a soldier. But what is he doing here? Perhaps he was posted to the Ministry of Information or the Air Ministry – but in that case he would have cleared off to Tours with the others, days ago. Well then, what? . . . The whole thing was clear to him. He stopped and pointed to an entry.

'Here we are.'

'I'm not going any farther,' said Philippe suddenly.

'What d'you mean?'

'I'm not going with you.'

'You'd rather be picked up by the Germans?'

'I just don't want to,' said Philippe, and stared at his feet. 'I've nothing to tell you, and I don't know anything about you.'

'So that's it,' said Daniel: 'so that's it!' He took the boy's head between his hands and forced him to raise his eyes.

'You know nothing about me, but I know all about you!' he said. 'I could tell you your whole story from A to Z!'

Staring fixedly into Philippe's eyes, he went on: 'You were with the Northern Armies. The men panicked, and you took to your heels. Later, I suppose, you couldn't find your unit again, so you came home. You found your family gone, so you put on a suit of civvies and made a beeline for the Seine with the idea of drowning yourself. It's not that you're particularly patriotic, but you can't bear the feeling that you're a coward. Am I right?'

The boy stood there motionless, but his eyes had grown round and large. Daniel's mouth was dry: he could feel anguish flooding through him like a tide. He repeated his question, but there was more of violence than assurance in his voice:

'Am I right?'

Philippe uttered a faint groan, and his body went limp. Anguish died away. Daniel caught his breath in a spasm of joy. His heart was madly hammering.

'Come upstairs,' he said in a low voice. 'I know a cure.'

'A cure for what?'

'For your trouble. I can teach you a lot of things.'

Philippe looked exhausted but relieved. Daniel pushed him into the entry. He had never dared to bring home with him the young professionals whom he had been in the habit of picking up in Montmartre and Montparnasse. But today the concierge and most of the tenants were haring along the roads between Montargis and Gien. This was a special occasion.

They climbed the stairs in silence. Daniel put his key into the lock, but he kept his grip on Philippe's arm while he did so. He opened the door and stood aside for the other to pass.

'Come along in.'

Philippe obeyed, moving like someone only half-awake.

'The door opposite – it's the living-room.' He turned his back on him, shut the front door, locked it, and put the key in his pocket. He found Philippe standing in front of the bookshelves, gazing with lively interest at a number of statuettes ranged along their top.

'I say, those things are pretty marvellous!'

'Not bad,' said Daniel: 'not at all bad. And the great thing about them is that they're *genuine*. I bought them from the Indians.'

'And that?' asked Philippe.

'That's the portrait of a dead child – from Mexico. When anyone kicks the bucket there, a corpse-painter is called in who proceeds to paint a portrait to look like life. That's an example of what they can do.'

'Have you been in Mexico?' asked Philippe, and there was a faint note of respect in his voice.

'I lived there for two years.'

Philippe was gazing ecstatically at the lovely face, so disdainful and so pale, that stared back at him from the remote distances of death with the serious, self-sufficient expression of an initiate. There's a resemblance between them – thought Daniel. Both of them fair, both of them insolent and pale, the one within the pictured semblance, the other outside it, the young creature who wanted to die, and the young creature who had died in fact, looked at one another. The only thing that separated them was death, nothingness, the flat surface of the canvas.

'It's marvellous!' said Philippe again.

An all-enveloping weariness swept over Daniel with the suddenness of a thunder-clap. He heaved a deep sigh and collapsed into an armchair. Malvina jumped on to his knee.

'Be a good little cat, Malvina,' he said, stroking her: 'be a beyoutiful little cat.'

He turned to Philippe, and spoke as though he were at the end of his tether:

'There's whisky in the liqueur cabinet: no, to your right, that small Chinese cupboard. You'll find glasses there, too. You must be the daughter of the house and do the necessary.'

Philippe filled two glasses, handed one to Daniel, and remained standing in front of him. Daniel emptied his drink at one gulp, and felt his spirits rise.

'If you were a poet,' he said suddenly, dropping into the second person plural, 'you'd realize what an extraordinary meeting ours was.'

The boy uttered an odd, provocative little laugh.

'How d'you know I'm not?'

He looked Daniel full in the face. A complete change had come over his expression, over his whole way of behaving, since he had entered the flat. It's fathers who get across him, thought Daniel with a sense of annoyance. He's not frightened of me any longer because he realizes that I don't belong in that category. He deliberately assumed an air of uncertainty.

'I'm just wondering,' he said, as though pondering a problem, 'whether you really interest me.'

'It might have been better if you had asked yourself that question earlier,' said Philippe.

Daniel smiled:

'It's never too late. If I decide that I find you a bore I can turn you out.'

'You needn't bother to do that,' said Philippe and turned towards the door.

'Stay where you are,' said Daniel: 'you know perfectly well that you need me.'

Philippe smiled with an air of easy laziness, and sat down on a chair. Poppaea brushed past him. He caught her and lifted her on to his knee. She made no protest. He stroked her gently, voluptuously.

'That's a point in your favour,' said Daniel with no little surprise. 'It's the first time she's ever allowed any stranger to do that.'

Philippe indulged in a self-satisfied smile.

'How many cats have you got?' he asked, dropping his gaze.

'Three.'

'That's a point in *your* favour!'

He scratched Poppaea's head, and the cat started to purr. He's a great deal more at his ease than I am, thought Daniel. He knows perfectly well that I like him.

His next question came suddenly. He asked it with the object of breaking down his visitor's self-possession.

'How did it all happen?'

Philippe spread his knees and let Poppaea go. The cat jumped to the floor and made good her escape.

'Since you've guessed the truth, there's no more to be said.'

'Where were you?'

'In the Nord – at a village called Parny.'

'And afterwards?'

'Nothing happened afterwards. We held on for two days until the tanks and aeroplanes began to take a hand.'

'Both at the same time?'

'Yes.'

'Were you frightened?'

'Not a bit. Or perhaps it is that fear isn't like what one expects it's going to be.'

His face had assumed a hard, old look. He stared before him with an expression of weariness.

'The other chaps ran, and I ran with them.'

'And then?'

'I walked for a bit, then I jumped a lorry. Later still, I walked some more. I got here the day before yesterday.'

'What did you think while you were walking?'

'I didn't think.'

'Why did you wait until today before trying to kill yourself?'

'I wanted to see my mother again,' said Philippe.

'And she wasn't here?'

'No, she wasn't here.'

He raised his head and looked at Daniel with sparkling eyes.

'If you think I'm a coward, you're barking up the wrong tree,' he said in a tone that was brusque and sharp.

'Really? – then why did you run away?'

'I ran because the others ran.'

'Still, you did want to kill yourself.'

'Have it your own way: yes, the idea did cross my mind.'

'Why?'

'It would take too long to explain.'

'What's the hurry?' said Daniel. 'Have some more whisky.'

Philippe poured himself out a glass. There was colour in his cheeks now: he giggled.

'If I hadn't to think of anybody but myself, I shouldn't in the least mind being a coward. I am a pacifist. What does military virtue amount to? – lack of imagination, that's all it is. The really brave chaps, when it came to fighting, were the hobble-dehoys, the fellows who were little better than animals. I had the bad luck to be bred up in a family of heroes!'

'I see,' said Daniel: 'Your father, I suppose, was a regular soldier?'

'A reserve officer,' said Philippe. 'But he died in '27 as a result of the first war. He was gassed a month before the Armistice. His glorious death gave my mother a taste for that sort of thing. She married again in 1933 – a General.'

'She looks like being disappointed,' said Daniel: 'Generals have a way of dying in their beds.'

'Not this one!' said Philippe, and there was an undercurrent of hatred in his voice. 'He's a regular Bayard, makes love, kills, prays, but never thinks at all!'

'Is he at the front?'

'Where d'you suppose he is? He's the kind of chap who'd work a machine-gun single-handed, or charge the enemy at the head of his men. You can rely on him to get 'em all mown down!'

'I can imagine him – black, hairy, with a large moustache.'

'Precisely,' said Philippe: 'women adore him because he smells like a goat!'

They looked at one another and laughed.

'You don't seem to care much about him,' said Daniel.

'I hate him!' said Philippe.

He blushed and stared fixedly at Daniel.

'I suffer from an Oedipus-complex,' he said. 'I'm a regular case-book type.'

'Is it your mother you're in love with?' asked Daniel with an air of incredulity.

Philippe said nothing. He had the self-important air of a victim of destiny.

Daniel leaned forward:

'Isn't it more likely to be your stepfather?' he said quietly.

Philippe gave a start and went scarlet: then, still looking at Daniel straight in the eyes, he burst out laughing:

'That's rich!' he said.

Daniel joined in the laughter. 'Well, but, look here,' he said, 'it was because of him that you wanted to kill yourself.'

Philippe continued to laugh: 'Nonsense! – of course it wasn't!'

'Then who was it because of? You made a beeline for the river though you were lacking in courage, though you loudly proclaim your detestation of courage. You're afraid he'll despise you!'

'What I'm afraid of is that my mother may despise me,' said Philippe.

'Your mother? I'm sure *she'd* understand.'

Philippe bit his lips, but said nothing:

'When I touched you on the shoulder you were terrified,' said Daniel. 'I suppose you thought it was he?'

Philippe jumped to his feet, his eyes shining: 'He ... he struck me!'

'When?'

'About two years ago, and ever since then I've had a feeling that he was always behind me.'

'Have you ever dreamed that you were lying naked in his arms?'

'You're crazy!' cried Philippe with genuine indignation.

'There's no doubt at all that the thought of him is an obsession with you. You go down on all fours, the General rides you, he puts you through your paces like a mare. Never, not for a single moment, are you yourself. Sometimes you think *with* him, sometimes *against*. You don't really care a hang about pacifism. You'd never have given it a moment's thought if your stepfather hadn't been a soldier!'

He got up and took Philippe by the shoulders:

'Do you want me to make you a free man?'

'How can you do that?'

'As I said before, I have much to teach you.'

'Are you a psycho-analyst?'

'Something of the sort.'

Philippe shook his head:

'Assuming,' he said, 'that what you say *might* be true, why should I interest you?'

'I have a passion for the human soul,' said Daniel with a smile. Then, with sudden emotion, he added: 'Yours, I should say, would be exquisite if only we could rid it of frustration.'

Philippe said nothing, but it was clear that he felt flattered. Daniel took a few steps up and down, rubbing his hands. 'We must begin,' he said with an air of gay excitement, 'by liquidating all moral values. Are you a student?'

'I was,' said Philippe.

'Law?'

'No, literature.'

'So much the better. In that case you will be able to understand what I am going to say: systematic doubt – see what I mean? Rimbaud's "deliberate disorganization". We must set about a complete process of destruction, but not merely in words – in acts. Everything you have borrowed from others will go up in smoke. What remains will be the essential you – agree?'

Philippe looked at him with eyes that expressed curiosity:

'Given the state of mind you're in,' went on Daniel, 'what risk can you possibly run?'

Philippe shrugged: 'None.'

'Good,' said Daniel. 'I here and now adopt you. We'll start

150

on the journey to hell right away, but, for heaven's sake,' he added with a sharp look, 'no transference business with me, please!'

'I'm not quite a fool,' said Philippe with an answering glance.

'When you reach the stage of chucking me away like an old glove,' said Daniel, his eyes still fixed on the young man's face, 'the cure will be complete.'

'Don't worry!' said Philippe.

'Just like an old glove!' said Daniel with a laugh.

'Just like an old glove!' echoed Philippe. They were both of them laughing. Daniel refilled Philippe's glass.

'Let's sit down over there,' said the girl suddenly.

'Why over there?'

'It looks nice and soft.'

'Oho!' said Pinette, 'so young ladies in post offices like things soft, do they?'

He took off his tunic and flung it on the ground.

'Perch your softness on my tunic,' he said. They settled down in the long grass at the edge of a wheat-field. Pinette clenched his left hand, keeping a watch on the girl out of the corner of his eye, put his thumb in his mouth, and pretended to blow. His biceps began to swell as though inflated by a pump: the girl giggled.

'Feel it.'

She put out a timid finger and touched Pinette's arm. As she did so the muscle disappeared, and Pinette made a noise like air escaping from a balloon.

'Oh!' she said.

Pinette turned to Mathieu:

'What d'you think Mauron'd say if he saw me sitting in a ditch without my tunic?'

'You can't see Mauron for dust,' said Mathieu.

'That's all right by me!' – then, leaning towards the girl from the post office: 'Mauron's the skipper,' he explained. 'He's busy taking a fresh-air cure!'

'A fresh-air cure?'

'Finds it healthier!' said Pinette with a chuckle. 'We're our own masters now – no one to give us orders – we can do as we like – go to the school, if you like, and make free with the skipper's bed: the village is all ours.'

'But not for long,' said Mathieu.

'All the more reason to make hay while the sun shines!'

'I'd rather stay here,' said the girl.

'Why? – haven't I just said there's no one to stop us?'

'There are still some people in the village.'

Pinette indulged in an arrogant stare:

'I was forgetting,' he said: 'you're a public servant, of course: got to watch your step. Different for us, there's no one *we* need bother about' – he treated Mathieu to a knowing grin – 'homeless, roofless, faithless, and lawless – that's what we are, just birds of passage. *You've* got to stay put, but *we're* on the wing – a gang of gipsies, wolves, beasts of prey – big, bad wolves, eh?'

He broke off a blade of grass and began to tickle her chin. His eyes were fixed on her. Still smiling, he began to sing:

'Who's afraid of the big bad wolf?'

The girl blushed, smiled, and chimed in:

'Not us! not us! not us!'

Pinette was delighted: 'Hey, my pretty' – there was an absent-minded look in his eyes – 'Hey! my pretty pet, pet, Miss pretty pet!'

Suddenly he stopped. The sky was red, the earth cool and blue-shadowed. Mathieu could feel, beneath his hands, beneath his buttocks, the swarming, tangled life of grass and soil and insects, a vast expanse of rank, moist hair running with lice. To feel it was agony. Cornered! Millions of men cornered between the Vosges and the Rhine – all possibility of existing like men taken from them. This flat forest of living things would still be there when they were dead. It was as though the world had no room for anything but fields and grass and a sort of impersonal ubiquity. Beneath his hands the earth was as tempting as suicide; the grass and the dense darkness with which it overlay the soil, the shackled thoughts creeping earthbound through this shadowed dusk, the spider beside his foot, motionless, until, on a sudden, it spread its giant's legs and vanished.

The girl sighed.

'What's the matter, baby?' asked Pinette.

She made no answer. Her small face, the face of a respectably brought-up young woman, was feverishly flushed. She had a long nose, a thin mouth, and a lower lip that projected slightly.

'What's the matter? – come on, tell me what's the matter?'

She remained silent. A hundred yards or so from them, silhouetted between sun and field, four soldiers were moving like vague shadows in a golden mist. One of them stopped and turned towards the east. He looked, in the glare, to be without solidity. He showed, not exactly black, but mauve, rather, against the red glow of the setting sun. He was bare-headed. The man behind bumped into him, and gave him a push. The upper parts of their bodies seemed to drift like twin ships upon the surface of the wheat. A third loitered at their heels, his arms raised, and, in his rear, a laggard was slashing with a switch at the growing crops.

'Come on!' said Pinette.

He had her chin in his hand and was staring hard into her face. Her eyes were brimming with tears.

'Not very cheerful company, are you?'

He tried to put a soldier's roughness into the words, but lacked the necessary assurance. When she spoke, the phrase she used, slipping from her child's mouth, seemed wan and faded:

'I can't help it.'

He drew her to him:

'Come now, you mustn't cry. *We're* not crying, are we?' he added with a laugh.

She let her head droop against his shoulder, and he stroked her hair. There was a look of pride on his face.

'They'll take you away!' she said.

'Bah!'

'They'll take you away!' she repeated, and began to cry again.

A hard look came into Pinette's face.

'I'm not asking for pity!'

'I don't want them to take you away!'

'Who's said anything about taking away? You're going to see how Frenchmen can fight: you'll have a ringside seat!'

She gazed down at him with wide, dilated eyes. Her fear was so intense that she had left off crying.

153

'You mustn't fight!'

'Tchk – tchk – tchk!'

'You mustn't fight, the war's over.'

There was amusement in the look he gave her.

'Ha!' he said, 'Ha! ha!'

Mathieu averted his eyes: he wanted to go away.

'We've only known each other since yesterday,' she said.

Her lower lip was trembling, her long face drooped. She had the noble, sad, frightened look of a horse.

'Tomorrow,' she said.

'There's plenty of time between now and tomorrow,' said Pinette.

'Between now and tomorrow there's only a night!'

'Precisely, a night!' he said with a wink. 'Time enough for a bit of fun.'

'I don't want a bit of fun!'

'Don't want a bit of fun? D'you really mean that – you don't want a bit of fun?'

She looked at him without answering.

'Are you unhappy?' he asked.

She continued to look at him, her mouth half-open.

'Because of me?'

He leaned across her. There was a look of tenderness on his face, but rather worn, rather haggard. Almost at once he drew back, his lips twisted in an unpleasant sneer.

'Come on,' he said: 'come on, don't take it so hard. There'll be others. There's as good fish in the sea as ever came out of it!'

'I'm not interested in the others!'

'You won't talk like that when you've seen 'em! They're proper cards – well set-up chaps, too, broad shoulders, narrow hips.'

'Who are you talking about?'

'The Jerries – who d'you think?'

'They're not men at all!'

'Choosy, aren't you?'

'They're just wild animals!'

Pinette gave her an impersonal sort of smile. 'That's where you're wrong,' he said quietly. 'They're fine-looking fellows, and good soldiers too: not up to French standards, perhaps, but good soldiers for all that.'

'So far as I'm concerned, they're just beasts!' she said again.

'I wouldn't be too sure. If you start saying that sort of thing, you'll look a bit of a fool when you have to change your tune. They're conquerors, and don't you forget it! You can't stand out against a whopping great bloke who's won the war. You'll have to go through it like the others: there's something about 'em, you know, and it'll get you. Just ask the Paris girls if I'm not right. High old times going on there: plenty of fun and games in Paris, I give you *my* word!'

She shook herself free of him: 'I hate you!'

'What's biting you, kid?' asked Pinette.

'I'm French!' said the girl.

'So are the women of Paris – doesn't make a scrap of difference.'

'Leave me alone,' she said: 'I want to go back!'

Pinette's face was white. He began to laugh.

'Don't be angry with him,' said Mathieu: 'It was only his fun.'

'He's gone a bit too far,' she said: 'What does he take me for?'

'It's not very pleasant to be defeated,' said Mathieu gently. 'It takes time to get used to the idea. You've no idea how nice he is as a rule, just a woolly little lamb!'

'Ha!' said Pinette. 'Ha! ha!'

'He's jealous,' said Mathieu.

'Of me?' asked the girl, once more tractable.

'You can't blame him for thinking of all the men who'll be trying to make up to you while he's away breaking stones, now, can you?'

'Or eating dandelion roots,' put in Pinette, still laughing.

'I won't have you getting yourself killed!' she declared.

He smiled:

'You're talking like a woman,' he said: 'like a small girl, a teeny, tiny girl,' he wound up, tickling her.

'Behave yourself!' she said, wriggling. 'Oh, do behave yourself!'

'Don't make yourself too miserable about him!' said Mathieu

in a sudden fit of irritation: 'everything'll go off quite quietly, you know. Why, we haven't any ammunition.'

They both, at one and the same moment, turned and looked at him. Their faces expressed dislike and a sort of numb frustration, as though he had interrupted them in the act of making love. Mathieu stared at Pinette without sympathy. A few moments passed, at the end of which Pinette dropped his eyes, and began moodily to tug at a tuft of grass between his legs.

A number of soldiers were sauntering along the road. One of them had a rifle. He was holding it like a candle, and playing the fool.

'Bleedin' comic!' said a dark, stocky little fellow with knock-knees.

The other took the barrel of his rifle in both hands, swung the weapon like a golf-club, and slogged with the butt at a stone, which jumped about twenty feet.

Pinette regarded their antics with a frown.

'Some of 'em getting out of hand already,' he said. Mathieu made no comment. The girl had taken Pinette's hand and was playing with it on her lap.

'You're wearing a wedding-ring,' she said.

'This the first time you've noticed it?' he asked, half-closing his hand.

'I noticed it before, all right. Are you married?'

'What d'you suppose I wear a wedding-ring for, if I'm not?'

'I see,' she said sadly.

'Just you watch!'

He pulled at his finger, grimacing with his face, wrenched off the ring and flung it into the growing corn.

'Oh, you didn't ought to have done that!' said the girl. She sounded shocked.

He took up a knife from the table, Ivich was bleeding: he drove it into the palm of his hand: acting: little gestures of trivial destruction that get you nowhere: and I took it all as a fine manifestation of freedom. Mathieu yawned.

'It was gold?'

'Yes.'

She leaned forward and kissed him lightly on the lips. Mathieu got up, and then sat down again.

'I'm off,' he said.

Pinette looked at him uneasily:

'Oh, don't go yet.'

'You don't want me.'

'Stay a bit longer,' said Pinette: 'you've got nothing to do.'

Mathieu smiled and pointed at the girl.

'She's not particularly keen for me to stay.'

'She? of course she is; she likes you.' He leaned over her, and there was a note of eagerness in his voice:

'He's my pal: you like him, don't you?'

'Yes,' said the girl.

She hates me – thought Mathieu – but he stayed. Time was standing still. It quivered and eddied above the russet plain. He knew that if he made any sharp, sudden movement, he would feel it in his bones like the twinge of an old rheumatic joint. He stretched himself on his back. The sky was pink and empty. If only one could fall headlong into the sky! But there was nothing he could do about it. We are earthbound creatures – and that is at the root of all our troubles.

The four soldiers whom he had seen moving slowly along the edge of the field had turned at its far end in order to regain the road. They were strung out in single file. They were men from a Sapper company. Mathieu did not know them by sight. The corporal, walking ahead of the others, had a faint look of Pinette. Like him he was in his shirt-sleeves, and his hairy chest was plainly visible. Behind him was a dark, sun-tanned fellow, his tunic thrown loosely about his shoulders. He was holding a wheatstalk in his left hand and extracting the grain with his right. Raising it to his mouth, he began to lick up the golden seeds with small, pecking movements of his head. The third, taller and older than the rest, was running his fingers through his fair hair. All were walking slowly, dreamily, with the easy carriage of civilians. The man who had been fidgeting with his hair dropped his hands, passing them gently over his neck and shoulders, as though enjoying the feel of a body that had suddenly emerged into the sunlight from its shapeless military chrysalis. They stopped, almost at the same moment, and stood, one behind the other, looking at Mathieu. Their eyes were the eyes of creatures belonging to a different age of the world's history. Mathieu felt as though he had melted into the grass: he was a meadow exposed to the fixed stare of animals. The dark fellow said:

'I've lost me belt.'

His voice did nothing to break the charm of the relaxed, inhuman world. The sounds it uttered were not words but just part of the rustle which made up the silence. A similar rustle came from the lips of his fair-haired companion.

'Don't worry – the Jerries would have took it in any case.'

A fourth man seemed to materialize noiselessly. He stopped and looked up. His face reflected the sky's emptiness.

'Hey!' he said.

He stooped, picked a poppy, and stuck it in his mouth. As he straightened up again he noticed that Pinette had his arms round the girl and was holding her tight. He started to laugh:

'Been pretty hot.'

'You said it, chum.'

'But it's cooling off now.'

'Seems like it.'

' 'bout time, too.'

The four heads nodded. The intelligence conveyed by the gesture was peculiarly French. Then, intelligence faded. All that remained was a sense of immense leisure. The heads continued to nod. 'For the first time in their lives,' thought Mathieu, 'they're knowing what it's like to have a rest.'

They were resting from forced marches, from inspections, from manoeuvres, from leaves, from waiting, and from hoping. They were resting from the war, and from a weariness more ancient still – the weariness of peace. In the middle of the growing crops, at the forest's edge, on the outskirts of the village, other small groups were similarly resting: troops of convalescents were roaming the countryside.

'Hey! Pirard!' shouted the corporal.

Mathieu turned his head. Pirard, Captain Mauron's batman, had halted at the roadside and was making water. He was a sly, brutish peasant from Brittany. Looking at him now, Mathieu felt a shock of surprise. The man's animal face was flushed by the setting sun; his eyes were dilated; gone was his habitual expression of distrust and shiftiness. For the first time, perhaps, he was seeing the signs written across the sky, and the mystic circle of the sun.

'Hey! Pirard!'

Pirard gave a start.

'What you up to?' demanded the corporal.

'Just takin' a breath o' air,' said Pirard.

'Cancher see there's ladies about?'

Pirard looked down at his hands. What he saw seemed to surprise him, for he hastily buttoned up his trousers.

'Did it without thinkin',' he said.

'Don't mind me,' said the girl.

She snuggled up against Pinette and smiled at the corporal. Her skirt was above her knees, and it never occurred to her to pull it down.

All was innocence in this new world. They looked at her legs, but with a sort of gentle and astonished melancholy. They were angels: the expression of their faces was quite without emotion.

'Well, so long,' said the dark-haired man; 'we'll be toddling.'

'Just taking a walk to get up an appetite,' said the tall, fair man with a laugh.

'Here's wishing you a good one!' said Mathieu.

They laughed. Everyone knew there was nothing to eat in the village. The spare rations in the Quartermaster's stores had all been looted early that morning.

'It ain't appetite that's the trouble.'

They none of them moved. They had stopped laughing now, and a flicker of uneasiness showed in the corporal's eyes. It was as though they were afraid to say good-bye. Mathieu was half-inclined to ask them to sit down.

'Come on!' said the corporal, but the calm authority of his tone was rather overdone. They started off again towards the road. Their departure tore a sudden hole in the coolness of the evening, through which trickled a few drops of time: the Germans took a leap forward; five steel fingers closed about Mathieu's heart. Then the bleeding stopped; time once again coagulated, and the scene reverted to a park in which angels were sauntering at their ease. 'How empty it all is,' thought Mathieu. Some vast, brooding figure had made off, leaving Nature in charge of a few second-line soldiers. *A voice runs be-*

neath the sun of an older world: Pan is dead, and some such dereliction was what they felt now. But what was it that had died this time – France? Christendom? Hope? Quietly the earth and the fields had turned back to their pristine uselessness. On the surface of these meadows that they could neither cultivate nor protect, men were now but parasites. The world seemed made anew, yet all about the evening stood the black fringes of the coming night, and in the depths of that night a comet would strike the earth. Were they going to be bombed? It might not be long before some such pleasant little attention was afforded them. Was this the first day of the world, or the last? The wheat, the poppies, now growing dark as far as eye could see, the whole prospect, seemed caught in a simultaneous crisis of birth and death. Mathieu let his eye roam over this peaceful ambiguity: he thought – it is the paradise of despair.

'Your lips are cold,' said Pinette.

He leaned to the girl and kissed her.

'D'you feel cold?' he asked her.

'No.'

'Do you like me kissing you?'

'Yes, very much.'

'Then why are your lips cold?'

'Is it true they rape the women?' she asked.

'You're crazy!'

'Kiss me!' she said passionately: 'I don't want to think about anything any more!'

She took his head between her hands and fell back upon the grass, pulling him down upon her.

'My pretty!' he said: 'my pretty!'

He covered her, and Mathieu could see no more than the tangle of their hair in the grass. But almost at once Pinette's face reappeared. The mask of sneering self-sufficiency had fallen from it. His eyes looked at Mathieu with the smooth and simple nakedness of an immense simplicity, but did not see him. They brimmed with loneliness.

'Darling, don't leave off, don't leave off!' sighed the girl.

But rigid, white, and blind the head stayed reared above the grass. Now, thought Mathieu, he is doing a man's work – and looked into the dark and clouded eyes.

Pinette lay with the girl crushed beneath him to the earth, making her one with the earth and the hesitant grasses. He held the goodness of the earth under the pressing weight of loins and belly. She was summoning him into her, and in her he was taking root. She was water, woman, mirror, giving back the reflection of the virgin hero with battles still to fight. Nature, in a breathless silence, supine beneath him, gave absolution for defeat, murmuring, 'Come to me darling, come.' But it was his will to play the part of the conquering male to the end. He pressed with his open palms against the earth. His arms, doubled behind him, looked like wings. He reared his head above the docility of her tangled hair. It was his will to be admired, reflected, and desired by her who lay beneath him in the deep darkness of unthinking surrender. It was his will to ignore the glory that was being transmitted to his body by the earth, like animal heat; to break free into the emptiness and anguish of a thought – 'What next?' The girl wound her arms about his neck and drew it down. His head plunged into the depths of love and glory, and the grasses met above it. Very quietly, Mathieu got up and moved away. He crossed the field. He caught a glimpse of one of the angels sauntering upon the road that still shone white between the dark stains of the poplars. The couple lay hid in the dark grass. Soldiers passed, carrying bunches of flowers. One of them, as he walked, raised the bunch he carried to his face, buried his nose in the flowers, and breathed in, with their fragrance, his idleness, his pain, the sense of a superfluity that nothing seemed to justify. The corrosion of the night lay on flowers and faces. In the darkness they all looked alike. I am like them, thought Mathieu. He walked on a little way, saw a star come out, and brushed past a shadowed saunterer who was whistling on his way. The man turned his head, and Mathieu saw his eyes. They exchanged a smile – one of those smiles that he had met with yesterday, a smile of friendship.

'Chilly,' said the man.

'Yes,' said Mathieu: 'it's beginning to get cold.'

They had nothing more to say, and the other moved on. Mathieu looked after him. Must men, then, lose everything, even hope, before one could read in their eyes all that a man might gain? Pinette was busy making love: Guiccioli and Latex were lying dead drunk on the floor of the Mairie: along the roads solitary angels walked at leisure, with only their pain for company. *No one needs me.* He sat down on the edge of the road because there was nowhere for him to go. Night entered into him through mouth and eyes, through nose and ears. He was no one now; he was nothing – nothing any longer but misery and darkness. The thought of Charlot came to him and he jumped to his feet – the thought of Charlot alone with his fear and his shame. *All the time I was indulging in romantic melancholy among those drunken beasts, he was alone, humble, and fearful – and I might have helped him.*

Charlot was seated just where he had left him, bending over his book. Mathieu went up to him and ruffled his hair.

'You're ruining your eyes!'

'I'm not reading,' said Charlot. 'I'm thinking.'

He had raised his head, and there was the hint of a smile on his thick lips.

'What are you thinking about?'

'About my shop – wondering whether it's been looted.'

'That's not very likely,' said Mathieu. He pointed to the darkened windows of the Mairie.

'What's going on in there?'

'Don't know,' said Charlot: 'there hasn't been a sound for some time.'

Mathieu sat down on a step.

'Not feeling too good, eh?'

Charlot smiled sadly:

'Was it because of me you came back?' he asked.

'I was feeling bored. It occurred to me that you might feel inclined for a bit of company. That suited me fine.'

Charlot shook his head but said nothing.

'Like me to go away?' asked Mathieu.

'No,' said Charlot. 'I don't mind you being here, but you can't help me. What can you say? – that the Germans aren't savages? – that one's got to keep one's courage up? – I know all that.'

He sighed and laid the book down beside him with great care.

'If you aren't a Jew,' he said, 'you can't possibly understand.'

162

He laid his hand on Mathieu's knee, and added, almost apologetically: 'It's not me that's frightened, but the Race deep down in me. There's nothing I can do about it.'

Mathieu was silent. They sat there side by side, saying nothing; the one without hope, the other powerless to help, both waiting for the darkness to cover them.

It was the hour at which objects overflow their contours and fuse together in the fluffy shades of evening. The windows slid with motionless movement into the dusk; the room was a pinnace adrift, the whisky bottle an Aztec god. Philippe was a long, grey weed, powerless to frighten. Love was much more than love, and friendship not quite friendship. Daniel, invisible in the shadows, was talking of friendship. He was no more than a calm, warm voice. He paused for breath, and Philippe took advantage of the silence to say:

'How dark it's getting: don't you think we might turn on the lights?'

'If the current isn't cut off,' said Daniel dryly.

He got up with an ill grace. The moment had come when he must submit to the ordeal of light. He opened the window, leaned out above the emptiness below, and breathed in the violet fragrance of the silence. How often, at this same time, I have longed to escape, and have heard the sound of mounting steps that have trampled on my thoughts. . . . The night was untamed and mild. The flesh, so often wounded by the darkness, had healed. A virgin night, deep, profound; a lovely night with never a man to be seen, an exquisite blood-orange without pips. Regretfully he closed the shutters and turned the switch. The room leaped from the shadows; the various objects took on familiar identity. Philippe's face pressed hard against his eyes. He felt within the focus of his vision the movement of this magnified head, precisely defined, freshly severed, disconcerted. Its two bewildered eyes held his own fascinated, as though he were seeing it for the first time. 'I've got to play a cautious game,' he thought. He was conscious of a feeling of embarrassment, raised his hand as though to dissipate a trick of the eyes, pinched the lapel of his coat between his fingers, and smiled. He dreaded being unmasked.

'What are you staring at me like that for? – d'you find me good-looking?'

'Very good-looking,' said Philippe in a colourless voice.

Daniel turned to the mirror, and studied, not without a feeling of pleasure, his dark and handsome face. Philippe had lowered his eyes and was sniggering behind his hand.

'You giggle like any schoolgirl.'

Philippe stopped: but Daniel would not leave the subject:

'What are you giggling *at*?'

'Oh, nothing special.'

The boy was half-drunk with wine, suspense, and weariness. Now's the moment, thought Daniel: but he must be careful to treat the whole thing as a joke, a sort of schoolboy prank. Provided he did *that* Philippe would let himself be tumbled on the divan, petted, kissed behind the ear. He would put up no sort of fight, but merely dissolve in helpless laughter. Sharply, Daniel turned his back on him, and took a few paces across the room. Too soon, much too soon: mustn't make a fool of myself. If I do that he'll simply run off in the morning and kill himself – if he doesn't try to kill me.

'Well, now,' he said.

'Well?' echoed Philippe.

'Look me in the eyes.'

He stared hard at the boy. His nod expressed satisfaction.

'You're no coward,' he said slowly. 'I'm certain of that.'

He extended his hand and tapped Philippe on the chest with one finger.

'Run away because you'd panicked? *that's* not the sort of thing you'd do. No, you just turned your back on the whole affair, left them to settle it without you. Why should you get yourself killed for the sake of France? – why indeed? *You* don't care a damn about France, do you, you young scamp?'

Philippe's only reply was a movement of the head. Daniel resumed his walking up and down the room.

'You're through with all that' – he said with an appearance of nervous gaiety. 'You've had a stroke of luck that never came *my* way. Oh,' he added hastily, gesturing with his hand, 'I'm not referring to our meeting. What I meant was that the *historical coincidence* has been a godsend for you. You want to undermine bourgeois morality, don't you? Well, you've got the Germans now to give you a helping hand. *They'll* make a clean sweep of all this junk right enough! You'll have the delightful spectacle of respectable householders positively crawling and licking the conqueror's boots, just asking to have their fat bums kicked. They're the people who have really been beaten in this war. What an opportunity for you to show your contempt!'

He laughed till the tears came. 'Oh, what a spring cleaning there's going to be!' he said: then, with a quick swing round: 'You've got to learn to love them.'

Philippe looked startled: 'Who've I got to learn to love?' he asked.

'The Germans: they are our allies.'

'Love the Germans? – but – but – I don't know them.'

'We'll get plenty of opportunity to know them, never fear. We shall be asked to dine with the Gauleiter, with the Field-Marshal. They'll trot us round in their great black Mercedes cars, while the Parisians'll have to trudge it on foot.'

Philippe stifled a yawn. Daniel took him by the shoulders and shook him.

'You've got to love the Germans,' he said with intense seriousness: 'that's going to be the first of your Spiritual Exercises.'

The boy showed no sign of being particularly thrilled at the idea. Daniel let him go, flung out his arms and intoned with mock solemnity:

'Voici venir le temps des assassins!'

Philippe yawned again. Daniel could see his pointed tongue.

'I'm sleepy,' said Philippe apologetically: 'I haven't shut my eyes for two nights.'

Daniel was half-inclined to show anger, but he too felt exhausted, as always when he had found a new object for his affection.

Desire for Philippe had left him with a sensation of heavy frustration. He longed suddenly to be alone.

'I'll leave you to yourself, then,' he said: 'you'll find pyjamas in the chest-of-drawers.'

'Thanks all the same,' said the boy, without much show of conviction, 'but I really ought to be getting home.'

Daniel smiled at him.

'Just as you choose, but you run the risk of meeting a patrol, and God knows what they'll do to you. You're as pretty as a girl, and all Germans are homosexual. Besides, even if you do get home safely, it'll be only to find what you're running away from. Aren't there photographs of your stepfather on the walls, and doesn't the room reek of your mother's scent?'

Philippe seemed not to have heard. He made an effort to get up, but fell back again on the divan.

'Haah!' he said in a drowsy voice. He looked at Daniel with a puzzled smile.

'Perhaps it *would* be better if I stayed here.'

'Good night, then.'

'Good night,' said Philippe with another yawn.

Daniel crossed the room. As he passed the fireplace he pressed a piece of the moulding, and one of the book-shelves turned on itself, revealing a row of yellow-bound books.

'Allow me to introduce you to hell!' he said: 'Later on, you must read them: they're full of you.'

'Of me?' said Philippe, not understanding.

'Yes, of your case.'

He readjusted the shelf and opened the door. The key was still on the outside. He tossed it across to Philippe.

'If you're afraid of ghosts or burglars, you can lock yourself in,' he said mockingly.

He shut the door behind him, groped his way in the darkness to the far end of his bedroom, switched on the reading-lamp, and sat down on the bed. Alone at last! Six hours of stumping the streets, and four more hard at it playing the part of Mephistopheles! I'm all in! He sighed with the sheer pleasure of solitude. Revelling in the thought that there was no one to see him, he pulled a mournful face. Then he smiled and stretched himself out as though in a lovely hot bath. He was accustomed to these long fits of desire in the abstract, and experience had taught him that he would suffer less if he lay down. The lamp threw a round patch of light on the ceiling: the pillow felt cool. Motionless, dead, smiling, Daniel lay there at rest. 'Peace, perfect peace: I have locked the front door and the key is in my pocket. Besides, he's dropping with sleep and won't wake up till midday. Pacifist! – *really!* On the whole, though, I haven't got much out of the adventure yet. There must be some weak spot on which I can play – if only I can find it.' With the Nathanaels and the Rimbauds Daniel was on his own ground, but he found the younger generation disconcerting. 'What an extraordinary mix-up – narcissism and social theories – it just doesn't make sense.'

All the same, by and large, things hadn't gone too badly. He'd got the boy safe there under lock and key. If the worst came to the worst, he could always play the card of systematic debauching. It flattered the victim, and it usually worked. . . . 'Sooner or later, I'll get you, and then I'll put your principles through the mangle well and truly, dear angel-face. Social theories, indeed! – you'll soon see what'll become of them!' The coldly calculated enthusiasm in which he had been indulging lay heavy on his stomach. What he needed was a good strong dose of cynicism to clear his emotional bowels. 'If I can keep him for a good long time, I'm in luck's way. I need a quiet life, with my little bit of relaxation always on tap when I feel like it. I'm through with the old racketing round with Graff and Toto, with my "aunt" from Honfleur, with Marius and "Sens Interdit": I'm through with hanging round the Gare de l'Est on the look-out for squalid little soldiers on leave with their smelly feet. I'm going to settle down (*through with the Terror*).' He sat up on the bed and began to undress. This time, he decided, it was going to be serious. He felt sleepy and perfectly calm. He got up to fetch his pyjamas, clearly conscious of how calm he felt. 'It really is extraordinary,' he thought, 'that I'm not all on edge.'

At that precise moment he got the feeling that there was somebody behind him. He swung round. There was nobody, but suddenly the calmness of his mood was shattered, rent in two. 'Just the same old business over again!' – he knew it all backwards, could foresee precisely what would happen, could reckon minute by minute the years of misery that lay ahead, the daily toll of long, long years heavy with boredom and hopelessness, and, at the end of them, the squalid, inevitable end. It was all there. He looked at the shut door. He was breathing heavily. 'This time,' he thought, 'it'll be the end of me,' and in his mouth he could taste the bitterness of all the agonies still to come.

' 'Tis a prarper blaze!' said an old man.

Everybody was out on the road, soldiers, old men and girls. The schoolmaster pointed with his stick towards the horizon. Perched on its ferrule was the glow of an artificial sun, of a ball of fire dimming the pale dawn. Roberville was burning.

' 'Tis a prarper blaze!'

'Aye, that 'tis.'

The old men stood, their hands behind their backs, rocking a little on their feet, and saying 'Aye, that 'tis' in their deep, calm voices. Charlot dropped Mathieu's arm.

'It's awful!' he said.

' 'Tis what allus comes to we country-folk,' replied one of the veterans, 'When 'tisn't war, 'tis hail or frost. There baint no peace anywheres for we country-folk.'

The soldiers were fumbling the girls in the darkness and making them giggle. Mathieu could hear behind him the shouts of urchins playing in the abandoned alleys of the village. A woman came forward: she was holding a baby in her arms.

'Is it the French as has done it?' she asked.

'You not caught on, Ma?' said Lubéron: 'it's the Fritzes.'

One of the old men tremblingly voiced his incredulity: 'The Fritzes?'

'Yes, Fritzes, Boches . . .'

The old man seemed to be unconvinced:

'Us had t' Boches here in other war, and they didn't do much 'arm. Germans be decent lads.'

'What they go and do a thing like that for?' demanded Lubéron indignantly: 'we ain't a lot of savages.'

'Why should it be they as done it? – how'll they manage for billets now?'

A bearded soldier raised his hand:

'Probably some of our little lot have been playing the fool and letting off at 'em. One man dead's enough for the Fritzes to burn down a whole village.'

The woman turned to him with a worried look.

'And what about you?' she asked.

'How d'you mean, what about us?'

'You're not going to play the fool?'

The soldiers laughed.

'Don't worry your head about that, lady. We know what's good for us!'

The exchanged conspiratorial looks under cover of their laughter.

'Oh yes, we know what's good for us! We're not likely to go looking for trouble, with peace breaking out, and all!'

The woman stroked her child's head. 'Is it really going to be peace?' she asked in quavering tones.

'Yes, it's peace all right,' said the schoolmaster with conviction: 'that's what we've got to remember.'

A sort of ripple passed through the crowd. Mathieu could hear behind him a confused medley of voices. They sounded almost happy.

'It's peace! it's peace!'

He watched Roberville burning and echoed their words: the war's over; it's peace! He looked at the road. Two hundred yards ahead it emerged from darkness, flowed, a white, glimmering stream, to his feet, and passed beyond, to lap against the houses with their closed shutters: a lovely road, a road of adventure, a road of danger, a road on which there was no turning back. It had recaptured the untamed wildness of the rivers of antiquity – tomorrow it would float into the village vessels filled with murderers. Charlot sighed and Mathieu silently pressed his arm.

'There they are!' said a voice.

'What d'you mean?'

'The Fritzes, there they are!'

There was movement in the darkness. Scattered skirmishers, their rifles under their arms, were emerging, one by one, from the dark waters of the night. They advanced slowly, cautiously, ready to open fire at the least alarm.

'There they are! there they are!'

Mathieu felt himself jostled and elbowed. The crowd about him swayed with an uncertain but clearly defined movement.

'Hey, boys, better get out of this!'

'You crazy? – they've seen us. Only thing to do is to wait for 'em.'

'Wait for 'em? – they'll shoot!'

A great sigh of hopelessness rose from the crowd. The school-master's thin voice cut through the stillness.

'Women to the rear! Drop your rifles, men – those who have them – and put your hands up!'

'Can't you see they're French, you fools!' exclaimed Mathieu, beside himself with anger.

'French . . .? where from?'

They were French, right enough, fifteen men under the com-mand of a lieutenant. Their faces were set and grimy. The village folk lined the road and looked at them with unfriendly eyes. French they might be, but they were from a strange and dangerous country. Frenchmen with rifles, Frenchmen in the dead of night, Frenchmen creeping out of the shadows, out of the war, bringing the war with them into this village to which peace had already come. From Paris, they might be, or Bordeaux – visitors only a degree less bad than Germans. They came on between twin hedges of hostile apathy, looking at nobody. The expression on their faces was one of pride. The lieutenant gave an order and they halted.

'What division do you belong to?' he asked. The question was addressed to nobody in particular. It was met by silence, and he repeated it.

'Sixty-First,' said a surly voice.

'Where are your officers?'

'They've hopped it!'

'What do you mean?'

'Hopped it,' repeated the soldier with obvious satisfaction. The lieutenant compressed his lips. He did not press his inquiry.

'Where is the Mairie?'

Charlot, always willing to oblige, stepped forward.

'On the left – far end of the street – 'bout a hundred yards up.'

The officer swung round and looked him up and down. 'Is that the way you speak to an officer? Have you forgotten how to stand to attention? Would it be too much to suggest that you say "sir"?'

For a few moments no one spoke. The lieutenant was looking hard at Charlot. The men crowded about Mathieu were looking at the lieutenant. Then Charlot straightened up.

'Beg pardon, sir,'

'That's better.'

The lieutenant looked contemptuously at the circle of faces, motioned with his hand, and the little group of soldiers moved on. The men of the Sixty-First watched the darkness swallow them without a word.

'I thought we were through with officers,' said Lubéron with an effort.

'Through with officers?' came a voice, bitter and exacerbated: 'You don't know officers: they'll bugger us about till we're all bleedin' stiffs!'

'They won't start any of their fighting here, will they?' asked one of the women suddenly.

A ripple of laughter greeted her words:

'What do *you* think, Ma?' said Charlot, good-humouredly: 'they're not nuts!'

Silence reigned once more. Every face was turned to the north. Roberville, isolated, out of reach, already legendary, was burning. It had been unlucky. It was in a foreign country, on the other side of a frontier. Fighting – fire – death – destruction: well, that's just too bad for Roberville: nothing much can happen to us! Slowly, nonchalantly, men began to drift away from the crowd and move towards the village. Better get their stuff in some sort of order so's to be ready when the Fritzes turned up at dawn.

'I'm off,' said Charlot.

'Going to turn in?'

'Seems to be the general idea.'

'Like me to come with you?'

'Don't bother,' said Charlot with a yawn. He moved off, and Mathieu was left alone. 'We're slaves' – he thought; 'nothing more or less than slaves.' But he felt no anger at his companions. It wasn't their fault. They had had ten months of hard labour. There had been a change-over of authority now, and they were about to pass into the hands of *German* officers. They would salute the Feldwebel and the Oberleutnant. It wouldn't make much difference. The officer caste is international. The hard labour would go on. That was all there was to it. 'It's at myself that I feel anger,' he thought, but resented doing so. To feel angry with himself was a way of setting himself above the rest.

Indulgent to others, severe with oneself – just another trick of pride. At once innocent and guilty, too severe yet too indulgent, impotent yet responsible, part of the general whole yet rejected by each several individual, perfectly lucid yet utterly deceived, enslaved yet sovereign. I'm just like everybody else.

Somebody clutched his arm. It was the girl from the post office. Her eyes were blazing.

'You must do something to stop him if you're his friend!'

'Eh?'

'He wants to fight: oh, do do something to stop him!'

Pinette appeared behind her. His face was pale and his eyes had a dead look. His lips were distended in a sinister grin.

'What do you want me to do, my dear?' Mathieu asked her.

'I've just told you – he wants to fight. I heard him say so. He went to the captain and told him he wanted to fight.'

'What captain?'

'The one that went by with his men.'

Pinette chuckled, his hands behind his back.

'That was no captain – that was a lieutenant.'

'Is it true that you want to fight?' asked Mathieu.

'You make me sick, the whole lot of you!'

'You see!' said the girl: 'you see! – he said he wanted to fight, I heard him!'

'But who said there's going to be any fighting?'

'Didn't you look at them? – they've got murder in their faces. He' – and she pointed to Pinette – 'he frightens me, he's a monster!'

Mathieu gave a shrug:

'But what can I do?'

'Aren't you his friend?'

'That's just why I can't do anything.'

'If you're his friend you ought to tell him that he's no right to get himself killed.'

She clung to Mathieu's arm:

'He hasn't any right to!'

'Why?'

'You know perfectly well!'

Pinette's smile was cruel and insensitive:

'I'm a soldier: it's my job to fight, that's what soldiers are for!'

172

'Then you shouldn't have come after me!'

She seized him by the arm, and added, in a trembling voice:
'You belong to me!'

Pinette shook himself free:
'I don't belong to anyone!'

'Yes, you do!' she said: 'you belong to me!' She turned on
Mathieu, passionately summoning him to her aid: '*You* tell him!
– tell him that he's no right to get himself killed! It's your duty
to tell him that!'

Mathieu said nothing. She advanced upon him, her face
ablaze. For the first time Mathieu saw her as desirable.

'You call yourself his friend, and you don't care whether he
gets hurt or not!'

'Certainly I care.'

'You think it's a fine thing for a boy like that to stand up to
a whole army, don't you? It's not even as though it would do
any good. You know perfectly well that no one's going to fight
now!'

'Oh yes, I know that all right,' said Mathieu.

'Then why don't you tell him?'

'Because he hasn't asked my opinion.'

'Henri, I *implore* you – ask him what he thinks. He's older
than you are, he must know.'

Pinette raised his hand as though to refuse her request. But
suddenly an idea seemed to occur to him, and he let it fall to his
side, screwing up his eyes with a sly expression which Mathieu
had never seen in them before.

'You want me to discuss with him what I mean to do?'

'Yes, since you don't love me enough to listen to what *I've* got
to say!'

'All right, then, I will – but you clear off first.'

'Why?'

'I'm not going to talk to him in front of you.'

'But why?'

'Because this isn't woman's business.'

'It's *my* business, since it concerns you.'

'Hell!' he said, by now thoroughly exasperated: 'you give me
the belly-ache!'

He nudged Mathieu in the ribs.

'There's no need for you to go away,' said Mathieu quickly: 'he and I'll take a stroll along the road: you wait here.'

'Oh yes, I know, and then you won't come back!'

'You're crackers!' said Pinette: 'where d'you *think* we're going? – we'll be within twenty yards of you — you'll be able to see us the whole time.'

'And if your friend tells you not to fight, you'll listen to him?'

'Sure,' said Pinette: 'I always do what he tells me.'

She clung to Pinette's neck:

'Swear you'll come back? – even if you decide to fight, even if your friend advises you to? Anything would be better than not seeing you again. Will you swear?'

'All right, have it your own way.'

'Say – I swear!'

'I swear,' said Pinette.

'And *you* swear you'll bring him back to me?' she said to Mathieu.

'Of course I do.'

'Don't be long,' she said, 'and don't go far.'

They went a few yards along the road in the direction of Roberville. Trees and bushes mottled it with shadow. After a few moments Mathieu turned his head. The girl from the post office was standing where they had left her, tense and upright, trying to make them out in the darkness. Another step, and she would vanish altogether. At that very moment her voice came to them:

'Don't go too far, I can't see you!'

Pinette began to laugh. He made a funnel of his hands and shouted back to her:

'Oho! Ohoho Ohohoho!'

They walked on: Pinette was still laughing.

'She wanted me to believe she was a virgin. That's what all the trouble's about.'

'Ah!'

'That's according to her – can't say I noticed it meself!'

'Some girls are like that: you think they're lying, and then you find they really are virgins.'

'Says you!' replied Pinette with a chuckle.

'It does happen sometimes.'

174

'Oh yeah? – an even if it does, it'd be an odd coincidence if it should happen to me.'

Mathieu smiled but said nothing. Pinette jerked his head up.

'Look here, you know, I didn't force her. When a girl's serious there's plenty of ways for her to keep a chap at a distance. Take my wife, for instance, we both wanted it bad, but there wasn't nothing doing before we got spliced.'

He clinched his words with a movement of the hand.

'Cross me heart! That little piece was just crazy for it – or I'm very much mistaken: honest, it was just doing her a favour!'

'What if you've started a kid?'

'What, me?' said Pinette, flabbergasted. 'You don't know what you're talking about. I'm one of your careful sort. My wife wouldn't have one because we was too poor, so I got in the way of watching meself. Oh no, there ain't nothing like that going to happen. She had her bit of fun, I had mine: we're quits.'

'It's difficult to believe that, if it really *was* the first time so far as she was concerned. Women don't often find the first time much fun.'

'Well then, wasn't that just too bad,' said Pinette, unsympathetically: 'In that case it was a proper trip-up for her!'

They relapsed into silence. A moment or so passed: then Mathieu raised his head and tried to see Pinette's face in the darkness.

'Is it true that they're going to put up a fight?'

'Yes.'

'In the village?'

'Where else d'you suggest?'

Mathieu felt his heart contract. Then, suddenly, he found himself thinking of Longin being sick under the tree, of Guiccioli sprawling on the floor, of Lubéron watching Roberville burning, and saying – 'It's peace.' He uttered an angry laugh.

'What are you laughing at?'

'I was thinking of the boys and of what a nasty surprise they've got coming to them.'

'You said it!'

'Is the lieutenant willing to take you on?'

'If I've got a rifle. He said, come along if you can find a rifle.'

'Your mind's made up?'

175

Pinette laughed savagely.

'It's . . .' began Mathieu.

Pinette swung round on him:

'I'm of age, I don't need any advice!'

'In that case,' said Mathieu, 'let's go back.'

'No,' said Pinette, 'let's walk a bit further.'

They walked on. Suddenly, Pinette said:

'Hey, jump into the ditch!'

'What?'

'Do as I say – jump!'

They jumped, scrambled up the bank, and found themselves in the middle of a wheatfield.

'There's a path over there to the left, that leads back to the village,' explained Pinette.

Mathieu stumbled and fell on one knee.

'What's all this damn' nonsense about?'

'Can't stick the sight of 'er, not now,' replied Pinette.

They could hear a woman's voice coming from the direction of the road:

'Henri! Henri!'

'Sticks like a limpet!' said Pinette.

'Henri, don't leave me.'

Pinette seized Mathieu's arm and pulled him down. They lay in the wheat. They could hear the girl running along the road. A wheat-ear rasped Mathieu's cheek: some small animal scuttled away between his hands.

'Henri! don't leave me! You can do what you like, but don't leave me! Come back, Henri! I won't say a thing, I promise, only come back! Don't leave me like this, Henri-i-i-i! Don't go away without giving me a kiss!'

She passed close by them: she was panting.

'Lucky the moon's not up yet,' whispered Pinette.

The smell of the earth was strong in Mathieu's nostrils: it was soft and damp beneath his hands. He heard Pinette's hoarse whisper, and thought: 'They're going to fight in the village.' The girl cried out to them twice more, her voice roughened with anguish. Then, suddenly, she turned on her heel, and started to run back the way she had come.

'She loves you,' said Mathieu.

'Oh, to hell with her!' replied Pinette.

They got up. Away to the north-east, Mathieu could see, just above the line of the wheat, a ball of flickering fire. *One man's enough for the Fritzes to burn down a whole village.*

'Well, what about it?' said Pinette in a challenging voice: 'what about you doing a bit of consoling of 'er?'

'She gets on my nerves,' said Mathieu, 'besides, I'm not particularly interested in women just at present. Still, it was wrong, you know, to do what you did, if you meant to drop her like a hot brick.'

'Blast the 'ole bleeding show!' said Pinette: 'According to you everything one does is wrong.'

'There's the path,' said Mathieu.

They walked on for a while. Pinette said:

'The moon!'

Mathieu, looking up, saw a second fire on the horizon, this time a blaze of silver.

'A reglar picture!' said Pinette.

'I don't think they'll get here before tomorrow morning,' said Mathieu. A moment later, he added, not looking at Pinette: 'You'll be killed to the last man.'

'That's war, that is,' said Pinette hoarsely.

'You've got it wrong,' said Mathieu: 'the war's over.'

'Armistice isn't signed yet.'

Mathieu took Pinette's hand and squeezed it gently; it was icy.

'Sure you really want to get done in?'

'I certainly don't want to get done in: I want to knock over a Jerry.'

'The two things go together.'

Pinette withdrew his hand without speaking. Mathieu wanted to say something. 'He's going to die for nothing,' he thought, and the idea stuck in his throat. But suddenly he felt cold. He said nothing. 'What right have I to stop him? what alternative can I offer?' He turned his head, looked at Pinette, and began to whistle softly. Pinette was far out of his reach, marching blindly through the darkness of his last night, marching but not advancing: for whither he was going he had already come: his birth and death had swung full circle, and met. He was marching under the moon with the imminent sun already shining on

177

his wounds. Over and done with was Pinette's pursuit of Pinette, for now he was wholly himself, a Pinette entire, close-packed in the final reckoning. Mathieu sighed, and in silence took his arm, the arm of a young employee of the Métro, noble, gentle, brave, and tender, who had been killed on 18 June 1940. Pinette smiled at him: from the depths of his past he smiled. Mathieu saw the smile and felt utterly alone. I can break the shell that separates us only if I am content to wish for myself no other future than his, no other sun than that on which, tomorrow, he will look for the last time: to find contentment in sharing his time, his very minutes and his death. Very slowly he said:

'It's I, really, who ought to go to the slaughter in your place, because I have so much less reason for living.'

Pinette looked at him happily. Once again they had become almost contemporaries.

'You?'

'I have been on the wrong tack ever since the word "go".'

'It's easy,' said Pinette: 'you've only got to come along of me. We can wipe the slate clean and start again.'

Mathieu smiled: 'One can wipe the slate clean, but one can't begin again,' he said.

Pinette put his arm about his neck.

'Delarue, dear old pal,' he said passionately, 'come with me. It'll be lovely having you: I shan't know any of the other chaps.'

Mathieu hesitated. To die, to enter into the eternity of a life that was already dead ... to die together. . . . He shook his head.

'No.'

'Why not?'

'I don't want to.'

'Scared?'

'No, it just seems to me stupid, that's all.'

To cut one's own hand with a knife, to throw away one's wedding-ring, to shoot off a rifle at the Jerries – and so what? To smash and destroy – *that* wasn't liberty, but a mere acting on impulse. If only I could be *reasonable*.

'Why is it stupid?' asked Pinette irritably. 'I want to bring down a Jerry: what is there stupid about that?'

'You can bring down a hundred, but it won't alter the fact that the war has been lost.'

'I shall save my honour!'

'In whose eyes?'

Pinette walked on with lowered head, saying nothing.

'Even if they put up a monument to you, even if they laid your ashes under the Arc de Triomphe, would all that be worth the burning of a village?'

'Let it burn,' said Pinette: 'that's the fortune of war.'

'There are women and children in it.'

'They'll be safe enough if they run off into the fields.'

His face was like the face of an idiot: 'The sooner the better!'

Mathieu laid his hand on his shoulder: 'You love your wife as much as all that?'

'What's my wife got to do with it?'

'Isn't it for her you want to bring down your Jerries?'

'I'm sick of all the nonsense you talk!' shouted Pinette: 'if that's all education's done for you, I'm glad I never had any!'

They reached the first houses of the village. Suddenly, Mathieu started to shout in his turn.

'I'm fed up!' he cried: 'fed up! fed up!'

Pinette stopped and stared at him.

'What's biting you?'

'Nothing,' said Mathieu, dumbfounded at his own behaviour. 'I think I must be going mad.'

Pinette shrugged his shoulders.

'I want to look in at the school: the rifles are in the class-room.'

The door was open: they went in. Soldiers were sleeping on the tiled floor of the entry. Pinette took his torch from his pocket. A little circle of light showed on the wall.

'In there.'

Rifles were lying about in piles. Pinette took one of them, looked it over by the light of his torch, put it down and took another which he examined with care. Mathieu felt ashamed of the way he had yelled. The essential thing is to know how to wait, and to keep one's brain clear. Rushes of blood to the head settle nothing. He smiled at Pinette.

'You look as though you're choosing a cigar!'

Pinette, satisfied at last, slung one of the rifles across his shoulder.

'This'll do: let's get going.'

'Give me your torch,' said Mathieu. He shone the beam over the rifles. There was something tedious about the look of them, something administrative. They might have been so many typewriters. It was difficult to believe that one could kill a man with things like that. He bent down and took one at random.

'What are you doing?' asked Pinette with a look of surprise.

'Can't you see?' answered Mathieu: 'I'm choosing a rifle.'

'No!' said the woman, and slammed the door in his face. He stood there on the steps, his arms dangling, and the cowed look he had when he could no longer bully. 'Old witch!' he muttered – loud enough for me to hear, but not loud enough for her to hear, too. No, my poor Jacques, *not* 'old witch', anything else, but *not* that. Look down with those blue eyes of yours, look down between your feet, where Justice, that lovely masculine toy, lies shattered: come back to the car with that step of yours which is so infinitely eloquent of melancholy resignation. It's up to God to settle accounts with you, but you'll manage to come out on the right side at the Day of Judgement (he went back to the car with that step of his which was so infinitely eloquent of melancholy resignation). No, not 'old witch' – he should have found a different epithet – 'old trout', 'old cow', 'old so-and-so', but *not* 'old witch'. You envy *him* his knowledge of slang. No, *he* would have said nothing at all, and these people would have opened their doors to us, would have given us their bed, their linen, the very shirts off their backs. *He* would have sat down on the edge of the bed, with his great hand on the red counterpane, would have blushed and said: 'They take us for man and wife, Odette.' And I should have said nothing, and he would have gone on: 'I'll sleep on the floor,' and I should have said, 'Nonsense, it can't be helped; after all, a night's soon over, and what does it matter? We must sleep in the same bed. Oh do come, Jacques, do come! Seal up my eyes, crush my thoughts, be *the man in occupation*, lie heavy upon me, be exigent and possessive, don't leave me alone with him.'

He was coming now, descending the steps, so transparent, so *foreseeable*, that he was like a memory. You will sniff, with a lift of the right eyebrow; you will drum with your fingers on the bonnet, you will look me through and through – but it was *his* sniff, *his* lift of the eyebrows, *his* searching and pensive look. There he was, leaning over her, a drifting presence in the deep, animal darkness, so that it seemed to her that she could stroke him with her finger-tips. He was a drifting shade, unsubstantial, old, a thing of habit. I can see through him the vague, solid mass of the farmhouse, the road, the prowling dog. Everything is new, everything except him. He is not a husband at all, merely a general idea. I call to him, but he gives me no help. She smiled at him, because they must always smile at one another, offering him the gift of nature's sweet tranquillity, the confident optimism of a happy woman. But deep down, she was melting into the darkness, liquefying, merging into the vast femininity of the night where somewhere, somewhere in her heart, Mathieu lay concealed. He did not smile. He rubbed his nose with a gesture that he had borrowed from his brother. She gave a start. What have my thoughts been doing? I must have been dozing on my feet. It's too soon yet for me to be an old and cynical woman. I've been dreaming. The words sank back into the dark obscurity of her throat. All was forgotten. Nothing remained on the surface but a flow of shared and tranquil generalities. She asked her question cheerfully:

'Well?'

'Nothing doing: they say they haven't got a barn – but I saw it with my own eyes, over there, on the other side of the yard. I find it difficult to believe that I look like a highwayman!'

'After fourteen hours on the road,' she said, 'I don't suppose that we can be a very reassuring sight.'

He looked at her with careful scrutiny, and she felt her nose gleam like a lighthouse beneath his gaze. He's going to tell me that my nose is shiny.

He said: 'You've got pouches under your eyes, my poor darling: you must be all in.'

With a quick movement she took her compact from her bag, and examined herself mercilessly in the mirror. I look a perfect sight! In the light of the moon her face seemed as though covered with black splotches. I don't mind looking ugly, but I can't stand being dirty!

'What do we do now?' asked Jacques uncertainly. She had

181

taken out her powder-puff and was dabbing at cheeks and eyes.

'That's for you to say.'

'I was asking you.'

He caught at the hand that held the powder-puff, and held it imprisoned in his own with an air of smiling authority. I was asking you. You know perfectly well that if I told you what I thought, you wouldn't take the slightest notice of it. But he had to have other people's ideas to criticize. It was the only way in which he could find out what he was thinking himself. She said the first thing that came into her head.

'Let's drive on: perhaps we shall find a better welcome somewhere else.'

'No, thank you! Once is quite enough for me! How I hate peasants!' he said violently.

'Why shouldn't we drive all night?'

He stared at her.

'*All* night?'

'We could reach Grenoble tomorrow morning. The Bleriots would let us rest in their house. Then we could start off again in the afternoon and sleep at Castellane. We should be in Juan by the day after tomorrow.'

'Not on your life!'

Very seriously he added:

'I am *far* too tired. I should fall asleep at the wheel, and we should find ourselves in the ditch.'

'I could take a turn at driving.'

'Darling, the sooner you realize that I'll *never* let you drive at night, the better. With your short-sightedness, it would be sheer murder. The roads are packed with carts, lorries, and cars driven by people who have never handled a steering-wheel in their lives, and who just started off wildly, in a panic. No, you need a man's nerves for this kind of job!'

Shutters were flung open: a head appeared at a window.

'There be folk here trying to get some sleep,' shouted a rough voice. 'If so be you've got to talk, for God's sake do it somewhere else!'

'Many thanks, sir,' said Jacques in tones of biting irony: 'you are very polite, and have been *most* hospitable!'

He flung himself into the car, slammed the door, and started up the engine, making as much noise as possible. Odette looked at him out of the corner of her eye. Much better say nothing: he's doing fifty at the very least, without lights, because he's terrified of planes. Luckily the moon is full.

She was thrown against the door: 'What are you doing?'

Scarcely slowing down, he had wrenched the car round into a side-road. They drove on for a while: then he braked sharply and brought the car to a standstill, some distance up the road, under a clump of trees.

'We're going to sleep here.'

'Here?'

He said nothing, but opened the door and got out. She followed him. It was almost chilly.

'How about sleeping in the open?'

'No.'

She looked regretfully at the soft, dark grass, bent down and touched it as though it had been water.

'Oh, Jacques, it would be lovely out here. We could bring a cushion and rugs from the car.'

'No,' he repeated, and added with determination: 'we'll sleep in the car. There's no knowing who's prowling the roads in times like these.'

She watched him walking up and down, his hands in his pockets. His step was young and jaunty. The wind was playing a devil's tattoo in the trees, and his movement seemed compelled to keep time to it. The face he turned to her was old and worried: there was a shifty look in his eyes. Something was wrong. It was almost as though he were ashamed. He turned back towards the car. The youth and magic of the leafy music seemed to possess him, to have run into his feet, so that he moved with an air of gaiety. He hates sleeping in the car: whom is he punishing – himself or me? She felt guilty, though she did not know of what.

'Why are you pulling such a face?' he asked: 'Here we are, on the open road, headed for adventure. This ought to be just your cup of tea.'

She looked down: I never wanted to come away, Jacques: the Germans don't bother *me*. I wanted to stay in my own home. If the war lasts, we shall be separated from him: we shan't know whether he is alive or dead. What she actually said was:

'I am thinking of my brother, and of Mathieu.'

'At this moment,' said Jacques with a sour smile, 'Raoul is in bed at Carcassonne.'

'But Mathieu isn't . . .'

'You'd better get this into your head,' said Jacques with a flare of temper: 'my brother was posted to a second-line formation, and is, therefore, in no danger whatsoever. The worst that can happen to him is to be taken prisoner. In your eyes all soldiers are heroes, but that is where you are wrong, my dear. Mathieu is pushing a pen in some headquarters or other. He is having an easier time than if he were out of the battle-zone altogether, probably a good deal easier time than we're having at this precise moment – what the army calls a cushy job: and very glad I am, for his sake.'

'It's not much fun being a prisoner,' said Odette without raising her eyes.

He turned a solemn look on her. 'Don't put things into my mouth that I never said! Mathieu's fate causes me great deal of anxiety, but he is strong and he is resourceful. Oh yes he is, a great deal more resourceful than you think, for all his happy-go-lucky ways. I know him much better than you do. All that perpetual hesitation of his is largely put on – all part of the character he has built up for himself. I can just see him acting as secretary to a German officer, or doing a job as a cook . . . it would fit him like a glove!' – he smiled, and repeated with relish: 'A cook, yes, just the very thing for him! If you really want to know what I think' – he went on confidentially – 'it is this, that a spell in a prison-camp will give him some much-needed ballast. He'll come back a different man!'

'How long will it last?' asked Odette, her heart in her mouth.

'How should I know?'

With a self-satisfied wag of the head he added:

'But this I can tell you – the war, so far as I can see, can't possibly last very long. The next objective of the German Army will be England . . . and the Channel is not very wide.'

'But the English will put up a fight,' said Odette.

'To be sure they will,' he threw out his arms in a gesture of despondency, 'but whether we ought to want them to, or not, I really am not prepared to say.'

What ought we to want? What ought *I* to want? When the war started, it had all seemed so simple. What they ought to want, she had thought, was victory on the 1914 model. But nobody, apparently, had shared her views. She smiled cheerfully, as she remembered having seen her mother do when the Nivelle offensive was opened. She had never wearied of saying, 'Of *course* we shall win! That's what we've got to say to ourselves all the time, we just *can't not* win!' But she had hated herself for talking like that, because she loathed war, even when it was victorious. People had shaken their heads and said nothing. It was as though she had been guilty of a lack of tact. So she had given up talking about the war at all, had tried to make herself as little conspicuous as possible. She had heard a great deal of argument about Germany, England, and Russia, but had never really begun to understand what it was that people wanted. 'If only he were here, he would explain it all,' she thought. But he wasn't here: he didn't even write. In nine months he had sent Jacques only two letters. What does he think? He must know, he must understand. But what if he didn't? Suppose no one understood?

On a sudden impulse, she looked up. She longed to see in Jacques' face that expression of comfortable certainty which still had the power, at times, of calming her; longed to read in his face the assurance that everything would be all right, that there were solid reasons for hope of which she knew nothing. Hope of *what*? Was it true that an Allied victory could profit nobody but the Russians? She scrutinized his too familiar features, and saw him, suddenly, as someone new and strange – eyes darkened by anxiety, a mouth that still retained a hint of arrogance – though it was the sulky arrogance of a child caught doing what it ought not to do. 'Something is wrong: he doesn't feel comfortable.' Ever since they had left Paris he had seemed as though not quite himself – sometimes over-violent, sometimes over-gentle. How frightening it was when men produced that impression of being obsessed by a sense of guilt!

'I'm dying for a smoke!'

'Haven't you any cigarettes left?'

'No.'

'Here,' she said: 'I've got four.'

He made a face and took one suspiciously.

'Straw!' he said, and slipped the packet into his pocket. At the first puff, Odette smelled the fragrance of burning tobacco. The longing to smoke caught her by the throat. For a long time now, even after she had ceased to love him, she had liked to feel thirsty when he drank, hungry when he ate, drowsy when she saw him sleeping. Such feelings were, in some sort, reassuring. It was as though he laid hold of her desires, and sanctified them in a fashion more virile, more moral, more definite than her own, so that she derived a certain vicarious satisfaction from what he did. But now . . .

She laughed softly: 'Give me just one.'

He looked at her as though he did not understand what she meant, then raised his eyebrows.

'Sorry, my poor darling: that was a purely automatic reflex on my part!' He took the cigarettes from his pocket.

'You can keep the packet,' she said: 'I only want one.'

They smoked in silence. She was afraid of herself, remembering the violent, irresistible desires that had swept her off her feet when she was a young girl. Perhaps that was all going to start over again. He coughed two or three times to clear his throat. *There is something he wants to say to me, but he's taking his time, as usual.* She went on patiently smoking. *He will approach his subject like a crab, sideways.* He was sitting very straight and upright. There was severity in the look he turned on her.

'Well, my dear –' he said.

She smiled at him vaguely – it seemed to be the only thing to do. He laid his hand on her shoulder.

'This is a pretty kettle of fish.'

'Yes,' she said, 'it certainly is.'

His eyes were still fixed on her. He crushed out his cigarette against the running-board of the car, and put his foot on it. Then, he moved closer to her, and when he next spoke it was with a vehemence that seemed designed to overcome some possible resistance.

'We should be running *absolutely no risk*.'

She made no reply, and he went on. His voice was quiet but insistent.

'I feel quite sure that the Germans will be on their best behaviour. They'll be *particularly careful* about that.'

It was just as she had always thought. She could read in his eyes the answer he wanted her to make.

She said: 'But one can never be quite sure, can one? Suppose they burned Paris to the ground and put everyone to the sword?'

He shrugged: 'Why should they? – how like a woman to suggest such a thing!'

He leaned close to her, and began patiently to explain.

'Listen to me, Odette, and try to understand. Once the armistice is signed, Berlin will quite certainly want France to take her place as one of the partners in the Axis. It may even be counting on our prestige in America to keep the United States out of the war. Do you see my point? We may be beaten, but we've still got a card up our sleeve. It may even be that our political bigwigs' – he gave a low chuckle – 'have an important part to play in the councils of Europe – provided, that is, they can rise to the occasion. Well, in view of all that, it is quite incredible that the Germans should run the risk of unifying French opinion against them by a display of useless violence.'

'I quite agree,' she said: but her nerves were on edge.

'Ah!'

He looked at her, and bit his lip. He seemed to be so thoroughly put out, that she added hastily: 'Still, one can never be sure, can one? Suppose they're fired on from windows?'

Jacques's eyes flashed.

'Had there been any danger I should have stayed. It was only because I was quite convinced there was none that I resigned myself to the idea of leaving.'

She remembered how he had come into the drawing-room; his quiet, tense manner; the way in which his hand had trembled when he lit a cigarette; the deliberate way in which he had said: 'Pack your things, Odette. I've got the car downstairs, and we're leaving in half an hour.' What was he getting at now? She did not at all like the sound of his voice.

'It might,' he said, as though closing the subject, 'have looked rather like abandoning one's post.'

'But you hadn't got a post.'

'I was in charge of our block of flats,' he said, and waved away any possible objection on her part. 'It may sound silly, and I took on the job only because Champenois asked me to. All the same, even in that *restricted field*, I might have been useful. Besides, we ought to set an example.'

The look she gave him was utterly devoid of sympathy. Yes, yes, yes, of course you ought to have stayed on in Paris, and if you think I'm going to say you oughtn't, you're very much mistaken.

He sighed: 'Well, no use crying over spilt milk. Life would be too easy if one were never confronted by a clash of loyalties. But I'm afraid I'm boring you, darling. These are masculine scruples.'

'But I think I can understand them.'

'Naturally, my dear, naturally.' There was something lonely, something virile, in the smile to which he treated her. He took her wrist in his fingers. A note of reassurance came into his voice. 'Nothing very much could happen to me: at the very worst, they might send all men of military age to Germany. Well, what of it? Mathieu is in the same boat – though, true, he hasn't got this cursed heart of mine – remember when that damn' fool of an M.O. turned me down?'

'Yes.'

'How wild I was! I'd have done anything to get taken on. Don't you remember how angry I was?'

'Yes.'

He sat down on the running-board of the car, rested his chin on his hands, and stared straight in front of him.

'Charvoz stayed,' he said, not shifting his gaze.

'Really?'

'Yes, I ran into him this morning, at the garage. He looked surprised when I told him we were going.'

'It's rather different for him,' she said automatically.

'That's true,' he said, bitterly: 'He's a bachelor.'

Odette was standing beside him, on his left. She could see the glint of his scalp through the thinning hair. So that's it! she thought.

His eyes were unfocused.

'There was no one I could have trusted to look after you,' he muttered.

She stiffened.

'What?'

'I said there was no one I could have trusted to look after you. I didn't dare to let you go off to your aunt alone.'

'Are you trying to tell me,' she said – and her voice was trembling – 'that you left Paris on my account?'

'It was a case of conscience,' he replied. He looked at her affectionately.

'You'd been so nervous all those last few days. I was frightened about you.'

Amazement kept her silent. Why had he got to say that? Why did he feel obliged to say that?

He went on with a sort of gaiety of manner. 'You kept the shutters closed; we lived all day long in darkened rooms: you began hoarding food: there were tins of sardines all over the place, and I think you were worried about Lucienne. You weren't the same after she left. She was frightened out of her wits, besides being as gullible as you make 'em, only too ready to believe stories of rape and atrocities.'

I won't say what he wants me to say, I won't! What is there left for me if I despise him? She took a step backward. He fixed a steely glare on her. It was as though he were saying – 'Out with it! come on, out with it!' Once more, beneath that eagle stare, beneath her husband's scrutiny, she felt guilty. Perhaps he *did* think I wanted to go: perhaps I *did* seem frightened: perhaps I *was* frightened without knowing it. What is the truth? Up till now it has always been what Jacques said: if I stop believing in him, in whom *can* I believe?

She looked away: 'I didn't want to stay on in Paris.'

'You were frightened, weren't you?' he asked in a tone of kindly indulgence.

'Yes,' she said, 'I was frightened.'

When she looked at him again he was smiling.

'Well, not much harm's been done,' he said. 'A night under the stars – not, perhaps, quite suited to our time of life, but we're still young enough to find it rather attractive.' He stroked the back of her neck. 'Remember Hyères, in '36? We slept in the tent – one of the happiest memories of my life.'

She said nothing. She had gripped the handle of the door, and

189

was clinging to it with all her strength. He choked back a yawn.

'It's terribly late: how about going to bed?'

She nodded assent. Somewhere a night-bird called and Jacques laughed.

'Nothing if not rural!!' he said. 'You lie on the floor of the car,' he added in a tone of affectionate concern: 'like that, you'll be able to stretch out your legs. I'll sleep in the driving seat.'

They got back into the car. He locked the right-hand door, and pushed the catch on the other.

'You all right?'

'Yes, perfectly all right.'

He took out his revolver and examined it with amusement.

'This is a situation that would have delighted my old pirate of a grandfather,' he said, adding gaily – 'There's something of the bold sea-rover in all the members of my family!'

She remained silent. He turned in his seat and touched her chin.

'Give me a kiss, darling.'

She felt his warm, open mouth pressing against her own. He just touched her lips with his tongue, as in the old days, and she shuddered. At the same moment she felt his hand creeping under her arm and caressing her breast.

'My poor Odette!' he said tenderly: 'poor little girl, you poor darling child.'

She flung herself back: 'I'm simply dropping with sleep!'

'Good night, sweetheart,' he said with a smile.

He turned round, folded his arms on the wheel, and dropped his head on his hands. She remained seated, rigid, filled with a sense of oppression, watching him. Two deep breaths: not yet. He was still fidgeting. She could think of nothing while he sat there still wakeful, with that picture of her in his mind. I've never been able to think while he was close to me. Ah, now he's off! He had uttered his three familiar grunts. She relaxed slightly. He's no better than an animal. He was sleeping. The war was sleeping. The whole world of men was sleeping, engulfed in that head of his. Upright in the darkness, with the chalky patches of the two windows on either hand, deep in a pool of moonlight, Odette kept her vigil. A memory came back to her from the distant past. I was running along a little pinkish road: I was twelve: I stopped, my heart beating with a sense of uneasy happiness: I said out loud – 'I am indispensable.' She repeated the words, 'I am indispensable' – but indispensable for what, she did not know. She tried to think about the war, and it seemed to her that she was just on the point of discovering the truth: 'Is it a fact that victory will profit nobody but the Russians?' Suddenly she gave up the attempt. Her joy was turned to a feeling of disgust. I don't know enough about it!

She wanted to smoke. I don't *really* want to: it's just nerves. The desire grew and grew, distending her breasts, peremptory and conquering, as in the days of her uncontrolled girlhood. He put the packet in his coat. Why should he smoke? In his mouth the taste of tobacco must be so terribly boring, so terribly ordinary. Why should he smoke rather than I? She leaned over him. He was breathing regularly. She slipped her hand into his pocket, and took out the cigarettes. Then, very quietly, she pushed back the catch of the door, and slipped out of the car. The moon seen through the leaves, and puddles of moonlight on the road, the freshness of the night air, the cry of a night-bird – all these things are *mine*. She lit a cigarette. The war is asleep, Berlin is asleep, Moscow, Churchill, the Politburo, our statesmen, all are asleep – the whole world is asleep. There is no one to see *my* night: I am indispensable. Those tins of food were for my adopted soldier-boys. It was suddenly borne in on her that she loathed the taste of tobacco. She took two more pulls at her cigarette, then threw it away. She could not think why she had wanted to smoke. The leaves rustled softly, the countryside creaked like a floor; the stars were wild animals. She felt frightened. He was sleeping, and she had rediscovered the mysterious world of her childhood, a forest of questions to which there was no answer. It was he who knew the names of the stars, the exact distance of the earth from the moon, the number of persons living in this part of France, their history, their employments. He is asleep; I despise him, and I know nothing about anything. She felt lost in a world of which she could make no use, in a world created to be *seen* and *touched*. She ran back to the car. She wanted to wake him, now, at once; to wake Science, Industry, and the Moral Code. She touched the handle, she leaned on the door, and saw, through the glass, a large open mouth.

What's the use? – she said to herself. She sat down on the running-board, and began to think, as she did every night, of Mathieu.

The lieutenant ran up the dark stairs. Mathieu and Pinette twisted at his heels. He stopped in the pitch darkness, pushed open a trap-door with the back of his neck, and they were dazzled by a silvery radiance.

'Follow me!'

They jumped into a cold bright sky that was full of memories and faint sounds.

'Who goes there!'

'It's me' – said the lieutenant.

' 'Shun!'

'At ease!'

They were on a square platform at the top of the church tower. It had a roof supported on four pillars, one at each corner. Between the pillars ran a stone parapet about three foot high. All about them was sky. The moon cast the shadow of one of the pillars on the floor.

'Everything all right here?' asked the lieutenant.

'All correct, sir.'

Three men stood facing him. All of them were tall and thin. All of them had rifles. Mathieu and Pinette felt shy and kept well behind him.

'Do we hang on here, sir?' asked one of the Chasseurs.

'Yes,' said the lieutenant, adding: 'I've got Closson and four of his chaps in the Mairie: the rest will be with me in the schools. Dreyer will be responsible for keeping contact.'

'What are our orders, sir?'

'Open fire at discretion: you can use up every scrap of ammo.'

'What's that, sir?'

The sound of muffled voices and shuffling feet came up to them from the street. The lieutenant smiled:

'Our friends of the Headquarters Staff. I've had to put them in the cellar over at the Mairie. They'll be a bit pushed for room, but it's only for one night. The Boches will take delivery when they've finished with us.'

Mathieu looked at the contingent of Chasseurs. He felt

ashamed for his companions. Not a flicker showed on any of the three faces.

'Listen,' said the lieutenant: 'at twenty-three o'clock the inhabitants of the village will assemble in the square. Don't fire on 'em. I am sending them off to spend the night in the woods. Once they're out of the way, open fire on anyone who crosses the street. And don't leave the church on any pretext whatever. If you do, we shall fire on you.'

He moved towards the trap-door. The Chasseurs looked Mathieu and Pinette up and down in silence.

'Sir,' said Mathieu.

The lieutenant turned round.

'I'd quite forgotten you. These chaps want to be in on the show. They've got rifles, and I've issued them with ammo. Do what you can with 'em. If their shooting's too bad, you'd better share out their ammo among yourselves.'

There was friendliness in the way he looked at his men.

'Good-bye, boys,' he said.

'Good-bye, sir,' they answered politely.

For a brief moment he seemed to hesitate, then, with a shake of the head, moved backwards down the first few steps, and let the trap fall. The three men on the roof looked at Mathieu and Pinette. Their eyes expressed neither fellow-feeling nor curiosity. Mathieu took two steps backwards and leaned against a pillar. His rifle embarrassed him: either he handled it with excessive unconcern, or else he held it like a candle. Finally, with great care, he laid it on the ground. Pinette joined him. Both of them were standing with their backs to the moon. The three Chasseurs, on the other hand, were full in its eye. The same black stubble stained all their chalky faces, and all of them had the same fixed stare of night-birds.

'Rather like a social call, isn't it?' said Pinette.

Mathieu smiled. The other three did not smile at all. Pinette went close to Mathieu and whispered in his ear:

'Don't seem to care for us much.'

'That's about the ticket!'

They felt too much embarrassed to say more. Mathieu leaned over the parapet and saw beneath him the dark, billowy foliage of the chestnuts.

'I'm going to have a word with 'em,' said Pinette.

'Much better not.'

But Pinette was already strolling across to the others.

'My name's Pinette, this bloke here's Delarue.'

He stopped and waited. The biggest of the three nodded, but furnished no information about himself or his companions. Pinette cleared his throat.

'We've come along to see a bit of fighting,' he said.

Still no reply. The tall, fair fellow scowled and turned away. Pinette seemed to be put out, and hesitated.

'What you want us to do?'

The tall, fair fellow was leaning with his back to the wall. He yawned. Mathieu noticed that he was a corporal.

'What you want us to do?' asked Pinette again.

'Nothing.'

'What you mean – nothing.'

'Nothing for the moment.'

'How about later on?'

'You'll be told.'

Mathieu smiled at them. 'Find it a bit of a bore having us here with you, eh? Rather be alone?'

The tall, fair man looked at him thoughtfully: then he turned to Pinette.

'What's your line?'

'Railwayman – Métro.'

The corporal gave vent to a bark of laughter. But there was no sign of amusement in his eyes.

'Think you're still a civvy – just you wait a bit!'

'Oh, you mean in the army?'

'Yes.'

'Observer.'

'And your pal?'

'Telephonist.'

'Second-line troops?'

'Yes.'

The corporal studied him attentively as though he found some difficulty in bringing his mind to bear on the problem.

'What's wrong with you? – you look hefty enough.'

'Bad heart.'

'Ever drawn a bead on a man?'

'Never,' said Mathieu.

The corporal turned to his companions. All three shook their heads.

'We'll do our best,' said Pinette in a tight little voice.

There was a long silence. The corporal looked at them and scratched his head. At last he heaved a sigh and seemed to have made up his mind.

'My name's Clapot, it's me as gives orders: the others are Chasseriau and Dandieu. Just you do what they tell you. We've been in action for a fortnight, and we've pretty well got the hang of it.'

'A fortnight?' said Pinette incredulously: 'How did that happen?'

'We were covering your retreat.'

Pinette blushed and hung his head. Mathieu felt his jaws contract. Clapot proceeded to explain in a more conciliatory tone:

'Delaying action.'

They looked at one another, but not a word more was said. Mathieu felt ill at ease. He thought: 'We shall never be one of them. They've been fighting for fifteen days on end, while we've been scuttling along the roads. Be a bit too easy if we joined up just in time for the peace celebrations. They'll never accept us, never. Our chaps are down there in the cellar, wallowing in filth and shame. Our place is at their side, and we've abandoned them at the last moment from motives of simple personal pride.' He leaned over. He could see the black houses, the glittering ribbon of the road. 'My place is down there,' and he knew in his heart that he would never again be able to go down from the tower.

Pinette was sitting astride the parapet, probably just to keep his spirits up.

'Get down off there!' said Clapot. 'You'll give our position away!'

'The Germans are a long way off.'

'What d'you know about it? Get down, d'you hear me?'

Pinette jumped down on to the roof with a bad grace, and Mathieu thought: 'They'll never accept us.' Pinette was getting on his nerves – continually moving about and talking when he'd much better have kept in the background, not opened his big mouth, and let the others forget all about him. He gave a jump. An enormous explosion, muffled and heavy, had gone off close to his ear. There was a second and a third: a brazen racket: the roof quivered under his feet. Pinette laughed nervously.

'No need to get the wind up: that's the clock, that is!'

Mathieu stole a glance at the Chasseurs, and noticed with satisfaction that they too had jumped.

'Twenty-three o'clock,' said Pinette.

Mathieu shivered. He was cold, but the feeling was not unpleasant. He was high up in the sky, above the roof-tops, and above the men in the village: he felt cold and it was dark. 'No, I shall never go down again: wouldn't go down for anything in the world!'

'There's the civilians starting off.'

They were all leaning over the parapet. He could see through the leaves a number of black animals moving about. It was as though he were looking down into the bottom of the sea. In the main street doors were being opened noiselessly. Women and children were creeping out. Most of them carried bundles or suit-cases. Small groups were forming in the roadway. They appeared to be waiting for something. Then they melted together into a single procession, which moved off slowly in a southerly direction.

'Like a funeral,' said Pinette.

'Poor devils,' said Mathieu.

'Don't you worry your heads about them,' said Dandieu with dry unconcern. 'They'll find their shacks waiting for 'em when they get back. The Germans don't often burn down whole villages.'

'How about that?' – and Mathieu nodded towards Roberville.

'That was different. It wasn't only us as fired on 'em: the inhabitants joined in.'

Pinette started to laugh.

'Not at all like here – the sods are too damn' frightened!'

Dandieu looked at him.

'You've not been fighting. Still, civilians didn't oughter set the ball rolling.'

'And whose fault was that?' asked Pinette in a fury: 'Whose fault was it we didn't fight?'

'Search me!'

'It was the officers' fault: it's the officers have lost the war!'

'Don't you go talkin' against the officers,' said Clapot: 'you've no call to do that!'

'And why not?'

'Not afore us, you haven't,' went on Clapot with determination: 'because you can take it from me that apart from one lieutenant – nor it wasn't his fault neither – all the rest stuck by us.'

Pinette tried to explain. He waved his arms at Clapot, then dropped them to his side.

'It's no good; we shan't never understand each other,' he said dejectedly.

Chasseriau looked inquiringly at him:

'What you come here for?'

'I told you: we come to do a bit of fighting.'

'But why? – you didn't have to?'

Pinette laughed in a foolish sort of way:

'Oh, I don't know – for a bit of fun, I suppose.'

'You'll get your fun all right,' said Clapot unsympathetically: 'I give you *my* word!'

Dandieu broke into a pitying laugh:

'Hear that? Popped in ter see us for a bit o' fun – just to see what scrapping's like. Wanted to score up a nice little target, like at the pigeons: an' they weren't even forced to!'

'And who forced you, you chump?' asked Pinette.

'Us? – that's different: we're Chasseurs.'

'What of it?'

'If you belong to the Chasseurs, you fight.'

He shook his head:

'If it warn't for that – you talks as how I was out to shoot men just for the fun of it.'

Chasseriau was looking at Pinette with mingled surprise and repulsion:

'Haven't you got it into your thick head that you're risking your skin?'

Pinette's only reply was a shrug.

'Because, if you have,' went on Chasseriau, 'you're an even bigger fool that I took you for. It don't make sense to risk one's skin if one isn't forced to.'

'We were forced to, all right,' said Mathieu suddenly: 'don't make any mistake about that. We were fed up, and we didn't know what to do.'

He pointed down at the schools:

'For us it was either the church tower or the cellar.'

Dandieu seemed to be impressed. Some of the harshness went out of his expression.

Mathieu pursued his advantage: 'What would you have done in our place?'

They none of them said anything. He pressed his point.

'What would you have done?'

Dandieu shook his head:

'I might have chosen the cellar: fighting's not much catch. Wait till you've had some.'

'Perhaps not,' said Mathieu: 'but it's not much catch either being cooped up in a cellar when others are fighting.'

'Don't suppose it is,' said Chasseriau.

Dandieu had to admit the force of this argument. 'Can't feel very proud of oneself I sh'd say.'

They seemed less hostile now. Clapot looked at Pinette with an air of surprise, then turned away and went over to the parapet. The expression of feverish hardness had gone: his face showed a certain vague gentleness. He stared out into the mild darkness, at the childlike and legendary countryside. Mathieu was hard put to it to determine whether the mildness of the night was reflected in his face, or whether the loneliness of his face was reflected in the night.

'Hi, Clapot!' said Dandieu.

Clapot straightened up. He was once more the alert specialist. 'What's up?'

'I'm going to have a nose round down there: think I saw something.'

'Righto!'

Just as Dandieu lifted the trap a woman's voice came up to them from below:

'Henri! Henri!'

Mathieu leaned out over the street. A few laggards were scuttling about aimlessly like frightened ants. He could see, close to the post office, a small patch of shadow.

'Henri!'

The expression of Pinette's face darkened, but he said nothing. Some women had taken the post office girl by the arm and were trying to lead her away. She was struggling with them and shouting:

'Henri! Henri!'

She broke free, rushed into the post office and shut the door.

'A pretty muck-up!' whispered Pinette.

He scraped the stone of the parapet with his nails.

'She ought to have gone with the others.'

'Certainly she ought,' said Mathieu.

'Get herself into trouble, that's what she'll do!'

'And whose fault will that be?'

There was no reply. The lid of the trap-door rose.

'Gimme a hand!'

They pulled the lid back and laid it flat on the roof. Dandieu emerged from the darkness. He was carrying two straw mattresses on his back.

'See what I've found!'

Clapot smiled for the first time. He seemed overjoyed.

'That's a bit o' luck,' he said.

'What are you going to do with those?' asked Mathieu.

Clapot looked at him with surprise:

'What you think one usually uses mattresses for – stringing beads?'

'Do you mean to say you're going to sleep?'

'We're going to have a bit of grub first,' said Chasseriau.

Mathieu watched them busying themselves round the mattresses, taking tins of bully from their haversacks.

'Don't they realize they're going to be killed?'

Chasseriau had discovered a tin-opener. He opened three tins with quick, precise movements. Then they all sat down and took their jack-knives from their pockets.

Clapot glanced at Mathieu over his shoulder.

'You two hungry?' he asked.

It was two days since Mathieu had last eaten. His mouth was filled with saliva.

'Not me,' he said.

'How about your pal?'

199

Pinette made no reply. He was leaning over the parapet, and his eyes were fixed on the post office.

'Come along and have some grub,' said Clapot: 'plenty for all.'

'Chaps as does the fighting's got a right to eat,' said Chasseriau.

Dandieu rooted about in his haversack and produced two tins which he offered to Mathieu. Mathieu took them and tapped Pinette on the shoulder. Pinette gave a start.

'What's up?'

'This is for you: eat.'

Mathieu took the tin-opener which Dandieu gave him. He applied it to the edge of the tin and pressed hard, but the blade slipped on the metal without penetrating it, jumped out of the groove, and struck his left thumb.

'Clumsy!' said Pinette: 'hurt yerself?'

'No,' said Mathieu.

'Come on, give it here!'

Pinette opened the two tins, and they ate in silence, standing close to one of the pillars. They were too shy to sit down. They dug into the meat with their knives, and pecked the pieces off the points. Mathieu munched conscientiously, but his throat felt paralysed. He could taste nothing, and found it difficult to swallow. Seated on the mattresses, the three Chasseurs were busy concentrating on the food. Their knives gleamed in the moonlight.

'To think,' said Chasseriau dreamily, 'we should be eating in the belfry of a church.'

In the belfry of a church. Mathieu looked down. Under their feet was the fragrance of spices and incense, coolness, and the stained-glass windows feebly shining in the shadows of the Faith. Under their feet was confidence and hope. He felt cold. He looked at the sky, breathed the sky, thought with the sky. He was naked on a glacier at a great height. Far below him lay his childhood.

Clapot had thrown his head back. His eyes were on the sky as he ate.

'Look at the moon,' he said in a low voice.

'What's that?' said Chasseriau.

200

'The moon: isn't it bigger than usual?'

'No.'

'Ah, I thought it was.'

Suddenly he lowered his eyes.

'Hey, you two, come and eat with us: don't stand about there!'

Mathieu and Pinette both hesitated.

'Come along!' said Clapot.

'Let's go,' said Mathieu to Pinette.

They sat down. Mathieu could feel Clapot's warmth against his leg. This was their last meal, and it was sacred.

'We got some rum,' said Dandieu. 'Not much, just enough for a spot all round.'

He passed his canteen. Each man put his lips where the last had drunk. Pinette leaned over to Mathieu.

'I rather think as how they've adopted us.'

'So do I.'

'They're not bad blokes: I like 'em.'

'Me too.'

Pinette straightened up with sudden pride. His eyes were shining.

'We should'a been like 'em if we'd bin told what ter do!'

Mathieu looked at the three faces and nodded his head.

'Aren't I right?'

'Perhaps.'

For the last few moments Pinette had been looking at Mathieu's hand. There was a ragged gash in the left thumb.

'That must have been the tin-opener.'

'An' you let it bleed, fathead?'

'I didn't feel anything.'

Pinette was delighted. 'What'd you do,' he grumbled, 'if I warn't here?'

Mathieu looked at his thumb. The fact that he had a body filled him with surprise. He was conscious of nothing – not of the taste of food, not of the sting of alcohol, not of the pain in his hand. It's as though I were made of ice. He laughed.

'Once at a night-club, I had a knife . . .'

He broke off. Pinette was looking at him with an expression of surprise.

'Go on.'

'Oh, nothing. I'm unlucky with sharp instruments.'

'Give me your hand,' said Clapot.

He had taken a roll of gauze and a blue bottle from his pack. He poured some of the burning liquid on Mathieu's thumb and bound it up. It looked like a doll. Mathieu smiled at it. All this trouble to prevent blood from flowing *too soon*!

'That's better,' said Clapot.

'Much better,' said Mathieu.

Clapot looked at his watch:

'Turn in, lads ... close on midnight.'

They bunched round him.

'Dandieu,' he said, with a jerk of the thumb at Mathieu: 'he'll be with you on guard.'

'Righto!'

Chasseriau, Pinette, and Clapot lay down side by side on the mattresses. Dandieu took a blanket from his pack and laid it over the three of them. Pinette stretched luxuriously, winked roguishly at Mathieu, and closed his eyes.

'I'm going over there,' said Dandieu: 'you stay where you are. If you hear any movement don't do a thing without telling me first.'

Mathieu settled down in his corner and raked the countryside with his eyes. It occurred to him that he was going to die, and the idea of such a thing appealed to him as being highly comic. He looked at the dark roofs, the mild, phosphorescent gleam of the road between the blue trees, at all the sumptuous, uninhabitable land, and he thought: 'I am going to die for nothing.' A faint sound of snoring made him start. The lads were already asleep. Clapot, his eyes shut, looked younger. He was smiling happily. Pinette, too, was smiling. Mathieu bent over him and looked down at his face. He thought: 'What a shame!' Dandieu, at the other end of the platform, was leaning forward, his hands on his thighs in the attitude of a goal-keeper.

'Hi!' said Mathieu in a low voice.

'Hi!'

'Footballer, aren't you?'

Dandieu turned towards him in surprise.

'How did you know?'

'It's obvious.' He added: 'Were you good?'

'With a bit of luck I might have been a pro.'

They exchanged a wave of greeting, and Mathieu went back to his post. He thought: 'I am going to die for nothing', and he was filled with self-pity. For a brief moment memories rustled about him like leaves in the breeze: *all* his memories: I was in love with life. An uneasy question stirred at the back of his mind. Had I any right to abandon my pals? Have I any right to die for nothing? He stood up and rested his hands on the parapet. He shook his head angrily. I'm fed up: the chaps down there can think what they like, the world can think what it likes. I'm through with remorse, with hesitations, with mental reservations. No one has the right to judge me; no one is thinking about me; no one will remember me; no one can make up my mind for me. He had reached a decision without remorse, with full knowledge of the facts. He had made up his mind, and, on the instant, his scrupulous, his sensitive heart went tumbling down through the branches. No more sentiment for him! that was over now. Here and now I have decided that death has all along been the secret of my life, that I have lived for the sole purpose of dying. I die in order to demonstrate the impossibility of living. My eyes will put an extinguisher upon the earth and shut it down for ever. The earth raised its topsy-turvy face to the dying man: the foundering sky swept across him with all its stars. But Mathieu kept watch without so much as deigning to pick up these useless gifts.

Tuesday, 18 June. 5.45 a.m.

'LOLA!'

She awoke, as she always did, with a sense of loathing, and, as she always did, crept back into the leavings of her rotten flesh.

'Lola! are you asleep?'

'No,' she said: 'what's the time?'

'Five-forty-five.'

'Five-forty-five? – and my little tough guy's awake, is he? That's something new for a change.'

'Come to me,' he said.

No, she thought; I don't want him to touch me.

'Boris . . .'

My body disgusts me even if it doesn't disgust you! it's a swindle, it's rotten – and you don't know it. If you did know, it would fill you with horror.

But already he had taken her by the shoulders; he was heavy upon her. It is *through a wound* that you will enter me. When he used to touch me in the old days, I became like velvet: now, my body is like dried earth: I crack and crumble under his fingers. He's tickling me. He rent her to the very roots of her belly, he was moving in her belly like a knife. On his face was a look of loneliness, of morbid concentration. She saw him as an insect, as a fly climbing up a window-pane climbing, falling, climbing again. She was conscious only of the pain he was causing her. He was panting, sweating. He achieved his orgasm. It is in my blood that he is spending himself, in all that is evil in me. She thought: 'Christ! he hasn't had a woman for six months: he's making love like a soldier in a brothel.' Something moved in her, a fluttering of wings: no, it was nothing. He clasped her to him, nothing about her moved except her breasts. With a little impulsive movement he separated himself from her, and her breasts made a sound like rubber suckers suddenly detached. She felt a wish to laugh, but one glance at his face killed the wish in her. His expression was hard and tense. He kissed her with the determination of a man intent on getting drunk. There is something he wants to forget. Finally, he fell upon her like one half-dead. Automatically she stroked his hair, the back of his neck. She felt cold and at peace, but she was conscious of something like the thundering of a bell that rose in her from belly to breast. It was Boris's heart beating within her. I am too old, much too old. These antics seemed grotesque to her. Gently she pushed him from her.

'Get off me.'

'What?' He had raised his head and was looking at her in surprise.

'It's my heart,' she said: 'it's beating too hard, and you're suffocating me.'

With a smile he stretched himself beside her, and lay there on his stomach, his face in the pillow, his eyes shut, and a comic little pucker at the corner of his mouth. She propped herself on her elbow and looked at him. So used to the sight was she, so much a habit had he become, that she could no longer see him any more than she could *see* her own hand. I felt nothing. And yesterday, when he came into the courtyard, looking as pretty as a girl, I felt nothing, nothing at all, not even the old feverish dryness in my throat, not even the old bushy heaviness at the pit of my stomach.

She gazed at the too familiar face. She thought: 'I am alone.' How often she had taken that little head in her hands and pressed it, that little head which had secreted so many sly thoughts. In those days she had fought, questioned, begged, so eager was she to open it like a pomegranate and lick out the contents. Then, at last, the secret had emerged, and, as in a pomegranate, had turned out to be no more than a few drops of sugary liquid. There was rancour in her gaze. She was angry with him for failing to stir her deeply. She looked at the bitter lines about his mouth. If he lost his gaiety of heart what would there be left? Boris opened his eyes and smiled at her.

'It's comic how happy I am just to have you here, old girl.'

She returned his smile. Now it's I who have a secret, and you can try till you're black in the face to get it out of me! He sat up, drew back the sheet, and studied Lola's body attentively. Lightly with his hand he brushed her nipples. She felt embarrassed.

'Just a marble statue,' he said.

She thought of the unclean beast that was proliferating in the fastness of her body, and the blood rushed to her face.

'I'm proud of you,' said Boris.

'Why?'

'Because you didn't give a damn for the chaps up at the hospital!'

Lola gave a suppressed chuckle:

'Didn't they wonder what you could see in an old bag of bones like me? Didn't they take me for your mother?'

'Lola,' said Boris reproachfully. Then he laughed, moved by some memory, and, for a moment, looked young again.

'What are you laughing at?'

'I was thinking of Francillon. His girl's a loose little fish, though she *is* only eighteen, and he said to me – I wouldn't mind doing a swap with you!'

'That was very polite of him,' said Lola.

A thought drifted like a cloud across Boris's face, and his eyes darkened. She looked at him, but there was no friendliness in her look. You've got your little troubles like everyone else. If I told you mine, what would you do? What would you do if I said: 'I've got a tumour of the womb: I've got to have an operation, and at my age that's sometimes dangerous'? You'd open those great tart's eyes of yours, and you'd say: 'It's not true! it can't be!' 'Yes it is,' I'd reply, and you'd say it wasn't possible, that things of that kind could perfectly easily be put right with drugs and ray-treatment, that I was exaggerating. Then I'd say: 'It wasn't to get my money that I went back to Paris, but to see Le Goupil, and he was quite definite.' You'd tell me that Le Goupil is a fool, that he's the last person in the world I ought to have consulted. You'd protest and deny, you'd dart your head this way and that like a trapped animal, and then at last, when you were cornered, you'd stop talking, and you'd look at me tragically, resentfully.

She raised her bare arm and took hold of Boris by the hair.

'Lie down, my little roughneck, and tell me what's the matter.'

'Nothing's the matter' – but his face belied his words.

'That's odd: it's not your way to wake up at five o'clock in the morning.'

He said again, but without conviction: 'Nothing's the matter.'

'I see how it is,' she said: 'you've got something to tell me but you want me to drag it out of you like a midwife.'

He smiled and laid his head on her breast, just below the shoulder. He took a deep breath, and said:

'How good you smell.'

She gave a shrug.

'Are you going to talk, or aren't you?'

He shook his head; it was as though he was terrorized. She said no more, but lay there on her back. All right, don't talk. It doesn't matter to me. He speaks to me and kisses me, but when I come to die I shall be alone. She heard Boris heave a sigh, and turned her face towards him. He had a sad, set expression on his face, an expression she had never seen before. She thought, without enthusiasm: 'Now, I suppose, I've got to start worrying about you!' She would have to question him, spy on him, draw conclusions from the way he looked, as in the old days of her jealousy, work away at him until at last he told her what he had been dying to tell her all along. She sat up.

'Give me my dressing-gown and a cigarette.'

'Why a dressing-gown? you're nicer as you are.'

'Give me my dressing-gown; I'm cold.'

He got up, brown and naked. She looked away. He took the dressing-gown from the foot of the bed and held it out to her. She slipped it on. After a moment's hesitation, he put on his trousers and sat down on a chair.

'You've found some pure young girl, and want to marry her, is that it?' she asked.

He looked so completely dumbfounded that she blushed.

'All right, I'm wrong,' she said.

There was a brief silence before she went on:

'What are you going to do when they discharge you?'

'I'm going to marry you.'

She took a cigarette and lit it.

'Why?' she asked.

'I've got to be respectable. I can't take you with me to Castelnaudary unless you are my wife.'

'What the hell are you going to do at Castelnaudary?'

'Earn my living,' he said severely. 'No, I'm not pulling your leg: I'm going to turn schoolmaster.'

'But why at Castelnaudary?'

'You'll learn soon enough. Castelnaudary it's got to be.'

'Are you trying to tell me that I shall be addressed as Madame Serguine; that I shall have to dress up and call on the headmaster's wife?'

'They call him the Principal there,' said Boris. 'Yes, that is precisely what you will have to do. And at the end of the school year, I shall have to make a speech at prize-giving.'

'Hm!' said Lola.

'Ivich'll come and live with us,' said Boris.

'But she can't stand me!'

'Perhaps not, but that is how it's going to be.'

'Does she want to?'

'Yes, she can't stick living with her in-laws. It's sending her crackers: you'd hardly recognize her.'

Silence. She watched him out of the corner of her eye.

'So it's all arranged, is it?' she asked.

'Yes.'

'And what if I don't like the arrangement?'

'Oh, Lola, how can you say that?'

'Naturally, you think I shall jump at the chance of living with you,' said Lola.

She fancied that she caught a gleam in his eye.

'You're not serious, are you?' said Boris.

'Perfectly serious. You're just a little roughneck, and rather too certain of your power to charm.'

The gleam vanished. He looked at his knees, and Lola noticed that his jaws were moving.

'You like the idea of that kind of life?' she asked.

'I'd like anything so long as I could live with you,' said Boris politely.

'You used to say you couldn't bear the thought of being a schoolmaster.'

'What else can I do? The whole trouble is,' he went on, 'that while I was fighting I didn't bother my head with problems, but now I just spend all my time wondering what I'm fit for.'

'You wanted to write.'

'I never thought seriously of writing. I've nothing to say. You see, I never believed I should come out of this business alive. I've been caught on the wrong foot.'

Lola looked at him attentively.

'Are you sorry the war's over?'

'It isn't over,' said Boris. 'The English are carrying on, and before six months are out the Yanks'll be in it.'

'But it's over for you.'

'Yes,' said Boris, 'it's over for me.'

Lola was still looking at him.

'For you and all Frenchmen.'

'Not for all of them!' he said fiercely. 'Some of them are in England, and they'll fight on to the end!'

'I see,' said Lola.

She drew at her cigarette and dropped the butt on the floor. Very quietly, she said:

'Is there any way you could get over there?'

'Oh, Lola!' said Boris, and there was admiration and gratitude in his voice: 'Yes, there is a way.'

'What way?'

'A plane.'

'A plane?' – she seemed not to understand.

'There's a little private flying-ground near Marignane, hidden away between two hills. A military plane landed there about a fortnight ago – engine trouble: it's being repaired.'

'But you can't handle a plane.'

'But I've got some pals who can.'

'Who are they?'

'One of them's Francillon – the chap I introduced you to, and then, there's Gabel and Terasse.'

'Did they suggest that you should go with them?'

'Yes.'

'Well?'

'I refused' – the words came tumbling out of his mouth.

'I see: you refused, but it wasn't final. You said to yourself – I'll break it gently to the old girl?'

'No,' he said.

He gazed at her tenderly. It was not often that his eyes had so melting a look: there was a time when I'd have killed myself for a look like that!

'You may be an old bit of nonsense, and rocky in the top story, but I can't leave you in the lurch. You'd do all sorts of ridiculous things if I weren't there to keep an eye on you!'

'When are we going to get married?' asked Lola.

'Whenever you like,' he said indifferently. 'All that matters is that we should be married by the beginning of term.'

'That's in September, isn't it?'

'No, October.'

'Good,' she said: 'we've plenty of time.'

She got up and began walking up and down the room. There were cigarette-ends on the floor, stained with lipstick. Boris bent down and picked them up with a stupid expression on his face.

'When are your pals starting?' she asked.

Boris carefully arranged the cigarette-ends on the marble top of the bedside table.

'Tomorrow evening,' he said, without turning round.

'As soon as that!' she said.

'Yes, they've got to be quick about it.'

'As soon as that!'

She walked to the window and opened it. She looked at the swaying masts of the fishing-boats, at the empty wharves, at the pink sky, and she thought: tomorrow evening. There was one more cable to cut, and only one. As soon as that was broken, she would turn round. Well, tomorrow evening's as good as any other time, she thought. The first golden gleams of sunrise were on the idle sea. Far off she could hear a ship's hooter. She waited until she felt truly freed, then turned to him.

'Go if you want to,' she said. 'I'm not holding you back.'

She got the words out with difficulty, but once they were spoken she felt empty and relieved. She looked at Boris, and thought, without knowing why: the poor boy, the poor boy.

Boris had jumped to his feet. He went across and took her by the arm.

'Lola.'

'You're hurting me,' she said.

He dropped his hand, but the look he gave her was suspicious.

'Won't it make you unhappy?'

'Yes,' she said, 'it'll make me unhappy, but I'd rather have it that way than see you school-mastering at Castelnaudary.'

He seemed slightly reassured.

'You couldn't live there any more than I could?' he asked.

'No more than you could.'

His shoulders drooped, and he hung his arms. For the first time in his life he seemed to feel that his body was an embarrassment. Lola was grateful to him for not showing his joy openly.

'Lola!' he said.

He stretched out his hand and touched her shoulder. She wanted to tear it away, but kept a tight hold on herself. She was smiling at him. She could feel the weight of his hand, and already he was hers no longer, but away in England. Already they faced one another as dead persons.

'I'd refused, you know,' he said in a trembling voice: 'I'd refused.'

'Yes, I know.'

'I'll be true to you. I won't sleep with any other woman.'

She smiled: 'My poor boy!'

He was in the way. She could have wished that the next evening had already come. Suddenly he struck his forehead.

'Hell!'

'What's the matter now?'

'I can't go! I can't go!'

'Why not?'

'Ivich! I told you she wanted to live with us.'

'Boris!' said Lola in a fury. 'If you won't stay for *my sake*, I forbid you to stay for hers!'

But her anger was something that belonged to a time already dead.

'I'll look after Ivich,' she said.

'You'll take her with you?'

'Why not?'

'But you can't stick her!'

'What's that got to do with it?' said Lola. She felt horribly tired: she said, 'Either get dressed or go back to bed. You'll catch cold.'

He took a towel and began to rub his body. How odd, she thought: he's just taken a decision that will change the whole course of his life. She sat down on the bed. He was rubbing away furiously, but his face was still gloomy.

'What's wrong?' she asked.

'Nothing. Everything's grand. I don't know what's biting you.'

She got to her feet with difficulty, grabbed his hair and forced his head up.

'Look at me: what's wrong?'

Boris turned his face away.

'It's only that I think you're rather strange.'

'What do you mean – strange?'

'Not seeming more put out at the idea of my going, I mean: I feel rather shocked.'

211

'So you feel shocked, do you!' said Lola: 'you actually feel shocked!'

And she burst out laughing.

6 a.m.

MATHIEU grunted, sat up, and rubbed his head. A cock crowed, the sun was warm and cheerful, though still low.

'Fine day,' said Mathieu.

No one replied. They were all kneeling behind the parapet. Mathieu looked at his wrist-watch and saw that it was six o'clock. He heard a distant, rhythmic rumbling. He crawled on all fours over to his companions.

'What is it? – a plane?'

'No: it's them: motorized infantry.'

Mathieu hoisted himself up till he could see over their shoulders.

'Don't be a damn' fool,' said Clapot: 'keep well down, they've got glasses.'

Two hundred yards before reaching the first of the houses, the road made a bend to the west, disappeared behind a grassy knoll, ran between the high buildings of a flour-mill, which masked it, and entered the village at an angle, from the south-west. Mathieu could make out a number of motor-vehicles very far away. They seemed not to be moving. He thought: 'Those are Germans!' and felt frightened, frightened in an odd, almost religious way: his emotion was, more truly, a sort of horror, such as is inspired by the supernatural. Thousands of foreign eyes were raking the village: eyes of supermen and insects.

He was overwhelmed by a sudden frightful realization: they *will see* my dead body!

'They'll be here any minute now,' he said, in spite of himself.

The others remained silent. A few moments passed, and then, in slow, solemn tones, Dandieu said:

'No use opening fire at that range.'

'Get back! – all of you,' ordered Clapot.

The four of them withdrew and sat down on one of the mattresses. Chasseriau and Dandieu had the appearance of two dried prunes, and Pinette was doing his best to look like them. Both had dirty faces and large, gentle eyes with no depth to them: 'My eyes are doggy,' thought Mathieu. Clapot was squatting on his heels: he talked back to them over his shoulder:

'They'll halt just outside the village, and send in motor-cyclists to recce. Don't fire on them whatever you do.'

Chasseriau yawned. The same sweetish, sickly yawn distended Mathieu's mouth. He tried to fight against his fear, to find some little warmth in anger. To himself he said: 'Christ! we're fighting men, aren't we, not victims!' – but his anger was not *genuine*. He yawned again. Chasseriau looked at him with sympathy.

'The waiting's always the worst part,' he said: 'you'll feel better later on.'

Clapot, still squatting on his heels, turned and faced them.

'Orders are simple,' he said: 'defend the approaches to the schools and the Mairie: they mustn't get near either of them. The chaps down there'll give us the signal. As soon as they start shooting we can open up – independent fire, and, remember, while they hold out our job's only to cover them.'

They looked at him with obedient and attentive faces.

'And after that?' asked Pinette.

'Oh, time enough . . .'

'I don't think they'll hold out long,' said Dandieu.

'You can never tell. They may have a light field-piece. It's up to us to prevent them from bringing it into action. We shan't have a clear field of fire, but nor will they, because the road enters the village at an angle.'

He got on to his knees and crawled to the parapet. Screened by a pillar, he looked out over the countryside.

'Dandieu!'

'Yes, Corporal!'

'Come over here.'

He gave his directions without turning his head.

'We'll face 'em, you and I, Dandieu: Chasseriau – you watch the right flank, and you, Delarue, the left. Pinette, you'd better get round to the other side in case they try a turning movement.'

Chasseriau dragged one of the mattresses to the parapet facing west. Mathieu took the blanket, made it into a pad, and dropped to his knees.

'I've got to turn my back on the buggers!' complained Pinette angrily.

'You've got nothing to grouse about!' said Chasseriau. 'I shall have the sun bang in me eyes!'

Flattened against his pillar, Mathieu looked straight down on the front of the Mairie. By craning his head slightly to the right, he could see the road. The square was a deep pit filled with poisonous shadow, a trap. It made him feel sick to look at it. In the chestnuts the birds were singing.

'Watch your step!'

Mathieu held his breath. Two motor-cyclists, dressed in black and wearing helmets, were dashing along the road; two super-natural messengers. He tried, in vain, to make out their faces: they had none. Two slim figures, four long, parallel legs, a pair of round, smooth heads with neither eyes nor mouths. They came on to an accompaniment of mechanical poppings. They had the stiff nobility of the figures that move forward on old-fashioned clocks when the hour strikes. The hour was just about to strike.

'Hold your fire!'

The motor-cyclists made the round of the square, their ex-hausts roaring. Some sparrows flew off, but, otherwise, nothing stirred. The treacherous square held death. Mathieu, fascinated, thought: 'They're Germans!' They caracoled past the Mairie, passing immediately beneath him – he could see their great leather paws trembling on the handle-bars – and turned into the main street. A moment later, they reappeared, sitting very up-right, screwed to their jolting saddles, and went at top-speed back along the road by which they had come. Mathieu felt pleased that Clapot had told them not to fire: to him the two figures had seemed invulnerable. The birds circled for another moment or two, then flew into the trees. Clapot said:

'That's our chaps!'

There was a screaming of brakes, car doors slammed. Mathieu heard steps and the sound of voices. A wave of sickness, like the oncoming of sleep, washed over him. He had to struggle to keep his eyes open. Squinnying them up he looked down at the road and felt in a conciliatory mood. If we went down now and threw away our rifles, they'd crowd round us: perhaps they'd say: 'Comrades of France, the war's over!' The steps drew nearer. They've done nothing to us, they're not thinking of us, they wish us no harm. Suddenly he shut his eyes: hatred would spout into the sky. They'll see my dead body: they'll kick it. He was not afraid of death, but he was afraid of hatred.

At last! A sharp crackling sounded in his ears. He opened his eyes. The road was silent and deserted. He tried to believe he had been dreaming. No one had fired, no one ...

'The bleedin' mugs!' muttered Clapot.

Mathieu gave a start:

'Who?'

'The blokes in the Mairie – opened up too soon. Must have been perishin' windy or they'd 'a' let 'em come on!'

Mathieu's gaze painfully retraced the road, slipping on the cobbles, on the tufts of grass in the cracks between them, until it came to rest on the corner. No one. Silence. *It is a village in August: the men are in the fields.* But he knew that on the other side of those walls were men planning his death. They're trying to do us as much damage as possible. He foundered in a sea of treacle: he loved the whole world, Frenchmen, Germans, Hitler. In a sort of clammy dream he heard a sound of cries, followed by a violent explosion and the clatter of broken glass. Then the firing started again. He gripped his rifle to keep it from falling.

'Too short with that grenade!' muttered Clapot.

The firing was continuous now. The Jerries were using their rifles. Two more grenades exploded. If it'd only stop, just for one moment, so's I could get a grip on myself? – but the cracking and banging and din of explosions went merrily on. Inside his head a cogwheel was turning, more and more quickly, and each cog was a rifle shot. Christ! – suppose I turned out to be a coward! – that'd be the last straw! He turned and looked at his companions. Squatting on their heels, with pale faces and shining eyes, Clapot and Dandieu were watching. Pinette had his back to him: he neck looked stiff and rigid, his shoulders were jerking. Must have an attack of St Vitus's dance, or a fit of uncontrollable laughter. Mathieu took shelter behind a pillar and cautiously poked his head out. He managed to keep his eyes open but could not bring himself to look in the direction of the Mairie. He gazed towards the south where all was empty, all was calm. That way lay Marseilles and the sea. There was another explosion, followed by a dry rattling on the tiles of the clock-tower. Mathieu screwed up his eyes, but the road streaked by beneath him. The objects upon it were all rushing along, intermingled, dwindled.

The whole thing was a dream. The pit grew deeper, seemed to hypnotize him – *the whole thing was a dream*. A wheel of fire kept turning, turning, like the spinning disc at a waffle-booth, and he was just about to wake in his bed when he noticed a toad crawling into action. For a moment he watched the squat creature with complete indifference, then the toad became a man. Mathieu saw with quite extraordinary clarity the two creases on the shaven back of his neck, his green tunic, his belt, and his boots of soft black leather. 'He must have got here across the fields, and now he's crawling towards the Mairie to throw his grenade.' The German was working his way forward with knees and elbows. His right hand, which he held in the air, was grasping a stick topped by a cylinder of metal, rather like a small saucepan. 'But . . .' said Mathieu: 'but . . . but' – the road stopped streaking by . . . the road came to a dead stop. Mathieu jumped to his feet and brought his rifle to his shoulder. A hard look had come into his eyes. He stood there, a foursquare object in a world of foursquare objects, with an enemy at the business end of his rifle – calmly aiming at the man's stomach. A momentary grin of superiority stretched his lips. The famous German army, the army of supermen, the army of locusts, was summed up in this poor devil, who looked touching because he was so wrong-headed, so bogged down in ignorance and error, so absorbed in what he was doing. He had all the comic intentness of a small child.

Mathieu was in no hurry. He kept his eye on his man; he had plenty of time. The German army *is* vulnerable. He fired. The man gave a funny little jerk and fell on his stomach, throwing his arms forward like somebody learning to swim. Mathieu found the sight amusing. He fired again, and the poor wretch took two or three strokes, dropping his grenade which rolled on the roadway without exploding. He lay quite still, inoffen-

216

sive, grotesque, smashed. 'I've put paid to *him*,' said Mathieu in a low voice: 'I've cooked *his* goose.' He looked at the dead man, and thought: 'They're just like everyone else.' He felt himself to be a fine fellow.

He was aware of a hand on his shoulder. Clapot was taking a look at the job done by this amateur. He stared at the squashed insect, nodded his head, then turned round:

'Chasseriau!'

Chasseriau crawled towards them on his knees.

'Lend an eye here,' said Clapot.

'I don't need Chasseriau,' said Mathieu angrily.

'They'll try to get their own back for that,' said Clapot. 'If they attack in strength, you'll be overrun.'

There was a burst of machine-gun fire. Clapot raised his eyebrows.

'Hullo!' he said, going back to his own post: 'things beginning to warm up good and proper!'

Mathieu turned to Chasseriau.

'I rather think we're giving Jerry a bit of a headache!' he said excitedly.

Chasseriau said nothing. He had a heavy, animal, almost sleepy, look.

'Notice how long they're taking?' said Mathieu in a strained voice: 'I should have thought they'd have settled with us in two shakes of a duck's arse!'

Chasseriau looked at him in astonishment, then glanced at his wrist-watch:

'Only three minutes since the motor-cyclist went by,' he said.

Mathieu's excited mood suddenly collapsed. He started to laugh. Chasseriau stared ahead of him. Mathieu looked at the dead soldier and laughed. For years he had tried, in vain, to act. One after the other his intended actions had been stolen from him: he had been no firmer than a pat of butter. But no one had stolen this! He had pressed a trigger, and, for once, something had happened, something definite. The thought made him laugh louder than ever. His ears were deafened by shouts and by the noise of explosions, but he scarcely heard them. He looked with satisfaction at his dead man. He thought: 'Bet he felt that all right! He knew what was happening to him: he understood!' *His* dead man, *his* handiwork, something to mark *his* passage on the earth. A longing came to him to do some more killing: it was fun, and it was easy. He would have liked to plunge Germany into mourning.

'Look out!'

A fellow was creeping along the wall, holding a grenade in his hand. Mathieu took aim at this strange, desirable creature. His heart was thumping against his ribs.

'Hell!'

Missed! The creature bunched up, became a bewildered man who was looking about him without understanding. Chasseriau fired. The man went slack like a spring, straightened up, sprang into the air, threshing with his arms, hurled his grenade, and crumpled up on his back in the middle of the road. At the same moment there was a crash of broken glass. In a blinding flash Mathieu saw a number of shadowy figures in contorted attitudes on the ground floor of the Mairie. Then everything went black. There were yellow spots in front of his eyes. He felt furious with Chasseriau.

'Hell!' he shouted in a blazing temper: 'Hell! Hell!'

'Shut up!' said Chasseriau. 'Anyhow, he missed. The boys are up on the first floor.'

Mathieu blinked his eyes and shook his head to get rid of the yellow spots which were dazzling him.

'I'm blinded,' he said.

'It'll pass,' said Chasseriau: 'just you plug that fellow I dropped if he makes a move.'

Mathieu leaned forward. He could see a bit better now. The Jerry was lying on his back. His eyes were wide open and his legs were twitching. Mathieu raised his rifle.

'Don't be a damn' fool!' said Chasseriau, 'wasting ammo like that!'

Mathieu lowered his rifle with a bad grace. 'The bugger may make a getaway,' he thought.

The door of the Mairie was flung open. A man appeared on the threshold, and advanced with a sort of nobility in his movements. He was naked to the waist. He looked like a lay figure. His face was dark red, as though it had been flayed. The skin was hanging in flakes. Suddenly he started to scream. Twenty rifle shots rang out simultaneously. He tottered, pitched forward, and collapsed on the steps.

'That was one of our lot,' said Chasseriau.

'No,' said Mathieu, speaking with difficulty because of his rage, 'he was one of ours, chap called Latex.'

His hands were trembling and his eyes hurt him. Tremulously he repeated what he had just said:

'Chap called Latex – had six kids.'

Suddenly he leaned over the parapet and aimed straight at the wounded man whose great eyes seemed to be fixed on him.

'You're going to pay for that, you sod!'

'You going crackers?' said Chasseriau. 'Didn't I say not to waste ammo?'

'Oh, go to hell!'

He was in no hurry to shoot. If the swine can see me, he won't enjoy what he sees. He got his sights on the man's head, and fired. The head lay there, smashed – but the man was still twitching.

'Swine!' shouted Mathieu: 'swine!'

'Look out! – for Chri' sake look out – left!'

Five or six Germans had just come into view. Chasseriau and Mathieu both opened fire, but the Germans were employing different tactics. They had taken cover behind the corners of the houses, and stood there, seemingly waiting.

'Clapot! Dandieu! Come over here!' shouted Chasseriau: 'there's something up!'

'Can't,' said Clapot.

'Pinette!' yelled Mathieu.

Pinette made no reply. Mathieu dared not turn round.

'Look out!'

The Germans had started to run. Mathieu fired, but they were already on the other side of the road.

'Christ!' said Clapot: 'there's some Jerries under the trees. Who let 'em get by?'

No one answered. The ground under the trees was alive with men. Chasseriau took a pot shot.

'Must be the knocking-shop! nothing else would have got 'em moving!'

The men in the schools had started shooting, and the Germans under the trees were returning their fire. The Mairie was silent. Smoke was billowing over the road, low down.

'Don't shoot into the trees!' shouted Clapot: 'just a waste of ammo.'

At that moment a grenade exploded against the wall of the Mairie at first-floor level.

'They're climbing the trees!' said Chasseriau.

'If they do, we'll get 'em!' said Mathieu. He peered into the leaves, saw a lifted arm, and fired. Too late: the Mairie went up in smoke, the windows were torn from their frames. For the second time he was blinded by the same horrible yellow flash. He fired at random, and heard the sound of large, ripe fruit tumbling from branch to branch. He had no idea whether the men were falling or going down of their own accord.

'Mairie's out of action!' said Clapot.

They held their breath – listening. The Germans were still keeping up their fire, but no reply came from the Mairie. Mathieu shuddered. Dead men. Joints of bleeding meat on the staved-in floors of empty rooms.

'Not our fault,' said Chasseriau: 'they were too many for us.'

Suddenly, great clouds of smoke began to billow from the first-floor windows. Through it, Mathieu could see flames, red and black. Someone in the Mairie began to scream. The voice was shrill, like a woman's and impersonal. Mathieu suddenly had the feeling that he was going to die. Chasseriau was firing away.

'You're daft!' Mathieu said to him: 'keeping it up on the Mairie. Who's wasting ammo now?'

Chasseriau was aiming at the windows of the Mairie. Three times he fired into the flames.

'It's that bloke screaming,' he said: 'I can't stick it!'

'He's still screaming,' said Mathieu. They listened, frozen with horror. The voice grew weaker.

'It's over.'

But even as he spoke the inhuman noise started again, a vast, solemn noise creeping up the scale. Mathieu, too, began shooting through the windows, but with no result.

'He won't die!' said Chasseriau.

All of a sudden the screaming stopped.

'Ouf!' said Mathieu.

'Through!' said Chasseriau: 'finished, burnt to a cinder!'

There was no sign of movement now, neither under the trees nor in the street. The sun gilded the burning front of the Mairie. Chasseriau looked at his watch.

'Seven minutes,' he said.

Mathieu turned and twisted in the flames, a blazing torch, the smoke in his throat, choking him. He had to lay his hands on his chest and move them slowly downwards to his stomach before he could convince himself that he was unscathed.

Clapot's voice came sharply.

'There's some of 'em on the roofs!'

'On the roofs?'

'Just opposite, they're firing at the schools. Hell, see what they're doing?'

'What?'

'Bringing a machine-gun into action. Pinette!' he shouted.

Pinette crawled back to them.

'Come over here – the chaps in the schools are going to get a spraying!'

Pinette raised himself on hands and knees. He looked at them with a vacant expression. His face was grey.

'Anything wrong?' asked Mathieu.

'Nothing wrong?' he replied curtly.

He dragged himself over to Clapot, and knelt by the parapet. 'Let 'em have it!' said Clapot: 'shoot down into the street to distract attention! We'll look after the machine-gun!'

Pinette said nothing but started to shoot.

'Better'n that, for Chri' sake!' said Clapot. 'You can't shoot if you shut your eyes!'

Pinette gave a start and seemed to be making a violent effort to control himself. A little colour had come back into his cheeks. He was aiming with his eyes wide open. Clapot and Dandieu beside him were firing continuously. Clapot uttered a shout of triumph.

'That's done it!' he cried: 'that's done it! we've silenced them!'

Mathieu strained his ears. The noise of the machine-gun had stopped.

'Yes,' he said, 'but the boys down there have stopped firing.'

The schools were silent. Three Germans who had been hiding under the trees, raced across the road and flung themselves against the door of the schoolhouse. It flew open. They rushed in, and reappeared a moment later, leaning from the first-floor windows, gesturing and shouting. Clapot fired and they vanished. A few moments later, Mathieu, for the first time that morning, heard the whine of a bullet. Chasseriau looked at his watch.

'Ten minutes,' he said.

'Yes,' said Mathieu: 'this is the beginning of the end.'

The Mairie was burning. The Germans had occupied the schools. It was as though France had been defeated a second time.

'Shoot! – for Chri' sake shoot!'

A few Germans showed themselves cautiously at the far end of the street. Chasseriau, Pinette, and Clapot fired at them. The heads disappeared.

'They've twigged us!'

Once more there was silence: a long silence. Mathieu thought: 'What are they up to?' In the empty street lay four dead men: a little further on, two more. The sum total of what we've been able to do. Nothing for it but to finish the job and get polished off. What difference has all this made to the Germans? – merely put their time-table out by ten minutes!

'Our turn now,' said Clapot suddenly.

A small, squat monster was moving towards the church. It glittered in the sun.

'Schnellfeuerkanon!' muttered Dandieu between his teeth.

Mathieu crawled towards them. They were still firing, though there was no one to be seen. The cannon seemed to be moving independently of human aid. They were firing from a sense of duty, because there was still some ammunition left. Their faces had a calm, tired beauty – the faces of their last hour.

'Back!'

A big man in shirt-sleeves appeared suddenly on the left of the gun. He made no attempt to take cover, but gave his orders quietly, with one arm raised. Mathieu stood up suddenly. The little figure with its bare throat inflamed him with desire.

'Back, and keep down!'

The gun's maw rose slowly in the air. Mathieu had not moved. He knelt there aiming at the Feldwebel.

'Hear what I said?' shouted Clapot.

'Shut up!' grumbled Mathieu.

He fired first. The butt of his rifle drove back against his shoulder. At the same moment there was a huge detonation like the amplified echo of his own shot. Everything went red before his eyes, and he heard a long-drawn-out muffled sound of tearing linen.

'Missed us!' exclaimed Capot: 'they're aiming too high!'

The Feldwebel was writhing on the ground, his legs in the air. Mathieu was just about to finish him off, when two soldiers appeared on the scene and carried him away. Mathieu worked himself backwards, still on his knees, and lay down beside Dandieu. Clapot already had the trap-door open.

'Come on, down with you!'

Dandieu shook his head.

'There are no windows on the floor below.'

They looked at one another.

'Must use up our ammo,' said Chasseriau: 'got much left?'

'Two magazines.'

'How about you, Delarue?'

'One.'

Clapot let the trap fall again.

'You're right,' he said: 'must use it up!'

Mathieu heard behind him the sound of rasping breath. He turned his head. Pinette was pale to the lips and breathing with difficulty.

'You been hit?'

Pinette looked at him with a wild expression.

'No.'

Clapot stared attentively at Pinette.

'If you want to go down, lad, nobody's going to stop you. It's a matter of ammo with us – got to use it up.'

'Hell!' said Pinette: 'why should I go down if Delarue's staying?'

He dragged himself to the parapet and started to fire.

'Pinette!' shouted Mathieu.

Pinette did not answer. Bullets were whining over them.

'Let him alone,' said Clapot: 'it'll take his mind off.'

The gun fired two shots in rapid succession. They heard a dull shock above their heads, and a shower of plaster rained down on them from the ceiling. Chasseriau took out his watch.

'Twelve minutes.'

Mathieu and Chasseriau crawled to the parapet. Mathieu squatted down beside Pinette, with Chasseriau on the right, standing, and leaning forward slightly.

'Not too bad, twelve minutes,' said Chasseriau. 'Not at all too bad!'

The air about them screamed, hurtled, and struck Mathieu full in the face. It felt hot and heavy like the flick of a damp rag. Mathieu collapsed in a sitting position. He was blinded by blood. His hands were red to the wrists. He rubbed his eyes, mingling the blood on his hands with the blood on his face. Chasseriau was sitting on the south side of the parapet, headless. Blood was spouting and bubbling from his neck.

'I can't stand it!' said Pinette: 'I can't stand it!'

He jumped up, ran to Chasseriau, and struck him full on the chest with the butt of his rifle. Chasseriau swayed and tumbled over the parapet. Mathieu, seeing him fall, felt no emotion. This was no more than the beginning of his own death.

'Independent fire!' shouted Clapot.

The square was suddenly alive with soldiers. Mathieu went back to his post and resumed firing. Dandieu was doing the same close by.

'It's just a massacre!' said Dandieu with a laugh. He dropped his rifle which fell into the street. He crumpled up on top of Mathieu with the words:

'Good lad! good lad!'

Mathieu pushed him away with his shoulder. Dandieu fell backwards, and Mathieu went on firing. He was still firing when the roof fell on top of him. A beam struck him on the head. He dropped his rifle and fell. Fifteen minutes! – He thought in a fury, I'd give anything just to hold on for fifteen minutes! The butt of a rifle was jutting from a pile of splintered wood and broken tiles. He seized it. It was sticky with blood, but still loaded.

'Pinette!' shouted Mathieu.

No one answered. The ruins of the roof obstructed the whole north side of the platform. The trap-door was blocked by a heap of beams and rubbish. An iron bar was hanging from the yawning rent in the ceiling. Mathieu was alone.

'Christ!' he said out loud. 'No one shall say we didn't hold out for fifteen minutes!'

He made his way to the parapet and stood there firing. This was revenge on a big scale. Each one of his shots avenged some ancient scruple. One for Lola whom I dared not rob; one for Marcelle whom I ought to have left in the lurch; one for Odette whom I didn't want to kiss. This for the books I never dared to write, this for the journeys I never made, this for everybody in general whom I wanted to hate and tried to understand. He fired, and the tables of the Law crashed about him – Thou Shalt Love Thy Neighbour as Thyself – bang! in that bugger's face – Thou Shalt Not Kill – bang! at that scarecrow opposite. He was firing on his fellow men, on Virtue, on the whole world. Liberty is Terror. The Mairie was ablaze, his head was ablaze. Bullets were whining round him free as the air. The world is going up in smoke, and me with it. He fired: he looked at his watch: fourteen minutes and thirty seconds. Nothing more to ask of Fate now except one half-minute. Just time enough to fire at that smart officer, at all the Beauty of the Earth, at the street, at the flowers, at the gardens, at everything he had loved. Beauty dived downwards like some obscene bird. But Mathieu went on firing. He fired. He was cleansed. He was all-powerful. He was free.

Fifteen minutes.

PART TWO

*

NIGHT, stars, a red glow in the northern sky: some hamlet burning. Eastward, westward, long flashes of heat, sharp, spasmodic; their guns. They're everywhere: tomorrow they'll get me. He entered the sleeping village, crossed the square, picked out a house at random, and went up to it. He knocked – no answer; pressed the latch, and the door opened. He went in: he closed the door: blackness. A match. He was in an entrance-hall; a mirror emerged mistily from the gloom: he looked at himself in it: I need a shave badly. The match went out. He had had time to see a staircase on his left, leading downwards. He groped his way towards it. The staircase twisted and Brunet twisted with it. He was conscious of a vague, diffused light – twisted once more, and was in a cellar. It smelt of wine and mushrooms. There were some casks in it, and a pile of straw. A large man, wearing a nightshirt and trousers, was sitting beside a fair woman who was half-naked and held a child in her arms. They looked at Brunet. The mouths of all three of them were open. They're scared. Brunet went down the remaining steps; the man was still looking at him. Brunet never stopped moving. Suddenly, the man said: 'My wife's sick.' 'What of it?' said Brunet. 'I didn't want her to spend the night in the woods.' 'I'm a funny person to tell that to,' said Brunet; 'doesn't mean a thing to me.' He was in the cellar now. The man looked at him defiantly. 'What you after, anyways?' 'I want to sleep here,' said Brunet. The man pulled a face; he was still staring hard. 'You a warrant-officer?' Brunet did not reply. 'Where are your men?' asked the man suspiciously. 'Dead,' replied Brunet, and went over to the pile of straw. 'What about the Germans?' said the man: 'where are they?' 'Everywhere.' 'They mustn't find you here,' said the man. Brunet took off his tunic, folded it up, and laid it on one of the casks. 'Hear what I said?' shouted the man. 'I heard, right enough,' said Brunet. 'I've got a wife and kid: I don't want to pay for any of your nonsense!' 'Take it easy,' said Brunet. He sat down. The woman looked at him with an expression of hatred. 'There are Frenchmen up there who are going to fight: you ought to be with them.' Brunet looked at her. She pulled her nightdress up over her breast: she shouted – 'Get out of here! You've lost the war, and now you're going to get us killed into the bargain!' 'Calm down!' Brunet said to her: 'all you need do is wake me when the Germans arrive.' 'What'll you do then?' 'Give myself up.' 'Dirty bastard!' said the woman: 'there are boys up there as are going to get killed!' Brunet yawned, stretched, and smiled. He had been fighting for a week without food or sleep. Twenty times he had been within an ace of staying where he lay, for good and all. No more fighting for him, now. The war was lost, and he'd got work to do. A lot of work. He lay down on the straw, yawned, and fell asleep. 'Get out!' said the man: 'here they are.' Brunet opened his eyes. He was aware of a large, red face, and could hear the cracking of rifles and the thud of explosions. 'Did you say they were here?' 'Yes; there's a scrap going on: you can't stay.' The woman had not moved. She was looking at Brunet with a savage glare, and holding her sleeping child in her arms. 'I'll clear off,' said Brunet. He got up, yawned, went over to where there was a ventilating shaft, rooted about in his haversack, and took from it a fragment of mirror and a razor. The man stared at him with loutish indignation. 'You're never going to shave?' 'Why not?' asked Brunet. The man's face was congested with fury. 'They'll shoot me if they find you here.' 'I shan't be long,' said Brunet. The man took hold of his arm and tried to push him out. 'I'm not having none of that! I've got a wife and kid: if I'd known I shouldn't have let you come in!' Brunet shook himself free. He looked with disgust at the great lump of flesh that seemed so determined to go on living, that would live on under every régime, humble, muddle-headed, close-fisted, of use to no one. The fellow made a rush at him. Brunet flung him against the wall. 'You keep quiet, or there'll be trouble!' The man said nothing. He was breathing heavily and rolling his drink-sodden eyes. He seemed to be gathering himself for a spring. He gave off a strong smell of death and dung. Brunet started to shave without soap or water. His skin smarted. Beside him the woman sat shivering with terror and hatred. Brunet hurried. If I'm too long about it she'll go mad. He put his razor back in the haversack: the blade'll do for two more shaves. 'There now, I'm through. Not worth making all that fuss, was it?' The man still said nothing. The woman screamed – 'Get out, you dirty beast, you filthy coward! you'll get us all shot!' Brunet put on his tunic. He felt clean, fresh, and stiff. His face was red. 'Get out! get out!' He raised two fingers in farewell. 'Many thanks,' he said. He climbed the dark staircase and crossed the entrance-hall. The front door was wide open. Outside was the white cascade of the day, the lunatic stammer of machine-guns. The house was dark and cool. He walked over to the door: he'd got to make a plunge into that surf of light. A small square, the church, the war-memorial, piles of manure in front of the houses. Between two blazing buildings the road looked pink under the morning sun. The Germans were there, thirty men or so, all busy, workmen on the job. They were firing on the church with a Schnellfeuerkanon, and being shot at from the tower. The place looked like a builder's yard. In the middle of the square, beneath the cross-fire, a number of French soldiers in shirt-sleeves, their eyes red with sleep, were tip-toeing along, with short, hurried steps, like so many competitors filing past the judges at a beauty contest. Their pale hands were raised above their heads. The sun played antics between their fingers. Brunet looked at them. He looked at the church-tower. To his right a large building was in flames: he could feel the heat on his face. 'Hell!' he said, and went down the three steps into the street. It was all over: he was taken. He kept his hands in his pockets: they felt as heavy as lead. 'Stick 'em up!' There was a German with his rifle pointing straight at him. He flushed. His hands rose slowly until they were in the air above his head: they shall pay for that with blood! He joined the Frenchmen and tripped along with them – it's just like a film, nothing looks real: those bullets won't kill anyone, and the gun's firing blank. One of the Frenchmen doubled up and fell. Brunet stepped over him. Without hurrying, he turned the corner of a brown house and emerged on to the main road at the same moment as the church-tower collapsed. No more Jerries, no more bullets, the film was over. He was in the open country. He put his hands back in his pockets. All round him were Frenchmen, a crowd of little Frenchmen in khaki; unwashed, unshaved, their faces black-ened with smoke, laughing, joking, talking together in low voices, a bobbing sea of bare heads and forage caps – not a helmet among them. There were recognitions and greetings. 'Saw you at Saverne in December! Hello, Girard, how goes it? Takes a defeat, don't it, to get one so's one can meet one's pals? Lisa O.K.?' A single German soldier, with a bored look and his rifle slung, was in charge of this herd of the undersized and vanquished, matching his long, slow stride to the patter of their progress. Brunet pattered with the rest, though in size he was the Jerry's equal, and was no less well-shaved than him. The pink road wound between stretches of grass. There was not a breath of air, only the stifling stillness of defeat. The men smelt strong. They chattered away and the birds sang. Brunet turned to his neighbour, a large, kindly-looking fellow who was breathing through his mouth. 'Where does this lot come from?' 'Saverne: we spent the night billeted in the farms.' 'I came on my own,' said Brunet. 'All this is a damn' nuisance, I thought the village was deserted.' A young, fair-haired chap, with a suntanned face, was walking a couple of files from him. He was stripped to the waist, and had a great bleeding scab between his shoulder-blades. To the rear of the column a vast hubbub had developed, a normal, everyday sound of shouts and laughter and the scrabbling of boots on the surface of the road. It sounded like the noise of wind in the trees. Brunet turned his head. By this time the number of men behind him had run into thousands. Prisoners had been mopped up from here, there, and everywhere; from the fields, from the hamlets, from the farms. Brunet showed head and shoulders above the rest, a solitary landmark in the undulating sea of heads. 'I'm Moulu,' said the big chap: 'from Bar-le-Duc,' he added with pride: 'know this part of the world like the back of me 'and.' At the side of the road a farm was burning. The flames looked black in the sunlight. A dog was howling. 'Hear that tyke?' said Moulu to his neighbour: 'bin and shut him up in the house.' The man he was speaking to hailed, obviously, from the North: he was fair, medium-sized, with a skin like milk, and bore a strong resemblance to the Jerry in charge of them. He frowned and looked at Moulu with large blue eyes. 'What's that?' 'The dog: he's inside.' 'Well, what of it?' said the northerner: 'it's only a dog' ... 'Ouah! ouah! ouah! ouah!' ... this time it was not the dog howling, but the young fellow with the naked back. Someone was dragging him along with one hand clamped over his mouth. Brunet had a glimpse of his large, pale, frightened face with its lashless eyes. 'Charpin don't seem too good,' said Moulu to the northerner. The other stared at him: 'Eh?' 'I said your pal Charpin don't seem too good.' The northerner laughed, displaying very white teeth: 'Always has bin a bit odd!' The road began to climb. All about them was a delicious smell of sun-warmed stone and wood smoke. Behind them the dog was still howling. They reached the top of the hill. The road began to descend steeply. Moulu jerked his thumb in the direction of the interminable column. 'Where's all this lot come from?' He turned to Brunet: 'How many should you say there are?' 'Don't know, maybe ten thousand, maybe more.' Moulu looked at him incredulously. 'Mean to say you can tell that just by looking at 'em?' Brunet thought of the Fourteenth of July, of the First of May, when they used to have chaps posted along the Boulevard Richard-Lenoir, whose job it was to estimate the numbers demonstrating by judging the time it took the columns to pass a given point. The crowd on those occasions had been silent and hot. If one was in the middle of them it was stifling. This one was noisy, but cold and dead. He smiled: 'I've got the trick of it.' 'Where we going?' asked the northerner. 'Search me!' 'Where are the Fritzes? Who's in charge of this little lot?' The only Fritzes they saw were the ones they passed along the road, amounting to about ten. The herd slid down the hill as though propelled by its own weight. 'Enough to make a bloke proper fed up!' said Moulu. 'You bet it is,' said Brunet. It *was* enough to make a bloke fed up. There were enough of them to overwhelm the Germans, strangle them, and make off across the fields. But what good would that do? On they trudged, straight ahead, as the road took them. A while back they had been at the bottom of the hill, in a kind of cup, now they were climbing, and felt hot. Moulu took from his pocket a bundle of letters held together by an elastic band, and for a while turned it over and over in his great clumsy fingers. Sweat made stains on the paper, causing the violet ink to run. Then he took off the elastic band, and started to tear the letters up. He did this methodically, without re-reading them, and scattered the fragments with the movement of a man sowing seed. Brunet followed their eddying progress with his eyes. Most of them fell, like showers of confetti, on the men's shoulders, and from there to their feet. One there was which fluttered for a moment or two and then settled on a tuft of grass. The blades bent slightly, upholding it like a canopy. There were other pieces of paper all along the road, some torn, some scrabbled up, some crumpled into balls. They lay in the ditches, among the broken rifles and dinted helmets. Where the writing was round and elongated, Brunet could make out an occasional sentence: eat well, don't expose yourself, Hélène has come with the children, all yours, darling. The road was one long, dirtied love-letter. Small flabby monsters crouched low on the ground, watching the gay convoy of defeated men with sightless eyes – gas-masks. Moulu nudged Brunet with his elbow and pointed to one of them. 'Lucky we didn't have to use 'em!' Brunet said nothing, and Moulu looked about for someone else to confide in. 'Hey! Lambert!' A man in front of Brunet turned his head. Moulu silently pointed to a mask, and they both began to laugh. The others near them joined in. They were filled with hatred of the parasitic grubs of which once they had been so frightened, yet had to care for and keep efficient. Now they lay beneath their feet, smashed, useless, and the sight of them was a further reminder that the war was over. Peasants, who had come as usual to the fields to work, watched the men pass, leaning on their spades. Lambert was in a gay mood, and shouted to them: 'Morning, daddy: we're the boys they called up!' Ten voices, a hundred, repeated the words with a kind of defiance: 'We're the boys they called up! we're the boys they called up – and we're going home!' The peasants said nothing. It was as though they had not heard. A fair-haired youth with frizzed hair, who looked as though he came from Paris, turned to Lambert. 'How long d'you think it'll be?' he asked. 'Pretty soon,' said Lambert; 'pretty soon, Goldilocks.' 'Really think so? – you sure?' 'Look for yerself. Where's the blokes who ought to be guarding us? If we was prisoners good and proper, we'd be regularly hemmed in.' 'Why did they capture us, then?' asked Moulu. 'Capture? – they didn't capture us – they've just put us aside so's we shan't get in the way while they're advancing.' 'Even so,' sighed Goldilocks, 'it might be quite a while.' 'You

daft? – why, they can't run fast enough to keep up with our lot!'
He was as merry as a cricket, and laughing all the while. Nothing for old Fritz to do: just a pleasure jaunt in the country with
a nice little bit o' skirt in Paris, a drink or two at Dijon, and a
bowl of bouillabaisse at Marseilles. Marseilles'll be the end:
damn it all, it must be! They can't go no further than Marseilles, 'cos of the sea! When they get there, they'll turn us loose.
We shall be home by the middle of August.' Goldilocks shook
his head – 'You're in a thundering hurry: they got to mend the
railways, haven't they? – so's they can get the trains running.'
'They can keep their trains for all I care,' said Moulu: 'if that's
all we're waiting for, I don't mind doing it on me flat feet!'
'Hell! – not for this baby! I bin walking for the last fortnight,
and I've just about had it. Bit of comfort's what I want!' 'How
about having a tumble with your girl?' 'What'll I use? I've done
so much footslogging, I don't seem to have nothing inside me
pants. All I want's a bit of sleep, with the bed to meself!' Brunet
listened to them. He looked at the backs of their necks, and he
thought what a lot of work there was for him to do. Poplars,
poplars, a bridge over a stream, more poplars. 'Makes a fellow
feel thirsty,' said Moulu. 'It's not the thirst I mind,' said the
northerner, 'so much as the hunger: haven't had a bite since
yesterday.' Moulu was sweating profusely as he jogged along,
and panting. He took off his tunic, put it across his arm, and
unbuttoned his shirt. 'Any'ow there's no one to stop a bloke
from taking off his coat,' he said with a grin. There was a sudden halt, and Brunet bumped into the back of the man in front
of him, who happened to be Lambert. Lambert turned round.
He had a Newgate fringe and sharp little eyes under thick-
growing black brows. 'Why can't yer look where yer going,
clumsy! Haven't you got eyes in yer face?' He looked at Brunet's
uniform with an insolent expression. 'Non-coms. is out – no
one's giving orders now – just reglar fellers, that's what we are –
all on us!' Brunet returned his look, but without anger, and
the man said no more. Brunet found himself wondering what
his job in civil life was likely to be: small shopkeeper? clerk? –
lower-middle-class, anyhow, that was quite certain. Must be hundreds of thousands like him – with no feeling for authority and
no sense of personal cleanliness. There'd have to be iron dis-

cipline. 'What we stopping for?' asked Moulu. Brunet made no reply. Another lower-middle-class product: not much difference between him and the other, except that he was stupider. Not easy material to work on. Moulu heaved a sigh of contentment, and began to fan himself. 'P'raps we got time for a sit-down?' He put his haversack by the roadside and squatted on it. The German soldier came up and stood staring at them with his long, handsome, expressionless face. There was a vague look of sympathy in his blue eyes. Speaking slowly and carefully, he said: 'Poor French – war over – you go home – home.' 'What's he say? – that we're going home? – should damn' well think we *are* going home! Hear that, Julien, says we're going home – ask him when!' 'Give us the low-down, Fritzy, *when* are we going home?' Their attitude to him was at once servile and familiar. He might represent the army of the victors, but he was only a footslogger after all! The German, still with his blank stare, repeated what he had already said: 'You go home – home!' 'Yes, but *when*?' 'Poor French, you go home!' The column started to move again ... poplars, poplars ... Moulu groaned: he was hot, thirsty, and tired: he wanted to stop. No one could check this plodding progress, because there was nobody in command. Somebody grunted, 'Me head's splitting,' and trudged on. The talk began to flag: there were long spells of silence. The same thought was in every mind: 'surely we're not going on walking like this all the way to Berlin?' But no one stopped. Each man followed the man ahead, pushed along by the man behind. A village. On the square was a pile of helmets, gasmasks, and rifles. 'Poudroux,' said Moulu: 'come through it yesterday.' 'So did I,' said Goldilocks, 'yesterday evening – in a lorry. Folk were all out on their doorsteps – didn't look too pleased to see us.' They were there now, on the doorsteps, their arms folded, silent: women with black hair, black eyes, and black dresses, and old men: all staring. Confronted by these spectators, the prisoners straightened up: their faces became peaky and cynical: they waved their hands, they laughed and shouted, 'Hello, ma! Hello, pa! – we're the lads! – war's over! – so long!' They passed in an agitation of greeting, ogling the girls, smiling provocatively. But the spectators said nothing – just looked. Only the grocer's wife, a fat, good-natured creature,

murmured – 'Poor boys' The man from the North smiled gleefully. 'Good thing we're not where I come from!' he said to
Lambert. 'Why?' 'They'd 'a' bin chucking the furniture at us!'
... A water-trough: ten, a hundred broke from the ranks in
their eagerness to drink. Moulu was one of them. He leaned
down clumsily, greedily. They slaked their weariness: their
shoulders moved spasmodically: the water ran over their faces.
The German guard seemed not to notice them. They could have
stayed in the village had they been brave enough to face the
inhabitants' hostile eyes: but they made no effort to do so. One
by one they came back, hurrying, as though they feared to miss
their places in the line. Moulu's run was like a woman's – knock-
kneed. They jostled one another, laughing and shouting, shame-
less and provocative as a crowd of nattering washerwomen, their
mouths gaping with merriment, their eyes abject like the eyes of
beaten dogs. Moulu wiped his lips. 'That was good, that was!
You not thirsty?' Brunet shrugged his shoulders but said nothing. Pity this mob wasn't surrounded by five hundred soldiers
with fixed bayonets, prodding the laggards and bashing the
chatterers with their butts! *That'd* take the grins off their faces!
He looked to right and left. He turned his head, seeking, in all
this forest of lost, hysterical features twisted into masks of irre-
pressible gaiety, for someone like himself. Where were the
Comrades? Not hard to tell a Communist when you see him.
Oh, for one face, one hard, calm, controlled face, for something
that might have betokened a man! But no: under-sized, nimble,
mean, they sloped along, their ferrety muzzles pressing ever
onwards, the facile mobility of their race showing through the
dirt, twitching their mouths like the mouths of puppets, com-
pressing or dilating their nostrils, wrinkling their foreheads,
making their eyes sparkle: no good for anything but to appraise,
to draw fine distinctions, to argue and judge and criticize, to
weigh the pros and cons, to savour objections, to demonstrate, to
draw conclusions – an interminable syllogism in which each one
of them was a term. On they slouched obedient, argumentative,
unworried by their fate. The war was over: they had seen no
fighting: the Germans weren't a bad lot: unworried because
they fondly imagined that they had summed up their new
masters, and were intent on hoarding the fruits of their intel-

ligence – that specifically French *article de luxe* – so that they could later use it to advantage with the Jerries as coin with which to buy a few trivial concessions. Poplars ... poplars: the sun blazing down on them: noon. 'That's them!' – gone suddenly all sign of intelligence from the crowded faces. A groan of delight rose from the vast concourse, not a cry, not even a murmur, but, rather, a sort of wordless, passive reflex of admiration, like the gentle sussuration of leaves under a shower of rain. 'That's them!' Back and forth the words passed down the line, travelling from man to man like a rumour of good news. The ranks crowded together, jostling into the gutter. A shudder went through the human caterpillar. A column of Germans was moving down the road; Germans in cars and tractors and lorries, freshly shaven, freshly rested, tanned, handsome, calm, remote as Alpine pastures. They had eyes for no one, but sat there staring southwards, driving into the heart of France, upright and silent: getting a free trip – foot-slogging on wheels – that's what I *call* a war – look at them machine-guns – and the mobile artillery – all A1 stuff – no wonder we lost the war! They were delighted that the Germans should be so strong, feeling themselves by so much the less to blame: 'unbeatable – say what you like – unbeatable!' Brunet looked at the defeated mob caught up in a frenzy of wonder and admiration, and he thought: 'This is the material I've got to work on – pretty poor stuff, but that can't be helped: it's all I have. One can always work on what's to hand, and there must be one or two in this little lot who will respond to treatment.' By this time the German column had gone by. The human caterpillar had crawled off the road on to what had been a basket-ball ground. The prisoners swarmed over it like an ooze of black pitch. They sat and lay about with old newspapers spread over their faces to keep off the sun. The whole place looked like a racecourse, or the Bois de Vincennes on a Sunday. 'What've we stopped for?' 'Don't know,' said Brunet. The sight of all these men stretched on their backs got on his nerves. He had no wish to sit down, but realized that he was being merely stupid. No use despising them: that was the surest way of bungling his job. Besides, there was no knowing how far they would have to go, and he'd got to husband his strength. He sat down. Behind him, first one German, then another, sauntered past. They grinned at him in friendly fashion, saying with kindly irony: 'Where are the English?' He looked at their boots of soft black leather, but said nothing. The Germans took themselves off, all but one lanky Feldwebel who stayed behind and said in tones of reproachful melancholy: 'Where are the English? – poor old Frenchies, where you think the English are?' No one answered him, and he stood there, shaking his head. As soon as the Jerries were at a safe distance, Lambert gave his answer between clenched teeth: 'Search me! but wherever they are you'll have to run pretty fast to get the English out of your hair!' 'Ouais!' said Moulu: 'Eh?' 'Perhaps,' explained Moulu, 'the English *will* get in Jerry's hair, but just at the moment he's in theirs, good and proper, and not so very far away, either.' 'Who says so?' 'It's a sure thing, you silly bugger. It's easy for them to talk big when they're tucked away in their island, but just you wait until the Fritzes have got across the Channel. If we French couldn't win the war, it's a damn' sure thing the *English* won't.' Where are the Comrades? Brunet felt lonely. Never, in all the past ten years, had he felt so utterly alone. He was hungry and thirsty, and he was ashamed of being hungry and thirsty. Moulu turned to him: 'They're going to give us some grub.' 'Really?' 'Seems the Feldwebel said so: there's going to be an issue of bread and bully.' Brunet smiled. He knew perfectly well that they were not going to be fed: but it was the only thing they could talk about, and they would never get sick of talking about it. All of a sudden, some of the men got up. Others followed suit. Soon they were all on their feet. They were starting off again. Moulu was furious. 'Who gave the order to move?' he grumbled. No one answered, and he shouted: 'Don't let's budge, boys: they're going to give us some grub!' Blind and deaf, the convoy scrambled back on to the road, and the march was resumed. A forest. Sunlight filtering pale and red through the leaves: three abandoned 75's still pointing threateningly to the east. The men seemed happy now because there was shade. A regiment of German Pioneers filed past. Goldilocks looked at them with a faint smile. It amused him to watch their conquerors between half-closed lids, to play with them like a cat with a mouse, to play with them from the remote heights of his superiority. Moulu gripped Brunet's arm and shook it. 'See that grey chimney over there?' 'What about it?' 'That's Baccarat!' He stood on tiptoe and made a funnel of his hands. 'Hey, boys, Baccarat!' he shouted: 'pass it along: we're just getting into Baccarat!' The men were tired: they had the sun in their eyes: apathetically, they repeated 'Baccarat! Baccarat!' but they didn't care a damn. 'Baccarat?' said Goldilocks to Brunet: 'Isn't that the place they make lace?' 'No,' said Brunet, 'glass.' 'Ah!' said Goldilocks, and his tone was vaguely respectful: 'Ah!' The town looked black under the blue sky. Gloom settled down on the column. 'Feels odd to be in a town again,' said somebody in a flat voice. They passed down a deserted street. Smashed glass lay on the road and the sidewalks. Goldilocks laughed, and jerked his thumb: 'Baccarat glass!' he said. Brunet raised his head. The houses were undamaged, but all the windows were out. Behind him he heard a voice – 'odd to be in a town'. A bridge. The column halted. Millions of eyes were fixed on the river. Five naked Jerries were playing about in the water, splashing and chattering. Twenty thousand grey-faced, sweating Frenchmen, stifling in their uniforms, stared at bellies and buttocks which, for ten months, had been secure behind a rampart of guns and tanks, but were now exposed to view. There was a sort of quiet insolence in their fragility. So that was what their conquerors looked like! – just a bunch of vulnerable white flesh! A sigh, low and eloquent, swept through the ranks. They had watched, without the slightest feeling of anger, the progress of a victorious army perched on its triumphal cars; but the sight of these naked Jerries playing leapfrog in the water seemed to them an insult. Lambert leaned over the parapet, looked at the river, and murmured: 'Must be nice!' The words expressed not so much a wish as a dead man's regret. Dead, forgotten, wrapped in the shroud of a war now over and done with, the crowd of prisoners moved on, parched, hot, choked with dust. A gate swung open with a squeal of hinges. Around them were high walls. At the far end of a huge courtyard, through a quivering curtain of heat, Brunet could see a barrack-building. All the shutters were closed. He moved forward. Somebody bumped into him from behind. He turned: 'No need to push – plenty of room for all of us.' He passed the gate. Moulu laughed with relief. 'Well, we're through with it for

one day!' – through with the world of civilians and conquerors,
with the poplars and the rivers glittering in the sun. They were
going to bury their filthy old war among these high buildings,
were going to stew in their own juice, unseen of the outer
world, isolated and alone. Brunet moved on, pushed from behind, to the farthest limit of the courtyard. He stopped at the
foot of a long, grey cliff. Moulu nudged him: 'Militia barracks.'
A hundred pairs of shutters hermetically sealed; a flight of three
steps; a padlocked door. To the left of the steps, a few yards
from the main building, a low, brick breastwork had been con-
structed, about three feet high and six long. Brunet went across
and leaned against it. The courtyard was filling up. A continual
stream of men was packing the first arrivals tight, forcing them
against the building. On and on they came. Suddenly, the gates
swung to and closed. 'Home at last,' said Moulu. Lambert eyed
the gate and said with satisfaction: 'There's one little lot
couldn't get in: they'll have to spend the night outside.' Brunet
gave a shrug. 'Doesn't make much difference whether one sleeps
in a street or a courtyard.' 'Oh yes it does!' said Lambert. Goldilocks nodded approval. 'At least *we're* not outside.' Lambert
went one better: '*We're* in a house without a roof.' Brunet
swung round. Standing with his back to the barrack-block, he
made a survey of his surroundings. Opposite, the courtyard
stretched down a gentle slope to the outer wall, on the top of
which two watch-towers had been built, a hundred yards apart.
For the moment they were empty. A row of posts had been
freshly set up to support a curtain of barbed-wire and rope which
divided the yard into two unequal parts. The smaller of these –
a relatively narrow strip of ground between the outer wall and
the posts – was unoccupied. The main body of prisoners was
crowded together in the other, between the posts and the buildings. The men looked ill at ease, as though they were temporary
visitors, and no one dared to sit down. They still had their
haversacks, and various odd bundles in their hands, and their
cheeks were runnelled with sweat. No longer was the gleam of
typical French intelligence visible on their faces. The sun shone
in their vacant eyes. They had taken refuge from the past and
from the immediate future, in a sort of uncomfortable, provisional, and minor death. Brunet refused to admit to himself

that he was thirsty. He had put his haversack on the ground, and was standing with his hands in his pockets, whistling. A sergeant gave him a military salute before coming up to him. 'What are we waiting for?' 'I've no idea.' The man was tall, thin, and tough-looking. Self-importance gave his large eyes a dead look. There was a thick line of moustache across his bony face. His movements had something violent and staccato about them – clearly the result of training. 'Who's in charge?' he asked. 'The Jerries, presumably.' 'In our little lot, I mean: who's responsible?' Brunet laughed in his face: 'Search me!' The sergeant's eyes expressed a mixture of suspicion and reproach. What he wanted was to be second-in-command, to combine the intoxicating satisfaction of obeying with the pleasure of giving orders. But Brunet had no intention of assuming control: he had ceased to command when the last of his men had fallen. He had other things to think about now. The sergeant showed signs of impatience. 'Why are these poor devils being kept hanging about on their feet?' Brunet said nothing. The sergeant gave him a furious look and resigned himself to the necessity of taking charge. He drew himself to his full height, made a megaphone of his hands, and shouted: 'Everyone sit! Pass it along!' Faces were turned uneasily in his direction, but nobody moved. 'Everyone sit!' repeated the sergeant: 'the whole lot of you!' A few men sat down, looking half-asleep: voices echoed the message – everyone sit down. A ripple went through the crowd: there was a general subsidence. The cry eddied above their heads – everyone sit – travelled to the far end of the courtyard, rebounded from the wall, and returned mysteriously distorted – everyone up – stay on your feet and wait for orders. The sergeant looked at Brunet uneasily: somewhere, over by the gate, he had got a rival. Some of the men jumped to their feet, hugging their haversacks, and looking about them with hunted eyes. But most remained seated, and, gradually, those who had got up sat down again. The sergeant contemplated the result of his labours, and uttered a self-satisfied laugh. 'It's only a matter of issuing orders.' Brunet looked at him and said: 'Sit down, sergeant – that's an order!' The sergeant hesitated, then lowered himself to the ground between Lambert and Moulu. He sat with his hands clasped round his knees, gazing up at Brunet, his mouth hanging half-open. Brunet explained: 'I stand because I'm a warrant-officer.' He wouldn't sit down. He had cramp in his calves and it was creeping up his legs, but he wouldn't sit down. Before his eyes were thousands of backs and shoulder-blades, twitching necks and jerking shoulders. The whole crowd seemed to have caught the fidgets. He watched it sweltering and shimmering: without either boredom or pleasure, he thought: this is my material: they're just waiting, rigid, expectant: they don't even seem to be hungry any more: the heat must have affected their stomachs. They're afraid and they're waiting. What are they waiting for? – an order, a catastrophe, or just nightfall? – it wouldn't much matter what, so long as it took them out of themselves. A fat reservist raised a white face and nodded in the direction of one of the watch-towers. 'Why aren't there any sentries up there? what's their little game?' He paused for a moment, the sun flooding his upturned eyes, then shrugged, and said in a voice that combined criticism with dis-appointment: 'Same trouble with them as with us – too much organization.' Brunet, the only man on his feet, looked at the carpet of heads: he thought: there are Comrades somewhere in this lot, but they'll be as hard to find as needles in haystacks. It'll take time to get them together. He looked up at the sky, at an aeroplane showing black against it, then lowered his eyes and turned his head. To his right he noticed a big fellow who had not sat down – a corporal. He was smoking a cigarette. The aeroplane passed overhead with a shattering din. The crowded faces lowered, then upturned, passed from black to white, like a field suddenly bursting into flower: in place of hard, black heads, thousands of camelias broke into blossom. Spectacles glittered like scraps of glass in a garden bed. The corporal had not moved. His broad shoulder blades were stooped, and he was staring at the ground between his feet. Brunet noted, with a little thrill of pleasure, that he was freshly shaved. The corporal turned, and it was he now who studied Brunet. He had large, heavy, deeply shadowed eyes. Had it not been for a broken nose he would have been almost good-looking. Brunet thought: 'I've seen that face before! – but where?' He could not remember; he had seen so many faces. He left off trying to remember: the point was not really important, and, anyhow, the man seemed

243

to have no recollection of him. Suddenly, Brunet uttered an ejaculation, and the other raised his eyes. But Brunet was still not satisfied. He had no wish to chum up with the chap, it was only that he had caught his attention by remaining on his feet and being freshly shaved and clean. 'Come over here,' he said, with no special eagerness. 'If you want to keep standing you can lean against this low wall.' The man stooped, picked up his bundle, and followed Brunet, stepping over the recumbent bodies. He was thickset, but decidedly putting on fat. 'Howya, chum!' 'Howya!' said Brunet. 'This pitch'll do for me,' said the man. 'You alone?' asked Brunet. 'My men are all dead,' replied the man. 'So are mine,' said Brunet. 'What's your name?' 'Didn't catch,' said the man. I said, 'What's your name?' 'Oh, Schneider – what's yours?' 'Brunet.' They relapsed into silence. What did I want to pick up this fellow for? – he's going to be a nuisance. Brunet looked at his watch: five o'clock. The sun was invisible now behind the buildings, but the sky was as oppressive as ever: not a cloud, not the suspicion of a breeze: a dead sea. There was no sound of voices. All round Brunet men were trying to sleep, their heads buried in their arms, but uneasiness was keeping them awake. They sat up, sighed, and began to scratch. 'Hi!' said Moulu: 'Hi!' Brunet turned. Behind him a dozen or so officers were marching along in charge of a German sentry. They were keeping close to the wall. 'So there's some of *them* about still!' muttered Goldilocks between his teeth: 'didn't all make a getaway then?' The officers, silent, and with their eyes averted, moved on. The men laughed in an embarrassed way, and deliberately turned from them as they passed. It was as though officers and men were both afraid of one another. Brunet caught Schneider's eye. They exchanged a smile. From the ground nearby came a little splutter of angry voices: the sergeant was having words with Goldilocks. 'Every bleedin' one of them!' Goldilocks was saying: 'in cars and trucks. Whole damn' lot of 'em cut and ran and left us to hold the baby!' The sergeant folded his arms: 'I don't like to hear men talking like that, not a bit I don't!' 'Only proves as how the Boches were right,' replied Goldilocks: 'They said when they nabbed us – the French Army – they said – is an army without a leader!' 'And what about the other war, didn't the

leaders win that?' 'They wasn't the same 'uns.' ' 'Course they
weren't the same 'uns – but the point is they had different
troops!' 'So it's us as lost the bloody war? Pore bloody second-
line crocks. Is that what you mean?' 'What I mean is,' said the
sergeant, 'that you buggered off in face of the enemy and surrendered France!' Lambert, who had been listening in silence,
went scarlet in the face and leaned across to the sergeant. 'See
here, pal, how comes it *you're* here if *you* didn't bugger off?
Suppose you think you died on the field of honour and've just
woke up in Paradise? My own notion is they caught you because
you couldn't run fast enough!' 'I'm not your pal – I'm a sergeant, and I'm old enough to be your father. If you want to
know, I didn't bugger off: they got me, because I'd no ammo
left!' Men were crawling towards them from all sides, and
Goldilocks called them to witness. 'Hear that, chaps?' he said
with a guffaw. Everyone laughed. Goldilocks turned on the
sergeant: 'That's right, daddy, that's right, you bin and shot
down twenty parachutists and stopped a bleedin' tank with yer
own bleedin' 'ands! I could say just the same. What's yer proof?'
The sergeant pointed to a faded patch on his tunic: his eyes
were blazing: 'Médaille Militaire – Légion d'Honneur – Croix
de Guerre – won 'em in '14, before you were so much as born:
them's my proof!' 'Where's yer ribbons?' 'I tore 'em off when
the Germans came.' There was a general outburst of shouting.
The men were lying on their stomachs, curled up like seals.
They barked, they yelped, their faces were suffused with passion.
The sergeant sat, cross-legged, dominating the lot of them, one
against a crowd. 'See here, you blighter,' shouted a voice, 'you
don't think I felt much like fighting, do yer, when the radio
kept on bawling that Old Man Pétain said France had asked for
an armistice?' – and another: 'Suppose you'd 'ave liked us to get
ourselves bumped off while the generals was doing a deal with
Jerry in one of them historic châteaux?' 'And why not?' replied
the sergeant in a fury: 'chaps are supposed to get killed in a
war, aren't they?' Indignation kept his audience silent for a
moment. He took advantage of the pause to say: 'Saw it all
a-coming a long time ago, I did – only had to look at you, the
lads of '40, skulkers, the lot of you, pretty boys without an ounce
o' discipline. No one could as much as say a word to you –

245

captain had to come cap in hand before you'd listen: "Sure I'm very sorry, I hope you don't mind, but would you be so very kind as to go on cookhouse fatigue?" Just you wait, said I to meself, one of these days there's going to be a bust-up, and what'll the little tough guys do then? – the fat'll be in the fire then all right, I said. Leave! When all the fuss about leave started, that's tore it, I said. Got too much spunk in you, I suppose: got to send you home to get rid of some of it with your girl friends! Think we had leave in '14?' 'Course you did!' 'How d'you know that, kid? Didn't happen to be there, did yer?' 'I didn't, but me old man did, and he told me!' 'Must've fought his war at Marseilles, your old man, 'cos we had to wait two years, and then some, before we got any leave! One chap might strike lucky, and then, when the next come along, all leave was suspended. Like to know how much time I spent at home in fifty-two months of war? Well, I'll tell yer – twenty-two days. Yes, twenty-two days, m'lad. Put that in yer pipe, and even so there was some as said I had all the luck!' 'All right, all right,' said Lambert, 'we don't want to hear the story of yer life.' 'I'm not telling you the story of m'life. I'm just explaining how it comes we won our war and you lost yours.' Goldilocks's eyes were ablaze with anger: 'since you're so clever, maybe you'll explain how you managed to lose the peace?' 'The peace?' exclaimed the sergeant in astonishment. There was a babble of voices: 'Yes, the peace, the peace, it was you as lost the peace!' 'You was the old soldiers, wasn't you?' said Goldilocks: 'well, what did you do for ter see as how your kids should be safe? Did you make Germany pay? Did you see she was disarmed? How 'bout the Rhineland? how 'bout the Ruhr? how 'bout the war in Spain? how 'bout Abyssinia?' 'And how about the Treaty of Versailles?' said a lanky fellow with a head shaped like a sugarloaf, 'did I sign that?' 'Suppose you think it was me as signed it,' said the sergeant, grinning with vexation. 'Got it in one, old cock: if it wasn't you, who was it? You voted, didn't you? *I* didn't – I'm twenty-two and I've never voted yet.' 'What does that prove?' 'It proves that you voted like a s—, and got us all in a proper mess. You had twenty years to prepare for this war or avoid it, and what did you do? Don't think I'm not as good as you, chum: if I'd had good leaders and the right

weapons, I'd have fought as well as you ever did. But what'd I
got to fight *with*? Just you tell me that: why, I didn't even have
enough ammo.' 'Whose fault was it, then,' asked the sergeant: 'who voted for Stalin? who was it went on strike just
because he was fed up, just because he wanted to get his own
back on the boss? Who was it demanded wage rises? Who was
it refused to work overtime? What about all the cars and bikes
as was never turned out? Who was it wot never thought about
nothing but bits of skirt and holidays with pay and Sundays in
the country and Youth Hostels and the pictures? Just a lot o'
slackers, that's what you were. *I* worked every bloody day of me
life, Sundays included ...' Goldilocks was now the colour of
beetroot. He crawled over to the sergeant, and yelled in his face:
'Just you say I was a slacker! just you say that again! I'm the
son of a widow, I am, and I left school at eleven, just so's I
could support my mother!' He didn't care a damn about having lost the war, but wouldn't stand for being told he'd
slacked at his work. Brunet thought: I might make something of him. By this time, the sergeant, too, was on all fours,
and the two men were bawling at one another, their faces only
a few inches apart. Schneider was leaning forward, as though
about to interfere. Brunet touched him on the arm: 'Leave
'em alone: keeps 'em occupied.' Schneider seemed perfectly
willing to acquiesce. He straightened up, with an odd look at
Brunet. 'Come on,' said Moulu, 'pipe down! what's the point
o' scrapping about it!' The sergeant sat down with a short
laugh. 'You're right there!' he said: 'bit late to start fighting
now: if he'd wanted a rough-house, he'd only to have a go at
the Germans!' Goldilocks, too, settled back into his former
position. 'You makes me sick!' he said. There was a long
silence. They sat side by side. Goldilocks began pulling up bits
of grass and amused himself by plaiting them. The others waited
a moment, then crawled back on all fours to where they had
been before. Moulu stretched himself and grinned. 'That sort of
thing ain't serious,' he said in conciliatory tones: 'not a bit
serious.' Brunet thought of the Comrades losing battle after
battle, going on with teeth clenched from defeat to defeat until
the day of final victory. He looked at Moulu: Don't know that
type. He felt the need to talk to somebody: Schneider happened

to be there, so he talked to him. 'You see, it wasn't worth interfering.' Schneider said nothing. Brunet laughed: 'That sort of thing's not serious,' he said, imitating Moulu. Still Schneider said nothing. The expression of his heavy, handsome face was non-committal. The sight of it irritated Brunet, and he turned away. He hated passive resistance. 'I could do with a bite,' said Lambert. Moulu jerked his thumb at the open space separating the outer wall from the posts. His voice, when he spoke, was low and fervent: his words were a poem. 'That's where the grub'll come: the lorries'll drive through them gates, and there'll be loaves of bread thrown over the wire.' Brunet looked at Schneider out of the corner of his eye. He laughed. 'You see?' he said: 'there'd have been no point in getting excited. Defeat, war – it's not *them* that matter: food's the important thing!' A flash of irony showed in Schneider's half-closed eyes. 'What they been doing to you, pal?' he asked in tones of sympathy: 'you don't seem to like 'em much.' 'Nothing,' replied Brunet curtly: 'hearing 'em's quite enough for me!' Schneider was looking down at his right hand which he kept half clenched. He stared at his nails. In his big, nonchalant voice, he said: 'It's difficult to help people when one don't like 'em.' Brunet frowned. They often used to print my mug in the *Huma*, and it's easy to recognize. 'Who said I wanted to help 'em?' 'We all of us ought to help one another.' 'Sure we ought,' said Brunet. He was irritated with himself: first, because he should never have lost his temper, but particularly because he shouldn't have let this uncooperative bloke see that he'd lost it. He made an effort to control himself, smiled, and said: 'I haven't got anything against *them*.' 'Against whom, then?' Brunet gave Schneider an appraising look. 'Against those who led 'em up the garden.' Schneider's laugh had an unpleasant sound. 'Who led *us*, you mean,' he said: 'we're all in the same boat.' Brunet felt his former irritation stirring again, but kept a strong hold on his temper. 'If you prefer it that way,' he said good-humouredly: 'but I don't mind telling you *I* never had any illusions.' 'Nor did I, but what difference does that make? Led up the garden or not, here we are.' 'What of it, here's as good as anywhere else.' He was quite calm now: he thought: my place and my work's wherever there's men to be found. Schneider was looking towards the gate. He said no more. Brunet looked at him without antipathy: what sort of a chap is he? – an intellectual? an anarchist? What was his job in civil life? Too much fat; looks as though he'd let himself go a bit: but he holds himself well: might be able to make use of him. The evening light was showing pink and grey on the walls, on the black town which was out of sight. The men's eyes had a fixed stare. They were looking through the walls at the town, thinking of nothing, moving scarcely at all. The vast patience of the soldier had descended upon them with the dusk. They were waiting. They had waited for letters, for leave, for the German attack, and this was their way of waiting for the end of the war. The war was over, and still they waited. They were waiting for the lorries loaded with bread, for the German sentries, for the armistice; were waiting just so that they might have a tiny patch of future before them, were waiting so as not to die. Far away, in the falling night, in the past, a church-bell sounded. Moulu smiled. 'P'raps that's the armistice, Lambert!' Lambert began to laugh. The two men exchanged a knowing wink. 'I did hear as how there was going to be a reglar blow-out,' he explained. 'That'll be for when peace is declared,' said Moulu. The thought made Goldilocks laugh: 'On the day peace is declared,' he said, 'I'm going to get so plastered that I shan't be sober again for a fortnight!' 'Not for a fortnight! – not for a month!' – came in a clamour of voices: 'we'll be dead to the world, then, all right!' One by one, with infinite patience, we shall have to destroy their hopes, prick their illusions, make them realize the hideous condition of their lives, see it naked and unadorned as it really is, disgust them with everything and everyone, beginning with themselves ... only *then* ... This time it was Schneider who looked at him. 'That'll be difficult,' said Schneider. Brunet waited, his eyebrows raised. Schneider said again: 'That'll be difficult.' 'What'll be difficult?' 'To give us a sense of solidarity. We're not a class – we're little more than a herd: not many workmen – just peasants and middle-class riff-raff. We've not even got jobs. We're just human beings in the abstract.' 'Don't you worry,' said Brunet in spite of himself: 'we'll have jobs all right.' 'Oh, I know all about that, but as slaves have jobs. That's not the kind of work that emancipates: we shall never be anything but make-weights. What common action can you ask of us? A strike gives the strikers a sense of their power. But even if every French prisoner folded his arms and did nothing, it wouldn't make a ha'porth of difference to the German economy.' They looked at one another coldly. Brunet thought: so you *have* recognized me! well, so much the worse for you. I shall keep my eyes skinned where you're concerned. A sudden hatred flared in Schneider's face, then quickly died out. Brunet did not even know against whom the hatred was directed. ... There was a cry of surprise and delight. 'A Fritz!' 'Where?' Everyone looked up. A soldier had just appeared on top of the left-hand watch-tower. He was wearing a helmet, holding a tommy-gun, and had a grenade stuck in his boot-top. He was followed by another with a rifle. ' 'Bout time they *did* do summat 'bout us!' said a voice. The feeling of relief was general. They were back at last in the world of men, with its laws, its routine, its rules and regulations; back in some sort of human society. All heads were turned towards the other tower. It was still empty, but the men waited confidently, as they might have waited for the post office to open or the Blue Train to run through a station. A helmet showed at wall level, then two more; two helmeted monsters carrying between them a machine-gun which they proceeded to set up on its tripod and level at the prisoners. No one was frightened. The prisoners settled down. The sight of the sentries upright on the wall gave assurance that nothing would happen that night: no order would come to wake the assembled men and turn them out again to march the roads. They felt secure. A tall, strapping fellow, wearing steel-rimmed spectacles, had taken a breviary from his pocket, and was reading it, muttering to himself. 'He's on the prowl!' thought Brunet, but anger slid over him without penetrating. He felt at peace. For the first time for fifteen years he was aware of time moving slowly, of a day ending in a fine evening without there being anything for him to do. The sense of leisure, forgotten since childhood, welled up in him. Stuck there, on top of the wall, was the sky, pink-flushed, quite close, unusable. He looked at it shyly, then turned his gaze on the men lying motionless at his feet. He sat down beside Schneider and unlaced his boots. He yawned. His body felt as useless as the sky. He said: 'It's beginning to get chilly!' Tomorrow he would set to work. By this time the colour of the earth was grey. He heard a sound as of something softly rattling, a tight, irregular sound. He listened, tried to make out the rhythm, and amused himself with the thought that it might be Morse. Suddenly, a thought came to him: 'Somebody's teeth are chattering.' He sat up. In front of him he could see a naked back covered with black scabs. It belonged to the man who had been making a noise on the march. He crawled over to him. The man had goose-flesh. 'Hullo!' said Brunet. The man made no reply. Brunet took a knitted woollen waistcoat from his haversack. 'Hullo!' he said again, and touched the naked shoulder. The man started to yell. He turned round and looked at Brunet. He was panting. His nose was running. The stuff was dribbling into his mouth. Brunet saw his face for the first time, the face of a handsome young man. His cheeks looked blue, and his eyes were deeply sunk. There were no lashes to his lids. 'Don't get into a flap, old man,' said Brunet quietly. 'I only wanted to give you this woolly.' The man took the waistcoat. He looked frightened. He put it on obediently and sat motionless, his arms outstretched. The sleeves were too long, and reached to the tips of his fingers. Brunet laughed: 'Turn 'em up.' The man made no reply. His teeth were still chattering. Brunet took him by the arm and rolled up the sleeves. 'It's timed for tonight,' said the man. 'Really?' said Brunet, 'and what's timed for tonight?' 'The hecatomb,' said the man. 'That's all right, then,' said Brunet. He felt in the man's pocket and brought out a dirty handkerchief, stained with blood. He threw it away, took out his own and held it out. 'Meanwhile, you'd better wipe your nose.' The man did so, stuffed the handkerchief into his pocket, and began to jabber. Brunet stroked his head as he might have done an animal's. 'You're quite right,' he said. The man grew calmer, and his teeth ceased to chatter. Brunet turned to the other men lying round. 'Anyone know this chap?' A small, dark fellow with a bright face raised himself on his elbows. 'It's Charpin,' he said. 'Keep an eye on him,' said Brunet: 'he may try to do something silly.' 'I'll keep an eye on him,' said the small man. 'What's your name?' asked Brunet. 'Vernier.' 'What's your line?' 'Used to be a printer in Lyon.' A printer! what a piece of luck! I'll have a word with him tomorrow. 'Good night,' said Brunet. 'Good night,' said the man. Brunet went back to his own place. He sat down and started to reckon up his resources. Moulu – small shopkeeper, almost for certain: not much to be got out of him – nor out of the sergeant, an incorrigible old sweat. Lambert, a grouser, disintegrated, for the moment, under the impact of his own cynicism: might be possible to win him over later. The man from the North – a hobbledehoy – negligible; Brunet had no use for hobbledehoys. Goldilocks, same stamp as Lambert, but with more intelligence, and a worker's self-respect, but, for the moment, completely at sea. The printer – probably a young Communist. Brunet glanced across at Schneider, who was sitting motionless, his eyes wide open, smoking: 'have to see about *him*.' The priest had laid aside his breviary and was talking. The young men were lying close to him and listening with expressions of pious familiarity. Three of 'em already: he's a faster worker than I am – at least in the early stages. Chaps like him are lucky, thought Brunet. They can work openly, and on Sundays they can say Mass. Moulu heaved a sigh: 'Won't come tonight.' 'Who won't come tonight?' asked Lambert. 'The lorries – too dark.' He lay down and put his head on his haversack. 'Look here,' said Lambert: 'I've got a ground-sheet: how many are we?' 'Seven,' said Moulu. 'Seven?' said Lambert, 'it'll take the lot of us.' He spread his ground-sheet in front of the steps. 'Anyone got some blankets?' Moulu produced one, the man from the North and the sergeant two more. Goldilocks had none, nor had Brunet. 'Don't matter,' said Lambert, 'we'll manage.' A face emerged from the darkness showing a timid smile. 'If you'll let me lie on your ground-sheet, I'll share my blankets.' Lambert and Goldilocks eyed the intruder coldly. 'No room for you, chum,' said Goldilocks, and Moulu added in a more friendly voice, 'We're a bunch of pals, see?' The smile vanished, swallowed by the darkness. A group had formed in the middle of this nondescript crowd. A perfectly casual group, without the bond of friendship or any real element of solidarity. But already it was closing its ranks against outsiders, and Brunet was part of it. 'Come over here,' said Schneider: 'we'll doss down together under my blanket.' Brunet hesitated: 'Don't feel particularly sleepy just now.' 'Nor do I,' said Schneider. They sat side by side while the others rolled themselves in their blankets. Schneider was smoking, concealing his cigarette in the palm of his hand because of the sentries. He brought a packet from his pocket and held it out to Brunet: 'Cigarette? – you'd better go behind the wall to light it, so's they can't see.' Brunet longed for a smoke, but he refused: 'Not at the moment, but thanks all the same.' He wasn't going to play the schoolboy, like a kid of sixteen. To disobey the Germans in little things was, to some extent, to recognize their authority. The first stars came out. From far away, on the other side of the wall, drifted the sound of music. There was no sweetness in it: it was the music of their conquerors. Sleep rolled like a tide over twenty thousand exhausted bodies, and each body was a wave. The dark surf moved like a sea. Brunet began to feel that he had had enough of doing nothing. A lovely sky was all right to look at for a bit, but he might just as well go to sleep. He turned to Schneider with a yawn. Schneider was off his guard. His cigarette had gone out and he had not relit it. It was dangling from his lower lip. He was staring gloomily at the sky. This was the moment to find out more about him. 'You from Paris?' asked Brunet. 'No.' Brunet assumed an air of frankness: he said, 'I live in Paris, but Combleux's my home town, near St Étienne.' Silence. After a brief pause, Schneider said regretfully, 'I'm from Bordeaux.' 'Ah,' said Brunet: 'I know Bordeaux well. Fine town but a bit on the gloomy side, eh? You work there?' 'Yes.' 'What at?' 'What at?' 'Yes.' 'I'm a clerk – solicitor's office.' 'Ah,' said Brunet. He yawned. He had got to find some way of getting a look at Schneider's army book. 'And you?' asked Schneider. Brunet gave a start: 'Me?' 'Yes.' 'Traveller.' 'What you travel in?' 'Oh, anything that happens along.' 'I see.' Brunet settled himself along the base of the low wall, and curled up. In a scarcely audible voice, as though he were taking toll of the day, before going off to sleep, he said: 'Well, here we are.' 'Yes, here we are,' said Schneider in the same voice. 'A proper muck-up.' 'I agree.' 'Well, if we'd got to be beaten,' said Brunet, 'it's just as well we got beaten quickly: less bloodshed that way.' Schneider laughed: 'Don't worry; they'll bleed us by instalments; the result will be the same.' Brunet glanced at him: 'Bit of a defeatist, aren't you.' 'I'm not a de-

253

featist, but I know defeat when I see it.' 'What defeat?' said Brunet: 'Defeat, my foot!' He broke off, expecting Schneider to protest. But he was wrong: Schneider merely sat and stared blankly at his boots, the cigarette-stub still hanging from the corner of his mouth. Brunet had gone too far to stop: he'd got to develop his idea, but it was *no longer the same idea*. If only the fool had asked a few questions, he'd have harpooned him! The thought of talking gave him no pleasure now: his words would just slide off this great indifferent lump of flesh without penetrating. 'It's just chauvinism that makes the French think they've lost the war! They always believe they're the only people in the world, and then, when their invincible army gets it in the neck, all the stuffing goes out of 'em.' A little nasal sound came from Schneider. Brunet decided to go ahead willy-nilly. 'This war's only just begun. In six months' time we'll be fighting from the Cape to the Behring Straits.' Schneider laughed: '*We?*' 'Yes, we Frenchmen,' said Brunet: 'we shall continue the war in other fields. The Germans'll try to militarize our industry: that's something the proletariat can and must stop.' Schneider showed no reaction: his athletic body lay there inert. Brunet did not like the way things were shaping. Heavy, disconcerting silences were *his* specialty. He had been manoeuvring so as to fight on his own ground, had been trying to make Schneider talk, and now it was he who had been compelled to do the talking. It was his turn, now, to be silent. Schneider still said nothing. This sort of thing might go on for a long time. Brunet began to grow uneasy. The fellow had got either too much or too little in his head. Not far from them somebody began to yap feebly. This time it was Schneider who broke the silence. He spoke with a kind of heat. 'Hear that? – thinks he's a dog!' Brunet shrugged, this isn't the moment to get sentimental over a chap who was having a bad dream: I've no time to waste. 'Poor devils!' said Schneider, in a deep voice thrilling with passion. Brunet remained silent. Schneider continued: 'They'll never go home, never!' He turned to Brunet, and there was hatred in his eyes. 'Hey! don't look at me like that!' said Brunet with a laugh: 'it's not *my* fault!' Schneider, too, began to laugh. His expression softened, and the fire died out of his eyes: 'You're right: it's not your fault.' Silence fell between them. An idea occurred to Brunet. He sidled up to Schneider, and said in a low voice: 'If that's how you feel, why don't you try to escape?' 'Bah!' said Schneider. 'Are you married?' 'Should jolly well think I am – got a couple of kids.' 'Don't you get on with your wife?' 'I? – why, we're a pair of turtle-doves!' 'Well, then?' 'Bah!' repeated Schneider: 'are *you* going to escape?' 'I don't know,' said Brunet: 'I shall have to think about it.' He tried to get a look at Schneider's face, but the yard was wrapped in darkness. It was impossible to see anything but the outlines of the watch-towers against the sky. 'I think I shall go to sleep,' said Brunet with a yawn. 'Same here,' said Schneider. They stretched themselves out on the ground-sheet, and pushed their haversacks against the wall. Schneider spread his blanket, and they both rolled themselves in it. ' 'Night,' said Schneider. ' 'Night.' Brunet turned on his back and rested his head on his haversack. He kept his eyes open. He could feel the warmth of Schneider's body, and guessed that he, too, was lying there with his eyes open. He thought: 'I *would* get mixed up with a chap like that!' Which of them, he wondered, had really been man-oeuvring the other? Every now and then, between the clumps of stars, a little falling brilliance streaked the sky. Schneider moved noiselessly under the blanket. 'You asleep, Brunet?' he whispered. Brunet said nothing: he was waiting. A few moments passed, and then he became aware of the sound of somebody breathing audibly through his nose. Schneider was asleep. Brunet kept his watch in solitude, the one spot of living light among these twenty thousand patches of darkness. He smiled and let himself relax: two Arab women were laughing in the little wood: 'Where is Abd-el-Krim?' The elder of the two replied: 'I shouldn't be surprised if he were at the clothing store.' And there, indeed, he was, sitting quite calmly in front of a tailor's bench, shouting – 'Murder! Murder!' He was tearing the buttons from his tunic, and each button, as it came away, made a dry, explosive sound, and gave off a flash. 'Behind that wall, quick!' said Schneider. Brunet sat up and scratched his head. The night seemed unfamiliar and full of noises. 'What's up?' 'Hurry! Hurry!' Brunet threw back the blanket and flung himself flat behind the little wall, next to Schneider. A voice was moaning – 'Murder!' Someone cried out in German, and there followed the dry rattle of a machine-gun. Brunet risked a peep over the wall. By the light of the flashes he could see a world peopled by stunted trees all raising their twisted, knotted branches to the sky. His eyes hurt him; his head felt empty. He said: 'Suffering humanity!' Schneider dragged him back: 'Suffering humanity, my foot! – they're busy massacring us!' 'Like dogs,' said the unidentified voice – 'like dogs!' The machine-gun had ceased firing. Brunet passed his hand over his eyes: he was fully awake by now. 'What's happening?' 'Don't know,' said Schneider: 'They opened fire twice, the first time, probably, in the air, but the second, they meant business!' All round them the jungle was rustling: what is it? – what is it – what's happened? Self-appointed leaders replied: 'Don't talk; don't move; lie still.' The towers were black against the milky sky: within them were men awake and watchful, their fingers on the triggers of machine-guns. Brunet and Schneider, kneeling behind the wall, could see far off the round eye of an electric torch. It came nearer, swung by an invisible hand. It swept with its light the expanse of grey, flattened grubs. Two harsh voices were speaking German. The torch was shone straight in Brunet's face, so that he was blinded and shut his eyes. A voice with a strong accent asked, 'Who was that who shouted?' 'I don't know,' Brunet replied. The sergeant got to his feet. He stood there, very straight under the beam of the electric light, at once correct and distant. 'One of the prisoners has gone mad: he started to cry out: his companions took fright and got up: it was then that the sentry fired.' The Germans did not understand. Schneider spoke to them in German. They grunted, and then, in their turn, began to speak. Schneider turned to the sergeant: 'They say find out whether anyone's been wounded.' The sergeant straightened up, put his hands to his mouth in a precise, rapid gesture, and shouted: 'Report casualties!' From all sides weak voices were raised in reply. Suddenly, two searchlights came into action. They shed a snowstorm of fairy radiance which passed over the supine crowd. Some Germans crossed the yard carrying stretchers. A number of French medical orderlies joined them. 'Where is this madman?' asked the German officer in a tone of command. Nobody answered, but the madman was in full view, standing up, his lips white and trembling, and tears running down his cheeks. The soldiers surrounded him and led him away. He made no attempt to resist, but went with them. His eyes had a dazed look, and he was wiping his nose with Brunet's handkerchief. All around were men sitting up, looking at the man who was sharing their suffering, but carrying it to the bitter end. There was a feeling in the air of death and defeat. The Germans disappeared. Brunet yawned. The light was stabbing at his eyes. 'What are they going to do with him?' asked Moulu. Brunet shrugged his shoulders. Schneider merely said: 'The Nazis don't like madmen.' Figures were moving about with stretchers. Brunet said: 'I think we can go to sleep again.' They lay down. Brunet uttered a laugh: in the very spot where he had been lying, there was a hole in the ground-sheet, a hole with charred edges. He pointed to it. Moulu's face was green: his hands were trembling. 'Oh!' he said: 'Oh! Oh!' Brunet smiled at Schneider: 'I rather think you saved my life,' he said. Schneider did not return the smile: he was looking at Brunet with a serious and perplexed expression: 'Yes,' he said slowly, 'I saved your life all right.' 'Many thanks,' said Brunet, and rolled himself in the blanket. 'I'm going to doss down behind that there wall,' said Moulu. The searchlights went out suddenly. The forest creaked, crackled, rustled, and whispered. Brunet sat up, his eyes full of sunlight, his head full of sleep. He looked at his watch: seven o'clock. The men were busy folding their ground-sheets. Brunet felt dirty and clammy. He had sweated during the night, and his shirt was sticking to his back. 'Christ!' said Goldilocks, 'I don't half stink and no mistake!' With an expression of gloomy interrogation Moulu looked at the closed gates. 'Another day without grub!' Lambert opened a peevish eye: 'Have a heart!' Brunet got up, glanced round the yard, saw a group of men clustered about a hose-pipe, and joined them. A fat fellow, stripped to the buff, was being sprayed. He was squealing like a woman. Brunet took off his clothes, waiting his turn, and received a hard, icy jet of water on his back and front. Then he put on his clothes again without drying himself, took hold of the hose, and played it on the next three men. The bath had only very few patrons: the men preferred their sweat. 'Who's next?' asked Brunet. He dropped the hose in a temper. He thought: 'No self-respect!' He glanced about him. That pretty well summed up the lot of 'em. The job he'd got on his hands wouldn't be easy. He flung his tunic over his arm in such a way as to hide the badges of rank, and approached a little knot of prisoners who were chatting together in low voices – a good opportunity to find out how the land lay. What's the betting they're talking about food! – not that he minded; food was as good a subject to start off with as any other – simple, concrete, and actual. When a chap's hungry, there's something to work on. But they were not talking about food. A tall, thin man with red eyes recognized him. 'You're the bloke as was next the loony, aren't yer?' 'Yes,' said Brunet. 'What'd he done?' 'Kicked up a row.' 'That all! Hell! – grand total four dead and twenty wounded!' 'How do you know that?' 'Gartiser said so.' Gartiser was a thickset fellow with flabby cheeks and a morose, self-important expression. 'You a medical orderly?' asked Brunet. Gartiser nodded: yes, he was a medical orderly, and the Fritzes had taken him to the stables behind the barrack-block, where he had had to look after the injured. 'Every man jack of 'em passed through my hands.' 'It's pretty rotten luck,' said a man standing by, 'to have one's number up like that just a week before going home.' 'A week?' inquired Brunet. 'Oh well, a week or a fortnight, whichever you like. They'll have to send us home, seeing as how they can't feed us.' 'What about the chap who went mad?' asked Brunet. Gartiser spat between his feet. 'Best not talk about him.' 'Why not?' 'They tried to make him keep quiet: one of 'em put his hand on his mouth, and got bitten for his trouble. My aunt! you should've seen 'em! – all shouting and jabbering their lingo – couldn't hear yerself speak – and then they got him in a corner of the stables, and started hitting him with their fists and beating him with their rifle-butts: they was thoroughly enjoying themselves by the end, and there was some of our chaps as egged 'em on, because they said that but for that son of a bitch nothing would have happened. He wasn't a nice sight when they'd finished with him – face all mashed up, and one eye hanging out. Then they put him on a stretcher and carried him away – I don't know where to, but they must have gone on having their bit of fun with him, because I heard him yelling up to three o'clock.' He took from his pocket a small object wrapped in newspaper.

'It's one of his teeth – I picked it up this morning where he fell down.' Very carefully he rolled up his package again, put it in his pocket, and said: 'Keepin' it as a souvenir, I am.' Brunet turned away and went slowly towards the steps. Moulu cried after him: 'Heard the result?' 'What result?' 'Result of the night's doings – twenty dead and thirty wounded.' 'Christ!' said Brunet. 'Not bad,' said Moulu. He smiled as though he were taking a vague sort of pride in the news: 'not bad at all, for the first night!' 'What they want to waste ammo for?' asked Lambert: 'they can get rid of us easy enough by leaving us to starve: they've begun already.' 'They're not going to leave us to starve,' said Moulu. 'What you know about it?' Moulu smiled: 'Just you keep an eye on the gate, same as what I'm doing: it'll take yer mind off, and that's the way the lorries'll come in.' The sound of an engine drowned his voice. ' 'Ware plane!' shouted the man from the North. It was a machine out for observation. It flew over them at a hundred and fifty feet, black and shining. It swooped over the yard and made a sharp left turn. Twice, three times, it repeated the manoeuvre. Twenty thousand faces gazed at it, following its every movement. The whole crowd turned when it turned. 'Suppose they'll start dropping bombs now,' said Curly, with assumed indifference. 'Drop bombs?' said Moulu: 'why should they want to do that?' 'Because they can't feed us.' Schneider, narrowing his eyes, and screwing up his face against the sun, looked at the aeroplane. 'More likely to be photographing us,' he said. 'Who?' asked Moulu. 'War correspondents,' explained Schneider briefly. Moulu's heavy jowl went a dark red; his fear had changed suddenly to anger. All of a sudden he stood up, stretched his arms heavenwards, and began to shout: 'Stick yer tongues out at 'em, chums, stick yer tongues out at 'em – seems they're taking our pictures!' Brunet was amused. A wave of anger had swept the crowd. One man was shaking his fist; another, shoulders back, stomach forward, had stuck his little finger in his flies and was pointing his thumb upward like a sexual organ. The man from the North went down on all fours, put his head down, and displayed his backside to the sky: 'Let 'em photograph that!' Schneider looked at Brunet. 'Still got guts, you see,' he said. 'Bah!' replied Brunet; 'doesn't prove a thing!' The aeroplane flew off into the eye of the sun.

'Think I shall see my mug in the *Franqueforteur*?' said Moulu. Lambert had disappeared. He came back in a great state of excitement. 'Seems we can fit ourselves out nice and cheap!' 'What you mean?' 'There's a lot of furniture behind the barracks, mattresses, crocks, water jugs, all to be had for the asking! But we'll have to go carefully, 'cos it's a matter of lifting 'em on the sly!' He looked round him with shining eyes. 'What you say we have a shot?' 'I'm on to it,' said Curly, jumping up. Moulu did not move. 'Come along, Moulu,' said Lambert. 'No,' said Moulu; 'I'm saving me strength – not moving till I've had something to eat.' 'Keep an eye on things here, then,' said the sergeant. He got up and ran after the others. When they had reached the corner of the building, Moulu shouted after them in a weak voice: 'Wasting yer strength, that's what yer doing, me lads.' He heaved a sigh, looked severely at Schneider and Brunet, and added in a whisper: 'Oughtn't even to raise me voice.' 'Coming?' asked Schneider. 'What use is a water jug?' asked Brunet. 'Might come in useful for washing one's feet.' Beyond the barrack-block there was another yard, and a long, single-storied building with four doors – the stables. In one corner, piled anyhow, were old palliasses, spring-mattresses, cots, rickety cupboards, and tables with nothing left but a single leg. The men were milling round the accumulated rubbish. One of them came back across the yard carrying a mattress, another with a wicker dress-stand. Brunet and Schneider made the round of the stables, and came on a grassy hillock. 'How about sitting down?' said Schneider. 'All right.' Brunet was feeling uncomfortable: what was the fellow after? – friendship? I'm a bit too old for that. On top of the hillock they saw three trenches newly filled. 'See?' said Schneider, 'they didn't kill no more than three.' Brunet sat down on the grass beside the graves. 'Lend me your knife,' he said. Schneider passed it across. Brunet opened it and began to cut off his badges of rank. 'That's silly,' said Schneider: 'N.C.O.s don't have to work.' Brunet shrugged his shoulders but said nothing, put the pieces of braid in his pocket, and got up. He went back into the main yard. The men were making themselves comfortable. A good-looking fellow with an impudent face was sawing backwards and forwards in a rocking-chair. A tent had been pitched, and two others had dragged a table in front of it and a couple of chairs. They sat there, celebrating their victory with a game of cards. Gartiser was squatting cross-legged on a sofa marked all over with burns. 'Reminds me of an old-clo' fair,' said Brunet. 'Or an Arab bazaar,' said Schneider. Brunet went across to Lambert. 'What have you got?' Lambert raised his head with a look of pride: 'Plates!' he said, and pointed to a pile of chipped and blackened dishes. 'What are you going to do with 'em? – eat 'em?' 'Leave him alone,' said Moulu: 'maybe it'll hurry up the grub.' The morning dragged on. The men relapsed into their former torpor. Some of them tried to sleep, others lay on their backs, their faces to the sky, their eyes open and staring. They were hungry. Curly was tearing up handfuls of grass from between the cobbles and chewing it. The man from the North had taken out his knife and was whittling a piece of wood. One group had lit a fire under a rusty saucepan. Lambert got up and went to have a look, but came back looking disappointed. 'Nettle soup!' he said, and dropped down between Goldilocks and Moulu: 'no nourishment in it.' The German sentries were relieved. 'Going off to their dinner,' said the sergeant with a vacant look. Brunet sat down next to the printer. 'Sleep well?' he asked. 'Not too badly,' said the printer. Brunet looked at him with approval. He had a neat, clean appearance: there was gaiety in his eyes. Worth taking a chance. 'I meant to ask you before – were you working in Paris?' 'No,' said the printer, 'in Lyons.' 'Where?' 'At the Levrault works.' 'Ah, I know the place: you put on a good strike there, in '36 – determined and well organized.' The printer laughed proudly. 'Did you know a chap called Pernu, who was there then?' 'What, Pernu, the Trades-Union delegate?' 'That's the man.' ' 'Course I knew him!' Brunet got up. 'Come for a walk round, there's something I want to talk to you about.' When they were in the further yard, Brunet faced him squarely. 'You a member of the Party?' The printer hesitated. Brunet said: 'I'm Brunet of the *Huma*.' 'So that's who you are,' said the printer, 'I rather thought you were.' 'You got many pals here?' 'Two or three.' 'Tough?' 'As tough as you're likely to meet, but I lost sight of 'em yesterday.' 'Try to find them again,' said Brunet, 'and bring them along to see me. We've got to organize a cell.' He went back to where he had been sitting beside Schneider. He gave him a quick, furtive look. Schneider's face was calm and inexpressive. 'What's the time?' he asked. 'Two o'clock,' said Brunet. 'Look at that dog,' said Curly. A large, black dog was crossing the yard with its tongue hanging out. The men were looking at it oddly. 'Where's it come from?' asked the sergeant. 'I don't know,' said Brunet. It had probably been in the stables. Lambert was leaning on his elbow, following the dog with appraising eyes. He said, as though speaking to himself, 'Dog-meat's not so bad as people say.' 'You ever eaten any?' Lambert made no answer. He sketched an irritable gesture, then lay down again apathetically on his back. The two men playing cards in front of the tent had left their hands lying, and had risen with a careless air. One of them was carrying a ground-sheet under his arm. 'Too late,' said Lambert. The dog disappeared behind the barrack-block. They followed it without any sign of hurry, and, in their turn, were lost to sight. 'Will they get him or won't they?' asked the man from the North. A moment later, the two men reappeared. They had got some bulky object wrapped in the ground-sheet, which they were carrying, one at each end, like a hammock. As they passed Brunet a drop splashed on the cobbles – a red drop. 'Inferior material,' said the sergeant: 'that ground-sheet's supposed to be waterproof.' He shook his head: 'Typical, ain't it?' he grumbled: 'how could we be expected to win the war?' The two men threw their load into the tent. One of them crawled in after it on all-fours, while the other set off in search of wood for the fire. Curly sighed: 'Well, there'll be two survivors, anyhow.' Brunet dropped off. He awoke with a start at the sound of Moulu shouting: 'There's the grub!' The gate was slowly swinging open. A hundred men were on their feet. 'A lorry!' The lorry drove in. It was camouflaged and had flowers and branches on its bonnet, a moving pageant of spring. The number of men standing had now risen to a thousand. The lorry turned into the space lying between the outer wall and the barrier. Brunet had got up: he was elbowed, pulled, pushed, and almost carried, to the wire. The lorry was empty. A Jerry, naked to the waist, and perched on the tail-board, sat indolently watching the surging crowd. He had a brown skin, fair hair, and long, delicate muscles. He looked like some luxury object, like one of the men who ski, half-naked, at St Moritz. A thousand pairs of eyes were turned on him. He seemed to find the sight amusing. He smiled at the spectacle of these famished night-prowling animals pressing against the bars of their cage the better to see him. He leaned back and asked a question of the sentries in the watch-tower, who answered him with a laugh. The crowd waited in a sort of daze, watching the movements of its master, growling with impatience and delight. The Jerry bent down, took a loaf of bread from the floor of the lorry, fished a knife from his pocket, opened it, sharpened it against his boot, and cut himself a slice. Someone behind Brunet started to breathe heavily. The Jerry raised the slice to his nose, and pretended to sniff at it ecstatically, his eyes half-closed. The animals growled. Brunet could feel about him a source of anger. The German took another look at them, grinned, raised the slice, held flat between thumb and first finger, and sent it spinning towards them like a quoit. But he had aimed too low – perhaps on purpose – and the bread fell between the lorry and the posts. Some of the men were already on the ground, trying to creep under the wire. The sentry on the watch-tower barked an order, and covered them with his tommy-gun. The men stood there, pressed against the fence, their mouths open and a mad look in their eyes. Moulu, wedged against Brunet, muttered: 'There's going to be trouble – wish I was out of this.' But the pressure of the crowd crushed the two men together. Brunet tried in vain to free himself. 'Get back!' he shouted: 'get back, you fools! – can't you see we'll have last night all over again!' The German in the lorry cut a second slice and sent it spinning towards them. It turned over in the air and dropped among the lifted faces. Brunet was caught in a vast surge of bodies: he felt himself being elbowed, thrust aside, struck at: he saw Moulu swept away in an eddy, his hands raised in the air, like those of a swimmer in water. 'The swine!' he thought: 'the swine!' He wanted to hit those about him with his fists, to kick them with his feet. A second slice fell, a third. The men were fighting to get at them. A great hulking fellow broke away, holding one of them clutched in his hand, but the crowd caught him. Finding himself surrounded, he stuffed his booty into his mouth, pushing it with the back of his hand so as to get it all in. At that, his pursuers let him go free, and he moved slowly away, rolling anxious eyes. The Fritz was having great fun, sending slice after slice skimming to right and left, sometimes pretending to throw, and stopping at the crucial moment, just to disappoint the assembled prisoners. A piece of bread fell at Brunet's feet. A corporal saw it and made a dive, knocking against Brunet as he did so. Brunet seized him by the shoulders and held him tight, while the mob rushed on the prize lying in the dust. Brunet deliberately put his foot on the scrap of bread, and trod it into the ground. But ten hands laid hold of his leg, forced it away, and scraped up the muddy crumbs. The corporal struggled violently: another piece of bread had just bounced off his boot. 'Let me go, you barstard! – let me go!' Brunet maintained his grip: the man tried to hit him, but Brunet parried with his elbow, and exerted all his strength to contract his arms. He was enjoying himself. 'You're choking me!' said the man in a weak voice. Brunet went on squeezing. He could see above him the white scud of bread: he squeezed and squeezed: he was enjoying himself. The man in his arms had, by this time, abandoned any attempt at resistance. 'All over!' said a voice. Brunet glanced over his shoulder. The Jerry was in the act of shutting his knife. Brunet opened his arms. The corporal swayed, took two steps sideways in an effort to regain his balance, fixed Brunet with a glare of brutish hatred, and started to cough. Brunet grinned. The man eyed his breadth of shoulder, hesitated, finally muttered 'Barstard!' and turned away. Slowly the crowd dispersed, disappointed, and by no means proud of the scene just enacted. Here and there, one, who had been luckier than the rest, munched shamefacedly, hiding his mouth with his hand, and rolling his eyes like a naughty child. The corporal stood leaning against one of the posts. A slice of bread was lying in the coal-dust between the lorry and the wire. His eyes were fixed on it. The German jumped down from the lorry, went along the wall, and opened the door of a small hut. The corporal's eyes were gleaming: he stood there, watching. Suddenly, the sentries turned away, and, at once he went down on all fours and started to creep under the wire, his arms outstretched. There was a shout. One of the sentries raised his rifle. The corporal tried to crawl back, but the other sentry motioned to him to stay still, and there he waited, white in the face, his hand still extended, his rump in the air. The German of the lorry had, by this time, returned to his vehicle. Without the slightest sign of hurry, he sauntered up to the wire, pulled the man to his feet with one hand, and, with the other, struck him as hard as he could. Brunet laughed till he cried. A voice behind him said quietly, 'You don't seem particularly fond of us.' Brunet gave a start, and turned. It was Schneider. There was a silence. Brunet's eyes were on the corporal, whom the Jerry was now pushing towards the hut, to an accompaniment of kicks. In a colourless voice, Schneider said: 'We're hungry.' Brunet shrugged: 'Why do you say "we"?' he inquired: 'don't tell me *you* took part in that scramble?' 'Of course,' Schneider replied: 'I behaved like everybody else.' 'That's not true,' said Brunet: 'I was watching.' Schneider shook his head: 'I didn't manage to get a bit – but that's not the point.' Brunet, his eyes lowered, was grinding scraps of bread into the ground with his heel. A strange sensation made him look up suddenly: at the same moment the glint in Schneider's eyes went dim, as though a light had been extinguished. There was nothing now in his face but a sort of apathetic anger which gave it a heavy look. 'I know we're greedy,' he said; 'I know we're cowardly and servile, but whose fault is that? Everything's been taken from us – our jobs, our families, our responsibilities. No man can be brave unless he's got something to do. Without that he just dreams. We've got *nothing* to do. We haven't even got our livings to earn. We don't count any longer, we live in a dream. If we are cowards, it's only in a dream world. Give us a job of work and you'll see us wake up quickly enough.' The Jerry had emerged from the hut. He was smoking. The corporal limped along behind him, carrying a spade and a pick. 'I've got no work to give you,' said Brunet, 'but a man can at least behave properly even if he hasn't got any work to do.' Schneider's eyelids twitched open, then fell again. 'I should have thought you would have been more of a realist. No one's going to object to your behaving properly, but what difference is it going to make? It won't help anyone, and will serve no purpose except to give you a feeling of personal satisfaction unless' – he added with irony – 'you believe in the value of good example.' Brunet looked at Schneider coldly. He said: 'You've recognized me, haven't you?' 'Yes,' said Schneider: 'you're Brunet of the *Huma*, aren't you? – I've seen your photo often.' 'Did you used to read the *Huma*?' 'Such a thing was not unknown.' 'Are you one of us?' 'No, but I'm not against you.' Brunet pulled a face. They walked back slowly towards the steps, picking their way over the recumbent bodies. The men, exhausted by the violence of their desire and of their disappointment, had once more lain down. Their faces were livid, and their eyes glittered. The card-players were still seated close to their tent. They had begun a new game. Ashes and bones lay beneath the table. Brunet glanced at Schneider out of the corner of his eye. He was trying to catch again the familiar something which had struck him on the previous evening. But he had been looking at the large nose, at the general layout of the face, for too long. The vividness of the first impression had gone dim. 'I suppose you know,' he muttered between his teeth, 'what happens to a Communist if the Nazis get him?' Schneider smiled but said nothing. 'We give short shrift to squeakers.' Schneider's smile never left his lips. 'I'm no squeaker,' he said. Brunet stopped dead: so did Schneider. Brunet asked a question: 'D'you want to work in with us?' 'What are you planning to do?' 'I'll tell you, but only when you've answered my question.' 'Why shouldn't I?' Brunet tried to read the expression on the large, smooth, rather soft-looking face. Still staring at Schneider, he said: 'It's not going to be easy, you know; just grinding on day after day.' 'I've nothing to lose,' said Schneider, 'and, anyhow, it'll be something to do.' They sat down again. Schneider stretched himself at full length, his hands behind his head. He shut his eyes and said: 'No, that doesn't worry me much. What does worry me is that you don't seem to be particularly fond of us.' Brunet, too, lay down. What, precisely, *was* this fellow? – sympathizer? Hm! well, he thought, it's your funeral. I'm not going to let you go. He slept and woke again. It was evening. He dropped off again. When next he woke, it was night: then, a little later, the sun was up once more. He sat up, looked about him, wondered where he was, remembered. His head felt empty. Goldilocks was sitting up too. There was something dazed and sinister about him: his arms were dangling between his spread knees. 'Not feeling too good?' asked Brunet. 'Feeling a bit mouldy: think they're going to give us anything to eat this morning?'

'I've no idea.' 'They going to let us starve?' 'I doubt it.' 'I'm bored,' yawned Goldilocks: 'not used to doing nothing.' 'Go and get a wash then.' The other looked at the hose-pipe, without enthusiasm. 'It'll be cold!' 'Come along.' They got up. Schneider was still sleeping: Moulu was still sleeping. The sergeant was lying on his back, his eyes wide open, chewing his moustache. All over the ground were thousands of eyes, thousands of open eyes, and others slowly becoming open under the warm influence of the sun. Goldilocks was unsteady on his feet. 'Hell! I can't even stand now: I shall just melt away!' Brunet unrolled the hose-pipe, fixed it to the tap, and turned the water on. He felt heavy. Goldilocks had stripped. He was hard and hairy with great lumps of muscle. His flesh reddened and contracted under the spouting water, but his face remained grey. 'My turn, now,' said Brunet. Goldilocks took hold of the hose. 'Weighs a ton!' he said. He let it go, then took it up again. He directed the jet on to Brunet, swayed on his feet, and suddenly let the pipe fall to the ground. 'Too much for me!' he said. They put on their clothes again. Goldilocks remained for some time sitting on the ground, holding a puttee in one hand. He looked at the water spreading between the stones. He seemed fascinated by the muddy streamlets. He said: 'We're losing our strength.' Brunet turned off the tap and helped the other to his feet. He led him back towards the steps. Lambert was awake; he grinned at them. 'You can't walk straight: look as though all the stuffing had been knocked out of you!' Goldilocks collapsed on the ground-sheet. 'I'm all in!' he muttered: 'won't catch me doing that again.' He stared at his great hairy hands: they were trembling: 'No reaction.' 'Come for a stroll,' said Brunet. 'Not on your life!' He rolled himself in his blanket and closed his eyes. Brunet moved off in the direction of the further yard. It was deserted. Thirty times round at the double. At the tenth circuit his head began to feel dizzy: at the nineteenth, he had to lean against the wall. But he kept at it: he'd got to master his body. He completed the total, and stopped, completely out of breath. His heart seemed to be beating inside his head: but he felt happy. The body is made to obey. I'll do that every day: I'll work it up to fifty. He did not feel hungry. He was glad that he didn't feel hungry. My fifth day of fasting, and I'm still in pretty good form. He went back into the main yard. Schneider was still asleep, his mouth wide open. All the men were lying down, motionless, speechless. They looked like corpses. Brunet would have liked a word with the printer, but the printer was still sleeping. Brunet sat down, his heart still thumping. The man from the North began to laugh. Brunet looked round. The man from the North went on laughing, his eyes fixed on the stick he was carving. He had already scratched a date on it, and was busy cutting a flower design with the point of his knife. 'What's biting you?' asked Lambert: 'think it funny, eh?' The man from the North never stopped laughing. Without raising his eyes, 'I'm laughing,' he explained, 'because I haven't had a sh—t for three days!' 'What's wrong with that?' asked Lambert: 'ain't got nothing to s—.' 'Some do, though,' said Moulu: 'I've seen 'em at it.' 'They're the lucky ones,' said Lambert: 'they're the chaps as brought some bully with 'em.' The sergeant sat up. He tugged at his moustache and looked at Moulu. 'What about them lorries of yours?' 'They'll come all right,' said Moulu: 'they'll come.' But his voice lacked conviction. 'They'd better hurry, then,' said the sergeant: 'or they won't find anyone here.' Moulu's eyes were still fixed on the gate. There was a gurgling, liquid sound. Moulu apologized: 'It's me stomach,' he said. Schneider had woken up. He rubbed his eyes, smiled, and said: 'Coffee, please . . .' 'and rolls,' said Curly. 'Rather have a bowl of soup,' said the man from the North, 'with a little red wine in it.' 'Anyone got any fags?' asked the sergeant. Schneider held out his packet, but Brunet restrained him with a look of annoyance: he did not approve of acts of individual generosity. 'Much better share 'em out.' 'Right you are,' said Schneider: 'I've got a packet and a half.' 'I've got one,' said Brunet. He brought it from his pocket and laid it on the ground-sheet. Moulu took a tin box from his haversack: 'Seventeen left.' 'That all?' asked Brunet: 'you not got any, Lambert?' 'No,' said Lambert. 'That's a lie,' said Moulu: 'you had a whole packet yesterday evening.' 'Smoked 'em all during the night.' 'Couldn't have done,' said Moulu: 'I heard you snoring.' 'Have it yer own way,' said Lambert. 'I don't mind giving the sarge one if he's got none, but I'm damned if I share 'em out! They're mine, aren't they? I can do what I like with 'em, can't I?' 'Lambert,' said Brunet, 'you can take your ground-sheet and bugger off if you like, but if you're going to stay here, you've got to develop the team spirit and get used to sharing things. Hand over those cigarettes!' Lambert shrugged and peevishly threw a packet on to Schneider's blanket. Moulu counted the cigarettes: 'Eighty: that works out at eleven each, and three over to draw lots for. Shall I hand 'em round?' 'No,' said Brunet: 'if you do that, some of the blokes'll have smoked 'em all by this evening. I'll keep 'em. You'll get three a day for three days, and two on the fourth: O.K.?' The others nodded. They realized vaguely that they were tacitly acknowledging one of their number as leader. 'O.K.?' Brunet repeated. They don't really care a damn. All they're interested in is eating. Moulu shrugged and said: 'O.K.' The others signified approval with nods. Brunet gave each man three cigarettes, and put the rest in his haversack. The sergeant lit one of his, took four puffs, stubbed it out, and put it behind his ear. The man from the North tore one open and put the tobacco in his mouth. 'Makes one feel less hungry,' he said, and began to chew. Schneider had said nothing all this while. He had been the heaviest loser on the deal, but he said nothing. Brunet thought: 'May turn out to be a pretty good recruit.' He let his mind run on Schneider, and then on something else. What was it, he wondered suddenly, he was thinking about? – and could not remember. He sat there for a while staring at nothing, and playing with a handful of pebbles. Then he got up heavily. The printer was now awake. 'Well?' asked Brunet. 'Don't know where they are,' said the printer. 'I've been round the yard three times, and can't find 'em.' 'Try again,' said Brunet: 'don't lose heart.' He sat down, looked at his watch, and said: 'That can't be right: what time do you make it, chaps?' 'Four-thirty-five,' said Moulu. 'Then I am right!' Four-thirty-five, and I've done nothing. I thought it was ten a.m. He felt as though someone had been filching time from him. 'And that printer who can't find his pals' ... Everything here is in slow motion, hesitating, delayed, complicated: it'll take months to get anything going. The sky was a crude blue: the sun struck at them with violence. Gradually, the heat diminished, the sky grew pink. Brunet looked at the sky. His mind was busy with the thought of gulls. He felt sleepy: his head was buzzing: he was not hungry. He thought: I've not felt hungry all day. He fell asleep, dreamed that he was hungry, and woke up. Still he was not hungry. He was conscious only of a slight feeling of nausea, and of a burning circlet round his skull. The sky looked blue and grey; the air was cool; from far away came the hoarse sound of a cock. The sun was hidden, but its beams made a golden haze above the wall. The yard was still streaked with long, violet shadows. The cock fell silent. Brunet thought: how quiet everything is. For a moment he felt as though he were alone in the world. He sat up with difficulty. The others were all around him, thousands of men, motionless and supine. He could almost believe that he was on a battlefield. But all the eyes were wide open. He could see heads thrown backward, matted hair, eyes fixed in a watchful glare. He turned to Schneider and saw that his eyes, too, were fixed. 'Schneider!' he said quietly: 'Schneider!' Schneider made no reply. Far away, Brunet could see a long, slavering snake: the hose-pipe. He thought: got to have a wash. His head felt heavy: he had the sensation that it was dragging him backwards. He lay down again: he seemed to be floating. 'I've got to have a wash.' He tried to get up, but his body would no longer obey him. His legs and arms were without substance; he could no longer feel them: it was as though they lay beside him like independent objects. The sun peeped over the wall. I've got to have a wash. It made him angry to think that he was just another corpse among all these assembled corpses with their eyes open. He began to fidget, sorted out his limbs, forced himself forward. At last he was on his feet: his legs were shaky, he was sweating. He took a few steps: he was afraid he might fall. He went across to the printer. 'Hullo!' The printer sat up and looked at him oddly. 'Hullo!' said Brunet. 'Not feeling too good?' said the printer: 'why don't you sit down?' 'I'm all right,' said Brunet: 'feeling fine, prefer to stand.' He wasn't at all sure, if he sat down, that he would be able to get up again. The printer remained sitting. He looked alive and fresh: his dark eyes were shining in his pleasant, girlish face. 'I've found one of 'em!' he said excitedly: 'chap by the name of Perrin: railwayman from Orléans. He's lost his pals and is looking for 'em. If he finds 'em, they'll come along, all three, at midday.' Brunet looked at his watch: ten o'clock. He wiped the sweat from his forehead with his sleeve: 'Good.' He had a feeling that he wanted to say something more, but did not know what. He stood there, for a moment, swaying above the printer, and repeating: 'Good, that's fine.' Then, with an effort, he resumed his walk. His head was burning. He let himself fall heavily on to the ground-sheet. He thought: 'I haven't had a wash.' Schneider was lying on one elbow, his head propped on his hand, eyeing him anxiously. 'Not feeling well?' 'Perfectly well,' said Brunet irritably. He took out a handkerchief and spread it over his face because of the sun. It was not exactly sleepy that he felt. His head seemed empty, and he had a sensation which resembled that of going down in a lift. A cough sounded above him. He whipped away the handkerchief. It was the printer, with three other men. Brunet looked at them in surprise. In a thick voice, he said: 'Midday already?' He tried to sit up. He was ashamed to have been caught napping. He was not shaved, he thought, but just as dirty as the rest of them. He made a violent effort and scrambled to his feet. 'Hullo!' he said. The newcomers were looking at him with curiosity. They were just the sort of fellows he liked: tough-looking, clean, with hard eyes. Good tools. They were looking at him. 'I'm their only hope,' he thought, and felt better. He said: 'What about a bit of a walk round?' They followed him. He turned the corner of the barrack-block, and went to the far end of the smaller yard. He looked round and smiled at them. 'I know who you are,' said one, a swarthy man with a shaven head. 'I rather think I've seen *you* somewhere,' said Brunet. 'I came to see you in '37,' said the swarthy man: 'my name's Stephen, and I was in the International Brigade.' The others, too, gave their names: Perrin from Orléans; Dewrouckère, miner from Lens. Brunet leaned against the wall of the stables. He looked at them, noting, without pleasure, that they were young. He wondered whether they were feeling hungry. 'Well,' said Stephen, 'what d'you want us to do?' Brunet kept his eyes fixed on them: he could not remember what it was he had meant to say. Not a word did he utter. He could see the astonishment in their eyes. At last he managed to unclench his teeth. 'Nothing. For the moment there's nothing we *can* do, except pick out the men we can count on, and keep in touch.' 'You like to come in with us?' asked Perrin: 'we've got a tent.'

'No,' said Brunet briskly: 'we'd better stay as we are. Get as many likely chaps as you can together, and try to find out something about what the others are thinking, and, remember, no propaganda at this stage: it's too soon.' Dewrouckère pulled a face. 'I know that already,' he said: 'they're thinking of nothing at all. Their minds are on their stomachs.' Brunet had a feeling that his head had begun to swell. He half-closed his eyes: he said: 'That may change. Any padres in your sector?' 'There are in mine,' said Perrin, 'and acting pretty funny, too.' 'Leave 'em alone,' said Brunet: 'don't let 'em twig what you're after. If they make any advances to you, don't frighten 'em off: got it?' They nodded assent, and Brunet said: 'We'll meet again, tomorrow at noon.' They looked at him. There was a hint of hesitation in their manner. He was conscious of a faint feeling of irritation. 'Get going! I'm staying here.' They moved off. Brunet's eyes were on them. He waited until they had turned the corner before taking a step forward. He was not sure that he wasn't going to fall. He thought: 'thirty times round at the double.' He took two steps and stopped, swaying on his feet. Anger brought the blood to his face. It was as though a hammer were beating inside his head: thirty times round, now, at once! He wrenched himself free of the wall. After going three yards he fell flat on his stomach. He got up and again collapsed, cutting his hand. Thirty times round every day. He clung to an iron ring embedded in the wall. He managed to struggle upright, and started off at a jog-trot. Ten times; twenty times. His legs were trembling; each stride he took was like a fall, but he knew that if he stopped he would collapse. Twenty-nine. After the thirtieth circuit, he rounded the corner of the building, still running, and slowed down only when he was back in the main yard. He stepped over the prostrate bodies, and reached the steps. No one had moved. They looked like so many dead fish, floating stomach-upwards. He smiled. He was the only man there on his feet. What I've got to do now is to shave. He took up his haversack, went over to a window, extracted his razor, propped his fragment of mirror on the sill, and began to give himself a dry shave. The pain made him half-close his eyes. He dropped the razor, bent to pick it up, let go of the mirror, which shattered itself at his feet, and fell to his knees. This time he *knew* that he could not get up again. He crawled back to his place on all fours, and rolled over on his back. His overworked heart was thumping in his chest. At each stroke, a sharp point of fire bored into his skull. Schneider silently lifted his head, and put a blanket, folded into four, behind his neck. Clouds were drifting across the sky: one of them looked like a nun, another like a gondola. Somebody pulled at his sleeve. 'Get up, we're going to move!' The words conveyed no meaning to him, but he scrambled to his feet. He was pushed towards the steps. The door was open. Prisoners, in an unbroken flow, were being swallowed up inside the barrack building. He could feel himself going upstairs. He wanted to stop, but the pressure from behind kept him moving. A voice said, 'Higher!' He missed a step and fell, his hand flung forward. Schneider and the printer each took one arm and half carried him. He tried to free himself but was not strong enough to do so. He said: 'I don't understand.' Schneider laughed quietly: 'What you need is food!' 'No more than you do!' 'You're bigger'n us, and got more flesh,' said the printer: 'you need more grub.' Brunet was beyond speaking. They hoisted him as far as the attic floor. A long, dark corridor ran through the building from end to end. On each side were boxes, separated from one another by a system of bars. They went into one of them. Three empty packing-cases; that was all. No window. There was a skylight to each two or three boxes. One of these, situated in the box next to theirs, let in a slant of light which threw shadows from the great wooden bars obliquely on the floor. Schneider spread his blanket, and on this Brunet subsided. For a moment he saw the printer's face bending over him. 'Don't stand there,' he said to him: 'find somewhere for yourself further off: we're meeting at noon.' The face vanished, and a dream began. The shadows of the bars crept slowly across the floor, crept, bending, over the prostrate bodies, scaled the packing-cases, bent and bent again, grew dim. Darkness climbed up the walls. Through the bars, the skylight looked like a bruise, a pallid bruise, a black bruise which turned, suddenly, to a bright and mocking eye. The bars resumed their progress, turning, turning. The darkness turned like the lamp of a lighthouse. The beast was in its cage. Men, for a moment, scurried, then disappeared. The ship drifted from the shore with all the convicts dead from hunger in their cages. A match sputtered: a word leapt from the darkness, painted in red letters, at an angle, on one of the packing-cases: FRAGILE. There were chimpanzees in the next cage, pressing inquisitive faces to the bars. They had sad and wrinkled eyes. Monkeys have sadder eyes than any animal except man. Something had happened, he wondered what. A catastrophe. What catastrophe? Perhaps the sun had gone cold? A voice sounded from the back of the cages: 'An evening will come when I shall tell you lovely things.' A catastrophe, everyone is in jug. What catastrophe? What will the Party do? A delicious taste of young pineapples, a young taste, and rather gay, rather childish. He was chewing pineapple, munching the sweet, resilient, fibrous substance. When did I last eat pineapple? I used to love pineapple. It is like defenceless wood, wood stripped of its bark. He chewed. The young and yellow taste of tender wood *climbed* softly from the back of his throat, like the sun hesitantly rising, expanding upon his tongue. There was something *he wanted* to say. What was it he wanted to say? – this syrup of diluted sun? I used to love pineapple, oh, a long time ago, in the days when I loved skiing, mountains, boxing, sailing yachts, women. Fragile. What is fragile? We are all fragile. The taste upon his tongue twisted and turned, a solar whirlpool, an ancient taste, a forgotten taste, I had forgotten myself, *the sun swarming in the leaves of chestnut trees, a shower of sun upon my forehead, I was reading in the hammock, the white house was behind me, behind me was Touraine, I loved the trees, the sun and the house, I loved the world and happiness, Oh once!* He moved; he struggled; there's something I've got to do, something I've got to do at once. He had arranged to meet somebody: it was important; but whom? Krupskaia. He fell back. Fragile. What have I done with my loves: they said to me, you do not love us enough. They had me. *I was a young and tender shoot all sticky with sap*, and they stripped me, when I get out of here I shall eat a whole pineapple. He half-sat up: an urgent meeting; then, again, fell back into calm childhood, in a park, *part the grasses and you will see the sun: what have you done with your desires?* I have no desires: I am a piece of dead wood: the sap is gone: the monkeys clinging to the bars were looking at him with feverish eyes: something had happened. He remembered, he started up, 'The printer,' he shouted: 'has the printer come?' No one answered, he fell back into sticky sap, into SUBJECTIVITY, we have lost the war and this is where I am going to die, Mathieu was leaning over him and whispering, you didn't love us enough; you didn't love us enough; the monkeys were chattering and laughing, slapping their thighs: you loved nothing, nothing at all! – the shadows made by the bars circled slowly across his face, darkness, sunlight, darkness: he found it amusing. I am a member of the Party; I love the Comrades, I have no time to waste on others, there's someone I've got to meet. 'An evening will come when I shall tell you lovely things, when evening comes I shall tell you that I love you.' He was sitting up, he was breathing hard, he was looking at them. On Moulu's face, turned to the ceiling, was an angelic smile; a cool shadow was stroking his face, creeping down his cheek: the sunlight was making his teeth shine. 'Moulu!' Moulu was still smiling. 'D'you hear 'em?' he said, but he did not move. 'Do I hear what? asked Brunet. 'The lorries.' He could hear nothing: he felt terrified of the huge wave of desire that suddenly swept over him, a desire to live, a desire to love, a desire to caress white breasts. Schneider was lying on his right: he called to him for help: 'Ho! Schneider!' 'Bad show!' said Schneider in a weak voice. 'You'll find the cigarettes in my haversack, three a day.' Slowly his buttocks slid along the floor: he found himself lying with his head thrown back. He stared at the ceiling: I do love them, of course I love them, but *they've got to serve*, what is the nature of my desire? The body, the mortal body, a forest of desires, on each branch a bird, they serve Westphalian ham on wooden plates, the knife cuts into the meat, when one draws it out, one can smell, still sticking to it, the faint odour of damp wood, they had me, I am no more than a desire, we are all of us lying in excrement, and this is where I am going to die. What desire? Somebody lifted him, somebody sat him up. Schneider made him swallow some soup: 'What's that?' 'Barley broth.' Brunet started to laugh; that was what it was, just that: this immense, this guilty desire, was nothing but hunger. He slept. Somebody woke him. He had some more soup. He could feel it burning his stomach: the bars circled, the voice was silent. 'Someone was singing.' 'Yes,' said Moulu. 'He's left off.' 'He's dead,' said Moulu, 'they took him away yesterday.' More soup, this time with bread. He said: 'That's better!' He sat up without help, he smiled: childhood, love, 'subjectivity', all that had been nothing, just a dream brought on by weakness. Light-heartedly he put a question to Moulu: 'So the lorries did come, after all?' 'Yes,' said Moulu, 'they came.' He was scraping away with a pocket-knife at a lump of bread, scooping bits out of it. He was carving it into a shape. Without looking up, he said: 'Bit of left-over bread, gone mouldy. If you eat the blue part it gives you the gripes, but some of the crust's all right.' He held out a sliver of bread to Brunet, and stuffed a similar one into his large mouth. He said, in accents of pride, 'Six days without grub: I was going crackers!' Brunet laughed, he was thinking of his 'subjectivity'. 'Me too,' he said. He fell asleep and was wakened by the sun. He still felt weak, but was able to get up. 'Has the printer been round asking for me?' he inquired. 'We haven't been paying much attention to visitors these last few days.' 'Where's Schneider?' asked Brunet. 'Don't know.' Brunet went out into the corridor. Schneider was talking to the printer: both of them were laughing. The sight irritated Brunet. The printer came up to him, and said: 'Schneider's found a job for us.' Brunet turned to Schneider. He thought – gets his foot in everywhere. Schneider was smiling: he said: 'We've been get-ting around a bit these last few days: we've found several new pals.' 'Hm!' ejaculated Brunet briefly: 'I'd better give 'em the once-over,' he said. He went downstairs, Schneider and the printer at his heels. In the yard he stopped, screwing up his eyes against the dazzle. It was a beautiful day. Several men were seated on the steps, quietly smoking. They looked thoroughly at home, like men resting after the week's work. Now and then one of them would nod his head and say something, at which all the rest nodded. Brunet looked at them angrily. He thought: 'Just settled in as easy as asking!' The yard, the watch-towers, the outer wall, *belonged to them*. There they sat, at their own front door, gossiping with rustic wisdom about every little thing that went on in the village. 'What can one do with chaps like that? They've got a passion for ownership. You could pop 'em in jug, and in three days you wouldn't know whether they were

276

prisoners or the owners of the prison!' Others were walking about in twos and threes, carrying themselves smartly, chatting, laughing, turning this way and that: a parcel of bourgeois taking a stroll. Several officer cadets passed, in fancy uniforms. They looked at nobody, but Brunet could hear their refined voices: 'No, old man, I think you've got it wrong: there *was* a question of their filing a petition, but nothing came of it. The Bank of France took a hand in the nick of time.' In the middle of one group, two men in spectacles were playing a game of chess on their knees: a little bald fellow was reading, and frowning over his book: now and again he laid it down, and excitedly referred to a large volume. Brunet passed behind him: the volume was a dictionary. 'What are you up to?' he asked. 'Learning German.' Round the hose-pipe several naked men were shouting, shoving, and laughing. Leaning against one of the posts, Gartiser, the Alsatian, was speaking German to one of the German sentries, who was nodding agreement. It had needed only a mouthful of bread! A mouthful of bread, and this sinister yard, where a beaten army had been lying at its last gasp, had been suddenly transformed into a seaside beach, a sun-bathing pitch, a fair-ground. Two men, stripped to the buff, were lying on a blanket, browning themselves. Brunet felt like kicking their golden buttocks. Burn down their towns, burn down their villages, drag them into exile, and they'll fight tooth and nail just to build up again their squalid, poverty-stricken contentment. And that's the material I've got to work with! He turned his back on them, and went into the further yard. He stopped dead in amazement. Backs, thousands of backs, the tinkle of a bell, thousands of bowing heads. 'Good God!' Schneider and the printer began to laugh: 'Just a little surprise for you: it's Sunday!' 'So that's it!' said Brunet: 'Sunday, of course!' He could scarcely believe his eyes. What stubborn idiocy! They had turned out a synthetic Sunday, like all the Sundays they had ever known in towns or countryside, just because they had seen on a calendar that it was Sunday. In the other yard it was a village Sunday, a main-street Sunday; here it was a Church-Sunday. It only needed a cinema to make it all complete. He turned to the printer: 'No flicks this evening?' The printer smiled: 'The padres are getting up a bit of a

277

"do" ...' Brunet clenched his fists. He thought about the priests. They've been working overtime while I've been sick! One never ought to be sick! Shyly, the printer said: 'Lovely day, isn't it?' 'Sure,' said Brunet, between his teeth, 'sure, it's a lovely day' – damn' sure, a lovely day, a positive peach of a day all over France – torn and twisted railway-lines glinting in the sun, and golden sunlight on the yellowing leaves of uprooted trees, water gleaming at the bottom of bomb-craters, dead men turning green in the cornfields, their upturned bellies chanting paeans to a cloudless sky. Have you forgotten so soon? The men before him looked as though they were made of rubber. They had their heads raised now, and were listening to the priest. Brunet could not hear what he was saying, but he had a clear view of his red face, his grey hair, his steel-rimmed spectacles, and his broad shoulders. He recognized him; it was the chap who had been reading his breviary on the first evening. He moved closer. A few paces from the preacher, the moustached sergeant, his eyes shining and a humble look on his face, was listening with passionate intensity. '... that many of you are believers, but that there are others who have been drawn here out of curiosity, out of a wish to learn, or merely because they have nothing else to do. You are all of you my brothers, my very dear brothers, brothers in arms, brothers in God, and it is to all of you that I am speaking now, Catholics, Protestants, atheists, seeing that the Word of God is for all men. The message that I bring you on this day of mourning, which is also God's day, may be summed up in three simple words – DO NOT DESPAIR ... for to despair is not only to sin against God's loving mercy. Even those of you who are not of my way of thinking will agree with me that despair is self-slaughter, is, if I may so describe it, moral suicide. There are, no doubt, among you, my dear brothers, some who, led astray by a sectarian education, have been taught to see in the wonderful events of our history, no more than a succession of accidents without meaning and without cohesion. Such men will go from this place saying that we were beaten because we lacked tanks, because we lacked aeroplanes. Of them Our Lord has said that they have ears but hear not, eyes have they, but see not. Doubtless, when the Divine Wrath was loosed upon Sodom and

Gomorrah, there were in those wicked cities sinners so hardened as to say that the rain of fire which reduced their homes to ashes was the result only of an atmospheric disturbance or a meteorite. Oh, my brothers, were not those men sinning against themselves? For if it was by accident only that the lightning struck down Sodom, then is there no work of man's hands, nor product of his patience and his industry, that may not, without rhyme or reason, be reduced to nothingness by blind forces. Why, if that is so, should men build houses for themselves, sow their fields, or raise up families? Today we are vanquished and imprisoned, humiliated in our legitimate pride of country, suffering in our bodies, and without news of our dear ones. Is it without design that these things have happened? Does their origin lie only in the interplay of mechanical forces? If that be true, my brothers, then I say unto you – despair, for there can be nothing more productive of despair than to suffer for no reason. But I, too, my brothers, would ask a question of these daring and emancipated thinkers. Why was it that we lacked tanks? Why was it that we lacked guns? No doubt they will answer me – because we did not produce enough. And in those words is suddenly revealed to us the countenance of that France of Sinfulness which, for a quarter of a century, has been forgetful of its duty to God. Why, and this is the point, did we not produce enough? Because we did not work. And whence, my brothers, came this wave of idleness which has descended upon us as once the locusts descended upon the land of Egypt? Because we were a nation divided by internal quarrels. The workers, led by cynical agitators, had grown to detest their employers: the employers, blinded by selfishness, cared nothing about satisfying even the most legitimate of claims. Our business men were eaten up with jealousy of our public functionaries, our public functionaries lived like the parasite mistletoe upon the oak. Our elected representatives in the Chamber, instead of discussing affairs of State calmly, and with only the general interest in mind, spent their time in brawling and hurling mutual insults, so that at times they came actually to blows. And what, my very dear brothers, was the cause of all this discord, all this conflict of interests, all this degradation of public conduct? The cause of it was this, that a sordid materialism had spread through the country like an epidemic. And what is materialism if not a turning away from God? A materialist holds that we are born of the earth, and that to the earth we will return. His sole concern is with his worldly interests. This, then, I say to the sceptics: You are right, my brothers, we lost the war because we lacked *material*. But your argument is only in part correct, because it is a *materialistic* argument. It is because you were materialists that you have been beaten. It was France, the eldest daughter of the Church, that inscribed in her annals the dazzling succession of her triumphs. It is France without God that has been laid low in 1940.' He stopped. The men were listening in silence, their mouths open. The sergeant was nodding approbation. Brunet turned his eyes to the priest, and was struck by his air of triumph. His gleaming eyes were darting hither and thither about the audience, his face was red. He raised his hand, and resumed his discourse. There was something almost gay in his passionate utterance: 'And so, my brothers, let us abandon the idea that our defeat was the effect of chance. It is our punishment, and it has been brought upon us by our own fault, not by chance, my brothers. Chastisement: that is the good news I bring to you today.' He paused again and gazed at the faces bent towards him in rapt attention, so as to judge of the effect produced by what he had said. Then, leaning forward, he continued in a more persuasive tone: 'That it is harsh news, unpleasing news, I agree: but it is good news, too. When a man believes that he is the innocent victim of catastrophe, and sits wringing his hands, unable to understand what has happened to him, is it not good news for him to be told that he is expiating his own fault? And that is why I say unto you, rejoice, my brothers, rejoice in the dark place of your suffering, for where there has been sin, there, too, is there expiation, there, too, is there redemption. I say unto you again, rejoice in the House of your Father, for there is yet another reason why you should do so. Our Lord, who suffered for all men, who took our sins upon Himself, who suffered, and still suffers, that He may expiate them, has chosen you. Yes, all of you, peasants, workers, men of the middle class, none of whom are wholly innocent, though, certainly, not the most guilty: you He has chosen to fulfil an incomparable destiny. As He suffered for us, so has He ordained

that you shall suffer that you may redeem the sins and the faults
of that France which God has never ceased to love, and has
punished with a heavy heart. It is for you, my brothers, to
choose. Either you may groan and tear your hair, saying, why
should these miseries have fallen upon me, on me rather than
upon my neighbour who was rich and wicked, on me rather
than on the men of politics who have led my country to destruction? – and, if you do that, then is there no meaning in anything, and all you can do is to die in rancour of heart and in
hatred: or, you can say, we were as nothing, and now are we
chosen out from all men to suffer, to make of ourselves a willing
sacrifice, to endure martyrdom. In that case, while a man raised
up by Providence, a worthy follower of those men whom the
Lord has always given to France when she found herself on
the brink of destruction . . .' Brunet tiptoed away. He found
Schneider and the printer leaning against the wall of the barracks. He said: 'He knows his job!' 'I'll say he does!' said the
printer. 'He sleeps near me at night, and nobody gets a chance
when he starts talking. He's got the boys just where he wants
'em!' Two men passed close to them, one of them tall, thin,
with a long face and spectacles, the other, small, fat, and with
a disdainful expression on his lips. The tall one was talking in
tones of sweet reasonableness: 'He spoke very well, very simply,
and he said things which needed to be said.' Brunet started to
laugh: 'God in Heaven!' They all walked on a little way. The
printer was looking at Brunet with trusting eyes. 'Well?' he
asked. 'Well?' echoed Brunet. 'What did *you* think of that
sermon?' 'There was good in it as well as bad. In a sense he's
doing our work for us. He explained that captivity wasn't going
to be all beer and skittles, and I rather think he'll keep that
stop out: it's to his interest, as well as ours, that he should do
so. So long as these blokes think they're going to see their best
girls in a month's time, there's no doing anything with 'em.'
'Ha?' the printer's handsome eyes were wide open, his face was
grey. Brunet went on: 'To that extent you might make use of
him. What you want to do is to get some of the boys away, on
the q.t., and say – "You heard the padre? He said things are
going to be pretty tough."' 'And you think they are?' – the
printer brought the words out with an effort: 'You think it'll

go on for a long time?' Brunet turned hard eyes on him: 'You
believe in fairies?' The printer swallowed hard, but said nothing. Brunet turned to Schneider and continued: 'I'm a bit surprised, though, to find 'em coming to heel so quickly. I thought
they'd wait and see. That sermon of his was a blatant political
programme, France, the eldest daughter of the Church, and
Pétain, the leader of the French. It's a fair bugger.' He turned
on the printer sharply: 'What do the boys round your part of
the world think of him?' 'They like him.' 'Do they, now?'
'They've not got much against him: he shares out everything
he has, but he doesn't let you forget it, always seems to be
saying, I'm giving you this for the love of God. Personally, I'd
rather not smoke at all than take his fags, but there's not many
thinks like me.' 'That all you know about him?' 'Well, I only
see him at night,' said the printer as though excusing himself.
'Where does he hide himself in the daytime?' 'Sick-house.'
'Mean to tell me there's a sick-house here?' 'Yes, in the other
block.' 'Is he a medical orderly?' 'No, but he's pally with the
M.O. in charge, plays bridge with him and two wounded
officers.' 'He does, does he?' said Brunet – 'and what do the boys
say about that?' 'They don't say nothing: they're inclined to think
it's true, but they'd rather not know for certain. I got it from
Gartiser, who's an orderly.' 'Good, that's something you can
give 'em to chew on. Ask them how they like the idea of the
padre always hobnobbing with the officers.' 'O.K.' Schneider
had been looking at them for the last few minutes with an odd
smile. 'The other block is where the Jerries hang out,' he said.
'Is that so!' said Brunet. Schneider turned to the printer: he was
still smiling. 'Your line's pretty clear – that the padre leaves his
own pals high and dry, and prefers to make up to the Jerries.'
'As a matter of fact,' said the printer, without much conviction,
'I don't believe he sees much of the Jerries.' Schneider shrugged
his shoulders in assumed impatience. Brunet had a feeling that
he was up to some game or other. 'You got the right to go into
the German block?' Schneider asked the printer, who shrugged
and said nothing. Schneider voiced his triumph. 'You see! I
don't care a damn what his intentions may be: for all I know he
may be perfectly sincere in his wish to save France, but *objectively* he's a French prisoner who spends his days in the company

of the enemy, and it's just as well the boys should know it.' The printer, now completely out of his depth, turned to Brunet. Brunet had resented Schneider's tone, but did not wish to give him the lie. 'You want to go carefully,' he said: 'no use trying to discredit him all at once. Besides, there are about fifty of his sort here, and you can't take 'em all on single-handed. What you want to do is to drop a few hints, seemingly casual hints, something like – the padre thinks it'll be longer than we think before we get home, and he ought to know, because he's always along of the officers, and has a good few chats with the Jerries. The great thing is to let them realize gradually that he isn't really one of them, see?' 'Yes,' said the printer. 'Any of our little lot see much of the padre?' 'Yes, one of 'em.' 'Sharp lad?' 'Pretty sharp.' 'Tell him to string him along, then: better put on an act of being convinced. We need an informer.' He leaned against the wall, thought for a moment, and then said to the printer: 'Go and talk to some of our chaps, two or three'll do – the newer lot, preferably.' As soon as they were alone, Brunet said to Schneider: 'I'd rather have waited a bit: in a month or two the boys'll be properly ripe. But these padres hold too strong a hand. If we don't start in at once, they'll get the lead of us. You still feel the same about coming in on the job?' 'What, exactly, is the job?' asked Schneider. 'Changed your mind? I just happened to think you wanted to stand in with us.' 'No, I haven't changed my mind: but I do want to know what working in with you means, that's all.' 'Well,' said Brunet: 'you heard the padre, didn't you? He's not by any means a lone performer: oh, no, in a month from now they'll be thick on the ground. But that's not all. It wouldn't at all surprise me if Jerry managed to scrape together two or three quislings from our little lot, and got them to try to win us over. Before the war, we could have put up a strong organized front against them, the Party, the Trade Unions, the Vigilance Committee: here, we've got nothing to fall back on. Our job is to build *something*. It may mean having to put up with a lot of palavering, and that's not the way I really like going about things, but we've no real choice. Our immediate objective must be to sift out the healthy elements, organize them, and get some sort of clandestine counter-propaganda going. The two main themes must be – that we don't refuse to recognize the armistice, and that democracy is the only form of government we are prepared to accept under present conditions. Useless to go further than that. We must move very cautiously in the early stages. It's up to me to collect any members of the Communist Party who may happen to be about. But they're not the only ones; there are the socialists, the radicals, and, generally speaking, all the fellows who can be vaguely classed as belonging to the Left, sympathizers, like you.' Schneider produced a wintry smile: 'The softies, in fact.' 'Let us rather say, the lukewarm,' said Brunet, and added hastily, 'not that a chap mayn't be both lukewarm and honest. I'm not quite sure that I know how to speak their language, but that kind of uncertainty can't bother you, since it's the one you habitually speak yourself.' 'O.K.,' said Schneider: 'what it comes to, I take it, is to some extent reviving the old Popular Front?' 'That mightn't be altogether a bad thing,' said Brunet. Schneider nodded: 'So that's to be my job: but are you quite sure it's *yours*?' Brunet looked at him in astonishment: 'Mine?' 'Oh,' said Schneider, as though the matter were one of complete indifference to him, 'so long as you're sure ...' 'Explain yourself,' said Brunet: 'I don't like hints.' 'But there's nothing *to* explain: all I meant to say was – what's the Party up to? what orders has it issued, what directives? I suppose you've been kept informed?' Brunet looked at him with a smile. 'I wonder whether you really see the situation as it is, even now? The Germans have been in Paris for the last fortnight: the whole of France is upside down: many of the Comrades are dead or captured, others have gone heaven knows where, with their Divisions, to Pau, to Montpellier, and so on, while others are safely in jug. If you really want to know what the Party is up to at this moment, the answer is that it is busy reorganizing.' 'I see,' said Schneider, with enthusiasm: 'and you're just trying to make contact with any Comrades who happen to be here: fine.' 'That's about the long and short of it,' said Brunet, as though anxious to bring the discussion to an end: 'if you're in agreement ...' 'Of course I'm in agreement, my dear fellow,' said Schneider: 'all the more so, since, really, it's nothing to do with me. I'm not a Communist. You tell me that the Party is reorganizing, and that's all I want to know. Still, if I were in your place ...' he fumbled in the pocket of his tunic as though feeling for a cigarette, but, at the end of a few moments, withdrew his hand and let his arm hang loosely against the wall: '... I should want to have a little more information. What, for instance, is to be the basis of this reorganization? – that's what really matters.' Without looking at Brunet, he went on. 'The Soviets are the allies of Germany.' 'That's where you're wrong,' said Brunet impatiently: 'they signed a non-aggression pact, of an entirely provisional nature. Just think for a moment, Schneider, what else *could* they have done after Munich?' Schneider heaved a sigh: 'Oh, I know,' he said: 'I know everything you're going to say. You're going to tell me that the U.S.S.R. had lost all confidence in the allies, and that it was temporizing until such time as it should feel strong enough to declare war on Jerry. Isn't that it?' Brunet hesitated: 'Not exactly,' he said: 'my own view is that they're quite convinced that Germany means to attack them.' 'But you do believe that they did all they could to postpone the event for as long as possible?' 'I imagine so.' 'In that case,' said Schneider slowly, 'I shouldn't, in your place, feel any too sure that the Party will take up a strong position against the Nazis. They might be afraid of injuring the U.S.S.R. if they did.' The look he turned on Brunet was full of uncertainty. It expressed melancholy and a lack of incisiveness. He had difficulty in keeping his eyes focused. Brunet turned away with a movement of impatience: 'Don't pretend to be more stupid than you are,' he said. 'You know perfectly well that it's not a question of the Party's *official* position. Since '39 it's been an illegal organization, and any action it takes must be clandestine.' Schneider smiled: 'Clandestine, yes, but what precisely does that mean? Will it, for instance, go on printing *L'Humanité* in secret? Besides, look here, of every ten thousand copies circulated, at least a hundred will fall into Fritz's hands: that is inevitable. An underground organization can, with a bit of luck, conceal the source of its literature, the places where it is printed, the editorial offices, etc. ... but not the literature *itself*, if only because pamphlets, and that sort of stuff, are printed with the sole object of being distributed. I should say that in three months, the Gestapo will know every detail of the Party's political programme.' 'What if they do? they can't hold the

U.S.S.R. responsible.' 'What about the Komintern?' asked Schneider. 'Do you really think that Ribbentrop and Molotov have never discussed the Komintern?' He spoke without aggressiveness, and his tone was perfectly neutral. All the same, there was something suspect in his unspectacular insistence. 'What's the use of indulging in armchair strategy?' said Brunet. 'What Ribbentrop and Molotov may have talked about I have no idea – not having been hidden under the table. All I know is – because the evidence is there for everybody to see – that contact between the U.S.S.R. and the Party has ceased.' 'And you really believe that?' asked Schneider, and then, after a moment's pause, continued: 'But even if it *has* ceased today, it will be re-established tomorrow. There is always Switzerland.' Mass was now over. Soldiers were drifting past, silent and with their minds elsewhere. Schneider lowered his voice: 'I am quite sure that the Nazis hold the U.S.S.R. responsible for the activities of the C.P.' 'Suppose they do,' said Brunet, 'what of it?' 'Let's assume that, in order to gain time, the U.S.S.R. muzzles the Communists of France and Belgium.' Brunet gave a shrug: 'Muzzle! what extraordinary ideas you have about the relations existing between the U.S.S.R. and the C.P.! Don't you know that the C.P. contains cells, and that those cells are made up of people who discuss and who vote?' Schneider smiled, and patiently continued: 'I've no wish to hurt your feelings. Let me put things a little differently. Suppose that the C.P., anxious not to make difficulties for the U.S.S.R., decides to muzzle itself . . .' 'Would there be anything so very new about that?' 'Not much, I grant you: after all, it's what you did at the outbreak of the war, isn't it? But you mustn't forget this – that, since then, the position of the U.S.S.R. has definitely deteriorated. Should England capitulate, Hitler would have his hands free.' 'The U.S.S.R. has had time to prepare: she is braced for the shock.' 'Are you quite sure of that? The performances of the Red Army this last winter were not particularly brilliant, and you said yourself that Molotov was temporizing.' 'If relations between the U.S.S.R. and the C.P. are as you describe them, the Comrades will know in good time all about the preparations of the Red Army.' 'The Comrades in Paris, yes: but what about *you*? It's *you* who are working *here*.' 'What are you getting at?' said

Brunet, his voice rising: 'what are you trying to prove? – that the C.P. has turned Fascist?' 'No, but that the Nazi victory and the German-Soviet Pact are two realities with which the C.P. has got to come to terms, however little they may like them. The point is that you've no sort of an idea *how* it'll come to terms with them.' 'Are you suggesting that I should sit still and twiddle my thumbs?' 'I'm not suggesting anything of the kind,' said Schneider: 'Surely, one can talk things over ...' – he paused, then, rubbing his great nose with his forefinger, continued: 'The C.P. is no more in sympathy with the Western democracies than the Nazis are – though for other reasons. So long as it was possible to imagine an alliance between the U.S.S.R. and the West, you took as your platform the defence of political liberties against Fascist dictatorship. You know even better than I do that those political liberties are illusory. Today the democracies are on their knees, the U.S.S.R. has drawn closer to Germany, Pétain has seized power. It is now within the framework of a Fascist Society, or of a Society of Fascist sympathies, that the Party has to carry on its work. And here are you, without leaders, without a political slogan, without news, reverting, on your own initiative, to that old and outworn platform. We were talking just now of the spirit of the Popular Front. But the Popular Front is dead: dead and buried. In '38, given the historical context, it had a meaning: today it has none. Look out, Brunet, or you'll find yourself working in the dark.' His voice had become suddenly edged. He broke off sharply, and continued more quietly: 'That was why I asked whether you were sure what your job was.' Brunet began to laugh: 'Come now,' he said: 'there's nothing very terrible about that. What we've got to do is get the boys together, try to neutralize the padres and the Nazis, and then just wait and see. We shall find out soon enough what's got to be done.' Schneider nodded approval. 'That's right,' he said; 'that's right.' Brunet looked him straight in the eyes: 'It's you I'm worried about,' he said: 'you seem such a pessimist.' 'Oh, me!' said Schneider with an air of indifference: 'If you really want to know, my opinion is that nothing we can do will be of the slightest importance – politically. The situation is abstract, and we are without responsibility. Those of us who are lucky enough to get home eventually, will find Society organized anew, with its own hierarchies and its own myths. There's nothing *we* can do to influence the future one way or the other. Still, if we can succeed in keeping up the lads' morale, if we can save them from despair, if we can give them something to live for *here* – no matter how illusory that something may be – the necessary effort is well worth the making.' 'That's the spirit!' said Brunet. A moment later he added: 'As this is my first day out, I'm going to take a bit of a walk: so long.' Schneider raised a hand in farewell, and strolled away. A negative type, an intellectual; why on earth did I get mixed up with *him*? An odd sort of chap altogether, sometimes so warm and friendly, at others, cold as ice, almost cynical. Where have I seen him before? Why does he say *the* Comrades in talking of the Party members, and not *your* comrades, as I'd have expected him to do? I *must* manage to get a squint at his army book. In the Sunday atmosphere of the yard, the men looked as though they were out for the afternoon. On all their scrubbed and freshly shaven faces was the same expression of *absence*. They were waiting for something, and the fact of waiting had conjured into being, outside the confining wall, a whole garrison town, with its gardens, its brothels, and its cafés. In the middle of the yard someone was playing a mouth-organ, and two men were dancing. The phantom town had grown, till its roofs and tree-tops were higher than the prison-wall, and seemed reflected in the blind faces of these ghostly corybants. Brunet made a half-turn and moved into the farther yard. Here the scene was different. The temporary church had been dismantled, and the men were playing at prisoners'-base, shouting and running like lunatics. Brunet climbed the little hillock behind the stables and had a look at the graves. He felt at ease. Someone had scattered flowers on the trodden earth, and planted three small crosses in a row. He sat down between two of the graves. There, beneath him, were the dead, laid at full length. They had attained to peace. Some day, it would come to him, too, innocence. He unearthed an old sardine-tin, empty and rusty, and threw it away. It was Sunday, the day of the week devoted to picnics and visiting the cemetery: I was walking on a hill and below me, in a town, children were playing at prisoners'-base. Their shouts came up to me. Where was that? He had forgotten. He thought: 'It's true enough that I've got to work in the dark.' But what alternative was there? – to do nothing? His natural vigour revolted against the idea. I should go home at the end of the war and have to say to the Comrades: 'Here I am: I just worked away at keeping alive.' A fine thing that'd be! How about trying to escape? He looked at the walls. They were not so high as to make an attempt impossible. It'd only be a matter of reaching Nancy. The Poullains would hide me. But there were the three dead men beneath him, there were the children shouting in the timeless afternoon. He laid his hands palm downward on the cool earth. He would not, he decided, escape. Elasticity – that was what he needed. Get the lads together, so that, little by little, they would take him as the focus of their confidences, of their hopes for the future, urge them to denounce the armistice, but be ready to modify his instructions so as to keep in step with the turn of events. The Party won't leave us in the lurch, he thought. The Party *can't* leave us in the lurch. He lay down at full length, in the same posture as the dead, there, on the earth, above the dead. He looked at the sky. He got up. Slowly he descended the little hill, feeling very much alone. Death was all about him like a smell, like the fag-end of a Sunday afternoon. For the first time in his life he was conscious of a vague sense of guilt: guilt, because he felt lonely, guilt, because he was alive and capable of thought, guilt, because he was not dead. Beyond the wall were houses, dark, dead houses, with dead eyes, an eternity of stone. This babble of the Sunday crowd had been mounting skyward since the beginning of time. It was only he that was not eternal. Eternity was upon him like a fixed stare. He walked. When he returned with the dying light, he had been walking all day. There had been something he had had to kill, but whether it had been killed he did not know. When one doesn't care a damn for anything, one gets moods. It is inevitable that one should. The corridor up on the attic floor smelt of dust; the cages gave off a droning sound: Sunday was dragging slowly to its end. The ground looked like a sky pricked with shooting stars: the men were smoking in the darkness. Brunet stopped dead. Addressing nobody in particular, he called out: 'Be careful with those cigarettes, we don't want the whole place to go up in flames.' The men groaned and grumbled under the impact of this voice striking down on them from above. Brunet became silent. He felt at a loss, in a way. He moved on a few steps. A red star leaped into life and rolled lazily as far as his feet. He put his foot on it. The night was mild and blue. The windows stood out clearly against the darkness. They had the purplish colour of specks that float before the eyes when one has been staring too long at the sun. He could not find his own cage. 'Hey! Schneider!' he shouted. 'Here I am,' came a voice: 'over here!' He retraced his steps. A man was singing very quietly, as though to himself: '*sur la route, la grand'route, un jeune homme chantait*'. Brunet thought: 'How they love the dusk.' 'Over here,' called Schneider: 'keep on as you're going, just another few steps: that's right.' He went into the cage, looked at the skylight through the tracery of bars, thought of a gas-jet springing into life in the blue darkness. He sat down in silence, his eyes still on the skylight. What had happened to the gas-jet? All round him was a sound of quiet whispering. In the morning these men shouted, but at night they murmured, because they loved the evening. Peace came on velvet pads at nightfall in this great dark box; peace and the dead years. It was almost possible to believe that they had loved their lives. 'What I used to like,' Moulu was saying, 'was taking me collar off, and settling down with a pint. Just about now's the time I'd be at the Cadran Bleu, having a drink and watching the folk go by.' 'Cadran Bleu?' asked Goldilocks, 'whereabouts is that?' 'Gobelins – corner of the Avenue des Gobelins and the Boulevard Saint-Marcel.' 'You mean somewhere near the Saint-Marcel Cinema?' 'Couple o' hundred yards away. Know it like the back o' me hand. I hang out just opposite the Lourcine barracks. After work I'd go home for a bite, and then clear off again, usually to the Cadran Bleu, sometimes to the Canon des Gobelins, but the Cadran Bleu's better, because there's a band.' 'Used to be some pretty good shows at that Cinema.' 'Don't I know it. Trenet, occasionally, and Marie Dubas. Often seen her there in the flesh – used to sport a small car, comic little affair.' 'Had a way of going there meself,' said Goldilocks: 'I live over Vanves way – many's the time I've walked home on me flat feet when it was a fine night.' 'Pretty long tramp, that.' 'Oh, well, one was young in those days!' 'It's not the beer as I miss,' said Lambert, 'but the red wine. Could knock back a coupla litres a day in me time, three, if I'd got a thirst on me. What you say to a nice bottle of Médoc now?' 'Three litres!' said Moulu: 'that's pretty good going!' 'Just about suit me!' 'Can't manage more'n one meself, turns acid on me.' 'Ought to stick to white.' 'Ah, now you're talking!' said Moulu: 'white's my ticket!' 'Ought to see the old girl at my place: sixty-one she is, but she can still take her coupla litres a day without winkin' – and red, at that.' He broke off and sat there, dreaming of the past. The others were dreaming too. Very quietly they listened to the voices that spoke for all of them, making no effort to interrupt. Brunet thought of Paris; of the Rue Montmartre, of a little bar where he'd been in the habit of taking a glass of white wine, well laced, after leaving the *Humanité* office. 'On a Sunday like this,' the sergeant was saying, 'I'd be off with the old lady to my allotment: 'bout fifteen mile outa Paris, it is – rather further nor Villeneuve-Saint-Georges, proper good for green stuff!' From beyond the bars a hoarse voice chimed in approvingly: 'Soil's good all round them parts.' 'We'd be thinking of making for home, 'bout now,' said the sergeant, 'or a bit earlier, maybe, when the sun started going down: don't much care for biking after dark. The old lady'd have a bunch of flowers on the handle-bars, and I'd have a sack of veg. on the carrier.' 'Wasn't keen about going out Sunday, meself,' said Lambert: 'too many people round: besides, I worked Mondays, and it was a goodish pull to the Gare de Lyon.' 'What you do at the Gare de Lyon?' 'Worked in the inquiry office – that big building just outside the main entrance. Any time you're thinking of taking a trip, just you let me know: I'll see you get a seat, even at short notice! – there's ways and means of fixing things like that.' 'Couldn't never stick staying at home,' said Moulu: 'gave me the willies. I'm on me own, see?' 'Quite often I didn't go out even of a Saturday,' said Lambert. 'How did you manage when you wanted a bit o' skirt?' 'Got 'em to come round to my place.' 'To your place?' said Goldilocks in astonishment. 'Didn't your mum have something to say to that?' 'No: used to get us a meal and then go off to the pictures.' 'Well trained, that's what she must'a been!' said Goldilocks: 'very different from mine – why, she'd give me a clout over the ear'ole if she so much as caught me with a girl, even when I was eighteen.' 'Still live with her?' 'Not now – got a little home of me own.' He stopped speaking for a moment, and then went on: 'Night like this I wouldn't 'a' gone out neither: I'd've stayed in and done a spot o' love-making.' There was a long silence: Brunet sat listening to them. He felt ordin-ary: he felt eternal. Almost shyly, he said: 'I'd have been in a bar on the Rue Montmartre, taking a glass of white wine, laced, with my pals.' No one said anything. Someone started singing 'Mon cabanon' at the top of his voice. 'Who's that?' asked Brunet of Schneider. 'Gassou; he's a tax-collector from Nîmes.' The voice sang on. Brunet thought: 'Schneider didn't say a word about how he used to spend Sunday.'

He awoke with a start. In his ears was the sound of a long, melodious call. What was it? The skylight-frame showed white, and on the white ceiling the bars cast shadows. Three o'clock in the morning. The vines were a sea of foam under the sprayed sulphur of the moon. The Allier was nuzzling past its tufted islands, and at Pont de Vau-Fleurville the vine-dressers stood stamping their feet as they waited for the three a.m. train. Brunet lay wondering happily what it could have been. He spoke the question aloud, and started suddenly, because some-body answered: 'Ssh! listen!' *I am not* in my bed at Mâcon, *this is not* the summer holidays. Again, that long impersonal call: three drawn-out whistles that slowly died away. Some-thing was happening. The great attic was filled with rustlings. The huge beast moved its length across the floor: from the depths of this ageless night came the voice of a look-out man – 'A train! a train! a train!' So, that was what it was – the first train. Something was beginning. The night, till then abstract, was taking on substance and life. The night was beginning to sing. Everyone began to talk at once. 'The train! the first train! The track has been repaired – got to hand it to the Germans – they certainly get a move on! – always have been good workers – well, it's in their own interest, isn't it? they got to get things going again – at this rate – just you see – where's it going? Nancy? – Paris, perhaps: try to find out whether there are any prisoners on it, prisoners going home.' Out there the train was rolling onward over the makeshift track, and the great dark building was all agog. Brunet thought: it's a munition-train. He tried, for prudence' sake, to turn his back on his childhood, tried hard to see in imagination the rusty rails, the tarpaulins, a waste of iron and steel. But he could not. Women were sleeping under the blue light of ceiling-lamps turned low, in a pervasive smell of wine and sausages: a man was smoking in the corridor, and the darkness, pressed against the windows, was giving back the reflected image of his face. Tomorrow morning, Paris. Brunet smiled, and lay down again, wrapped snugly in his childhood, under the whispering glimmer of the moon: tomorrow, Paris: he was dozing in the train with his head upon a soft, bare shoulder, and he awoke in a silken radiance, Paris! He looked to his left without moving his head. Six bats were clinging to the wall by their feet, their wings drooping like skirts. He was now wide awake. The bats resolved themselves into the shadows cast by hanging tunics. Moulu, of course, had kept his on: must make him take it off when he goes to bed, *and* change his shirt: he'll make us all chatty if he goes on like this. Brunet yawned: another day! What was it that had happened in the night? – Oh yes, the train. He started up, threw back the blanket, and sat down. His body felt like wood, a zigzag pattern of stiffness, a pleasing woodenness in muscles that had gone numb. He felt as though the hardness of the floor had passed into the very substance of his flesh. He stretched, and thought: 'If I get out of this mess, I'll never sleep in a bed again.' Schneider was still asleep, his mouth open and a look of distress on his face. The man from the North had an angelic smile: Gassou, his hair tousled, his eyes red, was picking crumbs of bread from his blanket and eating them. Now and again he opened his mouth and rubbed the end of his tongue with his finger, to get rid of a scrap of wool or fibre which had been sticking to the bread. Moulu was scratching his head in a puzzled manner. The lines of his face were accentuated by streaks of coal-dust. He had the look of someone who had been making a night of it. Must find some way of making him wash. Goldilocks was blinking. His face expressed gloom and bewilderment. Suddenly it cleared. 'Gawd!' he said. Only his head was visible above the blanket: his expression now was one of delight and astonishment. 'What's up, young 'un?' inquired Moulu. 'Look what I've got!' said Goldilocks. He threw back his blanket. His shirt was rucked up over his white, hairy legs. 'Gosh!' exclaimed Moulu: 'lucky bastard!' 'Lucky?' said Gassou disapprovingly: 'I should call it damned unlucky.' 'You're jealous!' said Goldilocks: 'bet you wouldn't mind being unlucky in that sort of way.' Moulu shook Lambert by the arm: Lambert started awake with a cry. 'Take a dekko there!' said Moulu. Lambert rubbed his eyes, looked and saw. 'Christ!' he said quite simply. He couldn't take his eyes off it. 'I believe it's a fake!' 'Fake!' said Goldilocks in disgusted tones: 'why, in civil life I could do twice as well as that every morning!' He was lying on his back, his arms folded, his eyes half-shut, an almost childlike smile on his face. 'I was beginning to get worried,' he said, glancing downwards and watching the effect of the rhythm of his breathing 'You see, I got a wife.' They laughed. Brunet looked away. He felt anger rising in him. 'Well,' said Moulu, 'it meant the knocking-shop for me, so each time it didn't happen I sort of saved money.' Their laughter redoubled. Goldilocks was stroking himself with a negligent and paternal hand. 'Heaven on earth!' he finished up. Brunet swung round. 'Cover yourself up!' he said between his teeth. 'Why?' asked Curly whose voice had gone hoarse with voluptuous delight. Gassou, who was educated, said, mimicking Brunet, *'Cachez ce sein que je ne saurais voir.'* 'You're just a lot of animals!' said Brunet curtly. They were staring at him. 'They don't like me one little bit' – he thought. Gassou muttered in an ill-tempered voice. Brunet leaned towards him: 'What's that you were saying?' 'What's the harm in talking about love now and then; it makes a bit of a change,' said Moulu with the bright cheerfulness of the peace-maker. 'Men only *talk* about love when they're impotent,' said Brunet: 'love's something to make when you can.' 'And when you can't?' 'You keep your mouth shut.' They looked furtive and embarrassed. Regretfully, Goldilocks pulled up his blanket. Schneider was still asleep. Brunet leaned across to the man from the North and shook him. The man from the North groaned, and opened his eyes. 'Physical jerks,' said Brunet. 'Ugh!' said the man from the North. He got up and took his tunic. They went down into the

stable yard. In front of one of the sheds the printer, Dewrouckère, and the three Chasseurs were waiting for them. While he
was still some distance away, Brunet shouted, 'Everything all
right?' 'Everything fine!' 'Hear the train in the night?' 'Yes, I
heard it,' said Brunet, irritably. But his feeling of annoyance
quickly subsided. These men were young, clean, full of vigour.
The printer was wearing his cap set sideways, with a jaunty air.
Brunet smiled at them. It started to drizzle. On the far side of
the yard, a crowd of men was waiting for Mass. Brunet noticed
with pleasure that it was smaller than it had been on the first
Sunday. 'You do what I told you?' Dewrouckère, without reply-
ing, opened the door of the shed. He had spread some straw on
the ground. Brunet was conscious of a damp smell of stables.
"Where'd you get it?' Dewrouckère smiled, 'There's ways.'
'Good,' said Brunet, and he looked at them with eyes of friendship. They went in and undressed, keeping on nothing but their
pants and socks. Brunet pushed his feet into the soft, crisp straw.
He felt satisfied. He said: 'Let's get started.' The men stood in a
row, their backs to the door. Brunet, facing them, went through
the movements by number. They copied him. Their breath came
through their closed lips with a hissing sound. Brunet looked at
them approvingly as they squatted on their heels, their hands
behind their heads – well set-up fellows, with young, taut
muscles. Dewrouckère and Brunet were stronger than the rest,
but the muscles of all of them stood up in hard, round balls. The
printer was too thin. Brunet looked at him with a certain
amount of anxiety. Suddenly an idea came to him. He stood up
and shouted 'Stop!' The printer seemed pleased at the order: he
was breathing hard. Brunet went across to him. 'You're too thin.'
'I've lost twelve pounds since the twentieth of June.' 'How d'you
know that?' 'There's a set of scales in the sick-house.' 'You've
got to put them on again,' said Brunet: 'you're not eating
enough.' 'Well, but how can I? ...' 'There's a perfectly simple
way,' said Brunet: 'we'll each give you some of our rations.' 'I
...' began the printer. Brunet stopped him: 'I'm doctor here,
and I order you extra food: O.K.?' he asked turning to the
others. 'O.K.' they said. 'Good: from now on you'll come round
all the rooms and collect it: and make it early!' Trunk swinging. At the end of a few moments, the printer began to sway on

his feet. Brunet frowned: 'What's wrong now?' The printer smiled apologetically: 'Finding it a bit tough.' 'Don't stop!' said Brunet: 'whatever you do, don't stop!' The trunks turned like so many wheels, the men flinging their heads skywards, then dropping them between their legs: up, down, up, down. *Enough!* They lay down on their backs to go through the abdominal exercises. We'll finish up with the back-throw: they like that – it makes them think they're wrestling. Brunet was conscious of his labouring muscles, of a long, dragging weariness in the groin. He was happy. This was the one good time of the day. The black rafters swung back and down, the straw seemed to jump to meet his face: he caught its yellow smell, his fingertips touched it well in advance of his toes. 'Get on with it!' he said: 'get on with it!' 'That catches you!' said one of the Chasseurs. 'So much the better. Get on! get on!' He stood up. 'Your turn now, Marbot.' Marbot had done some wrestling before the war. By profession he was a masseur. He approached Dewrouckère and seized him by the waist. It tickled, and Dewrouckère giggled. He let himself fall backwards on to his hands. Now, it was Brunet's turn. He felt a warm grasp on his thighs, and flung himself backwards. 'No! no!' said Marbot: 'don't tighten up like that! It's suppleness, not strength, as does it.' Brunet felt the strain on his legs: his muscles cracked. He was too old for this sort of thing: too muscle-bound. He could only just touch the ground with his fingers. He got up, feeling pretty pleased with himself, all the same, and sweating. He turned round and began to hop. 'Stop!' He turned round sharply. The printer had fainted. Marbot laid him gently on the straw. With a faint hint of reproach he said, 'It was too much for him.' 'Nonsense!' said Brunet, suddenly on edge: 'it's only that he's not used to it.' By this time the printer had opened his eyes. He was pale, and breathing with difficulty. 'How goes it, old man?' said Brunet affectionately. The printer smiled at him: his face expressed complete trust. 'I'm all right, Brunet: I'm all right. I'm sorry I ...' 'Cut it out!' said Brunet: 'You'll be all right when you get some more food in you. Enough for today, boys. Shower-bath, and then a run round!' Still in their pants, with their clothes under their arms, they raced away to the hose-pipe. They threw their clothes on to a ground-sheet, rolled them up into a water-tight bundle, and took a shower-bath in the falling drizzle. Brunet and the printer took hold of the pipe and played it on Marbot. The printer shot a worried look at Dewrouckère, cleared his throat, and said to Brunet: 'I'd like a word with you.' Brunet turned to him, still keeping hold of the nozzle. The printer lowered his eyes. Brunet felt slightly irritated. He disliked feeling that he could intimidate people. He said shortly: 'Three this afternoon, in the yard.' Marbot dried himself with a scrap of khaki shirt, and dressed. He said: 'Hey, boys, something's going on!' A great swarthy-looking fellow was holding forth in the middle of a group of prisoners. 'That's Chaboche, the secretary,' said Marbot in great excitement: 'I'm going along to see what's up.' Brunet watched him walk away. The silly ass hadn't waited to put his puttees on, and was carrying them, one in each hand. 'What d'you think it's all about?' asked the printer. He spoke in an impersonal sort of way, but his voice betrayed him. It was the voice in which they all spoke, a hundred times a day, a voice of hope. Brunet shrugged. 'I suppose the Russians have landed at Bremen, or the English have asked for an armistice. It's always the same kind of thing!' He looked at the printer without a trace of sympathy. The boy was just longing to join the others, but did not dare to do so. Brunet gave him no credit for his timidity. I've only to turn away, and he'll be off at once to stand like a deaf-mute in front of Chaboche, with goggling eyes, dilated nostrils, and his ears wide open, just waiting to be filled. 'Give me a sluice down,' he said. He took off his pants. His flesh rejoiced at the feel of the astringent shower; pellets of hail, millions of little pellets of flesh, vigour. He rubbed his body down with his hands, his eyes fixed on the gaping listeners. Marbot had slipped into the crowd, and was standing with his snub-nose upturned to the speaker. God in Heaven! if only they could get rid of all this ridiculous hoping! – if only they could be put to *doing something*! Before the war, work had been their touchstone: work had been their test of truth: work had decided their relations with the world. Now that they cared about nothing they had come to believe that anything was possible: they lived in a dream-state, no longer capable of knowing the truth when they saw it. Look at those three chaps walking over there, loping along with easy strides, and a sort of vegetable smile on their faces! – are *they* really awake? From time to time a word would ooze from their lips as though they were half-asleep: they seemed scarcely to notice that they were speaking. What were *they* dreaming about? From morning till night they just drifted, manufacturing, like an auto-toxin, the life of sensation which had been taken from them, telling one another, day after day, about all the things they had once done but could do no longer, building up a fantasy life full of blood and drama. 'That's enough!' the jet of water fell. The hose lay on the ground, setting up a boil of foam between the cobbles. Brunet dried himself. Marbot came back. On his face was a look of blind triumph. For a moment or two, he slouched round, before making up his mind to speak. With assumed detachment, he said: 'Seems we're going to have visitors.' The printer's face went a fiery red. 'What visitors?' 'Relations.' 'Is that so?' said Brunet ironically: 'and when's that to be, may I ask?' Marbot straightened himself with alacrity, and looked him in the face with the air of one imparting a thrilling piece of news: 'Today!' 'Oh, yeah?' said Brunet: 'and I suppose they've ordered in twenty thousand beds just so's the prisoners can have a tumble with their wives!' Dewrouckère laughed. The printer was too nervous not to follow suit, but there was still a hungry look in his eyes. Marbot smiled with complete self-assurance. 'This is official,' he said: 'Chaboche has just told us.' 'Oh, if Chaboche said so . . .' said Brunet with a glint of amusement. 'Says it's going to be posted up this morning.' 'Posted up, my foot!' said Dewrouckère. Brunet smiled at him: Marbot looked surprised. 'But this is the real thing: Gartiser's heard about it, too – got it from a German lorry-driver – seems they're coming from Épinal and Nancy.' 'They? – who's they?' 'Whole families – on foot, on bicycles, in carts and freight-trains. They slept on mattresses in the Mairie, and'll be along this morning with a petition for the German Commandant. Look! – there's the notice going up!' A man was busy sticking a sheet of paper to the door. There was a wild rush. A crowd was soon milling round the steps. Marbot swung his arm in a wide gesture: 'What'd I tell you?' he said triumphantly: 'how about your foot now, is *that* your foot?' Dewrouckère shrugged. Brunet slowly put on his shirt and trousers. He was annoyed at having been proved wrong. He said: 'So long, boys; don't forget to turn off the tap.' He sauntered across to the crowd round the door. There was just a chance that this might be another false alarm. He hated the little scraps of undeserved good luck which now and again came to fill the void in the lives of these lily-livered swine – an extra dollop of soup, visitors from outside. Things like that made his work all the harder. From some distance away, over the assembled heads, he could read the notice. 'The Camp Commandant hereby authorizes the prisoners to see the members of their families (close relatives only). A room on the ground floor will be set aside for the purpose. Until further orders, such visits will take place on Sundays, between the hours of 2 p.m. and 6. In no case will interviews be allowed to exceed twenty minutes. Should the behaviour of prisoners be found not to justify this exceptional act of clemency, all visits will be forth-with suspended.' Godchaux looked up with a happy chuckle: 'Must give credit where credit's due: they're not such a bad lot of buggers after all!' On Brunet's left, little Gallois began to laugh: it was an odd sort of sound, rather as though he were laughing in his sleep. 'What are you laughing at?' asked Brunet. 'It's coming,' said Gallois: 'slow but sure, it's coming.' 'What's coming?' Gallois looked put out. He made a vague gesture, stop-ped laughing, and said again, 'It's coming!' Brunet forced his way through the crowd, and got on to the staircase. All around him, the dark ground-floor was a struggling mob of men. The place resembled an ant-heap. Raising his eyes, he could see bluish hands on the banister rail, and a long, moving spiral of bluish faces. He pushed his way up, and was pushed by others. He clung to the rail and hoisted himself forward. He was crushed against the banisters which shook under the weight. All day long men were going up or going down without the slight-est reason. He thought – 'Nothing to be done: they're not wretched enough – not yet.' They had become gentlemen of leisure, property-owners: the barrack belonged to them. They organized expeditions on to the roof and into the basement. They had discovered some books in one of the cellars. There weren't, to be sure, any drugs in the sick-house, or food in the kitchens: still, there *was* a kitchen, and there *was* a sick-house: there was a secretariat, and there were even some barbers. They had a feeling that they were part of an organized society. They had written to their families, and, for the last two days, the life that is lived in cities had resumed its humdrum. When the Kommandantur had issued instructions that all watches must be set by German time, they had hastened to obey, even those among them who, from June onwards, had carried on their wrists, in sign of mourning, watches that they had let run down. The vague sequence of the hours, born and nourished among wild grasses, had become militarized: they had had handed to them German time, true conquerors' time, the same time as ticked away in Danzig and Berlin, sacred time. No, they were not yet wretched enough, for here they were organized, administered, fed, lodged, and governed; were, in fact, without responsibility. There had been the train in the night; and now their relations were coming to see them, loaded with tinned food and consolation. What a squealing, what tears, what a kissing there would be! It needed only that to complete the rot! So far, they've not, at least, been showing off: but now they're going to feel that they are objects of interest! Wives and mothers had had plenty of time in which to build up the myth of the heroic prisoner, and they were coming to infect them with it. He reached the attic floor, went along the corridor, entered his cage, and looked round with anger at his companions. There they were, lying about as usual, with nothing to do, dreaming away their lives, comfortable, and, all of them, well and truly hoaxed! Lambert, with raised eyebrows, and an expression of sullen surprise, was reading *Les Petites Filles Modèles*. It was pretty obvious that the news had not yet reached the attics. Brunet hesitated. Should I e tell them? He could imagine how their eyes would shine, how excitedly they would prattle. 'They'll hear it soon enough.' He sat down in silence. Schneider had gone to get a wash. The man from the North had not yet come in. The rest of them looked at Brunet in consternation. 'What's up?' he asked. At first there was no reply, then Moulu, lowering his voice, said, 'Chatts in No. 6!' Brunet gave a start and made a face. He felt nervous, and the feeling increased. He said angrily – 'I won't have lice in here!' – then he broke off sharply, bit his lower lip, and looked at his neighbours uncertainly. No one had reacted to his words. The faces turned to him were as blank and as vaguely sheepish as ever. 'What are we going to do about it, Brunet?'

asked Gassou. 'I know you don't like me, but when there's anything to be done, it's me you come to for advice.' Very quietly he replied: 'You wouldn't move when I told you to.' 'Where could we have moved to?' 'There were plenty of empty rooms, Lambert: I asked you to see whether there was anyone in the kitchen on the ground floor.' 'The kitchen!' said Moulu: 'no thanks! lying on stones gives yer the gripes, and it's a gloomy hole anyway.' 'Better gloom than lice. Lambert, I was talking to you. Did you go and look?' 'Yes.' 'Well?' 'Full o' blokes.' 'You ought to have had a look at it a week ago!' He felt the blood rushing to his head; his voice rose, he shouted: 'I'm not going to have any lice in here!' 'Keep yer hair on!' said Goldilocks: 'it's not our fault!' But the sergeant leapt to his defence. 'He's perfectly right to give you a dressing-down. I was all through the '14 war, and never got chatty: damned if I begin now just because a lot of scallywags like you can't even keep theirselves clean!' Brunet had recovered his temper. In a reasonable tone, he said: 'We've got to take immediate steps.' Goldilocks laughed: 'Righto! but what steps?' 'First,' said Brunet, 'you've all of you got to have a shower every day: second: each man's got to delouse himself every evening.' 'How do we do that?' 'You strip, and you go over your tunics, your pants and your shirts to see whether there are any nits in the seams. If any of you wear body-belts you want to be particularly careful, it's their favourite breeding-ground.' Gassou sighed: 'What fun we're going to have!' 'When you turn in,' Brunet continued, 'you must hang everything, shirt included, on a nail and sleep naked in your blankets.' 'Hell!' said Moulu, 'I shall die of bronchitis!' Brunet turned on him sharply: 'I was just coming to you, Moulu. You're a regular nest of the things, and that's got to stop!' 'It's a lie!' said Moulu, almost speechless from indignation: 'you won't find a thing on me!' 'Not at the moment, perhaps, but if there are any lice within a radius of ten miles, they'll make a bee-line for you as sure as we've lost the war!' 'Why should they?' asked Moulu primly: 'why me and not you? You've no call to talk like that.' 'Oh yes I have!' thundered Brunet: 'it's because you're as filthy as a pig!' If looks could kill, Moulu would have laid him flat. He opened his mouth to reply, but the others were laughing and shouting –

'He's right there! You stink! you're humming, you are! ye'r a mass of s—: fair takes me appetite away just to look at yer!' Moulu sat up and glared at them. 'I wash meself reglar,' he said with an air of surprise: 'probably more reglar than any of you, but I'm not like some as strips stark naked just so's to get looked at!' Brunet fixed him with a pointed finger: 'Did you wash yesterday?' ' 'Course I did!' 'Let's see your feet, then!' Moulu jumped up: 'What right 'ave you got ...' he twisted his feet under him and squatted on his heels like a Turk. 'F—d if I show me feet!' 'Take his boots off!' said Brunet. Lambert and Goldilocks flung themselves on Moulu, and pinned him to the floor on his back. Gassou tickled his legs. Moulu twitched, gurgled, dribbled, giggled, and heaved deep sighs. 'Oh! stop it, boys, don't be a lot of barstards, I'm ticklish, I am!' 'Keep still, then!' said the sergeant. Moulu relapsed into immobility, though little shudders still ran over his flesh. Lambert was sitting on his chest. The sergeant unlaced his right boot, and pulled it off. His foot came into view. The sergeant went pale, let go of the boot, and got up suddenly. 'Christ!' he said. 'You may well say Christ,' observed Brunet. Lambert and Goldilocks got up too, in silence. They gazed at Moulu in admiring wonder. Moulu resumed his seat, looking calm and dignified. A furious voice came from a neighbouring cage. 'Hi! what the hell are you boys in No. 4 doing! There's a god-awful stink coming from somewhere, like rancid butter!' 'Moulu's taking his boots off!' said Lambert with simple directness. They looked at Moulu's foot. His big toe was poking through a hole in his sock: it was quite black. 'Seen the soles?' asked Lambert: 'more like lace than socks.' Gassou had buried his nose in his handkerchief. Goldilocks was nodding his head with an expression almost of respect, and saying over and over again: 'You dirty old beast! you *filthy* old beast!' 'We've seen all we want to see,' said Brunet: 'hide it away for God's sake!' Moulu hurriedly put on his boot. 'Moulu,' went on Brunet solemnly, 'you're a public danger. You'll oblige me by going down and having a wash *now*. If you're not scrubbed and clean in half an hour, you'll have no supper, and you certainly shan't sleep in here!' Moulu turned on him with a look of hatred, but got up unprotestingly, merely saying: 'Throwin' yer weight about a bit, aren't yer?' Brunet was careful to say nothing. Moulu went out: the others laughed. But Brunet did not laugh. His mind was busy with the idea of lice. He thought: 'Anyhow, *I* shan't get any.' 'What's the time?' asked Goldilocks, 'me belly's fair sagging.' 'Noon,' said the sergeant: 'time for ration issue: whose turn for cookhouse fatigue?' 'Gassou.' 'Come on then, Gassou, jump to it!' 'Plenty of time,' said Gassou. 'I said jump to it. We always get our grub last when you're on the job.' 'Oh, shurrup!' Gassou slammed on his cap in a temper and went out. Lambert returned to his book. Brunet was aware of a nervous itch between his shoulders. Lambert was scratching his thigh while he read: Goldilocks was looking at him. 'Say, you chatty?' 'No,' said Lambert: 'but I've been tickling ever since the talk started.' 'Same here,' said Goldilocks, and began to scratch his neck. 'Don't *you* feel itchykoo, Brunet?' 'No,' said Brunet. None of them said any more. Goldilocks smiled nervously while he scratched: Lambert scratched and went on reading. Brunet dug his hands into his pockets and did not scratch. Gassou reappeared in the doorway: his face threatened trouble. 'You boys been having a bit of fun with me?' 'Hey! where's the bread?' 'The bread, you big chump! – why, there's no one downstairs, the kitchens aren't even open!' Lambert raised scared eyes. 'Meantersay it's going to be like it was in June all over again?' Their lazy and prophetic souls were always ready to believe the worst, or the best. Brunet turned to the sergeant. 'What time d'you make it?' 'Ten past twelve.' 'Sure your watch hasn't stopped?' The sergeant smiled and contemplated his watch with profound self-satisfaction: 'It's a Swiss watch,' he said, and left the words to speak for themselves. Brunet called to the men in the next cage: 'What time is it with you?' 'Ten past eleven,' came a voice. The sergeant was triumphant: 'What'd I tell you?' he said. '*You* told us it was ten past twelve, you gawk!' said Gassou resentfully. ' 'Course I did: ten past twelve by French time, ten past eleven by Boche!' 'That's a dirty trick to play!' said Gassou in a fury. He stepped over to Lambert, and flung himself down on his blanket. The sergeant quite unruffled, continued: 'Nice thing, just when France has taken the count, to abandon French time!' 'You're nuts! – there's no such thing as French time now: only Jerry time for everywhere between Marseilles and Strasbourg.' 'Maybe,' said the sergeant obstinately refusing to let himself be rattled: 'but I'd like to see the man who'd make *me* muck about with any new-fangled time!' He turned to Brunet: 'You'll be glad enough to go back to it,' he said, 'when Jerry's had a kick in the pants!' 'Cor! look at old Moulu all tarted up!' shouted Lambert. Moulu had just come into the room looking pink, fresh, and Sundayish. The others began to laugh. 'Pretty good, eh, Moulu?' 'What is?' 'Water!' 'Oh, it wasn't too bad,' said Moulu carelessly. 'That's all right, then,' said Brunet; 'from now on, you'll have foot-parade every morning.' Moulu showed no sign that he had heard: he was flaunting an important and mysterious smile. 'News, boys, get on your marks!' he said. 'News? what news?' Faces shone, flushed, brightened up. Moulu said: 'We're going to have visitors!' Brunet got up noiselessly and went out. Behind him he could hear the sound of voices raised. He hurried on, forced his way through the dense jungle of the staircase, and went down. The yard was swarming with men, all walking slowly round under the thin drizzle, in single file. Their eyes were turned inwards to the centre of the circle they were describing. Every window was festooned with staring faces. Something had happened. He joined the procession and followed it round, though without curiosity. Each day in this place there was something happening, men standing rock-still, seemingly in expectation of some imminent event, others circling them, all eyes. Brunet turned: Sergeant André smiled at him. 'Why, if it isn't Brunet! bet he's looking for Schneider!' 'Have you seen him?' asked Brunet quickly. 'Not 'arf I haven't!' replied André with a grin: ''s matter of fact, he's looking for you!' He addressed himself to the others: 'Them two,' he laughed, 'they're as thick as thieves, always together, or runnin' after one another!' Brunet smiled – thick as thieves? – and why not? He regarded his friendship for Schneider with a tolerant eye because it made no inroads on his time. It was like a steamer acquaintance and committed him to nothing. If ever they got home from their prison-camp they'd never set eyes on one another again. It was an unexacting friendship, without mutual claims or responsibilities, just a feeling of warmth in the pit of the stomach. André was walking round beside him, saying nothing. At the centre of this slow maelstrom was a zone of

304

absolute calm where a few men in greatcoats were squatting on the ground or sitting on their haversacks. André stopped Clapot who was just passing him. 'Who *are* them blokes?' 'Punishment squad,' said Clapot. '*What* squad?' Clapot threw off his hand impatiently: 'I just told you, punishment!' They resumed their circular progress, but without shifting their gaze from the motionless and silent group. 'Punishment!' grunted André: 'first time I've seen anyone doin' punishment here! – punishment for what? What they bin up to?' Brunet's face cleared. He had just caught sight of Schneider grounded on the rim of the maelstrom. He was looking at the men undergoing punishment, and rubbing his nose. Brunet liked Schneider's trick of holding his head sideways. He thought with pleasure: 'We'll have a chat.' Schneider was very intelligent; more intelligent than Brunet – not that intelligence is so very important, but it does make for pleasant personal contact. He laid his hand on Schneider's shoulder, and smiled at him. Schneider smiled back, but without gaiety. Brunet sometimes found himself wondering whether Schneider really enjoyed his company. They were never apart, but if Schneider had any real liking for him, he did not often show it. At heart, Brunet was grateful for this reticence: he had a horror of all forms of demonstrativeness. 'Found yer pal, Schneider, then?' said André. Brunet smiled: Schneider did not smile. 'Say!' said André to Schneider: 'what for those blokes doing punishment?' 'What blokes?' 'Them over there.' 'They're not doing punishment,' said Schneider: 'they're the Alsatians, can't you see Gartiser in the front row?' 'Oh, so that's it!' said André: 'so that's it!' There was a look of satisfaction on his face. He stood beside them for a moment or two, his hands in his pockets, informed, assuaged. Then, suddenly, he grew worried. 'What they there for?' Schneider gave a shrug: 'Go and ask 'em.' André, after hesitating a moment, strolled slowly over to the men with assumed indifference. The Alsatians were looking stiff and uneasy. In their insecurity, they sat very upright, their greatcoats billowing round them like skirts. They had the appearance of emigrants on the deck of a ship. Gartiser was squatting, tailor-fashion, his hands flat on his thighs, his great farmyard eyes goggling in his big face. 'Hullo, chaps!' said André: 'so there's nine of you, is there?' They said nothing.

André's inquiring face seemed to swim above their lowered heads. 'Nine?' Still no reply. 'I *thought* there were nine when I saw yer sitting here in a circle: Hey! Gartiser!' Gartiser had made up his mind to raise his head. There was a certain arrogance in the expression with which he faced André. 'How come all you Alsatians got together?' 'They told us to.' 'But what about the greatcoats and the kit? – tell you to take them did they?' 'Yes.' 'Why?' 'Don't know.' André's face was scarlet with excitement. 'Haven't you got *some* sort of an idea?' Gartiser said nothing. Behind him there was an impatient gabbling in Alsatian dialect. André, thoroughly offended, stiffened. 'I see. You wasn't so proud of yerselves last winter – *nor* so keen to chatter in yer lingo. But now we're beaten, you seem to have forgotten yer French.' The heads remained lowered. The sound of the voices talking Alsatian was like the natural and ceaseless rustling of leaves in the wind. André laughed and stared at his audience of bent heads. 'Not much of a go now being French, eh, boys?' 'Don't you worry about us,' said Gartiser sharply: 'we shan't be French for long!' André frowned, hesitated, tried to find a stinging reply, but failed to do so. He made a half-turn towards Brunet: 'So, that's that!' From behind Brunet's back came a sound of angry voices. 'What d'you want to talk to 'em for? Leave 'em alone, can't yer: they're just Boches, that's what they are!' Brunet looked at the speakers, at the pale, embittered faces, all of them the colour of sour milk: envy – the envy of little middle-class minds, of petty tradesmen jealous of men with an official position, of men with privileges, jealous now of Alsatians. He grinned and looked at the rancorous eyes. This little bunch of men were vexed at being taken for Frenchmen. Well, that was better than passive resignation – even envy was better than that; it was at least something to work on. 'Ever know one of 'em who'd have lent you a penny or given you a helping hand?' 'Not bleedin' likely! why, there was some of 'em actually had grub when we was first took – and what did they do? gobbled it up with us lookin' on, didn't care if we starved!' The Alsatians were listening. They turned their fair, pink faces and looked at the Frenchmen. Perhaps there'd be a fight. From somewhere a harsh shout sounded. The Frenchmen jumped back: the Alsatians sprang to their feet and stood at attention.

A German officer had just appeared at the top of the steps. He was tall and fragile-looking, with hollow eyes and a dark face. He began to speak. The Alsatians listened. Gartiser, red as a beetroot, was leaning forward. The French were listening, too, not understanding a word, but with faces that expressed tolerant attention. Their anger had gone cold. They had a feeling that they were taking part in some sort of official ceremony. There is always something rather gratifying about a ceremony. The officer spoke on; time passed. The stiff, strange language had a sacrosanct quality, like the Latin of the Mass. No one dared to envy the Alsatians now. They were robed in dignity, like a choir. André nodded; he said: 'Not such an ugly lingo, theirs, after all.' Brunet said nothing. Just a lot of monkeys, that's what they were! - couldn't even keep their anger going for more than five minutes! 'What's he saying?' he asked Schneider. 'Says they've been liberated.' The voice of the Commandant emerged in a series of enthusiastic jerks from his dark face: he was shouting, but there was no gleam in his eyes. 'What's he saying now?' Schneider translated in a low voice: 'Thanks to the Führer, Alsace will return to the bosom of the motherland.' Brunet glanced at the Alsatians: but their faces were slow to express their feelings, incapable of keeping pace with their passions. Two or three of them, nevertheless, had flushed red. Brunet felt amused. The German voice soared and darted, rising from level to level. The officer had raised his fists above his head and, with his elbows, was beating time to his paean. Everyone felt moved, as when the national flag goes by, as when the music of a military band is heard. The two fists opened; the fingers sprang into the air; the men trembled; the officer yelled 'Heil Hitler!' The Alsatians looked as though they had been turned to stone. Gartiser swung round on them, struck them to the earth with the lightning of his glance, then, facing the Commandant, he flung his arm forward and shouted 'Heil!' There was a scarce noticeable silence: then other arms rose in the air. In spite of himself, Brunet seized Schneider's wrist and gripped it hard. There was a sound of shouting. Somebody cried 'Heil!' enthusiastically, others merely opened their mouths without uttering a sound, like people in church pretending to sing. One big fellow, standing in the back row, had his head bent and his hands in his pockets. He seemed to be suffering. The arms fell. Brunet let go of Schneider's wrist. The French said nothing. The Alsatians resumed their attitude of attention. Their faces were white marble, blind and deaf beneath the golden flame of their hair. The Commandant barked an order. The column began to move. The French backed away. The Alsatians marched by between two hedges of curious eyes. Brunet turned round. He looked at the excited faces of his companions. He would have liked to see in them fury and hatred: all he saw was a sort of flabby, blinking avidity. Far off, the gate swung open. Upright, on the steps, the German Commandant looked at the receding column with a benevolent smile. 'All the same ...' said André, '... all the same ...' 'Hell!' said a great bearded fellow, 'and to think I was born at Limoges!' André nodded his head: 'All the same ...' 'What's wrong?' asked Charpin, the cook. 'All the same ...' said André. The cook had a gay and lively look. 'See here, pal,' he said: 'if you'd only to shout "Heil Hitler!" to be sent home, wouldn't *you* shout? It doesn't commit you to nothing. You just shout, but you don't say what you're really thinking ...' 'Oh, *I'd* shout anything,' said André; 'but it's different for them: they're Alsatians, they owe France a duty.' Brunet made a sign to Schneider. They made their escape and took refuge in the farther yard, which was deserted. Brunet leaned with his back against the wall of the recreation hut, facing the stables. Not far from them, seated on the ground, his arms round his knees, was a tall soldier with a pointed skull and thin hair. He did not bother them. He looked like a village idiot. Brunet kept his eyes on his feet. He said: 'See those two Alsatian socialists?' 'What socialists?' 'Among the Alsatian crowd: I saw 'em: Dewrouckère got into touch with 'em last week. They were as keen as mustard.' 'What of it?' 'They raised their arms with the rest of 'em.' Schneider said nothing. Brunet stared at the village idiot. He was a young fellow, with a well-modelled, aquiline nose, the nose of a rich man. His distinguished face, moulded by thirty years of middle-class living, with its fine-etched lines, its sensitive intelligence, had assumed the look of tranquil bewilderment that one sees in certain animals. Brunet shrugged his shoulders: 'They're all the same: one day, you meet a chap: he seems all right, but twenty-four hours later, he's a changed person, pretends not to recognize you.' He jerked his thumb towards the idiot: 'I've been used to working with men, not with objects like that!' Schneider smiled: '*That* was once an engineer in the Thompson Works – the kind of young fellow one says has a future before him.' 'Well,' said Brunet, 'he's got his future behind him now!' 'How many of us are there?' asked Schneider. 'Can't say for certain: the number varies: Let's assume it's about a hundred.' 'A hundred out of thirty thousand?' 'Yes, a hundred out of thirty thousand.' Schneider's question had been put in a perfectly colourless voice. He made no comment on Brunet's reply; but Brunet dared not look at him. 'There's something not quite right,' he went on: 'reckoning on the basis of '36, we ought to be able to count on one-third of the prisoners.' 'It's not '36 now,' said Schneider. 'I know that,' said Brunet. Schneider touched his nostril with the tip of his forefinger. 'Fact is,' he said, 'we're recruiting the grousers, which explains the instability of our group. A grouser is not necessarily a man with a genuine griev-ance: on the contrary, he's perfectly content, as a rule, to go on grousing. If you try to take his words at their face value, he'll pretend to agree, so as not to look like a pricked bubble, but no sooner is your back turned, than he evaporates into thin air. That's happened to me more than once.' 'And to me,' said Brunet. 'What we want to do is to enlist the real malcontents,' said Schneider; 'the sound Leftists who used to read *Marianne* and *Vendredi*, the chaps who honestly believe in democracy and progress.' 'I'm with you there,' said Brunet. He looked at the wooden crosses on the mound, and the grass gleaming under the drizzle. He went on: 'Every now and again I meet a chap dragging along like a sick man, and I say to myself, that's one of 'em. But what can you do? As soon as you try to talk to him he takes fright. It's as though they were suspicious of every-thing.' 'It's not exactly that,' said Schneider: 'the trouble with most of them, I think, is that they're ashamed. They know that they've been the losers in this war, that they're down, and that they won't get up again.' 'They don't really want to go on fight-ing,' said Brunet; 'they'd much rather think that they're down and out for good, it's more flattering to their self-importance.' A strange look came into Schneider's face: he said between his

teeth: 'What can you expect? it's a form of consolation.' 'How
d'you mean?' 'It's always consoling to think that one's not alone
in one's defeat, that it's the common fate.' 'The suicide mentality?' said Brunet with an air of disgust. 'Put it that way if
you want to,' said Schneider, and added quietly: 'Still, you
know, they are France. If you can't establish communication
with them, everything you do goes for nothing.' Brunet turned
and looked at the idiot. The vacant face seemed to fascinate him.
The idiot yawned voluptuously and his eyes watered: a dog
yawned: France yawned: Brunet yawned. He stopped yawning. Without raising his eyes, and in a low, hurried voice, he
said: 'Is there any point in going on?' 'Going on with what?'
'Our work?' Schneider laughed. The sound was dry and unpleasing. '*You* ask that of *me*?' Brunet looked up suddenly. On
Schneider's thick lips he caught the vanishing tail of a sad,
sadistic smile. 'What'll you do if you don't go on?' asked
Schneider. The smile had vanished. The man's face was once
again smooth, heavy, calm: a dead sea. I shall never really get
at the meaning of that face. 'What'll I do? – make a getaway
somehow, join up with the Comrades in Paris.' 'In Paris?'
Schneider scratched his head. 'You think things are the same
there as here?' asked Brunet sharply. Schneider thought for a
moment: 'If the Germans are behaving well.' 'You bet they're
behaving well – helping blind people across the street, I shouldn't
wonder.' 'In that case,' said Schneider; 'yes, I expect things are
about the same as here.' He sat up suddenly and looked at
Brunet with an air of curiosity unmixed with distress. 'What are
you hoping?' Brunet had gone stiff: 'I'm not hoping anything:
I never have hoped anything: I don't give a damn for hope:
I *know* ...' 'What is it you know?' 'I know that sooner or later
the U.S.S.R. will join in the dance: I know that she's biding her
time, and I want our lot to be ready.' 'Her hour's gone by,' said
Schneider. 'England'll be down and out before the autumn. If
the U.S.S.R. didn't intervene while there was still an opportunity
to build two fronts, why should she intervene now when there'll
be nobody to help her?' 'The U.S.S.R. is the land of the
workers,' said Brunet, 'and the Russian workers won't let the
proletariat of Europe be ground into dust under the Nazi jack-
boot.' 'Then why was Molotov allowed to sign the German-

Soviet Pact?' 'At that precise moment, it was the only thing to be done. The U.S.S.R. wasn't ready.' 'What proof have you that she's any readier now?' Brunet smacked the wall irritably with the palm of his hand. 'We're not at the Café du Commerce,' he said, 'and I'm not going to argue. I'm a militant, and I've never wasted my time in speculating about high politics. I had a job to do, and I did it. So far as everything else was concerned, I put my trust in the Central Committee of the U.S.S.R., and I'm not going to change my attitude now.' 'When I asked what you were hoping, I was perfectly right,' said Schneider gloomily, 'you live on hope.' The mournfulness of his tone drove Brunet to exasperation: he had a feeling that this misery of Schneider's was assumed. 'Schneider,' he said, without raising his voice, 'It is *conceivable* that the Politburo might founder in the depths of stupidity: by the same token, it is *conceivable* that the roof of this hut might fall on your head, but that doesn't mean you spend your time keeping a wary eye on the ceiling. You may say, of course, if you feel like it, that your hopes are founded on God, or that you have confidence in the architect – but any reply of that kind would be mere words. You know perfectly well that there are certain natural laws, and that it is the way of buildings to stay standing when they have been built in conformity with those laws. Why, then, should I spend my time wondering about the policy of the U.S.S.R., and why should you raise the question of my confidence in Stalin? I have complete confidence in him, *and* in Molotov, *and* in Jdanov – as much confidence as you have in the solidity of these walls. In other words, I know that history has its laws, and that, in virtue of those laws, an identity of interest binds the country of the workers and the European proletariat. I give no more thought to these things than you do to the foundations of your house. My knowledge is the floor under my feet and the roof over my head. In that certainty I live, and behind that certainty I shelter. That is what makes it possible for me to carry on with the concrete duties assigned to me by the Party. When you stretch out your hand to grasp your mess-tin, the mere fact of that gesture postulates a universal determinism. Similarly, with me: my every act, no matter how trivial, affirms implicitly that the U.S.S.R. is the advance-guard of World Revolution.' He looked ironically at Schneider, and said, in conclusion: 'That's me. I'm a militant and nothing but a militant.' Schneider's expression was still one of discouragement. His arms hung loosely, his eyes were lustreless. It was though he were deliberately concealing the nimbleness of his mind under a mask of heaviness. It was something that Brunet had noticed in him before now. Schneider was always trying to slow down his own intelligence, as though he wanted to bring it into step with that patient, dogged mentality which, doubtless, he believed to be the distinguishing mark of peasants and soldiers. Why? So as to assert in the very depths of his being a complete solidarity with them? So as to utter a wordless protest against intellectuals and leaders? So as to express his hatred of pedantry? 'All right, old man,' said Schneider, 'go on being a militant to your heart's content, only don't get wild when I say that your behaviour bears a marked resemblance to the talky-talky of the Café du Commerce. With infinite trouble we have got together a handful of unhappy idealists, and all we give them to bite on is a lot of talk about the future of Europe!' 'That's inevitable,' said Brunet: 'so long as there's no work for them to do, I can't give them a definite job. The only thing open to us is to talk and make contacts. But just you wait till they've been transported to Germany: there'll be something for them to do, then, all right!' 'Oh, I'll wait,' said Schneider in a sleepy voice: 'I'll wait: doesn't seem as though I'd got much alternative. But the padres and the Germans won't wait, and their propaganda, oddly enough, is a good deal more effective than ours.' Brunet looked him straight in the eyes: 'What exactly are you getting at?' 'I?' said Schneider with an air of surprise: 'nothing at all. We were saying, a while back, how difficult it is to find recruits.' 'Am *I* to blame,' said Brunet with sudden violence, 'if the French are a lot of no-goods without either courage or initiative? Am *I* to blame if ...' Schneider sat up and broke in sharply on his words. His face had gone hard, and he spoke now so quickly, so disjointedly, that it was as though *someone else* had stolen his voice in order to heap insults on Brunet: 'You're ... you're always ... it's *you* who are the no-good,' he shouted: '*You!* It's easy to be superior when you've got a party behind you, when you've been trained up in a political dogma and got used to taking hard knocks: it's easy to despise a lot of poor devils who don't know whether they're going or coming!' The only effect this outburst had on Brunet was to make him feel guilty because he had lost his patience. 'I don't despise anyone,' he said: 'as for the boys here, naturally I take extenuating circumstances into account.' Schneider was not listening. His great eyes were dilated, he seemed to be waiting for something to happen inside himself. All of a sudden he resumed his shouting: 'Yes, you *are* to blame! of course you're to blame!' Brunet looked at him without understanding. An unhealthy colour had flooded Schneider's face: it was something more than anger that was finding vent in his words, it was something closer to long-standing hatred, like one of those suppressed enmities which one finds in families, a grievance that has been damped down for years, and at last bursts out with a kind of wild joy. Brunet looked at the massive incarnation of fury before him, at this man who looked more like a hedgerow preacher than anything else, and he thought – 'something's going to happen!' Schneider seized him by the arm and pointed to the engineer from the Thompson Works who was innocently twiddling his thumbs. There was a moment's silence, because Schneider was seething too violently for speech. Brunet felt cold and calm. When other people lost their tempers, it always made him feel calm. He waited. He wanted to find out the truth about Schneider. Schneider made a violent effort to control himself. '*That's* one of the no-goods who's got neither courage nor initiative! – just such another man as me, as Moulu, as all of us – except you, of course. It's *true* that he's become a no-good, it's *true*, so true that he's convinced of it himself. It happens that I saw him at Toul in September. He had a horror of war, but he accepted this war because he thought there were good reasons why he should fight, and I swear to you he wasn't a no-good then! ... This is what *you've* made of him! You're all in cahoots, Pétain with Hitler, Hitler with Stalin: the whole lot of you are busy explaining that these poor devils are doubly guilty, guilty of having made war, guilty of having lost it. You're running round, taking from them all the reasons which they thought made it necessary for them to fight. *He* thought he was embarked upon a Crusade for Justice and the Rights of Man, and now you want to persuade him that he was just cheated into taking part in an Imperialist war. He doesn't know what he wants: he's not even sure what he's done. It's not only the armies of his enemies that have triumphed, but their ideology as well. He's bogged down! he's fallen slap out of the world of men, out of history, with a bunch of nations that have no longer got the principle of life in them. He's trying to build up some kind of defence-mechanism, to think out the whole situation in which he finds himself; to get it straight, from the beginning. But what with? He no longer has the necessary tools. Even his power to think straight is down and out! He's suffering from the iron that has entered into his soul, and it's *you* who are to blame!' Brunet could not keep himself from laughing. 'Who d'you think you're talking to?' he asked, 'me or Hitler?' 'I'm talking to the leader-writer of the *Humanité*,' said Schneider: 'to a member of the C.P., to the fellow who, on 29 August 1939, filled two pages with paeans of praise on the occasion of the signing of the German–Soviet Pact!' 'So that's the trouble,' said Brunet. 'Yes, that's the trouble.' 'The C.P. was opposed to the war, as you perfectly well know,' said Brunet without any show of anger. 'Certainly, it was opposed to the war, we all know that, it didn't give us much of a chance not to! – it was opposed to the war, and it approved the very act which made the war inevitable!' 'No,' said Brunet very firmly: 'the Pact was our one chance of preventing it.' Schneider burst into a laugh. Brunet smiled but said nothing. Suddenly, Schneider stopped laughing. '*Look* at me! I always have a feeling that you're conducting some sort of post-mortem. More than once I've caught you studying us all with a kind of cold concentration: it's as though you were drawing conclusions from what you saw. Well, what are those conclusions? – that I'm just a waste-product of the historic process: all right, that's O.K. by me: I'm a waste-product sure enough, but I'm not dead, Brunet, oh no, I'm certainly not dead! – unfortunately! I've got to go on living my degradation, with the taste of it in my mouth – though that's something you could never understand. *You* deal in the abstract, and it's you, and others like you, who have made of us the scraps and waste-products that we are.' Brunet remained silent. He was looking at Schneider. Schneider seemed to be hesitating, but there was a look of terror in his hard eyes. He gave the impression of a man who has, on the tip of his tongue, words which, once said, could never again be unsaid. All of a sudden, the colour drained from his face. A film of sheer panic seemed to form on his eyes. He shut his mouth in a grim, hard line. For a moment he stayed like that: then, in calm, monotonous tones he continued: 'Well, we're all of us washed up, and that goes for you, too: it's your excuse. Oh, I know that you still think of yourself as a manifestation of the historic process, but that attitude on your part is purely intellectual now. Your heart's no longer in it. The C.P. will be re-established, but without you, and on principles of which you will know nothing. You could quite easily escape, but you don't dare, because you're afraid of what you'll find *outside*. The iron has entered into your soul, too!' Brunet smiled. No, that wasn't the way: they wouldn't get a rise out of him like that. This sort of talk was just words which didn't in the least concern him. Schneider was silent now, and faintly quivering. Actually, nothing had happened, nothing at all. Schneider had not confessed anything, had not revealed anything – he was just a man whose nerves had let him down. As for that refrain of his about the German–Soviet Pact – he had heard all that a hundred times since September ... The soldier must have realized that they had been talking about him. Slowly he unfolded his full length, and moved off on his long, spindly legs, sidling like a frightened animal. *What* was Schneider? – a bourgeois intellectual, an anarchist of the Right? an unconscious Fascist? The Fascists, too, had been opposed to the war. Brunet turned and looked at him. What he saw was a down-at-heel, perplexed soldier, who had nothing left to defend, nothing more to lose, a man who just stood there rubbing his nose with an absent-minded stare in his eyes. 'He wanted to *hurt* me' – thought Brunet. But he could not feel any resentment. In a very quiet voice he asked a question: 'If that's the way you think, why did you come in with us?' Schneider looked old, used-up. In tones that expressed nothing but wretchedness he said: 'So as not to be alone.' There was a silence, then, Schneider raised his head and showed a wavering smile. 'One's got to do something, hasn't one? – doesn't much matter what. We may not agree about some things ...' he broke off. Brunet said nothing. A few moments passed; Schneider looked at his watch. 'Time for our visitors – you coming?' 'I'm not sure,' said Brunet: 'you go along, I may join you later.' Schneider threw him a brief glance, as though he had half a mind so say something: then he turned away, moved off, and disappeared. The incident was closed. Brunet put his hands behind his back and started to walk up and down the yard under the thin rain. He was thinking of nothing. He felt within himself a hollow, echoing void. On his cheeks and hands he could feel the impact of tiny damp particles. The iron in the soul – all right, but what then? 'Just a lot of psychological balderdash,' he said to himself scornfully. He came to a stop, thinking of the Party. The yard was empty; a grey, disembodied place, smelling of Sunday, a land of exile. Suddenly he started to run, and dashed into the other yard. The men were crowding round the barrier, silent, all heads turned towards the gate. *They* were there, on the other side of the confining walls, exposed to the damp, thin drizzle. Brunet noticed Schneider's muscular back in the front row. He forced his way between the intervening bodies, and laid a hand on his shoulder. Schneider turned. His smile was warm and friendly. 'So, you did come after all!' he said. 'Yes, I came.' 'It's five past two,' said Schneider: 'they're going to open the gate.' Close beside them a cadet officer leaned towards his friend and murmured: 'Perhaps there'll be some girls!' 'It'll be fun to see civilians again!' said Schneider excitedly. 'This reminds me of Sundays at school.' 'Were you a boarder?' 'Yes; we used to line up outside the door of Big School, to see the parents arrive.' Brunet smiled, but said nothing. He didn't give two hoots for civilians, but he felt happy because the presence of all these chaps gave him a sensation of warmth. The gate swung back with much creaking of hinges. A murmur of disappointment was audible in the assembled ranks: 'Aren't there any more than that?' They numbered about thirty. Above the sea of heads, Brunet caught sight of the tiny black, packed group, doggedly waiting under a roof of umbrellas. Two Germans went forward to meet them, all smiles and affability, verified their papers, and then stood back to let them pass. There were men and women, all dressed in black, looking like members of a funeral procession in the rain. They were carrying suit-cases, bags, and baskets covered with napkins. The women's faces were grey. They looked hard, and their eyes were tired. They advanced slowly, brushing against one another, embarrassed by the staring eyes that seemed to be devouring them. 'Hell! – what a dowdy lot they are!' sighed the cadet officer. 'They've got possibilities,' said his friend: 'look at that kid over there, with the dark-haired woman.' Brunet scanned the visitors with a sympathetic eye. Dowdy they certainly were. The women's faces were harsh and set. They looked as though they had come to say to their husbands – 'That was a fool's trick of yours to get nabbed! – how d'you think I'm going to manage, left on my own like this, and with a kid to look after?' Still, there they were. They had come on foot or in carts, carrying baskets crammed tight with food, the kind of women who are always to be seen waiting outside hospitals, barracks, and prisons: pretty, young creatures, with shy eyes, accustomed to go about their daily tasks in mourning black. It was not without emotion that Brunet noticed on their faces the tell-tale traces of wretchedness and poverty, which was all that peace had brought them. With just such looks of feverish disapproval, mingled with loyalty, must they have taken meals to their husbands when they were engaged in a sit-down strike. The men, for the most part, were old and sturdy, with quiet, tranquil eyes. They walked slowly, heavily. They were free. They had won their own war when they were young, and their consciences were clear. This defeat was not *their* defeat, yet they accepted it as their responsibility, carrying the burden of it on their broad shoulders, because, when one has produced a child, one has got to pay for any damage it may do. They were neither angry nor ashamed. They had come to see precisely what mischief the young hopeful had been up to now. On these rustic faces Brunet suddenly discovered what he himself had lost – the meaning of life. These are the kind of men I used to talk with. They made no attempt to understand, but listened with just such an expression of calm thoughtfulness. They groused a bit: but once they had grasped what one was after, they never forgot it. He felt the recrudescence of an old desire: to work, and to feel upon him the eyes of those who were adult and responsible. He shrugged his shoulders, turned from his contemplation of the past, and looked at the *others*, at the crowd of tense, expectant prisoners with

317

their twitching, inexpressive faces. That's where I belong. They were standing on tiptoe, stretching their necks for a glimpse, looking at the visitors with monkey eyes of fear and insolence. They had counted on this war to make men of them, to give them their rights as the heads of families, their share of glory as war veterans. It was to have been for them a solemn initiation, a means of freeing them from the crippling shackles of that *Great* war, that *World* war, which had stifled their youth with memories of splendour. This war of theirs was to have been greater and still more world-wide. By firing on the Jerries they were to have accomplished that ritual massacre of fathers which marks the entry of each new generation into life. But as things turned out, they fired on nobody, indulged in no massacre. The whole thing had gone wrong. They had remained minors, and their fathers were still leading the procession, very much alive, hated, envied, adored, feared, while their sons, twenty thousand warriors, remained bogged down in a rancorous childhood. All of a sudden, one of the old men turned and faced the prisoners. The watching heads drew back. He had heavy, black brows and red cheeks: he was carrying a bundle at the end of a stick. He approached the barbed wire, gripped it with his hand, and stared across out of large and bloodshot eyes. The gaze was almost that of an animal, slow, fierce, inexpressive, and beneath it the men waited, withdrawn, holding their breath, ready to kick back if they were goaded. They stood there in expectation of a blow. The old man spoke: 'So there you be,' he said. Someone muttered, 'Yes, daddy, it's us all right!' The old man said: ' 'Tis a pitiful sight.' The cadet officer cleared his throat and blushed. Brunet could read the expression of his face – a furious, frustrated defiance: yes, daddy, this is us: twenty thousand chaps who wanted to be heroes and threw down their arms without striking a blow. The old man nodded his head. Heavily, in deep tones, he said: 'Poor lads!' Tension relaxed: faces smiled: heads were stretched forward. The German sentry came up. Very politely he touched the old man on the arm, and signed to him to move on. The old man barely turned his head. 'Can't you allow a body a minute?' he protested: 'Why, I be only just come!' He winked conspiratorially at the prisoners who smiled in response. They felt happy because of an old man

318

whose glance was warm and friendly, because of a tough old fellow from down their way. They felt as though freedom had been conferred on them by proxy. The old man asked: 'Things not too bad?' Brunet thought, now they'll all start whining. But twenty voices replied cheerfully, 'Not too bad, daddy, we'll get along all right!' 'That's fine, then,' said the old man: 'that's fine.' He had no more to say to them, but still stood where he was, a clumsy, stocky, rugged figure. The sentry took him gently by the sleeve. He hesitated, scanning the assembled faces. It was as though he were trying to pick out his son's. A deep-buried thought seemed to be struggling for utterance. Slowly it rose to his eyes. He showed signs of embarrassment. At last, in his gnarled old voice he said: 'You know, lads, it warn't your fault!' No one answered. The men stood stiffly before him, almost at attention. He tried to express himself more plainly: 'No one at home thinks as it were your fault.' Still, there was no answer. He said: 'Well, so long, lads,' and turned away. Then, all of a sudden, the crowd was swept as by a wind: voices were raised in passionate farewell: 'So long, daddy! So long! See you soon! See you soon!' The volume of their voices swelled as he moved away, but not once did he turn his head. Schneider said to Brunet – 'You see!' Brunet gave a start: 'See what?' he asked, but knew perfectly well what Schneider meant. Schneider said: 'It only needs someone to show a little confidence in us.' Brunet smiled, and said: 'Do I still look like a surgeon at a post-mortem?' 'No,' said Schneider, 'not now.' They looked at one another, and their eyes were the eyes of friends. Suddenly Brunet turned away and said: 'Look at that old girl!' She was limping along, and, as they stared, came to a halt; a small, grey, figure. She dropped her bundle in the mud, shifted into her right hand the bunch of flowers she was carrying in her left, and raised her right arm above her head. There was a moment's pause. It was as though that arm had risen of its own accord, in triumph, dragging at her neck and shoulder. Then, she threw the flowers from her, but the movement was awkward, and they dropped to the ground at her feet. They lay there, scattered, wild flowers of every description, cornflowers, dandelions, and poppies. She must have gathered them from the roadside. The men fought for them, scrabbling on the ground, gripping the stalks in muddy fists. Laughing, they got to their feet, displaying the flowers as though they were taking part in an act of homage. Brunet felt a lump in his throat. He turned to Schneider and said angrily: 'Flowers! what would it have been like if we'd won the war!' There was no trace of a smile on the woman's face. She took up her bundle and moved on: only her back was visible, waddling along in a mackintosh. Brunet opened his mouth to say something, but he saw Schneider's face and thought better of it. Schneider elbowed his way out of the crowd. He looked thoroughly upset. Brunet followed, and touched him on the shoulder. 'Anything wrong?' Schneider raised his head, and Brunet looked away. The thought of what his own face must look like, what the face of a surgeon at a post-mortem must look like, embarrassed him. 'Anything wrong? he said again, and stared down at his feet. They were standing alone in the middle of the yard. It was still raining. Schneider said: 'It's just that I'm a bloody fool!' There was a short silence, then he went on, 'Seeing these civilians again, that's the trouble.' Brunet, still looking down, said, 'I'm quite as much of a bloody fool as you are.' 'It's different in your case,' said Schneider, 'you've nobody belonging to you.' He paused for a moment, then, unbuttoning his tunic, and fumbling in the inside pocket, brought out a note-case that looked curiously flat. Brunet thought: He's destroyed everything. Schneider opened the note-case. There was nothing in it but one photograph, about the size of a post-card. Schneider held it out to Brunet without looking at it. Brunet saw the face of a young woman with brooding eyes. Beneath the eyes there was a smile. He had never seen anything quite like it. This girl looked as though she knew all about concentration camps, wars, and prisoners herded into barracks, knew about all those things, but, nevertheless, could still smile. It was to the conquered, the deported, the waste-products of history, that she offered the gift of her smile. In vain did he try to discover in her eyes the base, the sadistic, light of charity. Her smile told of confidence: it was a calm smile, a tribute to the strength in others. It was as though she were asking them to show mercy to their conquerors. Brunet had seen many photographs of late, and many smiles, but they, too, had suffered the devastation of war, so that he had found it impossible to look at them. But at this one he could look. It was a new-born smile, and it seemed to be addressed to *him*, to him alone, to Brunet the prisoner, to Brunet the waste-product, to Brunet the victorious. Schneider was leaning over his shoulder. 'It's getting dog-eared.' 'Yes,' said Brunet, 'you ought to trim the edges.' He handed back the photograph, it was glittering with rain-drops. Schneider wiped it carefully with his sleeve, and put it back in his note-case. To himself, Brunet said: 'Is she pretty?' He did not know. He had not had time to notice. He raised his head and looked at Schneider. He thought: 'Her smile is for him.' It was as though he saw him now with other eyes. Two men passed them, both of them young, both of them Chasseurs. They had put poppies in their buttonholes. They were quite silent, and their lowered eyes gave them an odd look, as though they had just taken Communion. Schneider gazed after them. Brunet hesitated. An almost forgotten word rose to his lips. 'I find them touching,' he said. 'Do you seriously mean that?' asked Schneider. Behind them the hedge of curious faces had disintegrated. The visitors had gone into the barracks. Dewrouckère sloped up, followed by Perrin and the printer. 'Of course,' thought Brunet: 'it's three o'clock.' There was a secretive look on the three faces. It occurred to Brunet, with a little shock of irritation, that they had been talking among themselves. That was one of the things that was bound to happen. While they were still some distance away, he called out – 'Hullo, boys!' They came up to him, stopped, and exchanged nervous glances. 'Come on, out with it,' said Brunet bluntly: 'what's the trouble?' The printer fixed him with his fine, uneasy eyes: he looked sullen: he said: 'We've done what you told us to do, haven't we?' 'Yes,' said Brunet impatiently, 'yes, you certainly have: what about it?' The printer could say no more. It was Dewrouckère who spoke for him, keeping his eyes down: 'We'd like to go on, and we will go on for as long as you want us to: but it's sheer waste of time.' Brunet remained silent; Perrin said: 'The boys won't listen.' Still Brunet said nothing. The printer went on in a colourless voice: 'Only yesterday, I got into a scrap with a fellow because I said the Jerries were going to deport us to Germany. He was plain crazy. He said I was a member of the Fifth Column.' All three looked up and stared at Brunet stolidly.

'Things have reached such a point that one can't say a word against the Germans.' Dewrouckère took his courage in both hands and looked Brunet full in the face. 'See here, Brunet,' he said, 'it's not that we're refusing to do the job, and if we've started off on the wrong foot we'll try again. But you've got to understand the position. We move about all over this camp. Hardly a day passes but we talk to a couple of hundred or so. We know what the feeling in this place is like; you, naturally, know far less about it than we do, you don't, you can't, realize what it's like.' 'Well?' 'With feeling as it is at present, if the twenty thousand prisoners here were liberated tomorrow, it'd mean twenty thousand additional Nazis.' Brunet felt his face going red. He looked at each of them in turn. 'Is that your opinion?' he asked. 'Yes,' said all three. 'You're all agreed on that?' They all said 'Yes' again, and at that he suddenly burst out: 'There are workers and peasants in this lot. You ought to be ashamed even to think that they'd become Nazis. If they do, it'll be your fault. A man's not a block of wood: he's a living, breathing, and *thinking* human being, and if you have failed to win these chaps over, it's because you don't know your job!' He turned his back on them, took three paces, and then swung round, his finger pointing: 'The truth of the matter is, you all think yourselves superior. You despise your comrades. Just you remember this, a member of the Party despises nobody!' He saw the bewilderment in their eyes, and the sight made him still angrier. 'Twenty thousand Nazis!' he shouted: 'You're plumb bats! You'll do nothing with them if you despise them. Try, for a beginning, to understand them. These boys have got the iron in their souls. They don't know which way to turn. They'll follow the first man who shows confidence in them!' Schneider's presence rasped his nerves. 'Oh come on!' he said to him. Just as he was moving away, he turned to the three others who were standing silent and discomfited. 'I consider that you have failed. I am prepared to overlook this failure. But don't let me have any more of your nonsense. Report again tomorrow.' He ran up the stairs, Schneider panting behind him. He went into the cage, flung himself down on his blanket, stretched out his hand, and picked up a book – Henri Laverdan's *Leurs Sœurs*. He read with concentrated attention, line by line, word by word, until he calmed down. When the light began to fail, he laid the book aside, and remembered that he had eaten nothing. 'D'you keep my bread for me?' Moulu held it out, Brunet cut off the piece he would give next day to the printer, stowed it in his haversack, and began to eat. Cantrelle and Livard appeared in the doorway. It was the time of evening when visits were paid. 'Hullo!' said the inmates, without looking up. 'Anything nice to tell us!' asked Moulu. 'They do say as some of the chaps have got blotto,' said Livard. 'And who pays for that? – us, as usual!' 'What's the news?' asked Moulu. 'One of the N.C.O.s has made a getaway.' 'Made a getaway, why?' asked Goldilocks, surprised into plain speaking. Those present took a little time to digest the information. They looked vaguely startled, slightly horrified, as they might have done, before the war, if, in the bored crowd filling the Underground, a madman had unexpectedly started making a noise. 'Made a getaway,' repeated Gassou, slowly. The man from the North laid down the stick he was busy carving. He seemed a bit restless. Lambert munched in silence, his eyes fixed in a hard stare. After a moment's silence, he said with an unpleasant laugh: 'There's always some as is more in a hurry than the rest.' 'Perhaps,' said Moulu, 'he likes walking!' Brunet dug out the mouldy fragments with the point of his knife, and let them fall on his blanket. He felt uncomfortable. The murky outer air had drifted into the room. Out there, in the dead town, a hunted man was in hiding. Here are we, eating, and tonight we'll have a roof over our heads. Rather reluctantly, he asked: 'How'd he manage it?' Livard looked at him with a consequential air: 'Guess.' 'How should I know? – over the back wall?' Livard shook his head with a grin. He took his time; then, triumphantly: 'By the front gate,' he said, 'at four o'clock this afternoon, under the Jerries' noses!' The others seemed struck all of a heap by this news. For a moment or two Livard and Cantrelle revelled in the general amazement; then Cantrelle proceeded to explain in precise, rapid words. 'His old woman came to see him with a suit of civvies in her bag. He changed in a cupboard, and then just walked out with his arm in hers!' 'Didn't anyone stop him?' asked Gassou indignantly. Livard shrugged his shoulders: 'Stop him? – why should anyone do that?' 'If I'd seen him going out,' said Gassou, 'I'd have called a Jerry and had him locked up!' Brunet looked at him in amazement: 'Have you gone stark mad?' 'Mad?' said Gassou with a spurt of ill-temper. 'What's this poor country of ours coming to? Chap tries to do his duty, and the only thanks he gets is to be called mad!' He glanced round the circle to see whether the company was with him, and then went on, with even greater vehemence. 'You'll soon see whether I'm mad when they put a stop to visiting! After all, they let our people in of their own free will – they didn't *have* to, don't you agree, boys?' Moulu and Lambert nodded, and Gassou added severely, 'For once in a way the Fritzes behave decently, and what happens? – we do the dirty on 'em! They'll be properly wild when they find out what's happened – and who's to blame 'em?' Brunet opened his mouth to say just what he thought of this argument, but Schneider, with a quick glance, got in before him: 'Gassou,' he said, 'what a nasty piece of work you are!' Brunet held his tongue, but his thoughts were bitter: 'He barged in with that bit of abuse to prevent me from passing *judgement* on him. He doesn't *judge* Gassou, he never *judges* anybody. He's ashamed for all of them because I'm here: whatever happens, whatever they do, he'll always be with them against me!' Gassou glared at Schneider; Schneider glared back, and Gassou looked away. 'All right!' he said, 'all right, just you wait till they put a stop to visits, and then see whether I'm mad or not! – doesn't matter to me, my folk are at Orange.' 'I'm an orphan, if it comes to that,' said Moulu: 'but, after all, one ought to have some consideration for others.' 'You're a fine one to talk, I must say,' said Brunet: 'you who wash yourself carefully every day just so's your pals shan't get lousy!' 'That's quite different!' said Goldilocks sharply: 'We all know Moulu's filthy, but it's only the chaps in this room as suffer. We're talking of a bloke who don't care whether he lets down twenty thousand provided he can do what he likes.' 'If the Jerries get him and put him in choky,' said Lambert, '*I* shan't do any crying.' 'Only six weeks before we're all demobilized,' said Moulu, 'and off our fine gentleman goes! Couldn't do like the rest of us, could he, and just wait?' For once in a way the sergeant was in agreement. 'Typical of the French character,' he said with a sigh: 'that's why we lost the war.' Brunet gave a nasty laugh: 'All the same, you'd be damn' pleased to be in his shoes: trouble with you is you're ashamed you didn't make a bolt for it yourselves!' 'That's where you're wrong,' said Cantrelle sharply: 'if he'd taken a risk, any sort of a risk, say of a bullet in the backside, one would have thought – he's a barstard and a hot-head, but at least he's got guts. Instead of which, he slips away on the q.t., hiding behind a woman like a bleeding coward. I don't call that an escape: I call it an abuse of confidence.' Brunet felt as though cold water was running down his spine. He sat up and looked at each of them in turn, straight in the eyes. 'All right, if that's how you feel, I give you fair warning. Tomorrow evening I'm going to hop over the wall and make a bolt for it. It'll be interesting to see whether anyone gives me away.' There was a general atmosphere of embarrassment, but Gassou wasn't going to let himself be put out of countenance. 'No one'll give you away. You know that perfectly well: but when I get out of here I'll bloody well give you something to remember me by, because you can be quite sure that if you escape, we're the ones that'll have to pay for it.' 'Something to remember you by?' said Brunet with an insulting laugh: 'I should like to see you try!' 'Well, if necessary, we'll get up a party to do the job.' 'Time to talk about that in ten years' time – when you get back from Germany.' Gassou was about to say something, but Livard got in first: 'No point arguing with him: they're letting us out on the 14th – that's official.' 'Oh, that's official, is it?' asked Brunet, still laughing: 'Suppose you've seen it in writing!' Livard made as though not to answer him. Instead, he turned to the others, and said: 'Not in writing, I haven't, but it's as good as.' Faces lit up in the darkness like radio valves, with a dark, muffled glow. Livard looked at them with a good-natured smile, and proceeded to expatiate: 'Hitler said so!' 'Hitler!' – Brunet was dumbfounded. Livard ignored the interruption and went on: 'not that the bugger's what you might call up my street – he's our enemy all right, and as for Nazism, well, I'm neither for it nor against it. It may work with the Jerries, but it don't suit the French temperament. All the same, I will say this for Hitler, he sticks to his word. He said he'd be in Paris on the 15th June, and there he was, sure enough – even a bit ahead of time.' 'And he's said something about let-

325

ting us go?' inquired Lambert. 'Well, didn't he say "On the 15th June I shall be in Paris, and on the 14th July, you'll be dancing with your wives"?' A timid voice piped up: it belonged to the man from the North: '*I* thought what he said was *we'll* be dancing with your wives – we – the Fritzes.' Livard gave him a withering look: 'Were you there, may I ask?' 'No,' said the man from the North: 'but I was told about it.' Livard broke into contemptuous mirth. 'If it comes to that,' said Brunet, 'were *you* there?' ' 'Course I was there: it was at Hagenau. We were holding an advance post – I'd been out, and when I got back he'd just finished speaking.' He nodded his head, and repeated with considerable self-satisfaction: 'On the 15th June we shall be in Paris, and on the 14th July, you'll be dancing with your wives.' By this time the others were in a cheerful mood. 'Ha!' they said, and quoted his words: '15th June, Paris, and on the 14th July we'll be dancing.' Women, dancing! Hunching their shoulders, throwing back their heads, grasping their ground-sheets like partners, they began to dance. The floor creaked: they were waltzing and revolving under the stars between the cliff-like buildings of the Chateaudun street-junction. Gassou, in softened mood, leaned across to Brunet, and embarked on a logical explanation. 'Hitler's not mad, you know. Why should he want to plump down a million prisoners in the middle of Germany – a million mouths to feed?' 'To make 'em work,' said Brunet. 'Cheek by jowl with the German workers? What'd the Jerries' morale be like after they'd talked with us for a bit?' 'In what language?' 'Any language – pidgin German, Esperanto, anything you like. The French workman is born cunning: he's a natural grumbler and stubborn as you make 'em: in less than no time he'd be taking the stuffing out of them Jerries, and you can be pretty sure that old Hitler knows all about that! You can bet your life, he's pretty shrewd! I agree with Livard – I don't like him, but I respect him – and that's more'n I'd say about a lot of people.' The others solemnly nodded their heads in agreement. 'He loves his country – only fair to grant him that.' 'He's a man with an ideal – mayn't be the same as ours, but one's got to take off one's hat to him.' 'All opinions are worthy of respect – provided they're sincere.' 'That go for ours too? – what about our Deputies, what sort of ideals have they got, beyond filling their pockets, keeping themselves in bits of skirt, and having a good time generally – on our money? Things are a bit different in Germany, I can tell you. You pay your taxes, but at least you know where the money goes. Each year you get a letter from the Collector: "Dear sir, you have paid so much. It represents this or that amount of medical supplies for the sick, or so many miles of motor-road." I know what I'm talking about!' 'He never wanted to make war on us,' said Moulu: 'it was us as declared war.' 'Not even us, it wasn't; it was Daladier, and he did it without even consulting the Chamber.' 'Just as I said: well, he couldn't take that lying down, now, could he? You've asked for me, he said, and here I am. And in less than two years he'd got us where he wanted us. So what's he going to do now. D'you think it's any fun for him to have a million prisoners on his hands? You wait a bit, and see. In a few days he'll say: "You're a damn' nuisance, boys," he'll say, "just you go home and stay there." Then he'll turn round on the Russkies and they'll hammer each other flat. Why should we bother? He'll take back Alsace, of course – that's a matter of prestige – and good riddance, say I; never could stick them Alsatians!' Livard went off into a fit of silent laughter, as though at some private joke. He looked thoroughly self-satisfied. 'If only we'd had a Hitler,' he said: 'Hitler, with the French army behind him,' said Gassou, 'why, there'd have been no holding him. He'd have been in Constantinople by this time, because' – he went on with a broad wink – 'the French soldier's the best in the world when he's properly led.' How ashamed Schneider must be feeling, thought Brunet, and dared not look at him. He got up and turned his back on the best soldiers in the world. No point in staying here, he thought, and went out. On the landing he paused, and looked at the staircase spiralling downwards into the darkness. At this time of night, the door would certainly be locked. For the first time he felt himself a prisoner. Sooner or later he would have to return to his gaol, lie down on the floor next to the others, and listen to them dreaming. Below him, the whole barrack building was alive with sound. A noise of shouting and singing filled the well of the staircase. The floor creaked. He swung round. Schneider was walking towards him down the twilit corridor, crossing, one by one, the last beams of daylight filtering through the windows. I'll say: 'Don't tell me you've got the nerve to stand up for 'em now!' Schneider was close to him. Brunet looked, but said nothing. He leaned his hands on the banister rail and Schneider leaned beside him. Brunet said: 'Dewrouckère was right.' Schneider made no reply. What was there for him to say? A smile, a few red flowers in the rain, that's all they need to give them a little confidence, and a little's all they need: confidence! my hat! In a fury he broke out: 'There's nothing to be done with them! nothing! nothing! nothing!' Confidence was *not* enough! Confidence in whom? Confidence in what? What they needed was suffering, fear, and hatred: what they needed was the spirit of revolt, massacre, and an iron discipline. When they'd got nothing more to lose, when life would seem even worse than death. ... They leaned there together above the blackness that smelled of dust. Schneider lowered his voice: 'Are you really planning to escape? Brunet looked at him without answering. Schneider said: 'I shall miss you.' Brunet said bitterly, 'You'll be the only one as will.' On the ground floor some men were striking up a chorus: 'Drink up: drink up: let's take a cup: here's to wine and women' – escape? – pull a fast one on twenty thousand blokes? – leave 'em to stew in their own juice? – has anyone ever got the right to say, there's nothing more to be done? Suppose they *are* waiting for me in Paris? The thought of Paris filled him with a sense of disgust so violent that he was amazed. He said: 'No, I'm not going to escape: I only said that because I'd lost my temper.' 'But if you really believe there's nothing more to be done?' 'There's always something more to be done. One's got to do the work that lies to hand, with such tools as one can find. We must wait and see.' Schneider heaved a sigh. Brunet said sharply: 'It's you who ought to escape.' Schneider shook his head: Brunet said shyly, 'You've got a wife waiting for you.' Again Schneider shook his head. 'Why don't you?' Brunet asked: 'there's nothing to keep you here.' Schneider said: 'It'd be worse everywhere else.' Drink up: drink up: let's take a cup: here's to wine and women! Brunet said, 'And now for Germany!' For the first time, and rather shamefacedly, Schneider echoed him: 'And now for Germany: that's the next step!' – and to hell with the King of England who has declared war on us!

Twenty-seven men: the freight-van creaked: the canal slid by. Moulu said: 'Things not so knocked about as one might have expected.' The Germans had left the sliding-doors open, and daylight filtered into the van with a swarm of flies. Schneider, Brunet, and the printer were seated on the floor in the opening of the door, dangling their legs outside. It was a fine summer's day. 'No,' said Moulu with satisfaction, 'not at all too bad.' Brunet looked up. Moulu was standing up, obviously pleased by the spectacle of the fields and grass-land slipping by. It was warm. The men gave off a strong smell. Someone at the far end of the van was snoring. Brunet leaned out. He caught the glitter of German helmets in the open truck, above an array of rifle-barrels. A fine summer's day in a peaceful world. The train rumbled on: the canal glided slowly by. Here and there a bomb had torn a hole in a road or scarred a field. At the bottom of the craters water reflected the sky. The printer said, as though speaking to himself: 'Easy enough to make a jump for it.' Schneider jerked his shoulder in the direction of the rifles: 'They'd knock you over like a rabbit!' The printer said nothing. He leaned out as though about to take a dive. Brunet held him back by the shoulder. 'Be easy enough,' said the printer again, like someone in a hypnotic trance. Moulu patted him on the back of the neck: 'What's the point, seeing as how we're off to Châlons?' 'But is that so, is that really where we're going?' 'You read the notice, same as I did.' 'But it didn't say nothing about Châlons?' 'P'raps not, but it did say we were staying in France, didn't it, Brunet?' For a moment or two, Brunet said nothing. *It was true* that the evening before there had been a notice stuck on the wall, signed by the Commandant: 'The prisoners in the Camp at Baccarat will remain in France,' but that didn't alter the fact that here they all were in a train, being carried off to some unknown destination. Moulu pressed his question: 'Is it true, or isn't it?' From behind them came impatient voices: 'Of course it's true! Why you trying to put the wind up us? – you know perfectly well it's true!' Brunet glanced at the printer, and said quietly: 'Yes, it's true.' The printer sighed. He was smiling now, and looked reassured. 'Trouble is, railway journeys always take me like this.' He laughed gaily: still turned to Brunet, he said: 'I've only been in a train about twenty times all told, I suppose, in my life, and it always takes me like this.' He laughed, and Brunet thought: 'He's in bad shape.' Lucien was seated slightly behind them, his hands clasped round his ankles. He said: 'My people were to have come on Sunday to see me.' He was young, gentle-looking, and wore spectacles. 'Wouldn't you rather find them waiting for you at home?' asked Moulu. 'That's all very well,' said the boy, 'but seeing as how they was to have come Sunday, I'd rather we hadn't started till Monday.' Protests rose from all sides. 'Here's a chap as'd like to have been stuck there another three days! There's some as don't know when they're well off! If we'd waited any longer, we might have been there till Christmas!' Lucien smiled sweetly: 'You see,' he explained, 'they're not as young as they were, and I don't like the idea of their being put to all that trouble for nothing.' 'Bah!' said Moulu: 'when you get home, it'll be you as'll be waiting for them!' 'That's what I'd like,' said Lucien: 'but no such luck: it'll take 'em at least a week to demobilize us.' 'Who knows?' said Moulu, 'who knows? – Jerry's a quick worker.' 'All I'm bothering about,' said Jurassien, 'is being home in time for the lavender picking.' Brunet turned his head. The van was full of white dust and white smoke. Some of the men were standing, others sitting. He could see across the bent trunks of this forest of legs, a collection of placid faces, each of them wreathed in a vague smile. Jurassien was a great lout of a fellow, who looked tough, had had his head completely shaved, and wore a black bandage across one eye. He was squatting tailor-fashion in order to take up less space. 'Where you from?' asked Brunet. 'Manosque: I was in the merchant navy. Now I live ashore with my wife, and I don't like the idea of her having to do all the cutting without me.' The printer was still staring at the rails. 'It was high time,' he said. 'What's the trouble, lad?' asked Brunet. 'High time they let us go – high time.' 'Why so?' 'It was getting me down,' said the printer. Brunet thought: He too! but seeing the feverish eyes in their dark sockets, he said nothing. He'll find out soon enough – he thought. Schneider said: 'That's right; it was no laughing matter. How you feeling now?' 'Oh,' said the printer, 'I'm fine now.' There was something he wanted to explain, but he could find no words for his thought. He made a gesture as

though to excuse his silence, and merely said: 'I'm from Lyons.'
Brunet felt embarrassed. He thought: I'd forgotten he was from
Lyons. I've been making him work for the last two months, and
I don't really know a thing about him. Now he has a grudge
against me – he's suffering badly from prison-sickness. The
printer had turned his head, and Brunet could see behind his
eyes a sort of anguished gentleness. 'Is it *certain* we're going
to Châlons?' asked the printer suddenly. 'Still on that lay!' said
Moulu impatiently. 'What's it matter?' asked Brunet: 'even if
it's not Châlons, we shall get home sooner or later.' 'It *must* be
Châlons!' said the printer: 'it must just be Châlons!' The words
sounded almost like a prayer. 'If it hadn't been for you, you
know,' he said to Brunet: 'I should have taken a chance ages
ago!' 'If it hadn't been for me?' 'Yes: as soon as I felt that there
was somebody ready to take responsibility, I, well, I *had* to
stay.' Brunet said nothing: he thought – 'It was I who made all
that difference' – but the knowledge gave him no pleasure. The
printer went on: 'I should have been back in Lyons by this time.
I've been in the army since October '37 – and that's a pretty
serious matter. It means I've forgotten my trade.' 'You'll find it
comes back pretty quick,' said Lucien. The printer shook his
head with a look of profound wisdom: 'Not so quick as all
that,' he said. 'It won't be any too easy starting in again – as
you'll find out soon enough.' He sat motionless, his eyes staring
at nothing. He said: 'When I was at home of an evening with
my old parents, I used to give everything a good polishing: I
hated having nothing to do – and I wanted the whole place to
look spick and span.' Brunet glanced at him out of the corner
of his eye. He had lost his neat, sprightly appearance; his words
came lolloping out of his mouth, and there were scattered tufts
of black hair on his thin cheeks. A tunnel swallowed the vans
ahead of them. Brunet looked at the black hole into which the
train was plunging. He turned sharply to the printer. 'If you
really want to take a chance, now's the moment!' 'What?' said
the printer. 'You've only got to make a jump for it as soon as
we're inside the tunnel.' The printer stared at him. Then, all
went black. He coughed. The train slowed down. 'Jump!' said
Brunet, coughing too: 'go on, jump!' There was no reply. The
daylight began to show grey through the smoke. Brunet wiped

331

his eyes. All of a sudden the van was filled with sunlight. The printer was still where he had been. 'Why aren't you gone?' asked Brunet. The printer blinked his eyes and said: 'What's the point if we're really on our way to Châlons?' Brunet answered with a shrug, and looked at the canal. There was a tavern standing on the bank, with a man drinking. They could see his cap, his glass, and his long nose, over the top of the hedge. Two other men were walking along the tow-path. They were wearing straw-hats and talking quietly together. They did not even turn their heads to look at the train. 'Hullo!' shouted Moulu: 'Hullo, chums!' But already they were out of sight. A brand-new café came in sight – '*À La Bonne Pêche*'. The metallic neighing of a mechanical piano struck on Brunet's ears, then died away: it must be the Jerries in the truck who were hearing it now. Brunet saw a château which was not yet within their range of vision, a white building flanked by pointed towers. A small girl in the park, holding a hoop, stared at them with solemn eyes. It was as though all of France – an innocent and outmoded France – was in that young face watching them. Brunet looked at the little girl and thought of Pétain. The train swept across her contemplative gaze, across her own especial future of quiet games and healthy thoughts and trivial worries, on towards fields of potatoes and factories and armament works, on to the real, dark future that lay ahead waiting to receive a world of men. The prisoners standing behind Brunet waved their handkerchiefs. But the child made no reply, only stood there, clasping her hoop. 'They might at least give us a hullo,' said André: 'they were glad enough to see us in September when we was off to get our faces bashed in just to protect 'em.' 'Yes,' said Lambert, 'but the trouble is that there wasn't any bashing.' An old man was fishing, seated on a camp-stool. He never so much as looked up. Jurassien laughed: 'Just sunk back into their old, easy-going ways, that's what they've done.' 'So it seems,' said Brunet. The train rolled on through a land at peace: fishermen, taverns, straw-hats, and the quiet summer sky. Brunet glanced over his shoulder. The faces he saw were discontented but fascinated. 'Between ourselves,' said Martial, 'I don't blame the old boy. In a week's time, *I* shall be off for a day's fishing.' 'What sort of fishing? just hook and line?' 'Not on your life! –

fly.' The liberation had become something they could almost touch, a picture with, for background, this familiar countryside, these calm waters. Peace, work, the old man coming home at night with his bag of carp. In a week's time they would be free. The proof of it was there before them, gentle, insinuating. Brunet felt ill at ease. It is a bad thing to be the only one in a crowd who has a true vision of the future. He turned his head away and watched another set of rails branching off from the track they were on. He thought: 'What can I say? – they won't believe me.' By rights he ought to be rejoicing: at long last they were about to have understanding forced upon them: at long last he would be able to get to work in good earnest. But against his shoulder and along his arm he could feel the feverish heat of the printer's body, and his heart was heavy with something very like remorse. The train began to slow down. 'What's up?' 'Points,' said Moulu with complacent knowingness. 'Not much of this line I'm not familiar with: used to go on it reglar ten years ago – every week. We shall go off left here, see if we don't. That right-hand track goes to Lunéville and Strasbourg.' 'Lunéville?' said Goldilocks: 'but I thought we had to go through Lunéville?' 'I *know* this line, I tell yer. Probably a block down Lunéville way, and we've gone round by Saint-Dié to avoid it, and now we're working back.' 'Does Germany lie over there to the right?' asked Ramelle in an anxious voice. 'Yes: we shall swing left here – Nancy, Bar-le-Duc, Châlons.' The train came to a halt. Brunet turned and looked at them. Their faces were calm and peaceful. A few of them were smiling. Only Ramelle, the music-teacher, was biting his lower lip and fingering his spectacles in a worried and unhappy manner. All the same, no one spoke. Suddenly a shout from Moulu broke the silence: 'Hey! my pretties! blow us a kiss!' Brunet swung round sharply. There were six of them, in light summer dresses: they had fat, red arms and healthy complexions. Six pairs of eyes were watching from behind the gate of a level-crossing. Moulu was busy blowing kisses. None of the girls smiled. One of them, large, dark, and far from plain, began to sigh: the sighs distended her ample bosom. The other five were staring with wide and mournful eyes. Six mouths, in six rustic and inexpressive faces, puckered up like those of children on the verge of tears.

'Come on!' said Moulu: 'give us a sign of life!' – then, moved by sudden inspiration, he added – 'spare a kiss for a lot of poor devils on their way to Germany!' Protesting voices were raised behind him: 'Don't say things like that, it's unlucky!' Moulu glanced over his shoulder: he was completely at his ease. 'Stow it! I only said that to get a smile out of 'em!' The men, now, were laughing and shouting: 'Come on, girls, don't be shy!' The dark-haired one was still staring hard with frightened eyes. Hesitatingly, she raised one hand, put it to her flaccid lips, and jerked it forward with the movement of a mechanical doll. 'You can do better than that!' said Moulu: 'that's not good enough for us, you know!' A furious voice shouted at him in German, and he hurriedly withdrew his head. 'Bloody fool!' said Jurassien; 'they'll be shutting the door on us if you're not careful!' Moulu made no reply: he was grumbling away to himself – 'proper bitches, the girls in this dump!' There was a sound of creaking: the train began to move: the men stopped talking: Moulu, his mouth hanging half-open, stood waiting. They were gathering speed. Brunet thought: now's the moment. There was a noise of banging and a sudden shock. Moulu lost his balance and caught at Schneider's shoulder. He gave a cry of triumph: 'What did I tell yer, boys! – we're off to Nancy!' Everyone started laughing and shouting. Ramelle could be heard saying nervously, 'are you *sure* we're going to Nancy?' 'Look for yerself,' said Moulu pointing to the track. Sure enough, the train had diverged to the left. It was strung out now in the arc of a circle. By leaning well forward it was possible to see the small locomotive. 'Is this the direct route?' Brunet turned his head. Ramelle's face was ashen: his bloodless lips were still trembling. 'Direct route?' asked Moulu with a laugh: 'd'you think they're going to make us change?' 'All I meant was, are there any other systems of points?' 'There certainly are,' said Moulu: 'one just before we get into Frouard, and another at Pagny-sur-Meuse. But we haven't got to worry. We've turned left, and left we shall keep for Bar-le-Duc and Châlons.' 'When can we be sure of that?' 'What more d'you want? we *are* sure.' 'But what about the points?' 'Oh,' said Moulu, 'if that's what's bothering you, the second lot are the ones that matter. If we went right *there* it'd mean Metz and Luxembourg. The third lot don't count: a swing right would only take us to Verdun and Sedan, and why in the world should they be sending us there?' 'So it's the second lot of points that are important?' said Ramelle, 'the ones that are coming next? ...' He relapsed into silence, and lay curled up with his knees drawn to his chin, looking lost and cold. 'Oh, give it a rest!' said André: *'you'll see soon enough!'* Ramelle did not answer. Silence lay heavy on the van; the men's faces were without expression, but rather tense. Brunet heard to his left the sound of a mouth-organ. André gave a start: 'Hey! cut it out – we don't want no music!' 'I've got a perfect right to play the mouth-organ,' said a voice from the shadows. 'We don't want any music!' said André. The man stopped his playing. The train had gradually been gaining speed. It ran across a bridge. 'That's the last of the canal,' remarked the printer with a sigh. Schneider was sleeping where he sat, his head jerking to the movement of the train. Brunet felt bored. He looked out at the fields, thinking of nothing. A few moments later the train began to slow down. Ramelle straightened up: his face looked haggard. 'What's happening!' 'Don't get the wind up: it's only Nancy,' said Moulu. The side of a cutting rose above the level of their heads, topped by a wall with a cornice of white stone. On top of the cornice there was an iron paling. 'Must be a road up there,' said Moulu. Brunet felt suddenly as though he were crushed under an enormous weight. The men all round him leaned out, supporting themselves on his shoulder. They were staring upwards. Great puffs of smoke drifted into the van. Brunet started to cough. 'Look at that chap, up there,' said Martial. Brunet tilted his head back: it struck something hard: hands were pushing him. There was a man leaning on the paling. They could see, through the iron lattice-work, his black jacket and striped trousers. He was carrying a leather brief-case, and seemed to be about forty. 'Hullo!' called Martial. 'Good morning,' said the man. His face was thin, its expression hard. He had a neat moustache and very light blue eyes. 'Hullo! ... Hullo! ...' cried the prisoners. 'How are things going on in Nancy?' asked Moulu: 'town been much knocked about?' 'No,' said the man. 'Good,' said Moulu: 'good.' The man said nothing. He was staring hard at them with an air of curiosity. 'Business starting up again?' asked

Jurassien. The engine whistled: the man curved his hand round his ear: 'What's that?' Jurassien gestured over Brunet's head, in an attempt to convey the fact that he could not talk any louder. Lucien said: 'Ask him about the prisoners from Nancy.' 'What about them?' 'Ask him if he knows what's happened to them.' 'Pipe down,' said Moulu: 'chap can't hear hisself speak.' 'Hurry up and ask him: we shall be off again in a minute.' The whistling had stopped. Moulu shouted: 'Business as usual?' 'Plenty doing with all these Germans in the place.' 'Cinemas reopened?' asked Martial. 'What's that?' shouted the civilian. 'Hell!' said Lucien: 'I'm sick of cinemas. For God's sake let's give 'em a rest! Here, let me do the talking!' Without pausing for breath, he added: 'How about the prisoners?' 'What prisoners?' 'Weren't there any prisoners from here?' 'Yes, but they're not here any longer.' 'Where they gone to?' shouted Moulu. The civilian looked at them with an air of mild astonishment. 'Germany, of course.' 'Stop pushing!' said Brunet. He braced himself with his two hands against the wall of the van. The men were crowding on top of him: they were all speaking at once: 'Germany? – you crazy? – you mean Châlons! Germany, indeed! who says they've gone to Germany?' The civilian made no reply. He fixed them with his untroubled gaze. 'Shut up, boys!' said Jurassien: 'don't all talk at once!' There was silence, and Jurassien shouted: 'How d'you know?' The sound of a voice raised in anger reached them. One of the German sentries jumped, with fixed bayonet, from the truck and ran up the train. Ill temper had flushed his face scarlet. He began to yell in very rapid German. His voice was hoarse. Brunet felt himself suddenly freed from the enormous weight that had been pressing on him. The men must have sat down suddenly. The sentry stopped talking. He stood in front of them, his rifle resting on the ground. The civilian had not moved. He was still where he had been, leaning over the paling, and looking at them. Brunet could feel behind him all the fevered faces raised in a mute questioning. 'The bloody fool!' muttered Lucien at his back: 'the bloody fool!' The man up on the road was motionless and dumb, useless from their point of view, yet filled with some secret knowledge. The engine whistled. A great eddy of smoke poured into the van: the train gave a shudder and began to move. Brunet coughed: the sentry waited until the truck passed him, and threw his rifle into it. Brunet could see two pairs of hands, projecting from greenish sleeves, catch him by the shoulders and hoist him up. 'What's that barstard know about it, anyhow?' 'Yes, what does *he* know? They went off somewhere, and he saw 'em go: that's all there is to it.' There was an outburst of angry voices at Brunet's back: he smiled, but said nothing. 'He was only guessing,' said Ramelle: 'he *guessed* they were going to Germany.' The train began to move faster, past long, empty platforms. Brunet saw a notice-board with the words – EXIT: SUBWAY. The train drove onwards. The station was dead. Brunet could feel the printer's shoulder trembling against his own. The printer gave vent to a fit of temper. 'Dirty swine, to say a thing like that if he didn't know for sure!' 'That's right,' said Martial: 'a proper barstard!' 'Nothing to worry about,' said Moulu: 'he's probably nuts ...' 'Nuts!' said Jurassien: 'did you look at him? – nothing nuts about that bugger – *he* knew what he was doing all right!' Brunet turned his head. Jurassien showed a nasty smile: 'One of the Fifth Column,' he said. 'How about if he was right?' inquired Lambert. 'For God's sake! – if *you* want to go to Bocheland, get on with it, but don't come putting the wind up us' 'Well, anyhow,' said Moulu, 'we shall know when we get to the next set of points.' 'When'll that be?' asked Ramelle. His face looked green: he was drumming with his fingers on the skirt of his greatcoat. 'Quarter of an hour – twenty minutes.' The others said no more, but sat there waiting. Brunet had never seen their faces so tense, their eyes so fixed, since catastrophe had overtaken them. Silence fell, heavy and complete. There was nothing to be heard but the creaking of the train. It was hot. Brunet would have liked to take off his tunic, but he was wedged between the printer and the wall of the van, and could not move. Sweat was trickling down his neck. The printer, without looking at him, said: 'I say, Brunet.' 'What?' 'Were you joking just now when you told me to jump?' 'Why d'you ask that?' The printer turned his face with its air of childlike charm, which wrinkles, dirt, and stubble were alike incapable of ageing, and looked at him. He said: 'I just couldn't stick being packed off to Germany.' Brunet said nothing: 'I

337

just couldn't stick it, it'd kill me.' Brunet gave a shrug: he said: 'We'll all be in the same boat.' 'But we'll all die, it'll kill the lot of us.' Brunet freed one hand and laid it on his shoulder. 'Get a hold on yourself, boy,' he said with a sudden display of affection. The printer was trembling. Brunet said to him, 'If you start talking like that you'll end by putting the wind up everybody.' The printer swallowed: all the fight seemed to have gone out of him. He said: 'You're right, Brunet.' He made a little movement, expressive of despair and helplessness. Very sadly, he added: 'You're always right.' Brunet smiled at him. A moment or two passed: then the printer began again in a dull voice: 'Then you *were* pulling my leg?' 'What d'you mean?' 'When you told me to jump – you were pulling my leg, weren't you?' 'Oh, forget it!' said Brunet. 'If I jumped now,' said the printer, 'would you hold it against me?' Brunet looked at the glitter of the rifle barrels projecting from the truck. 'Don't be a fool,' he said: 'you'd only get yourself bumped off!' 'Let me take a chance!' said the printer: 'let me take a chance!' 'This is the wrong moment,' said Brunet. 'I don't care!' said the printer: 'if they take me to Germany, I shall die in any case, and one way's as good as another!' Brunet remained silent. The printer said: 'All I want to know is, would you hold it against me?' Brunet's eyes were still on the rifle barrels. Slowly, coldly, he said: 'Yes, I would: I forbid you to do anything of the sort!' The printer hung his head, Brunet could see his jaw moving. 'What a brute you are!' said Schneider. Brunet turned his head: Schneider was looking at him with a hard expression in his eyes. Brunet did not answer him: he pressed against the door. He would have liked to say – 'Can't you see that if I don't forbid him to jump, he'll get himself killed?' – but could not, because the printer would have heard him. He had an uncomfortable feeling that Schneider was passing judgement on him. He thought: 'What nonsense!' He looked at the skinny back of the printer's neck; he thought: 'Suppose he really did die in Germany? – Hell! – what's the matter with me?' The train slowed down; they had reached the points. All of them knew perfectly well that it was because of the points that they were stopping, but not a word was uttered. The train came to a standstill. There was silence. Brunet raised his eyes. Moulu was leaning across him, looking at the track, his mouth open. His face was livid. The chirp of crickets could be heard coming from the grass that grew on the embankment. Three Germans jumped down on to the permanent way to stretch their legs. They sauntered past the van, laughing. The train began to move. They made a half-turn, and rejoined their truck at the run. 'It's left, all right, boys!' yelled Moulu: 'we're going left!' The van creaked and vibrated: it felt almost as though the rails would be torn from the sleepers. Once again, Brunet was conscious of ten heavy bodies leaning on his shoulders in their eagerness to see out. The men shouted – 'We're going left! we're going left! we're off to Châlons!' Laughing faces, blackened by smoke, appeared in the doorways of the other vans. André shouted: 'Hey! Chabot! we're for Châlons!' Chabot, who was leaning out of the fourth van from them, laughed and shouted back: 'And about time too!' Everyone was laughing. Brunet heard Gassou's voice: 'They were just as windy as us!' 'What did I say, boys?' said Jurassien: 'he was a Fifth Columnist all right?' Brunet looked at the printer. The printer said nothing. He was still trembling, and a tear was running down his left cheek, making a furrow in the grime and coal-dust. Somebody started to play a mouth-organ: somebody else struck up a song: 'Kaki, my sweet, I'm ever thine!' Brunet felt horribly depressed. He watched the track slipping by: he wanted to jump. Theirs was the front van: behind them, the whole train was singing. It was like a pre-war excursion. He thought: 'There's a nasty shock waiting for them.' The printer heaved a sigh of relief: 'Ah-h-h!' he sighed. He gave Brunet a shrewd look. '*You* thought it was going to be Germany!' Brunet stiffened slightly; he felt that his prestige had suffered, but he said nothing. The printer, by now, was in a friendly mood, and hastened to add: 'Everyone can make a mistake sometimes: as a matter of fact, I thought so too.' Brunet still said nothing. The printer started to whistle. A few moments passed, and then he said: 'I'll send her word before I show up.' 'Who's her?' asked Brunet. 'My girl,' said the printer. 'If I don't do that she might throw a faint.' 'You got a girl, at your age?' asked Brunet. 'You bet your life!' said the printer: 'we should have been married by this time if it hadn't been for the war.' 'How old is she?'

'Eighteen.' 'Did you meet one another through the Party?' 'N-no, not exactly,' said the printer: 'it was at a dance.' 'Does she think the same as you?' 'What about?' 'Everything.' 'Damned if I know what she thinks!' said the printer: 'actually, I don't believe she thinks at all. She's just a kid, but she's a decent sort, and a good worker ... and steady.' He brooded for a while, then: 'I think it was that got me down: I was feeling bored with her. You got a bit of skirt, Brunet?' 'No time for that,' said Brunet. 'How d'you manage, then?' Brunet smiled: 'Oh, just a pick-up now and again when I feel like it.' 'I couldn't live like that,' said the printer. 'Don't you ever feel you'd like a place of your own, with a wife and all?' 'I should never be there.' 'Yes, of course, I see that ...' – the printer seemed slightly abashed. As though to excuse himself, he said: 'I don't need much – nor does she: three chairs and a bed.' He was smiling at nothing in particular. He said: 'If it hadn't been for this war, we should have been happy.' Brunet felt irritated: he looked at the printer without sympathy. The thinness of the man's face made it easy to read, and Brunet deduced a strong desire for simple happiness. He said quietly: 'This war wasn't a matter of chance. You know well enough that it's impossible to live under an oppressive system.' 'Oh,' said the printer, 'I'd have dug a little hole for myself.' Brunet raised his voice, and said sharply: 'Then why are you a Communist? Communists aren't content to dig holes for themselves.' 'Because of the others,' said the printer: 'there was a terrible lot of poverty where I lived, and I wanted to see that changed.' 'When a man joins the Party, nothing but the Party matters,' said Brunet. 'You must have known what you were letting yourself in for.' 'Oh, I knew all right,' said the printer quickly: 'have I ever refused to do anything you asked? – only, don't you see – this is the way I figured it – when I'm with my girl, the Party's not looking on. There are moments when ...' He looked at Brunet and broke off short. Brunet said nothing: he thought – 'He's acting like this because he thinks I've made a mistake. One ought to be infallible.' It was getting hotter and hotter. His shirt was soaked with sweat: the sun was beating straight on his face. It was important to know *why* all these young men had joined the C.P. When the reason's been based on some sort of generous impulse, there always comes a moment when the enthusiasm begins to flag. *And what about you, why did you join?* Oh, well! all that is so long ago that it has ceased to matter. I'm a Communist because I'm a Communist – that's all there is to it! He freed his right hand, wiped the sweat from his forehead, and looked at his watch. Half-past four. What with all these détours, we're nowhere near getting there. Tonight the Jerries'll bolt the doors and we shall sleep in a siding. He yawned and said: 'Schneider, you're not doing much talking!' 'What d'you expect me to talk about?' asked Schneider. Brunet yawned again: he looked at the track streaming by. A white face was grinning at him from between the rails – ha, ha, ha – his head was falling. He awoke with a start. His eyes were hurting him. He pushed his way backwards in order to avoid the sun: someone had said 'Condemned to death!' – his head fell: he awoke again, and raised his hand to his face. His chin was wet: I've been dribbling – must have gone to sleep with my mouth open. It was something he had a horror of doing. 'Want to pumpship?' A hand pushed an empty bully-beef tin at him: it felt warm. 'What's that for?' he said – 'Oh, thanks.' He emptied it out of the door. The yellow liquid rained down on to the line. 'Hey! pass it up quick!' He handed it back without turning his head: it was taken from him. He wanted to go to sleep again. Someone tapped him on the shoulder. He took the tin and emptied it. 'Let me have it,' said the printer. Brunet held out the tin to him, and he struggled, with difficulty, to his feet. Brunet's fingers were damp, and he dried them on his tunic. A moment later, an arm was extended above his head, and the tin was again tilted. The yellow water fell in a scatter, and was left, a puddle covered with white bubbles, in their wake. The printer resumed his seat, wiping his fingers. Brunet let his head droop on the printer's shoulder. He could hear the music of the mouth-organ, could see a lovely garden full of flowers. He fell asleep. He was awakened by a violent jerk. 'What's up?' he exclaimed. The train had come to a halt in open country. 'What's up?' 'Nothing,' said Moulu: 'you can go to sleep again; it's only Pagny-sur-Meuse.' Brunet turned his head: peace lay over the scene. The men had grown accustomed to their new happiness. Some were playing at cards, some were singing; yet others, silent as though magicked, seemed to be telling stories to themselves. Their eyes were full of memories which, now at last, they could let come to the surface, untrammelled, from the depths of their hearts. No one was taking any notice of the fact that the train was standing still. Brunet was fast asleep. He dreamed of an unfamiliar plain, where men, naked and thin as skeletons, were seated about a great fire. When he awoke the sun was low on the horizon, the sky was mauve, two cows were grazing in a meadow, and the train was still motionless. The men were singing. German soldiers were picking flowers on the grassy embankment. One of them, a fattish little man with a great spread of shoulder and pink cheeks, approached the prisoners. He had a daisy between his teeth, and was smiling broadly. Moulu, André, and Martial smiled back at him. For a moment, the German and Frenchmen remained all looking at one another and smiling. Then Moulu said quickly: *'Cigaretten, bitte schön, cigaretten.'* The soldier seemed to turn the matter over in his mind. He glanced hastily at the embankment where his two companions were bending over the grass. Only their rumps were visible. He hurriedly felt in his pocket, and threw a packet of cigarettes into the van. Brunet heard behind him a noise of scrambling. Ramelle, who was not a smoker, stood up and shouted: *'Danke schön!'* to an accompaniment of smiles. The squat little German made signs to him to hold his tongue. Moulu said to Schneider: 'Ask him where we're going.' Schneider said something to the soldier, in German. The soldier answered with a grin. The others had, by this time, finished picking flowers, and approached the train, holding bunches in their left hands, upside down. The party consisted of a sergeant and two privates. They seemed to be in an hilarious mood, and were laughing a good deal as they talked. 'What are they saying?' asked Moulu, smiling likewise. 'Wait a moment,' said Schneider impatiently, 'and let me see if I can understand.' The soldiers indulged in a final pleasantry, and then started to move, unhurriedly, back to their truck. The sergeant stopped to make water against one of the wheels. He stood with his legs apart, buttoning up his flies. He took a quick look at his men, and, while their backs were turned, jerked a packet of cigarettes into the van. 'Ha!' said Martial with a chuckle: 'they're not a bad lot of buggers!' 'It's because we're

342

being released,' said Jurassien: 'they want to make a good impression on us.' 'Maybe,' said Martial: 'actually, it's all propaganda.' 'What were they saying?' Moulu asked Schneider. Schneider did not answer: there was an odd expression on his face. 'Yes,' chimed in André, 'what were they saying?' Schneider swallowed with difficulty; he said: 'They're from Hanover – been in action in Belgium.' 'Where did they say we're going?' Schneider spread his arms, smiled apologetically, and said: 'Trèves.' 'Trèves?' commented Moulu: 'and where may that be when it's at home?' 'It's in the Palatinate,' replied Schneider. There was a scarcely noticeable silence, then Moulu said: 'Trèves, in Bocheland? – then they must have been pulling your leg.' Schneider said no more. Moulu went on with calm assurance: 'One doesn't go to Bocheland by way of Bar-le-Duc.' Schneider still remained silent. André asked with an air of nonchalance: 'Were they having a joke with you, or what?' 'Must have been,' said Lucien: 'they were having you on.' Schneider broke his silence. 'They weren't joking when they told me that,' he said reluctantly. 'Didn't you hear what Moulu said?' exclaimed Martial angrily: 'Bar-le-Duc's not on the way to Bocheland. It doesn't make sense.' 'One doesn't go by Bar-le-Duc, I agree,' said Schneider: 'one branches to the right.' Moulu began to laugh. 'Poppycock! I suppose you'll allow I know this route better than any of you? Well, the line to the right goes to Verdun and Sedan. If you continued on in that direction you might find yourself in Belgium, but not in Germany!' He turned to the others with the reassuring air of one who knows. 'I used to travel this district every week – twice a week, sometimes,' he added, and his face expressed a desperate conviction. There was a chorus of voices: 'He knows! He can't be wrong!' 'One goes via Luxembourg,' said Schneider, speaking with an effort. Brunet had the impression that now he had started, he meant to drive the truth into their heads. He was pale, and avoided their eyes as he spoke. André thrust his face close up to Schneider, and shouted: 'Why should we have come this roundabout way?' The men behind chimed in: 'Yes,' they said, 'why? They wouldn't be such fools if they could take us round by Lunéville.' Schneider was scarlet. Suddenly he swung round towards the back of the van, and confronted the men who were making all the noise. 'I know nothing about it!' he shouted angrily: 'nothing! – maybe it was because the track's destroyed, or because there are German troop-movements going on. It's no use your trying to make me say more than I know. You can believe what you damn' well please!' A shrill voice sounded above the hubbub. 'No need to lose your tempers, chums: we shall soon know for certain.' The others repeated the words: 'That's right – we'll soon know, what's the point of squabbling?' Schneider sat down without saying any more. From the next van but one emerged a curly head, and a boy's voice shouted: 'Where d'they say we're going?' 'What's he want to know?' 'He's asking where we're going.' There was a roar of laughter. 'Couldn't have chose a better moment to ask!' Moulu leaned out, put his hands to his mouth, and yelled – 'Up me backside!' The head disappeared. Everyone laughed. Then the laughter stopped. Jurassien said: 'What about a game, boys? – takes the mind off.' 'All right – come on.' The men squatted tailor-fashion round a greatcoat folded into four. Jurassien took up the pack and dealt. Ramelle sat biting his nails in silence. The mouth-organ was playing a waltz. A man was standing against the end wall, smoking a German cigarette. He looked thoughtful. As though he were speaking to himself, he said: 'It's good to have a smoke.' Schneider turned to Brunet: 'I couldn't tell them a lie,' he said, and there was something almost defensive in the tone of his voice. Brunet's only answer was a shrug. Schneider went on: 'I just couldn't.' 'Not that it'd have done any good if you had,' said Brunet. 'It's better: they'll have to know sooner or later.' He noticed that he had spoken with gentleness, and felt irritated with Schneider – because of the others. Schneider gave him an odd look: 'Pity you don't know German.' 'Why?' asked Brunet, surprised. 'Because breaking the news might have been more up your street.' 'You're wrong,' said Brunet wearily. 'But you always wanted it to be Germany.' 'Yes, I suppose I did.' The printer was trembling again. Brunet put his arm round his shoulder and pressed it with a clumsy show of affection. Silently, he drew Schneider's attention to him, and said: 'Shut up!' The smile with which Schneider looked at Brunet expressed astonishment: it as good as said – since when have you bothered about sparing other people's feelings? Brunet turned away his head, only to see before him the printer's hungry, supplicating gaze. The printer returned his look. His lips moved, his great, soft eyes turned in his shadowed face. Brunet was on the point of saying, 'I wasn't so wrong, was I?' – but bit back the words. He looked at his legs hanging motionless above the wheels, and began to whistle. The sun went down. The heat grew less. A small boy was chasing cows with a stick. They galloped across a field, then quieted down and ambled majestically on to the road. A boy going home; cows making for the byre. It was a sight to make the heart sore. Very far off, high above the meadow, black birds were turning and twisting. Not all the dead had been buried. Brunet was beyond knowing whether this heart's anguish were his own or others. He turned and looked at his companions, trying to see them objectively. Their faces were grey and preoccupied, almost peaceful. He recognized their expression: it was the curious mental emptiness of crowds just before they are shaken by a gust of anger. He thought – 'That's fine! – that's as it should be!' – but without any sense of pleasure. The train shuddered throughout its length, continued on its way for another few minutes, then stopped. Moulu leaned out and stared at the horizon. 'Points a hundred yards ahead.' 'Don't you realize,' said Gassou: 'they're going to shunt the train and leave us here till morning.' 'Fine state of nerves we'll be in by that time,' said André. Brunet could feel in his very bones the dead-weight of the train's immobility. Someone said: 'It's the cold war all over again!' A dry cackle ran through the van: it was laughter: it died out. Brunet heard Jurassien say imperturbably – 'Trump you once – trump you twice!' He felt another jerk, and turned. Jurassien's hand, holding an ace of hearts, hung motionless in the air. The train moved slowly forward. Moulu was watching. A moment later, it gathered speed. Two rails leapt into view from under the wheels, two parallel flashes of light that showed for a moment and then vanished, over to their left, among the fields. 'Hell!' said Moulu: 'Oh, bloody hell!' There was complete silence. The men had understood. Jurassien let his ace fall on the coat, and took the trick. The train was running smoothly, with a regular puffing sound. The setting sun turned Schneider's face red. The air felt suddenly much cooler. Brunet looked at the printer and gripped

345

him sharply by the shoulders: 'No funny business, boy: no funny business!' The thin body went taut under his fingers: he tightened his grip, and the body grew slack. Brunet thought: 'I'll keep a hold on him till nightfall.' When darkness came, the Jerries would shut the door. By morning he would have calmed down. The train ran on under the mauve sky, in complete silence. They knew now – in each separate van they knew. The printer had dropped his head on Brunet's shoulder, like a woman. Brunet thought: 'Have I any right to keep him from jumping?' But he kept a tight hold of him. He heard a laugh at his back, and a voice: 'The old woman wanted a kid! I'll have to write and tell her to get the neighbour to do the necessary!' They all laughed. Brunet thought: 'The laughter of despair.' Laughter filled the van, and a rising anger. Somebody spluttered through his mirth – 'What bloody fools we were! – what complete, bloody fools!' A field of potatoes – a steel works – mines – forced labour: what right have I, what right, to hold him back? 'Bloody fools!' said the voice again. Anger rumbled and rose. Brunet could feel beneath his fingers the twitching of the thin shoulders, the movement of the slack muscles. He thought: 'He'll never be able to stick it.' He tightened his hold – by what right? – he tightened it still more. The printer said, 'You're hurting me' – Brunet maintained his grip – this is a life vowed to Communism so long as he lives, he belongs to us. He looked at the small, squirrel face: for so long as he lives – yes – but is he still alive? – he's finished, the springs are broken – he'll never work again. 'Let me alone!' shouted the printer; 'for Chri' sake let me alone!' Brunet was conscious of the queerness of his position, keeping tight hold of this rag of a man, this member of the Party, who would never again be of the slightest use. He wanted to speak to him, to cheer him, to help him, but could not do so. His words belonged to the Party; the Party alone gave to them any meaning they might have. Only within the Party could Brunet love, persuade, console. Now that the printer had got himself into a position where he was outside the range of that immense and wheeling light, Brunet could have nothing more to say to him. Nevertheless, the boy was still a suffering human being. ... death either way. Oh, let him decide for himself! If he could make a getaway, so much the better for him:

346

if he stayed, his death might be of some use to the cause. The laughter grew louder. The train was running slowly; it seemed to be on the point of stopping. Inspired by a sudden cunning, the printer said: 'Pass me the tin, I want to pumpship.' Brunet said nothing but looked at him, and what he saw was death – the vast freedom of death. 'Hell!' said the printer: 'why can't you pass me the tin – d'you want me to wet my pants?' Brunet turned his head: 'Tin up!' he shouted. Out of darkness aglow with anger came a hand holding the tin. The train slowed down still more. Brunet hesitated. He dug his fingers into the printer's shoulder, then, suddenly, relaxed his grip, and took the tin. How bloody silly it all was! how bloody silly! The men had stopped laughing. Brunet felt his elbow jarred: the printer had dived under his arm. He stretched out his hand: it closed on emptiness. The dark mass, bent double, had fallen, was falling, ponderously through the air. Moulu uttered a cry: a shadow struck the embankment, legs apart, arms flung wide. Brunet waited for the rifle-shots; the sound of them was *already* in his ears. The printer rebounded from the side of the cutting. They could see him standing upright, now, a figure of blackness, a figure of freedom. Brunet *saw* the flash of the rifles – five frightful jets of flame. The printer began to run along the train: he had been seized with panic, was trying to climb back again into the van. Brunet shouted to him: 'Get on to the bank! for God's sake, get on to the bank!' All the men were shouting: 'Jump!' they cried – 'Jump!' The printer did not hear. He was running as hard as he could. He was drawing level with them. 'Brunet!' he called out: 'Brunet!' Brunet could see his terrified eyes. He yelled at him the one word 'Embankment!' but the man seemed deaf, to be nothing now but a pair of enormous eyes. Brunet thought: 'If he can climb back quickly, he may have a chance.' He leaned out. In a flash Schneider realized what he was after, and flung his arm round him to keep him from falling. Brunet stretched out his arms. The printer's hand touched his. The Jerries fired three times: the printer slumped backwards and fell. The train drew away from him. The printer leaped once into the air and fell. The sleeper and the clinkers beneath his head were black with blood. The train jerked to a standstill. Brunet collapsed on top of Schneider: between his clenched

347

teeth he said: 'They must have seen perfectly well that he was trying to climb back: they shot him down just for the fun of the thing!' The body was lying some twenty yards away, already a mere object, already free. *I'd have dug a little hole for myself.* Brunet noticed that he was still holding the bully-beef tin: he had reached out his hand to the printer without letting go of it. It was warm. He let it fall on the stones of the permanent way. Four Jerries jumped out of their truck and ran to the body. Brunet could hear the men behind him growling. Their anger was no longer under control. From one of the trucks ahead ten Germans emerged. They clambered up the embankment and faced the train, tommy-guns levelled. None of the prisoners showed any sign of fear. Someone behind Brunet shouted 'Barstards!' The big German sergeant, with a look of fury on his face, bent over the corpse, lifted it, let it fall back and gave it a kick. Brunet struggled round: 'Hey! you'll have me over if you're not careful!' At least twenty of the men were leaning out. He saw twenty pairs of eyes with murder in them. There was going to be trouble. He shouted – 'Don't jump, boys! you'll only get yourselves slaughtered!' He got to his feet with difficulty, fighting for his freedom. 'Schneider!' he shouted. Schneider had got up, too. Each had his arm round the other's waist. With their free hands they clung to the jambs of the door. 'No one's leaving this van!' The men pushed. Brunet could see their hatred, *his* hatred, the tool ready to *his* hand, and he felt afraid. Three Germans approached the van, their rifles pointed at its occupants. Brunet recognized the big fellow with the curly hair who had tossed the cigarettes to them. His eyes were the eyes of a murderer. The Frenchmen and the Germans glared at one another: *this was war.* For the first time since September '39, this was war. Gradually the pressure relaxed. The men drew back. He could breathe again. The sergeant walked up to the van: *'Hinein!'* he shouted: *'Hinein!'* Brunet and Schneider were pressed against a wall of chests. Behind them the Jerries were closing the sliding doors. The van was plunged in darkness. It smelled of sweat and coal-dust. It was filled with a low mutter of anger. Feet were stamping on the floor: the sound was that of a crowd on the march. Brunet thought: 'They won't forget this: the game's won!' He felt ill, and was finding it hard

348

to breathe. His eyes were wide open in the darkness. Now and again he felt them swell, so that they seemed to be two great oranges about to start from their sockets. In a low voice he called: 'Schneider! Schneider!' 'Here I am,' said Schneider. A hand found his and pressed it. 'That you, Schneider?' 'Yes.' They stood side by side, hand in hand, both silent. There was a jerk: the train creaked into motion. What had they done with the body? He could feel Schneider's breathing close beside his ear. Suddenly Schneider withdrew his hand. Brunet tried to retain it, but Schneider shook him off and melted into the darkness. Brunet was alone, rigid and uncomfortable. The place was hot as an oven. He stood there on one foot: the other was jammed in a confusion of legs and boots. He made no attempt to free himself. He was obsessed by the need to feel that everything about him was provisional, that he was *passing through* something, that his thoughts were *passing through* his head, that the train was *passing through* France. Ideas leapt from his brain, vague, indistinct, and fell on to the railway track behind, even before he had had time to identify them. He was moving farther and farther and farther away. Only when life was moving at this speed was it endurable. Complete immobility. Speed slid by and dropped at his feet. He knew that the train was moving, grinding, bumping, shuddering its way onward, but he was no longer conscious of movement. He was in a great dust-bin. Somebody was kicking about inside it. Behind him, on the embankment, lay a body, limp and boneless. Brunet knew that they were moving farther from it with each passing minute. He longed to feel the reality of their movement, but could not. Complete stagnation reigned. Above the dead body, above the inert freight-van, the darkness wheeled. It alone was living. To-morrow's dawn would cover all of them with the same dew. Dead flesh and rusted steel would run with the same sweat. Tomorrow the black birds would come.

READ MORE IN PENGUIN

In every corner of the world, on every subject under the sun, Penguin represents quality and variety – the very best in publishing today.

For complete information about books available from Penguin – including Puffins, Penguin Classics and Arkana – and how to order them, write to us at the appropriate address below. Please note that for copyright reasons the selection of books varies from country to country.

In the United Kingdom: Please write to *Dept. EP, Penguin Books Ltd, Bath Road, Harmondsworth, West Drayton, Middlesex UB7 ODA*

In the United States: Please write to *Consumer Sales, Penguin Putnam Inc., P.O. Box 12289 Dept. B, Newark, New Jersey 07101-5289.* VISA and MasterCard holders call 1-800-788-6262 to order Penguin titles

In Canada: Please write to *Penguin Books Canada Ltd, 10 Alcorn Avenue, Suite 300, Toronto, Ontario M4V 3B2*

In Australia: Please write to *Penguin Books Australia Ltd, P.O. Box 257, Ringwood, Victoria 3134*

In New Zealand: Please write to *Penguin Books (NZ) Ltd, Private Bag 102902, North Shore Mail Centre, Auckland 10*

In India: Please write to *Penguin Books India Pvt Ltd, 11 Community Centre, Panchsheel Park, New Delhi 110017*

In the Netherlands: Please write to *Penguin Books Netherlands bv, Postbus 3507, NL-1001 AH Amsterdam*

In Germany: Please write to *Penguin Books Deutschland GmbH, Metzlerstrasse 26, 60594 Frankfurt am Main*

In Spain: Please write to *Penguin Books S. A., Bravo Murillo 19, 1° B, 28015 Madrid*

In Italy: Please write to *Penguin Italia s.r.l., Via Benedetto Croce 2, 20094 Corsico, Milano*

In France: Please write to *Penguin France, Le Carré Wilson, 62 rue Benjamin Baillaud, 31500 Toulouse*

In Japan: Please write to *Penguin Books Japan Ltd, Kaneko Building, 2-3-25 Koraku, Bunkyo-Ku, Tokyo 112*

In South Africa: Please write to *Penguin Books South Africa (Pty) Ltd, Private Bag X14, Parkview, 2122 Johannesburg*

READ MORE IN PENGUIN

Penguin Twentieth-Century Classics offer a selection of the finest works of literature published this century. Spanning the globe from Argentina to America, from France to India, the masters of prose and poetry are represented in by the Penguin.

If you would like a catalogue of the Twentieth-Century Classics library, please write to:

Penguin Marketing, 27 Wrights Lane, London W8 5TZ

(Available while stocks last)

BY THE SAME AUTHOR

Also published, the first and second volumes of The Roads to Freedom *trilogy, with introductions by David Caute:*

The Age of Reason

Set in the volatile Paris summer of 1938, *The Age of Reason* follows two days in the life of Mathieu Delarue, a philosophy teacher, and his circle in the cafes and bars of Montparnasse. Mathieu has so far managed to contain sex and personal freedom in conveniently separate compartments. But now he is in trouble, urgently trying to raise 4,000 francs to procure a safe abortion for his mistress.

The Reprieve

September 1938: in a heatwave Europe tensely awaits the outcome of the Munich conference. In Paris people are waiting too, among them, Mathieu, Jacques and Philippe – not one of them ready to fight. Sartre depicts a powerful montage of that critical week when Europe, in its pathetic longing for a reprieve, blinkered itself against the threat of war.

and

Nausea

In this, Sartre's first published novel and his first extended essay on the existential philosophy that was to make him world famous, Antoine Roquentin, an introspective historian, records the disturbing shifts in his perceptions and his struggle to restore meaning to life in a continuing present and without lies.

'*La Nausée*, Sartre's celebration of the horror of the contingent, is one of the very few unadulterated and successful members of the genre "philosophical novel". It is unique in Sartre's work, and I think in literature generally, a young man's *tour de force*' – Iris Murdoch

also published:

Words
In Camera and Other Plays